Rousseau's Legacy

Rousseau's Legacy

Emergence and Eclipse
of the Writer in France

DENNIS PORTER

New York Oxford   Oxford University Press   1995

Oxford University Press

Oxford   New York
Athens   Auckland   Bangkok   Bombay
Calcutta   Cape Town   Dar es Salaam   Delhi
Florence   Hong Kong   Istanbul   Karachi
Kuala Lumpur   Madras   Madrid   Melbourne
Mexico City   Nairobi   Paris   Singapore
Taipei   Tokyo   Toronto

and associated companies in
Berlin   Ibadan

Published by Oxford University Press, Inc.,
200 Madison Avenue, New York, New York 10016

Library of Congress Cataloging-in-Publication Data
Porter, Dennis, 1933–
Rousseau's legacy : emergence and eclipse
of the writer in France / Dennis Porter
p. cm.   Includes index.
ISBN 0-19-509107-8
1. French literature—History and criticism—Theory, etc.
2. Rousseau, Jean-Jacques, 1712–1778—Influence.
3. Authorship—Social aspects—France—History.
4. Politics and literature—France—History.
5. Literature and society—France—History.
6. Authors and readers—France—History.
7. France—Intellectual life.
8. Autobiography.
I. Title.   PQ71.P67   995
840.9'007—dc20   94-26408

1003502738

1 3 5 7 9 8 6 4 2

Printed in the United States of America
on acid-free paper

For my friends, wherever they are

Contents

Rousseau's Legacy

Liberté, égalité, fraternité . . . Why does nobody add Culture?

JOSEPH BRODSKY

Novelists who are more intelligent than their books should go into another line of work.

MILAN KUNDERA

Autobiography—that is the unprecedented decadence of literature.

LOUIS ALTHUSSER

Introduction

I am impressed at how the occupation of writer confers on its practitioners the right to speak out for humanity as though they incarnated it.

FRANÇOIS MAURIAC

This book makes the claim that French literary culture is currently undergoing a major transformation that is the equivalent of a paradigm change; that the transformation is visible in the fate of a certain idea of "the writer" which first emerged almost two hundred and fifty years ago; that the change is bound up with the unprecedented historical events of the past couple of decades; and that although the transformation is particularly marked in France because of the apparent normativity of its cultural and political history since the late eighteenth century, it has important ramifications for other Western and even non-Western countries.

My interest in the emergence and eclipse of a certain idea of "the writer" goes back to 1989 and the bicentennial of the French Revolution, when I was in Paris for the summer. In spite of the widespread national consensus apparent then that late-twentieth-century France is in so many respects the democratic and republican heir of that eighteenth-century revolution, press reports and opinion pieces during the previous eighteen months had confirmed that there remained predictably wide differences of opinion concerning the meaning of the Revolution in the late twentieth century and the significance of its various phases. There was also obvious discomfort in official circles about how it should be celebrated and especially about which phases to celebrate—and not simply because France had just undergone its first experience of "cohabitation" in the life of the Fifth Republic, with a socialist president (François Mitterand) and a conservative cabinet and head of government (Jacques Chirac). Moreover, if this were true of the phases of the Revolution, it was even more so with respect to its actors, from Mirabeau and Sieyès to Danton, Robespierre

3

and Saint-Just. Who, if any, were to be its heroes? This was fortunately not a decision that had to be made in 1989.

In the end, in officially sponsored events the emphasis fell not on the emergence of the National Assembly out of the Estates General nor on the storming of the Bastille or the people under arms, nor, of course, on the radicalization of the Revolution in subsequent years that led up to the Terror, but on the Declaration of the Rights of Man and of the Citizen, of August 1789, and the apparent universalism of a message that, it has long been claimed, inaugurated a new age for humanity and modern political culture. This choice of focus was in itself symptomatic of a further turn in contemporary France's relationship to its revolutionary past, for it is a recognized historical fact that the celebrated Declaration has not always held pride of place even among champions of the French republic, and that its career in France has been very different from that of the Bill of Rights in the United States. For two hundred years following the original Declaration, it has meant different things to different political formations; throughout the nineteenth century and into our own time, the eighteenth-century language of "rights" was an object of suspicion across the political spectrum, not least on the far Left, where it was typically taken to be the expression of bourgeois individualism.[1]

One effect of the bicentennial year and of the understandable impulse to memorialize the world-historical event that apparently marked the origin of modern France's national identity was that the malaise of French left-wing intellectuals became even more acute—a malaise that had remained relatively masked during the French Socialist and Communist parties' long period of opposition under the Fifth Republic, but that became obvious not long after their accession to power in the early eighties. It was increasingly and widely commented on in the course of the decade; the Socialist government was perceived to be adopting many of the social and economic policies traditionally associated with the French Right.

The malaise of French left-wing intellectuals in the eighties had, of course, its own well-documented earlier phases that, depending on one's perspective, reached back some twenty years to the events of May 1968 and the Warsaw Pact invasion of Czechoslovakia of the same year, or over thirty years to 1956 and the Soviet invasion of Hungary, or even further back to the immediate postwar period, the beginnings of the Cold War, and the age of Stalinist show trials in the Soviet Union and its satellite nations.

This is not the place to retrace the by-now-familiar ground of French left-wing intellectuals and their relationship to the Communist Party—the familiar ground of schism, denunciation, disillusionment, ostracism, and recantation—nor is it the place to recall the kind of erratic, step-by-step abandonment by former believers of their faith in Bolshevik-style revolution and its various avatars in the third world.[2] It is worth recalling that from the mid-seventies on, in the wake of the revelations concerning the

Soviet Gulags by Solzhenitsyn and others, a younger generation of so-called *nouveaux philosophes* mounted a critique against the generation of their fathers, whom they took to task for their incomprehension of the totalitarian implications of the historicist philosophers they had championed and their blindness to the reality of Soviet terror.[3] Yet none of this quite prepared French intellectuals—any more than those of other Western nations—for the abrupt collapse, beginning in late 1989, of Communist regimes in central and Eastern Europe preparatory to the ultimate dismantling of the Soviet Union itself. The substance and form of the events of that and the following years reinforced fundamental revisionist tendencies already at work and reached into every corner of French sociopolitical, and cultural life.[4]

It is probably true that by the late eighties relatively few French left-wing intellectuals still took for granted the Sartrean axiom, proclaimed at the beginning of the sixties, that Marxism was the unsurpassable critical philosophy of the age, and that it only needed to be wedded to other bodies of theory—existentialism, sociology, and/or psychoanalysis—in order to furnish a comprehensive account of the hidden rationality of human history and the form a future, nonexploiting, nonalienating society should take. Yet the faith in the rationality and necessity of the tradition of revolution itself had remained largely intact, even if the experience of the events of May 1968, in particular, had at least undermined the status of the universal intellectual as the interpreter of that history, as conscience and prophet of humanity at large, or what Michel Foucault once called "the master of truth and justice."[5]

In any case, when the bicentennial events of the summer of 1989 in Paris were followed, later that same year, by a wave of new democratic movements in central and Eastern Europe that challenged the legitimacy of long-entrenched Communist regimes, the significance of the legacy of revolution was once again on the agenda and the malaise of left-wing French intellectuals was notably heightened. The celebration of the bicentennial had, it seemed, been upstaged by what looked to some like a counterrevolution, or at the very least a liberal revolution, whose models, if they existed at all, antedated 1789 and all that, and were perhaps Anglo-American rather than French. In light of the universal revulsion expressed for the Bolshevik model of revolution throughout the former satellite states of the Soviet Union, it seemed essential to reexamine the filiation frequently claimed between the eighteenth-century Revolution and its twentieth-century avatars.

In 1990, at the annual meeting of the Twentieth French Studies Colloquium, I presented a paper entitled "Paradigm Lost: French Intellectuals in a Bicentennial Year." My purpose was to explore briefly the relationship of twentieth-century French intellectuals to the French Revolution and the revolutionary tradition in light of recent events, and to speculate on whether the Humpty Dumpty of revolution to which so many French intellectuals had deferred for so long could ever be put back together again in a recognizable form.

Tony Judt, referring to the years immediately following the Liberation, summarizes the significance of that revolutionary tradition as follows:

> One hundred and fifty years after Saint-Just, the rhetorical hege-
> mony exercised by the Jacobin tradition had not only not dimin-
> ished, but had taken from the experience of the Resistance a re-
> newed vigor. The idea that revolution—*the* Revolution, any
> revolution—constitutes not only a dramatic break, the moment of
> discontinuity between past and future, but also the only possible
> route from the past to the future so pervaded and disfigured French
> political thought that it is hard to disentangle the idea from the
> language it has invested with its vocabulary and its symbols. (*Past
> Imperfect*, 42).

Yet over the past decade or so that process of disentangling has been moving forward.

Some ten years before the bicentennial François Furet had, of course, affirmed that "The French Revolution Is Over."[6] But it finally took the acute discomfort of a left-wing government in power for the first time in the Fifth Republic at the beginning of the eighties, as well as the wholesale rejection of the Bolshevik or related models of revolution at the decade's end to leave a two-hundred-year-old left-wing intellectual tradition in France apparently with nowhere to go. It was as if, by an ironic effect of historical anamorphosis, after exactly two hundred years the image of revolution suddenly ceased to appear as the incarnation of social hope and finally revealed to almost everyone its bloody, despotic face instead. All those who, from approximately the beginning of our century, had affirmed the continuity of revolutions and their emancipatory power—from the French down through the Russian, the Chinese, the Cuban, and the Viet-namese—were obliged, once and for all, to consider a continuity of a kind they had largely preferred to overlook.[7]

One suggestive approach to the exploration of such a continuity was made by Mona Ozouf, a French historian associated with the influential new interpretation of the Revolution. She expressed her views in an essay published in 1988, "The French Revolution and the Idea of a New Man." This essay goes a long way toward explaining why the Revolution took such a radical turn:

> For those who suggested it or supported it, the ambition to create
> a new man is precisely that which gives the French Revolution its
> premonitory character as a result of which it anticipates future rev-
> olutions and the regimes born from them. Whoever undertakes to
> create a new man sets out to seize possession of the most insignifi-
> cant of thoughts, abolishes the distinction between private and pub-

lic, wages war against the inner life, plunges into a project of absolute visibility in which all imprecision is unacceptable, and thereby
refutes democracy: that is why the case for establishing the connection between the Revolution that was the daughter of the Enlightenment and the Gulag could be made.[8]

What Ozouf captures so well here is the kind of revisionist thinking
forced on the French intellectual class even before the virtually unprecedented, and certainly unanticipated, political change of the bicentennial
year itself. Moreover, it was against such a background that I became
interested in the origins of the two-hundred-year-old tradition which had
suddenly been overtaken by the history whose triumphant course it had
long claimed to have mastered. I began to read the eighteenth-century philosophes again, focusing on a more specific figure whose importance in
French cultural life was undeniable and whose history goes much further
back than that of the intellectual (although in the twentieth century the
two have tended to merge), namely, "the writer."[9]

It became clear to me that a new and influential idea of "the writer"
emerged in mid-eighteenth-century France; that it was different from the
concept of "the author" of works in one or more classic literary genres
such as epic, tragedy, comedy, narrative history, or various forms of poetry; that it was distinct from the notion of "the man of letters," whether
in the eighteenth-century sense of *"homme de lettres"*[10] or in the late-
nineteenth-century sense; and that although "the writer" partly overlapped
with the philosophe in the eighteenth century, or with the intellectual in
our own time, "the writer" has proved to be a more complex figure who,
in retrospect, has been just as influential. Lastly, it also appeared to me
that, like the intellectual and for related reasons, "the writer" is also undergoing a significant eclipse in the final decade of our own century.

This is not to say that I am again arguing, though with a different
terminology, that "the writer"—after God, man, the author, the novel,
and art itself—is dead. In particular, I am not using the term in the same
way that "the author" was used in poststructuralist and other circles in
the late sixties and seventies. The "eclipse of the writer" is to be construed
more in terms of a paradigm change and is by no means synonymous
with Roland Barthes's affirmation of "the death of the author" or Michel
Foucault's theorizing on "the author function" in "What Is an Author?"
However, in a characteristic Nietzschean exercise in demystification, in
that essay Foucault does emphasize the fact of the historicity of cultural
concepts. He argues that, far from being the originating subject of a text,
as he was assumed to be since the early nineteenth century, "the author"
is a construction of a given discursive regime and therefore varies according to historical periods and their normative discourses. Furthermore,
in tracing the changing understanding of the role of the author in the literary sphere—from the typical anonymity of the European Middle Ages

down through a cult of the author in the nineteenth century and a return to a different form of anonymity in the age of poststructuralism—Foucault articulates a position that is of obvious relevance to my purpose insofar at it points to the historically and culturally bounded character of our understanding of the role of the one who writes, and to the relationship of that understanding to discursive and nondiscursive practices.[11]

For reasons I shall develop, from the vantage point of the late twentieth century, the most potent and most enduring prototype of the figure of "the writer" is furnished not by Montesquieu, Voltaire, D'Alembert, or even Diderot but by the combined life and works of Jean-Jacques Rousseau. Although in the twentieth century there has been a marked tendency to isolate aspects of Rousseau's oeuvre and divide it up among different academic disciplines, Rousseau himself clearly had a preromantic sense of the unity of his philosophical, political, historical, literary, and pedagogical writings, while at the same time affirming their intimate connection to the man who lived and suffered in the world. In any case, it is the assumption of this book that it is with Rousseau that "the writer" appears virtually fully formed on the European scene as a cultural hero of a new age of revolution, an age that has endured up to the present time but has now effectively come to an end.

On the one hand, Rousseau was obviously associated with the philosophes in promoting those fundamental changes in the culture of politics in the decades immediately preceding the Revolution that have been so well described by recent historians of France. On the other hand, his thought and behavioral practice represent a radically new departure within the sphere of the new "literary politics" that Tocqueville discusses in Book 3 of *The Old Regime and the Revolution*. No other prerevolutionary thinker corresponds more obviously than Rousseau to the Tocquevillean thesis of the fatal divorce between practical politics and the ideal sphere of literature and philosophy, the consequences of which are pointedly summarized by Roger Chartier as follows: "The politicization of literature was at the same time a 'literarization' of politics transformed into an expectation of rupture and a dream of an 'ideal world.' "[12]

Rousseau is of crucial importance to me because he created a body of work that combined a radical critique of contemporary European society, including an outline for radical political change, with a condemnation of Enlightenment culture itself and of the philosophes who were its proponents. He was also the first in his time to add to this mix an expressed determination to tell the whole truth about his personal life; sociopolitical critique and a suspicion of the whole sphere of the aesthetic overlap with confession. The demand for a thoroughgoing reform of the practices and institutions of old-regime sociopolitical and cultural life constituted for Rousseau no more than half of a broader project that also required making his private life public or turning himself into both subject and object of his writing in the cause of a new openness among men in a more open, virtuous, and egalitarian society in which art had no obvious role. The ultimate goal was the moral and political regeneration of humanity.

In short, to engage in the kind of sloganeering of which Rousseau himself was past master, one might say that his originality consisted in the coupling of the late-nineteenth-century intellectual's *j'accuse* with his own *je me confesse;* and the reflexive pronoun of the French in the second case focuses more sharply than the English equivalent on the importance of the self as both object and agent of the action. Thus the first two *Discourses,* The *Social Contract,* The *Letter to D'Alembert on Theater* and The *Confessions* are complementary aspects of a single program that also encompasses the (re-)education of heart and mind *(Emile)* and the task of moral regeneration *(Julie, or The New Héloïse).*

"The writer," in the special sense that interests me, and of which Rousseau appears as the earliest complete embodiment, is not to be confused with "writer" in the generic sense. I am, in fact, using the word partly in the same way that Milan Kundera does in a number of short essays and dialogues that first appeared in the mid-1980s and have been collected and published in English under the title *The Art of the Novel.* In these essays, Kundera—who was, of course, an early example of the post-fifties, anticommunist dissident artist and victim of central European totalitarianism—makes a number of important distinctions of a kind that prove particularly helpful for someone who is attempting to understand the cultural mutation we are currently undergoing with respect to "the writer."

In the sense I am giving it here, then, "writer" is a normative idea. It is not more or less synonymous with poet, dramatist, novelist, essayist, man of letters, or someone who simply earns a living by means of his writings (although the figure is also typically associated with work in one or more of the traditional literary genres and frequently does live off his published work). That is why, in order to avoid confusing my use of the word with its generic use, I have chosen to put "the writer" in quotation marks whenever the special meaning is intended.

The kind of distinction I have in mind emerges clearly in a speech Kundera gave when accepting the Jerusalem Prize in 1985:

> It is with profound emotion that I receive today the prize that bears the name of Jerusalem and the mark of that great cosmopolitan Jewish spirit. It is as a novelist that I accept it. I say *novelist,* not writer. The novelist is one who, according to Flaubert, seeks to disappear behind his work. To disappear behind his work, that is, to renounce the role of public figure. This is not easy these days, when anything of the slightest importance must step into the intolerable glare of the mass media, which, contrary to Flaubert's precept, cause the work to disappear behind the image of its author. In such a situation, which no one can entirely escape, Flaubert's

remark seems to me a kind of warning: in lending himself to the role of public figure, the novelist endangers his work; it risks being considered a mere appendage to his actions, to his declarations, to his statements of position.[13]

Ex post facto, Kundera clearly associates himself with the modernist movement that affirmed the autonomy of the work of art; and his focus is on the current situation of all those who are practitioners of a specific literary genre, although his particular concern is with the fate of the novelist. In any case, his comments on the pressures to which the novelist is subject in the modern world fill out further the definition of "the writer" that I began to sketch earlier in connection with Rousseau. The important points are that Kundera takes the proper relationship between an author and his work to be reversed in the case of "the writer"; that the novelist in our time risks turning into a mere public figure who is sought out chiefly for his easily summarisable opinions; that part of the reason for this is that it is his "image" and his most easily transportable ideas, and not his literary work, which are the focus of interest; and that, finally, as the choice of the word "image" suggests, the contemporary mass media play a major role in forcing the wrong kind of public attention on the literary artist.

Kundera's understanding of the opposition between "the novelist" and the figure I am calling "the writer" is made even more explicit in the definition of "novelist" he gives in a section of *The Art of the Novel* entitled "Sixty-three Words." The passage is also significant, from my point of view, because it confirms the idea that "the writer" is not simply a recent phenomenon but has a relatively long history:

> NOVELIST (writer). I reread Sartre's short essay "What Is Writing?" Not once does he use the words "novel" or "novelist." He only speaks of the "prose writer." A proper distinction. The writer has original ideas and an inimitable voice. He may use any form (including the novel), and whatever he writes—being marked by his thought, borne by his voice—is part of his work. Rousseau, Goethe, Chateaubriand, Gide, Malraux, Camus, Montherlant.
>
> The novelist makes no great issue of his ideas. He is an explorer feeling his way in an effort to reveal some unknown aspect of existence. He is fascinated not by his voice but by a form he is seeking, and only those forms that meet the demands of his dream become part of his work. Fielding, Sterne, Flaubert, Proust, Faulkner, Céline, Calvino.[14]

When I came upon this passage, I was gratified to discover that Rousseau heads Kundera's representative list of "writers," since it confirmed a judgment I had previously come to independently. Since Kundera is concerned with categories of European writers more or less independent of historical context, he does not comment on questions of cause and effect, emergence and eclipse. Nevertheless, although not everyone would necessarily agree with the particular assignments of authors he makes to his two categories, his definition of the opposing figures is a historically precise and illuminating one.

It certainly works in the case of Rousseau. In spite of his retreat from Parisian society, Rousseau would undoubtedly have rejected from the beginning Kundera's postromantic plea for the self-effacement of the authorial self in literary art. Rousseau believed in voice, not form; in personality, not impersonality; in the possibility of unmediated communication between author and reader. Through writings in a variety of fields and genres, he made "a great issue of his ideas" and expressed himself on many of the important sociopolitical and cultural issues of his day. Moreover, he also insisted on public recognition of himself as a figure to be reckoned with. Along with the imperative to tell the whole, unadorned truth about the self, therefore, another crucial and related characteristic of "the writer" projected by the *Confessions* is the kind of position-taking and militancy we associate with the philosophe in the eighteenth century and the intellectual in ours—though typically Rousseau's is a militancy that is without the satirical worldliness or the interest in aesthetic issues one associates with his contemporaries Voltaire or Diderot. Rousseau was in his way already engagé, was "un écrivain de combat," long before those phrases gained notoriety in the middle decades of our own century.

In opposition to the dominant neoclassical aesthetic of the French eighteenth century, then, Rousseau as "writer" affirmed, on the one hand, the vital continuity between his life and writing—between "bio-" and "graphy"—and asserted, on the other hand, the preeminence of ideas and his own commitment to a sociopolitical cause. At the same time, in his frequent expression of distaste for the sphere of the aesthetic as such, for formal values, experiment, and an open-ended spirit of play (of the kind often associated with Diderot, for example), Rousseau also furnished a model of "the writer" as "antinovelist" in Kundera's sense. Thus, when Rousseau did indulge himself by writing a novel, *Julie, or The New Héloïse,* he found it necessary to apologize for it first. Art was figured as at best a distraction from the serious issues of life and at worst as positively corrupting.

As Kundera also notes in connection with one of Rabelais's many word coinages, "the writer," unlike the novelist, is typically someone who has little patience with the disruptive energies of the comic muse; he is what Rabelais called an *agélaste,* "a man who does not laugh, who has no sense of humor" ("Sixty-three words," 159). Among Europe's major writers, one would be hard put to find one who more obviously conformed to the idea of the *agélaste* than Rousseau as his famous critique of Molière's *Misanthrope* confirms. The Calvinist moral fervor he brought to bear in his assaults on manners, social life, and political institutions in the *ancien régime* also informed his understanding, or lack of understanding, of art.

The idea of "the writer" transmitted by Rousseau to subsequent generations, starting with the preromantic and romantic generations, then, is of someone who puts his or her private self on display for the purpose of personal witness, self-affirmation, and sociopolitical emancipation, and whose writings address themselves directly to humanity at large. This idea of "the writer," with different emphases at different historical moments, has persisted through the end of the nineteenth century and into our own times, when various forms of engagement have typically been combined with exercises in autobiographical witness. Thus, although even in the French tradition itself not all writers after the early nineteenth century have by any means been "writers" in the sense I am giving the word (one thinks immediately of such antithetical types as the aesthete, the *poète maudit,* and the *poète pur*), "the writer" has nevertheless been a normative figure in modern European culture, at least until the political upheavals in Eastern and central Europe of the last few years finally revealed the historical boundedness of that figure. Moreover, the importance of the idea and image of "the writer" is not limited to France or even to Europe, but extends to all those countries that for one reason or another have been open to the influence of the European revolutionary tradition and post-Enlightenment literary culture.

It is, in other words, appropriate to speak of Rousseau's legacy down to recent times in a way that it would not make sense to do for, say, Voltaire, Diderot, Hugo, Balzac, Flaubert, or even Baudelaire among major authors—although, as I will show later, the latter was largely instrumental in articulating a new idea of the modernist poet that came to constitute a formidable challenge to the Rousseauist model of "the writer."

It will in any case be the task of this book, first, to describe more fully Rousseau's self-understanding and self-representations that gave rise to the idea of "the writer" and, second, to trace the evolution of that idea over some two and a half centuries in a series of chapters that focus mainly on the autobiographical and relevant theoretical writings of a number of major French authors.

In order to make clear the approach I intend to adopt in completing this task, it is perhaps useful to begin with a denial and with two observations of a general order. As far as the denial is concerned, let me emphasize that I am interested in Rousseau's "legacy" and not in his "fault,"[15] although I do certainly feel that in a great many spheres he has proved an unfortunate guide. One sign of his enduring importance is to be found in the fact that although he has over the centuries been blamed for a great many things—though it seems unfair to blame a writer for his influence—Rousseau's contributions to political theory and to literature have helped change modern life and culture to such an extent that they can hardly be thought of without reference to him.

As for my two observations, first, as I conceive the figure, "the writer" is not a pure transhistorical category, any more than the intellectual is; it implies the idea of discontinuity as well as continuity. There is continuity because of the effect of identification and modeling themselves; there is discontinuity because, as the references made in the works I shall focus on confirm, although authors themselves frequently choose models from earlier eras when they embark on a career of writing, their individual social circumstances and their generational relation to historical events are nevertheless typically so different and so unpredictable that deformations relative to the original model are inevitably produced.

Second, I shall not be proceeding as a sociologist or even a cultural historian might, by invoking large numbers of practitioners and integrating them into some functional model of French society, or quoting a wide range of literary and non-literary materials, but as a student of literature whose focus is more specifically textual. And it is in this connection that it seems particularly appropriate to refer to the important theoretical work of Bourdieu.

To write a book at the present moment on a specifically French idea of the writer without some reference to Bourdieu's contributions seems difficult, even if only to distinguish one's own approach from that of "the genetic sociology" with which he has so brilliantly illuminated the whole field of cultural production. Apart from everything else, Bourdieu identifies the struggle over the definition of "writer" and over who does or does not merit that designation as central to the dynamic of transformation that characterizes the literary field. Nevertheless, the present work makes no attempt to compete with that "rigorous science" of the literary and artistic fields he has constructed on the recently vacated sites of various Marxisms and of French structuralism. It is not part of my purpose to try to reconstitute for a given historical moment the specific economy of those fields in their relational wholeness and of the competition between cultural producers for the positions and for the symbolic power available within them.

My project is a much simpler one. In Bourdieu's terminology, it can be said to be less synchronic than historical; its focus is on agents rather than structures, on "position-takings" *(prises de position)* rather than "positions." Consequently, the material discussed is typically composed of autobiographical or critical works, statements of position, and manifestos in which writers of all kinds articulate their resistances or allegiances to the established political, social, and cultural institutions, ideologies, or aesthetic practices of their age. I will, of course, inevitably touch on many of the questions having to do with the role of culture in social reproduction, with dominant and dominated schools, groups, or movements, with attacks on or defenses of the autonomy of art and literature, with symbolic as opposed to economic or political capital, and with the relations between the field of literature proper and what he calls "the field of power." In exploring the emergence and eclipse of a normative type over such a long period, I am particularly interested in the relationship between a number of writers and a single more or less remote "great predecessor" who contributes positively or negatively to their own self-definition and who has a profound influence on the terms of the debate in a succession of historical presents. Rousseau could, in fact, be described as one of the most categorical and original of "position-takers," who at a critical historical juncture gave an incisive new inflection to the literary field—not least because in at least one important sense he is Bourdieu's "great predecessor," too, insofar as in early modern Europe he was able to open up the question of the complicity between institutionalized culture and political power.[16] Nevertheless, from a Bourdieusian point of view the present work may appear to conceive of literary history as "a summit conference among writers" on which he heaps his scientific scorn ("Field of Cultural Production," 32).

The authors I shall be concerned with, then, are representative only in the sense that they are for the most part major figures who help to illuminate the hold of a normative idea over French literary culture across almost two hundred and fifty years. It is, however, important to note that although they do offer the advantage of bringing the questions that interest me sharply into focus, apart from Rousseau himself a great many other authors from the same tradition might have been chosen with almost equal effect. Furthermore, although some, (like Sartre, Duras, and, not least, Althusser) tend to conform more closely than others to the idea of "the writer" embodied by Rousseau—if one makes the appropriate adjustments for the very different historical circumstances in which they wrote—others (Stendhal, Baudelaire, or Barthes) acknowledge the normative power of the idea while at the same time reacting against it. In other words, I shall, as it were, be looking at examples and counterexamples, pro and contra, although because of the profound politicization of French social and cultural life following the Revolution, even the counterexamples have been subject to the influences of the same literary culture in which "the writer" in various avatars exercised a remarkable power of attraction for over two centuries.

For Stendhal, Baudelaire, and Barthes, commitment and confession remain, so to speak, an available choice or cultural temptation that in their fiction, their poetry, and their writerly essays, respectively, they typically resist. They are conscious of the Rousseauist claim that a writer's life should be produced in the public sphere in order to authenticate his or her literary art and reinforce the hold of his or her ideas, but they are conscious of the politicization of all aspects of social life that often manifests itself in the denigration and marginalization of art and of the aesthetic sphere in general. Like Kundera and this book, however, they also emphasize the various risks for literature and for the culture at large in dogmatically affirming the existence of an unproblematic continuity between art and life, on the one hand, and art and society, on the other.

The limitations of the idea of "the writer" have become very clear in the age of the mass media, in part—as Kundera, among others, has already suggested—because by their very nature the contemporary media promote the "image" of a person and elide the printed text, diffuse the informal spoken word, and merely refer to the formal, written one. Moreover, the vast expansion of the different media has given rise to a remarkable new vogue in various forms of confessional writing and quasi-confessional talk. (This has also been associated with the emergence of modern feminism since the late sixties, generating concepts such as "herstory," but is by no means limited to works inspired by feminist theory.) As a result, in contemporary France, as elsewhere, one has the sense that the difficult art of writing has fallen victim to the glamour of "the writer's" life; the rare counterexample of a Samuel Beckett, a Thomas Pynchon, or a Maurice Blanchot (who refused to allow himself to be photographed) [17] is the kind of exception that proves the rule. Given the current taste for various forms of memoirs (more or less fictionalized), autobiographical reportage, journals of mental or physical illness, romans à clef, and the intimate interview, it is not only in the popular mind that writing often seems to have been reduced to narrating the triumphs and scandals, maladies and addictions of a "writer's" life.[18] The focus in such cases has clearly been displaced from the art object to the artist, from the written word to "the writer."

One sign of the fact that one becomes a writer, in the generic sense as well as my specific sense, not naturally and innocently but by cultural choice is the frequency with which, over the past couple of centuries, writers of various kinds have referred to a moment of decision early in life concerning their future career. There are certainly writers in whom the idea of authorship and the literary works produced seem to be unproblematically fused. Yet at least from Rousseau's time on, there are a great many in whom the gap between a culturally available role and the work to be written is clear. The desire to become a writer frequently precedes any clear sense of how and what to write; it is less a question of work to be done than of a particular kind of life to be lived. That is why the idea of "the writer" in the Rousseauist mold came to exercise such a power of attraction. For reasons that I shall explore later, what appeals is a fantasized social role and a way of life that is in the public eye.

A historian of books and of publishing, Robert Darnton, makes clear how, from the closing decades of the *ancien régime* in France, a career in letters was increasingly perceived by talented but socially marginal members of the third estate as a potential path to social advancement and a prized place in the world.[19] The success of the heroic generation of philosophes and men of letters—from Voltaire to Diderot, d'Alembert, d'Hol-

bach, and Rousseau—invited emulation. In the decades following the Revolution the influence of the romantic movement conferred a new and spiri-
tually elevated aura on certain categories of writers that in some ways has
persisted down to this day.

It is for this reason that, in reflecting on her choice of a writing career
in *Memoirs of a Dutiful Daughter,* Simone de Beauvoir remembers her
fifteen-year-old former self answering the classic question "What do you
want to be when you grow up?" with the immediate response, "A famous
writer."[20] The revealing aspect of that response lies less in the career
named than in its modifier, though in the milieu in which Beauvoir was
raised prestige automatically attached itself to a certain class of writer at
least. Fame, in any case, is the spur, and it takes the form of a way of life
to which public homage of one kind or another is paid. Moreover, as the
autobiographical writings of a great many other writers confirm, Beauvoir's retrospective formulation of the issue is far from atypical.

When he was not yet Stendhal, the young Henri Beyle implicitly expressed the potential dichotomy between "writer" and "writing" in the
form of the un-Rousseauist wish "to write comedies like Molière and live
with an actress."[21] Here, too, it is no accident that the promise of an
erotic satisfaction associated with the life of a man of the theater is as
integral to the fantasm as the comedies that are to be written. A few decades later, in a moment of bitter romantic backlash, Flaubert also illuminated satirically the gap between a desirable role and the actual works
associated with it in the antihero of *A Sentimental Education,* Frédéric
Moreau. In the famous opening chapter of that 1869 novel, one of the
futures the young *bachelier* fantasies for himself on the deck of the Paris-
bound steamer is that of writer. In Frédéric's case, as in countless unre-
corded cases—Flaubert intended him to be perceived as a representative
young man of his time—the desire precedes the act of ever putting pen to
paper, and it characteristically comes to nothing.[22]

It should come as no surprise, therefore, that almost a century later
such an assiduous reader of the Flaubertian oeuvre as Jean-Paul Sartre
placed the issue of the idea of the man of letters in France and a culture's
representations of him at the center of his satirical autobiography. In fact,
the misguided cult of the great author and the culture that produced it are,
as much as the cult of the bourgeois family, the main targets of Sartre's
Words. If one bears in mind the entropic associations Flaubert wove
around the notion of "an education" in his novel, *A Writer's Education*
might be a fitting subtitle for Sartre's 1964 autobiography. *Words* focuses
on a boy's choice of a social role; it is, among other things, the story of
the way in which an early familial and cultural history had to be overcome
if the politically engaged "writer" was to emerge. In any case, many of the
issues that Sartre thematizes in *Words* have their source in the new literary
and publishing culture that began to emerge in the mid-eighteenth century.

A further important dimension of Sartre's critical account of the man of letters as cultural hero in France has to do with the way in which visual representation is crucial in diffusing an appropriate image of the figure— visual representation that by the late nineteenth-century included preeminently photography. Through the discovery of the significance of photographic images in the life of his grandfather, Charles Schweitzer, Sartre became aware in retrospect of the self-deluding character of the process of ego identification to which Lacan was to give a famous psychoanalytic turn in his discussion of the mirror stage.

There was, of course, a tradition in painting and in the plastic arts in general, of reproducing images of great writers or other men and women of genius long before the invention of photography. But from the mid-nineteenth century on photography proved to be a far more powerful medium for the production and dissemination of cultural models, in part because of its amazing capacity for the rapid diffusion of a variety of images and in part because of a general democratic leveling and the widespread improvement in the conditions of material life, such that its distinguished subjects no longer seemed so remote from average middle-class circumstances.

As far as the issues of representation and self-representation of "the writer" are concerned, photography is important for a number of reasons. To begin with, after mass circulation print journalism, it was the first example of what we now mean by "the media" and therefore played a pioneering role in generating some of the social effects we associate with the media in general. In this respect, it is characteristic of photography—as it is of film, radio, television, and video—that its logic was at least twofold. First, it fed the appetite for an ever more comprehensive coverage of its subjects. With the rapid improvement of the technology, it could quickly produce not just one image or even two, but dozens of different images, and it could record these images of its subjects not just in a studio or a well-lighted salon, but in all kinds of places and under all kinds of lighting conditions. Second, in large part as a function of this diversity, photography increasingly tended to blur the division between the public and the private sphere as far as its subjects were concerned. Writers, like other previously remote figures in a nation's political and cultural life, became increasingly public personalities. They could be framed not simply at a podium or even in their own study, but surprised in more or less informal circumstances, *en famille,* about town, with their hair up or down, and with or without their wives, mistresses, or other lovers. Finally, captured in the poses of heroic political activists demonstrating in the street or mounting the barricades, they could also become icons of utopian hope or resistance.

Moreover, the logic of photography was given a powerful new impetus with the invention, in turn, of the movie camera, sound recording, and video. The new capacity for representation and display that began in the age of Niepce, Daguerre, and Fox Talbot has culminated in the 1990s with the phenomenon of the videotaped interview, the T.V. talk show or up-scale, bookish French equivalents such as "Apostrophes" and "Bouillon de Culture." Although it does not seem to be the case that the fully literate sections of populations in Western countries are reading, proportionally, less serious literature than they were fifty or a hundred years ago, the image and status of the writer have undergone a substantial modification of a kind that is especially visible in France. That country finds itself in the paradoxical situation that most of those who were once used to living by the pen now achieve success in large part thanks to the mass media. Those whose peculiar aura derives in the popular mind from a quasi-magical power over the written word are promoted as often as not through the abundant use of the spoken word and visual images. A writer's fame and broad popularity require the consecration of media other than print.

It is in the light of this that I think one should understand Foucault's warning of the risks involved in responding too freely to the solicitations of the media: "Little by little, from the book to the review, to the newspaper article to television, we come to summarize a work, or a problem, in terms of slogans. . . . We can see the slide where philosophical thought, or a philosophical issue, becomes a consumer item."[23] In short, it is no accident that the 1989 *New History of French Literature* ends its critical survey of close to twelve hundred years of literature in French with an entry entitled "Friday Night Books," which is devoted to the phenomenon of a T.V. personality's book program that knowingly contributed to the cult of the writer.[24]

It is against this background that one should, I think, understand Barthes's observation in his poststructuralist autobiography, "I daresay there isn't a single adolescent today who has the fantasm of *being a writer*."[25] Although it is not without ambiguity in the context, Barthes seems here to be using the word writer (écrivain) in its old generic sense as more or less synonymous with the fin de siècle "man of letters": he means writer, not "writer." As he does throughout the autobiographical essay from which this quotation comes, Barthes is lamenting the fact that, late in his own career, one kind of literary culture, and the social status and behavioral practices associated with it, have come to an end. The literary life led by a Flaubert in the mid- to late nineteenth century, or even a Proust or a Gide down through the opening decades of the twentieth, had ceased to be the focus of adolescent desire in the culture, although the prestige of "the writer" at the time Barthes was writing remained very high. Although he does not formulate the issues as such, Barthes is here acknowledging the point made by social historians concerning the way in which the Second World War and its aftermath had enhanced the prestige of the philosopher at the expense of the prewar "man of letters."[26]

If there is an eclipse of the writer in France, then, it is not simply because since Beckett and Ionesco began writing in the fifties no other important playwrights have emerged or, with the possible exception of Marguerite Duras and Michel Tournier, no major new novelists have appeared since Camus. One might even make the case that the culture's creative genius has flowed elsewhere, namely, into philosophy, critical theory, the social and natural sciences, and technology, and that one of the most interesting French writers of recent decades was himself a critic, theorist, essayist, travel writer, and autobiographer, Roland Barthes. In any case, how many major works of world literature appear in a century in a given country, even if that country is possessed of a substantial literary tradition?

The eclipse is visible elsewhere. It has to do with the diminution within the culture of the cult of the written word in general. It is also manifest in the depreciation, first, of the writer/novelist in the turn-of-the-century mode of Proust or Gide and, more recently, of "the writer" in the tradition that extended from Rousseau through Sartre and into the eighties. It is, of course, the eclipse of this last figure that concerns me. Having for so long been relatively overvalued in French culture, literary prose, like poetry since symbolism, is now in the process of being marginalized, if not everywhere undervalued. Yet this is paradoxically the case at the same time that those media which consecrate value are more than ever willing to confer on writers themselves the star status they otherwise reserved for royalty, film stars, and athletes—provided, of course, that they behave like "writers" and make themselves accessible, that there be a perceptible continuity between their work and their lives. Truth, as always, is assumed to be secretive, but it is now located not so much in a work as in the living presence, the man or woman, who stands behind it.

As Rousseau demonstrated over two and a half centuries ago, the kind of accessibility demanded depends on a willingness to make one's private life the material of one's art and to establish a personal relationship with one's readers. Accessibility, however, has its cost. As even Rousseau's example suggests, "confessions" always risk degenerating into "True Confessions"; and in our time in the United States there is a politics as well as a prurience of abuse that has typically come to take the mass-market form of "My Life as Victim." What has also become very apparent in recent decades is that autobiography, like biography, is the genre of those who, like Rousseau, do not believe in literature.

Finally, with the sudden loss of the revolutionary paradigm of social change autobiography has been detached from a sense of sociopolitical mission; confession survives without *engagement* and has become an end in itself. The genre that was brilliantly reinvented by Rousseau in the eighteenth century now typically takes the form of more or less fictionalized episodes from lives in progress, of romans à clef, of reminiscences, and, increasingly, of tape- or video-recorded interviews that are reproduced verbatim in one medium or another. As a consequence, "the writer" as media star has come to be perceived as fascinating and intelligent but no more serious than other media personalities or assorted gurus. Like the work of art, the literary artist also loses his or her aura as a condition of mechanical reproduction and imagistic overexposure.

If my final chapter before the epilogue is devoted to Marguerite Duras, therefore, it is no accident. The case of her life and work is particularly fascinating because more than any other it embodies the current dilemma and the most recent modes of self-presentation of "the writer." She is probably the most photographed and most interviewed literary intellectual of her generation in France. At the same time there is a rare exemplarity about the way in which, starting with the early *Sea Wall (Un barrage contre le Pacifique)*, she has used again and again material from her own life in an increasingly direct form. If anything, the commitment to candor and to bearing painful witness have become even more dominant in such relatively· recent works such as *Pain (La Douleur)* and *The Lover (L'Amant)*. Her career in letters has come to be increasingly identified with a kind of heroic shamelessness that originated with Rousseau and, in a postreligious age, is perhaps the closest one can approach to literary martyrdom. Furthermore, her celebrity status largely depends on it.

From the point of view of the argument I develop here, the posthumous appearance of Louis Althusser's autobiography, *The Future Lasts a Long Time*,[27] in 1992 was an unexpected bonus at a moment when I had already completed a substantial portion of my book. Up to a certain point in his life and career, as the most influential Marxist theorist of his generation Althusser had clearly appeared to be a critical philosopher and political thinker in a recognizably Rousseauist mold. It was only as a consequence of his murder of his wife in November 1980 that he turned to autobiography as such to explain the circumstances and causes of that act.

Moreover, Althusser was self-conscious in recognizing the importance of Rousseau's legacy, not simply in the sphere of political thought but also relative to the practice of "confession" itself: "Finally, I found in the *Confessions* the unique example of a kind of 'autoanalysis,' entirely devoid of self-satisfaction, in which Rousseau manifestly made discoveries about himself in the process of writing and of reflecting on the most significant experiences of his childhood and his life, and, for the first time in the history of literature, *on sex* and on the admirable theory of the 'sexual supplement' that Derrida has given a remarkable analysis of as a figure of castration" (*Future*, 212–13). With *The Future Lasts a Long Time* Althusser followed Rousseau's lead and thereby realized a previously undisclosed ambition to be a "writer." With the publication of that book his oeuvre as a whole comes to have a distinctly Rousseauist look; that is, it combines theoretical and polemical writings of a primarily political character with a suspicion of the aesthetic and a penchant for personal witness and autobiographical revelation.

At the same time, it is symptomatic of the sociocultural change I have been describing here that Althusser's final work should reach his readers only from beyond the grave, and that although he remained unrepentant in his commitment to the communist cause, its publication occurred against the background of the virtually complete loss of faith in France not only in communism and Marxism but also, for the first time since the end of the *ancien régime,* in revolution as a way of change. The case of Althusser confirms by opposition the fact that after more than two centuries the idea of the "writer," like the French Revolution with which it was associated almost from the beginning, is over.

Given the great influence he exercised in the last decade or so of his life, it seems appropriate to give the last word on the brief historical trajectory of "the writer" traced here to Michel Foucault. His deeply ambivalent relationship to those working in that tradition, as well as to "the general intellectual," is illuminating, and it is something I will return to at the end. Of the generation of intellectuals that first came to prominence in the 1960s, he was one of the first to articulate the idea that the age of historicisms and of "the great faiths" was ending even in France. Further, by the end of his life Foucault seemed to be making a transition to something new, the starting point for which was the critique of the uses of confession to be found in the first volume of his counterhistory of sexuality, *The Will to Know.* A renewal of interest in ethics went along with the openness to aesthetics, at least in relation to the self, and a readiness to engage in debate with thinkers from the English-speaking world as well as with the tradition of the Frankfurt school and Jürgen Habermas.

Finally, there was in Foucault's life and work a visible ambiguity in the attraction of anonymity or of self-effacement, on the one hand, and openness to a public role, on the other. The ambiguity is effectively summed up in the cryptic final remarks of an interview he gave in English in 1983. In response to a query as to how he felt about "a popular status" consecrated by a column on him in *Time* magazine, he deliberately left open the question of the relationship between an author and his work as well as that of the degree to which a private life should be made public: "As far as my personal life is uninteresting, it is not worthwhile making a secret of it. By the same token, it may not be worthwhile publicizing it."[28]

CHAPTER 1

Jean-Jacques Rousseau:
Putting the Polis
in Command

TRANSPARENCY: A very common term in political and journalistic discourse in Europe. It means: the exposure of individual lives to public view. . . . The urge to violate another's privacy is an age-old form of aggressivity that in our day is institutionalized (bureaucracy with its documents, the press with its reporters), justified morally (the right to know having become first among the rights of man), and poeticized (by the lovely French word transparence).

MILAN KUNDERA

Given the argument I am developing in this book, it should be pointed out right away that what interests me here is not Rousseau but "Rousseau," not the man or his writings for their own sake but what he has come to mean in the light of his legacy. My focus is on those aspects of his life and work that contributed after the fact to the emergence of a cultural hero of a novel type or normative idea that I am calling "the writer." I am concerned with a new practice of writing and the self-representations of its first important practitioner, whose influence has been determinative in a number of important ways far beyond the romantic period in which it is usually assumed to have been ascendant.[1]

To this end, the purpose of the present chapter is primarily to set the scene, to delineate clearly from the point of view of the late twentieth century the bundle of features that constitute the idea of "the writer" Rousseau was the first to embody so completely. Since this will necessarily involve covering ground that may be more or less familiar, I should point out that my intention is less to be original on the subject of the thinker who has generated at least as many books and articles as any other canonical writer in the French tradition than to establish Rousseau's own originality.

The assumption that the heroic generation of philosophes contributed powerfully to a radical transformation of political and literary culture in the decades leading up to the Revolution is a commonplace of French historical writing that in one form or another is as old as the eighteenth

After Albrier, "Jean-Jacques composing his *Emile* in the valley of Montmorency."
(Photo Bibl. Nat.)

century itself. Further, as I indicated in my introduction, the idea that by the 1750s and 1760s a new public literary sphere had emerged in France—and, along with it, a radically different form of political culture—has more recently become a virtually uncontested belief, although in some ways it, too, traces its source at least as far back as Tocqueville. Crucial to this argument are ideas such as the following: that Enlightenment thinkers were committed to the public use of private reason in all spheres of human life, including religion and politics, in ways laid out by Kant in his famous

Allan Ramsay, *Jean-Jacques Rousseau*
(National Gallery of Scotland)

essay "What Is Enlightenment?"; that men of letters imbued by the spirit
of critical philosophy acquired a new importance as advocates of the progress of civilization and political reform; that new or transformed social
institutions such as the salon, the café and, periodical literature emerged
to facilitate the exchange of ideas and the formation of judgments outside
the traditional circuits of power and influence that were the royal court
and the academies; and that the upshot of all these changes was the formation for the first time in France of "public opinion" as a cultural and
political force to be reckoned with.[2]

Jeaurat de Berty, *Revolutionary Allegory*
(Musée Carnavalet)

It is against this background of change that the claim that Rousseau nevertheless constituted something radically distinct and original in the Western cultural tradition has to be understood. This, too, is a notion that had its origins in Enlightenment France among the actors themselves, for reasons I shall return to. However, a significant aspect of Rousseau's radical difference is caught in a concise aside by Mona Ozouf that focuses on the importance in French revolutionary thought of "the idea of a new man":

> In any case, apart from Rousseau, none of the philosophes believe in regeneration [*renouveau*], either politically or ethically. Voltaire, Diderot, d'Holbach, d'Alembert, they are all committed to transformations that are specific, concerted, and slow. They are all held back by the idea that, as d'Alembert puts it, against an enemy who is multiform and who has already advanced too far one is obliged to fight the war inch by inch. Rousseau alone breaks with this concern for the limits of the possible.[3]

But it is not only in the debate over the production of a new man that he stands apart from his contemporary philosophes.

Rousseau, of course, had no hesitation in making a claim for his originality on a number of occasions. Although he would not necessarily have recognized himself in the portrait of "the writer" I am sketching here with the hindsight of close to two and a half centuries of historical change, he provides a wonderful opening for my purpose with the celebrated first lines of his *Confessions:* "I am undertaking an enterprise that is without precedent and that will never be imitated. I want to show my fellow men a man in the whole truth of his nature, and that man is myself."[4]

It is a fundamental premise of this book that in these first two sentences Rousseau was both right and massively wrong. He was right because in the very act of uttering these words the eighteenth century's most disturbing original thinker did indeed inaugurate something important in the French literary tradition; he was massively wrong because the subsequent history of "the writer" in France and elsewhere has involved repeating in a variety of guises the enterprise of autoportraiture to which he refers.

Western literature did not, of course, wait until the mid-eighteenth century to conduct literary exercises in self-analysis or even autobiography (although the word itself is, in fact, a late-eighteenth-century coinage that first appeared in English). As his very choice of a title suggests, Rousseau was very aware of the dominant model furnished by Saint Augustine's narrative of Christian witness centered on retrospective self-accounting, the acknowledgment of one's sins, and an act of conversion. Relatively closer to hand, there were also what might be called the pagan countermodels of the European Renaissance—essays of critical and stoic self-reflection in the style of Michel de Montaigne or energetic narratives of turbulent artists' lives like Benvenuto Cellini's. Even closer in time were the confessional works of the pietists and other unorthodox Christian sects. Moreover, the eighteenth-century sentimental tradition clearly promoted in a number of genres the externalization of intimate impressions, thoughts and feelings of a kind often associated with autobiography. In memoirs—apparently genuine or fictionalized—journals, and exchanges of letters, authors took up the task of giving more or less detailed accounts of their inner lives and their often painful, ennobling, or insalubrious encounters with the world.[5]

The originality of Rousseau's *Confessions* lies elsewhere. What, along with a new frankness, he powerfully inaugurates—and not simply for French literary culture—is an identification between life and writing that is alien to the ethos of French classicism. It is an identification that in retrospect we can see contributed in a crucial way to establishing the very image of "the writer." If the *Confessions* is such an influential work, it is in large part because it affirms the intimate association between the unfolding of a singular life and the activity of authorship; self-revelation and self-representation come to be integral to a practice of writing assumed as a vocation.

Along with the claim to tell the whole, unadorned truth about the self, another crucial and related characteristic projected by the *Confessions* is that of writing conceived of as contestation and risk-taking, as resistance to a given order of things and even as a sacrifice of self. Such attitudes appear obliquely in the opening lines just quoted as an insistence on the unprecedented nature of the enterprise. They also appear directly in the famous prefatory note that precedes the first page of the text in the Geneva manuscript—a note that is, in almost equal parts, a demand for love, a symptom of paranoia, a plea for understanding, and an affirmation of defiance:

> Here is the only portrait of a man, painted exactly and truthfully from nature, that exists and probably ever will exist. Whoever you are, who through my destiny or my trust have been made the judge of this volume, I beg you on the grounds of my misfortunes and of all you hold most dear *[par vos entrailles]*, as well as in the name of the human species, not to annihilate a useful and unique work, a work that may serve as a primary piece of evidence in the comparative study of mankind, which is still to be undertaken, and not to efface from the memory of my honor the only sure monument of my character that has not been deformed by my enemies. Finally, even if you were yourself one of my implacable enemies, cease to be one toward my ashes, and do not pursue your cruel injustice unto that time when neither you nor I will any longer be alive, so that you may for once bear witness to the fact of having been generous and good when you could have been destructive and vengeful—if it be true that the evil addressed to a man who has never

> committed any, nor wanted to commit any, may be called ven-
> geance. (*Confessions*, 2)

What one observes above all in this prefatory note is the nature of the self-representation and the emotive style of address. That is, on the one hand, it already points toward the self-portrait of persecuted genius that will follow in the body of the text and, on the other, it is characterized by a rare paranoid fierceness of tone. At the same time, there is the claim that the will to tell the truth about the author's life and times encounters circumstances that make truth-telling peculiarly difficult. From the beginning, Rousseau defines his situation as marginal to the established social order and adopts a stance that is oppositional. He represents himself to his reader as one against many, as alone against an uncomprehending public sphere. Hence the desire to enlist his reader's understanding for a cause that is claimed to be that of truth and justice itself.[6]

Moreover, extrapolating from his own situation, in the body of the *Confessions* Rousseau will go on to identify in the malevolence that surrounds him symptoms of the need for the moral regeneration of modern man and of that sociopolitical order that had corrupted his originally benevolent nature: he will, as he puts it with reference to the *Discourse on the Origin and Foundation of Inequality among Men,* show mankind that "the true source of its misfortunes is in its supposed perfection."[7] *J'accuse* alternates in the text of the autobiography itself with *je me confesse.*

At the same time, the *Confessions* consciously brings together the moral ethos of the eighteenth-century sentimental tradition—inaugurated in European literature by such figures as Samuel Richardson and l'abbé Prévost and given such triumphant form in his own *Julie, or The New Héloïse* (1761)—with the same century's philosophical ambition to construct a new and reformed collective future. Yet Rousseau transcends both the sentimental and philosophic traditions in his insistence on the need for radically new beginnings on the individual as well as the collective level.

Man was to be reinvented. And in order for this to happen the whole truth of his nature had to be revealed, even if that meant that the *Confessions* sometimes reminds us of the fact that the eighteenth century was also a great age of erotic and libertine literature, of Sterne, Cleland, Laclos, Crébillon fils, Sade, and Casanova, as well as of the novelists just referred to. Although this is not an affiliation Rousseau would have cared to affirm, much of the interest and originality of his autobiography have, in fact, to do with its scandalous aspects of which those that concern his erotic life are among the most prominent. In this connection, it is characteristic that, in the narrative of his encounter with the Venetian courtesan Zulietta, he justifies the shocking details on the grounds of his commitment to candor and rejects what he calls "a false sense of decency" (la fausse bienséance) (378). If, as Foucault claimed, for a long time in modern European history sex was taken to be the secret of secrets of an individual life, then Rousseau was one of the first to exploit that view so forcefully.[8]

Rousseau did not, of course, wait until a relatively late work such as the *Confessions* to articulate the attitudes and the self-understanding of his role in the world that he expresses there. There is, on the contrary, a single-mindedness and a continuity in his thinking in this respect that goes back to his earliest works of cultural criticism and philosophical critique. The claim to uniqueness and the spirit of contestation referred to above are combined early on with a will to sociopolitical intervention that, along with "confessionalism," is the other leading attribute of "the writer."

Among other things, as I shall go on to argue, Rousseau is also the first modern theorist of alienation of a kind with which the twentieth century has been especially familiar. Moreover, in turning against the culture of the Enlightenment and the idea of the sovereignty of autonomous reason in which his fellow philosophes believed, he aimed some of his fiercest critiques at "the republic of letters" to which he at one time had seemed to belong.

A closer look at some crucial works will give greater consistency to the idea of "the writer" that Rousseau came to exemplify for subsequent generations. Along with the *Confessions,* two works that are of particular relevance to my purpose are the *Discourse on the Sciences and the Arts* (1750) and the *Letter to D'Alembert on Theater* (1758). The First Discourse and the *Letter,* taken together, are in many ways Rousseau's equivalent of Sartre's *What Is Literature?* written two centuries later; and it is part of the thesis of this book that there is significant continuity between them, between the theory of *engagement* propounded in the 1940s and the profound distrust of the sciences, the arts, and literature expressed by Rousseau.

From the perspective of the late twentieth century, it is even possible to assign a precise date to the beginning of the paradigm change I associate with Rousseau's example—of the emergence of "the writer" as cultural hero on the scene of European culture—namely, early October 1749. I have in mind, of course, the First Discourse and what, as a consequence of Rousseau's genius for self-dramatizing episodes, has come to be known as the "illumination de Vincennes'; the first new beginning referred to in his writings concerns his own inner life.

As Rousseau explains both in Part 2 of his *Confessions* (1769–71) and in the second of his four *Letters to Malesherbes* (1762), it was on his way to visit Diderot in prison at Vincennes that he came across the announcement of the topic proposed by the Académie de Dijon for an essay competition: "Whether the reestablishment of the Sciences and the Arts has contributed to the purifying of manners." It was, as we know, in response to this topic that he wrote the first of the critical pamphlets to be marked by the reforming zeal and the polemical truculence which characterize his work as a whole.

The reason the episode concerned has been designated the "illumination de Vincennes" is because, a decade or so after the fact, Rousseau implicitly associates his coming upon the topic proposed by the academy with a religious conversion; like Saint Paul on the road to Damascus or Saint Augustine in the garden in Milan, he discovered that he was the recipient of a message from a mysterious and authoritative source, a message that in an instant was to change him forever: "At the moment of reading, I saw another universe and became another man." The change was instantaneous, not to say miraculous.[9] Moreover, that the experience involved was in some sense providential was confirmed for him by the fact that it was registered in his body as a kind of biblical "fear and trembling": "[W]hen I arrived at Vincennes, I was in a state of agitation bordering on delirium" (*Confessions*, 416). Given Rousseau's familiarity with the founding texts of the Christian tradition, it is hard to imagine he did not interpret the experience as a sign that he had effectively been singled out for a mission that was to change his life, although he leaves his reader to draw that inference.

However, if in Rousseau's representation the episode resembles a religious conversion, from the point of view of the late twentieth century it can also be said to have the character of an ideological interpellation in the sense Althusser once gave the term in a celebrated essay;[10] the topic apparently posed in all innocence by a learned academy for a competition was interpreted by its recipient as a coded message that addressed him personally and had the character of a solemn mandate. Rousseau was changed by "a letter" that, in the Lacanian scheme on which Althusser relies, enabled him to interpret the desire of the Other, the big Other that is the sociosymbolic order in which we are immersed and in which we are obliged to assume a given role at the cost of alienation. Thenceforth, as the *Confessions* indicate in the very different discourse of their time, the author discovered his vocation; he had been invested with a new sociosymbolic identity that had the effect of eliminating doubt and flooding his life with purpose.

A second famous anecdote connected with this same experience—though not an anecdote Rousseau himself narrated—is almost equally suggestive of what it was that Rousseau inaugurated when he was preparing to write the essay that was to launch his career as thinker and "writer." The claim goes that on his arrival at Vincennes not only did Diderot encourage him to participate in the competition, he also anticipated Rousseau's future as "antiphilosophe" by affirming, "You will take the position that no one else will take."[11] *Se non è vero è ben trovato*, since whether or not they were indeed Diderot's words, they do confirm the character of the mandate that Rousseau took up from his First Discourse on; it is a mandate that was to be fulfilled through the act of writing conceived not as art but as a form of oppositional action designed to reform from the ground up an increasingly corrupt world. In this respect the question posed by the academy and the argument Rousseau developed in response to it are also of the highest significance. The first work by which he was to come before a wider public was a polemic against the science, literature, and art that were largely constitutive of what we mean by the Enlightenment. The position he took is that there are values to be defended in this world and work to be done that transcend those activities.

In short, the sociosymbolic identity assumed from Rousseau's First Discourse on is that of "writer" in the sense I am giving the word. And it is important to note the novelty of such an identity in the mid-eighteenth century: its emergence is part of the history of our cultural modernity that for almost a hundred nears now has preoccupied such important thinkers as Max Weber, Walter Benjamin, Theodor Adorno, Max Horkheimer, Jürgen Habermas, Michel Foucault, and Jean-François Lyotard.

Four years after the "illumination de Vincennes," another, even more politically pointed question posed by the Académie de Dijon concentrated Rousseau's attention in a way similar to that of 1749, namely, "What is the source of inequality among men, and is it authorized by natural law?" On this occasion it was, according to his account in the *Confessions,* while wandering through the forest of Saint-Germain in the company of Thérèse Le Vasseur that he found the necessary inspiration for his response. It was in that less than pristine corner of "primitive nature" that Rousseau apparently first pictured to himself what life must have been like in human prehistory and decided to reveal to contemporary Europeans the misconceptions they had about their condition and the fact that the source of their discontents was in themselves. Particularly striking is the prophetic tone of voice; given the question posed, the effect is, for good or ill, to inject the eloquence of religious preaching into a political discourse that addresses humanity at large: "Exalted by these sublime meditations, my soul rose toward the Divinity, and observing from there my fellows following the path of their prejudices, their errors, misfortunes, and crimes, I cried out in a weak voice that they could not hear, 'Fools who always complain about nature, understand that all your miseries are of your own devising' " (460).

As the references to the works under discussion suggest, central to the vocation of "the writer" as practiced by Rousseau are two very distinct genres, the critical philosophical essay and autobiography. The *Discourse on the Sciences and the Arts* and the *Discourse on the Origin of Inequality* are the first in a series of polemical essays of moral and sociopolitical philosophy—what nowadays we call "culture criticism"—that made Rousseau both famous and controversial in his lifetime; the passages in which

Rousseau evokes his 1749 "illumination" and the inspirational walk of 1753 in the forest of Saint-Germain are both from the *Confessions,* the work of his that in many ways has proved the most durable.

If the philosophical essay and autobiography have anything in common, it is that they are both characterized by a relative formlessness. Although in the case of the essay the theory and practice of classical rhetoric did lend a certain formal structure to the presentation of ideas, neither genre was subjected to the strict codification associated with, say, the different genres and subgenres of poetry or drama in the neoclassical aesthetic. As a result, the author was apparently free to argue his case directly or to indulge in a proto-romantic expressivity that was unconstrained by the external constraints of "mere form." To anticipate a little, one can say that it is characteristic of "the writer" Rousseau was struggling to become that he had no faith in the formal properties of "literature" to articulate the truths of his being, as the *Discourse on the Sciences and the Arts* implies: form divorced from content is perceived instead as an alienation of the self. Thus, integral to the appeal of Rousseau's work as a whole, from the First Discourse virtually to the end of his career, is this guiding belief in the possibility of a nonalienated way of being and of communicating in the world. The mark of a powerful personality overwhelms the depersonalizing constraints of form and at the same time breaks with literary convention by establishing a new and more intimate relationship with the work's reader.[12]

Through his two favorite genres also Rousseau characteristically associates the public and the private spheres: the first two Discourses belong to what is one of the most public of genres, the genre that is directly concerned with the *res publica* in a rhetorical style familiar from classical literature, that of the moral and sociopolitical essay in which the writer's self is ostensibly least at issue;[13] the *Confessions* belongs to the category of works whose material concerns by definition some of the most intimate aspects of the private life. In this respect the autobiographical writings have a great deal in common with the related genre of letter writing of which Rousseau was almost equally fond.

From the circumstances and topics of Rousseau's earliest critical writings, it is possible to extrapolate the general direction taken by him as moral philosopher, culture critic, political theorist, pedagogue, and "Legislator" in such subsequent works as the other Discourses, *Emile, The Social Contract,* and the *Considerations on the Government of Poland.* Outside his correspondence, it was not until a decade or so after the early Discourses that Rousseau began to write works with an important autobiographical component (from, say, the *Letters to Malesherbes* of 1762); it was, however, a form of writing that he returned to frequently thereafter down through the turbulent and fragmented final work on which he was still working at the moment of his death in 1778, *The Reveries of a Soli-*

tary Walker. In other words, the critical philosophical essay and autobiography in one form or another constitute the bulk of Rousseau's writings and are intimately associated with posterity's sense of his importance and uniqueness;[14] no author in the modern world had previously combined in that way political and sociocultural critique with confessional writing, although a great many would do so over the following centuries.

However, as far as "confession" is concerned, it is impossible in the late twentieth century not to observe in passing that to the two distinct, though occasionally overlapping, forms of "confession" long associated with the religious and literary spheres[15] one must add the practice of "confession" as an instrument of political terror. There is a sense in which all confessions are "forced confessions," although it would be cynical as well as cruel to confuse the "confessions" wrung, say, from the broken defendants of Stalinist show trials with those that proceed from the burden of psychic guilt. Nevertheless, precisely because in the *Confessions* and elsewhere Rousseau goes out of his way to offer himself up to public scrutiny, he challenges the very legitimacy of the idea of a separate and inviolable private sphere—"the right to privacy"—that is central to the theory of political liberalism. The implied ideal of the *Confessions* is what Jean Starobinski, following Rousseau's own lead, called "transparency."[16] But the lesson of the twentieth century has been that "transparency" on Rousseau's terms is an illusion, and a dangerous one at that. Since through his practice Rousseau implies that the virtuous man is by definition also a good citizen who has nothing to hide, he casts suspicion on those who refuse to show and tell all; it is an attitude that by implication legitimates the practice of surveillance and social control on condition that the political order be a legitimate one.

The First Discourse was, of course, written as a response to a question posed by the Académie de Dijon for an essay competition in 1749, and a clue to the reason why that question was, in effect, experienced by Rousseau as an interpellation is related to a key term in the title: "Whether the reestablishment of the Sciences and the Arts have contributed to the purifying of manners" *[épurer les moeurs]*.[17] As posed, the subject is tendentious enough: it invites a response that assumes a moral function for art and learning and it foregrounds a highly charged word, "épurer," that already had longstanding ethical and aesthetic as well as medicinal connotations. One can only suppose that the provincial academicians from Dijon who asked the question expected, if not an outright affirmative answer, at the very most a "Yes, but . . . ." Such an answer would have associated Rousseau with the philosophical mainstream of his age, which asserted that progress in all aspects of human affairs depended on the perfection of the sciences and the arts. Such, in any case, was the line of thought that stretched from Voltaire's *Philosophical Letters* (1734) and *The Century* of *Louis XIV* (1751) through d'Alembert's *Preliminary Discourse* in the *Encyclopédie* (1751–52) down through Condorcet's *Sketch for a Historical Picture of the Progress of the Human Spirit* (1793). Yet with a symptomatic gesture that can, in retrospect, be perceived as an opening on to Rousseau's whole future career as moral philosopher and political thinker, in the opening sentence of the Discourse he restates the question, with a notable addition: "Whether the reestablishment of the Sciences and the Arts have contributed to the purification *or the corruption* of manners" (5; emphasis mine).

The effect of Rousseau's metonymic slide is to highlight what was to become for him the kind of master signifier that stabilizes an ideological field, fixes meanings, and mobilizes interventionist energies. Surrounded by "corruption," he will make "purity"—or its virtual synonym in the context, "virtue"—the goal to be pursued throughout his life, on both the individual and the collective level, even when, as is sometimes the case, he is also succumbing to the temptations of the world. Moreover, to move from the title to the text of Rousseau's first important work is to realize how a whole critical essay is organized in terms of a series of equivalences and oppositional terms centered on the opposition "corruption"/"purity" as a kind of nodal point: nature, being, freedom, virtue, truth, vigor, manliness, simplicity, utility, and industriousness line up against civilization, appearance, enslavement, moral corruption, deception, masquerade, degeneration, effeminacy, politeness, luxury, leisure, philosophy, literature, the arts, and even learning (in the form of "the sciences").

Further, what the former equivalences presuppose in comparison with the latter, is a spirit of sacrifice: whereas the latter may be said to be associated in one way or another with the Freudian pleasure principle (although some of them are clearly at its destabilizing outer limit), the former have the quality of an ethical imperative; they smack of "duty" and "responsibility," of a giving up of self to that which, whether within or without (God, nature, empire, nation, class, leader, or, in Rousseau's case, "Geneva"), transcends the self. It is the spirit of sacrifice in a noble cause that gives rise to the militant tone of the First Discourse: the essay is the kind of moralistic and civic call to order familiar enough from the tradition of republican Roman discourse, but that seems decidedly out of place in the Paris of Louis XV, as Rousseau himself was aware. It is therefore characteristic of the moral ethos and argument of the First Discourse that it should end with a comparison between "two great Peoples," namely, Athens and Sparta, of which the first "knew how to speak well *[savait bien dire]*, and the other to act well *[bien faire]*" (30). From the beginning (political) action is elevated above (aesthetic) performance.

One does not have to read very far into the text of the First Discourse, then, to realize that at its heart is a fierce and generalized suspicion of the pursuit of knowledge for its own sake and especially of art and literature. Moreover, as far as the latter are concerned, they are required to justify themselves on grounds that transcend the aesthetic in the direction of morality and politics.

In this connection it is interesting to note that in his recent, posthumously published autobiography, *The Future Lasts a Long Time,* Louis Althusser praises Rousseau for his understanding of the important connection between art and ideology.[18] The most influential Western Marxist theorist of his generation clearly shared his eighteenth-century predecessor's suspicion of the sphere of the aesthetic to the point of claiming that Rousseau was one of the earliest thinkers to formulate the concept of hegemony (although the Enlightenment philosopher did not, of course, use that Gramscian term): "I take Rousseau to be the first theorist of hegemony— after Machiavelli" (212).[19]

Althusser claims to have discovered the theory of hegemony in Rousseau's Second Discourse, *On the Origin of Inequality* (1755), but the First Discourse is, in fact, even more explicit on the subject:

> Whereas the Government and Laws provide for the security and the well-being of the collectivity of men, the Sciences, Letters and the Arts, though perhaps less despotic and less powerful, hang their garlands of flowers over the iron chains that weigh men down, stifle in them the feeling for the original liberty they seemed born for, make them love their slavery, and turn them into what are known as civilized Peoples. (*Sciences,* 6–7)[20]

In short, the sciences, literature, and the arts are a crucial factor in seducing humanity into overlooking the lack of freedom and injustices of its sociopolitical condition.

From the point of view of twentieth-century Marxist theory, the concept of hegemony, along with Althusser's revisionist theory of the functioning of ideology,[21] forced attention on cultural production as, in spite of appearances, a site of political conflict, as a relatively autonomous practice characterized by fundamental class antagonisms. Yet two centuries earlier Rousseau had already understood that to take hegemony seriously is to believe in the necessity, under certain conditions, of banning books or of the policing of thought; in a conflict between the demand for freedom for art and for the institution of social justice, there is no doubt where Rousseau stood, any more than Althusser. Moreover, Rousseau's writings may be regarded as the site in which a disturbing connection is made between censor in the antique republican Roman sense and the modern meaning of the term.[22]

The great originality of Rousseau's opening pamphlet in what was to be his lifelong adversarial relationship with Enlightenment culture appears not only in the fact that he anticipates the twentieth-century concept of hegemony but that the First Discourse as a whole also has the character of what, after Nietzsche and Foucault, would come to be known as a "genealogy" or critical counterhistory. The work is, in effect, a "Genealogy of Science, Literature, and Art" in which Rousseau discovers the masked origins of the arts and sciences in vice and amour propre as well as in a form of the will to power: "Astronomy is born of superstition; Eloquence of ambition, hatred, flattery, deceit; Geometry of avarice; Physics of a vain curiosity; and all of them, including Morality itself, of our vices: we would have fewer doubts about their advantages if they owed them to our virtues" (17).

Perhaps nowhere is the gap separating Rousseau from virtually all other major thinkers of the Enlightenment period more obvious than in this denunciation of the sciences and arts. If one contrasts the statement here with the argument made in the Kant essay referred to earlier, "What is Enlightenment?" the fundamental differences are obvious. In arguing for an idea of Enlightenment that is synonymous with humanity's acceptance of its maturity as free and autonomous beings who are guided in the public sphere by the sole light of their individual reason and are prepared to debate any issue, Kant gives his essay the brave motto "Aude sapere" ("Dare to know"). It would not be inaccurate to formulate the meaning of Rousseau's First Discourse as virtually the opposite: "Noli audere sapere" ("Dare to remain ignorant").

Ironically enough, in the light of subsequent history, Kant even assumes that although rulers might be misguided enough to impose a given religious faith, "they have no interest in assuming the role of guardians over their subjects so far as the arts and sciences are concerned," [23] which is, of course, precisely what Rousseau proposes. In any case, he concludes that the arts and sciences are corrupt in their origins, in their objects of study and representation, and in the negative influence they exercise on politics and morals.

It is not, therefore, surprising that it is Kant rather than Rousseau who has come to be regarded by a critical tradition in German philosophy as the first theorist of modernity. The reason for this is that he was the first to break out of the premodern, holistic world of ideas and affirm the existence of three distinct forms of knowledge—the scientific/technological, the moral-practical, and the aesthetic—and to affirm the importance of maintaining their autonomy. If this is how we are to understand modernity, then it clearly follows that, insofar as he privileges the moral-practical sphere, Rousseau is premodern and even archaizing, in ways to which I shall refer later.

It may well be that from the perspective of the twentieth century there is something naive in Kant's uncritical celebration of reason, as German thinkers from Weber through Benjamin, Horkheimer, and Adorno and down to Habermas have not been slow to point out. Yet "the dialectic of Enlightenment" on which they have focused has nevertheless implied the existence of positive as well as negative reason; and it is a position that Foucault belatedly associated himself with in an important lecture for which he borrowed Kant's title. He associates himself there with the idea of the bifurcation that so preoccupied the Frankfurt school between emancipatory reason and the instrumental, coercive kind. His lecture formulates the opposition in terms of "the growth of autonomy" and "the growth of capabilities," in the sense of technologies of control, disciplines and procedures of normalization.[24]

Rousseau, on the other hand, seems to have had trouble seeing anything other than the negative side of reason—which makes him perhaps the first of the great modern "masters of suspicion."[25] One cannot imagine Kant ever asserting, as Rousseau does notoriously in the *Discourse on the Origin of Inequality*, that a "state of reflection is a state against Nature, and that the man who meditates is a depraved animal" (138). In this and other of Rousseau's works then, it is clear that the critique of the Enlightenment associated in different ways with Marx and Nietzsche as well as with Weber and the Frankfurt school, Althusser and Foucault, among many others, itself had its origin in the age of Enlightenment.

Perhaps the most notable aspect of the First Discourse is, however, that Rousseau justifies his attack on Enlightenment culture not simply in Kantian moral-practical terms, but in terms in which the political assumes the role of master discourse; in other words, morality tends to be collapsed into an exclusively political morality. The fact that, in lieu of the author's name, the title page originally bore the clearly honorific phrase "By a Citizen of Geneva" immediately alerts the reader to the political dimension of the work, as well as to its character as a demand for acknowledgment from a homeland the author had left at the age of fifteen. In any case, the human virtue Rousseau chiefly celebrates in the First Discourse contains something of the antique meaning of the word; that is, it is associated with honor and self-mastery. Above all, perhaps, it is civic virtue of the kind that makes for the social order, power, and stability of collectivities and nations. The point of view adopted is that of polis or state and not that of the individual, in spite of his references to the loss of individual freedom that characterizes those states in which learning, literature, and the arts flourish.

Consequently, it is not surprising that Rousseau's ideal states turn out to be Sparta and republican Rome, where ascetic values virtually excluded aesthetic ones. "Oh! Sparta," he eulogizes, "the eternal opprobrium of a false doctrine! Whereas the vices produced by the fine arts entered Athens, whereas a Tyrant there assembled with great care the works of the Prince of Poets, you banished from within your walls Arts and Artists, Sciences and Scientists" (*Sciences*, 12). Moreover, Rousseau goes on to endorse the affirmation of Fabricius Luscinus, the third century B.C. Roman general and censor, famed for his poverty, austerity, and incorruptibility, that the mission of Rome was to subdue and impose morality: "Let others distinguish themselves with their vain talents; the only talent worthy of Rome is to conquer the world and to make virtue reign" (15). In the context of the urbane forms of sociability and taste associated with the literary, artis tic, and philosophical culture of the mid-eighteenth century, the "virile virtue" invoked here appears to be disturbingly single-minded and antique.[26]

The open *Letter to D'Alembert on Theater* of 1758 effectively consecrated Rousseau's break with his erstwhile friends and collaborators, the philosophes, including in particular Denis Diderot and Jean Le Rond D'Alembert, the coeditors of that great summum of Enlightenment thought, the *Encyclopédie* (1751–65). In his open letter Rousseau in effect gives his most complete response to the Sartrean question "What is literature?" And the response is, of course, that it is not much or, at least, not much that is good.[27] The *Letter* is Rousseau's longest sustained attack on the most social and urbane form of literary expression. It is significant because in refuting D'Alembert's mild plea, in his article on Geneva in the *Encyclopédie,* that the Calvinist republic allow theatrical productions for the sake of "urbanity" and the improvement of taste, Rousseau develops further the themes of his First Discourse of almost a decade earlier.

Given the character of his writings in the intervening years, the fervor of his refutation of D'Alembert hardly constitutes a surprise, especially in light of the fact that Voltaire, who was a devotee of theater and was living nearby at Saint-Jean, was an interested party. From Rousseau's point of view, D'Alembert's inconsiderate proposal amounts, in effect, to an assault on the "Geneva" of his own fantasy scenario, that is, on the utopian idea of a republican city-state characterized by virtue, thrift, egalitarianism, unity, and faith, and consequently free of the inequities and ostentation of old-regime monarchy. Rousseau's Geneva is an anti-Paris, the antithesis of the metropolis whose reputation for idle living, corruption, and debauchery, associated in part with gambling and with theater, was an important topos of eighteenth-century French literature.

In any case, to admit theatrical performances into such an achieved social totality was, for Rousseau, to introduce once again the vices of representation, critical worldliness, irony, detachment, doubt, pleasure, and play on the part of the authors; masquerade and immorality on the part of actors and actresses; and leisure, luxury, display, and effeminacy on the part of the audience. Perhaps even more than the other arts discussed in the First Discourse, theater and all those associated with it (from playwrights, actors, and actresses to its philosophical apologists and the members of the public who constituted its audience) were in their way the agents of such "corruption."

The *Letter* makes clear that no figure exemplified so notoriously the dangerous, seductive power of theater for Rousseau as did Molière, a preeminent "man of the theater" who virtually singlehandedly created French classical comedy and whose patrons had been the royal court and seventeenth-century Parisian salon society. Molière's comedies constituted the most compelling evidence against theater for "the citizen of Geneva," inasmuch as an enormous talent can be seen to have been put in the service of wit and worldliness and a skeptical ethic of accommodation that undermines the very idea of a non-alienating society characterized by political virtue, moral seriousness, natural hierarchy, and social harmony.[28]

At the heart of Rousseau's polemical essay there is, of course, the celebrated defense of Alceste, the central character of *The Misanthrope*, against his author. The section is illuminating, in the first place, for the obvious way in which Rousseau identifies with Molière's comic hero and in particular with the cleansing energy of his "hate": "What is Molière's Misanthrope then? A good man who hates the morals of his time and the wickedness of his contemporaries; who precisely because he loves his fellow men hates in them the evils they do to each other and the vices these evils cause" (49). In the second place, the passage is suggestive insofar as it throws light on the fantasmatic character of Rousseau's reasoning and the connection made between the private man and his social world.

On the level of the social world, to identify with the Misanthrope is to believe in the possibility of a homogeneous and transparent society, characterized by total honesty, complementarity, and reciprocity in its relations—in other words, an impossible and probably totalitarian society or one that can only exist as social fantasy. On the level of the private man, to identify with the Misanthrope is to fail to appreciate the underlying comic structure of the character, that is to say, the way in which Alceste lives a contradiction; Alceste is a comic character, not a model of moral rectitude in a hypocritical world, because of the antagonism he visibly embodies, namely, that between a dogmatic moral stance and a passion, between contempt for the insincerity of human social relations and desire for a coquette who is a living incarnation of that insincerity. As he indicates in a brilliant sentence, Rousseau was aware of this—"Making his Misanthrope fall in love was nothing; the stroke of genius was in making him fall in love with a coquette" (75)—but he resents the resulting ridiculousness of the figure. It is as if Rousseau, in this case at least, wants to deny the possibility of the divided self or subjectivity in the modern psychoanalytic sense of the word; in the face of so much evidence in himself and others, Rousseau clings to the dangerous illusion of homogeneity and transparency within and without, of full accessibility of self to self and of self to others.

It is for similar reasons that he also indignantly condemns the art of acting as such; there is for him an implied connection between the social role-playing of the characters who surround Alceste in Molière's play and those who earn a living from pretending to be that which they are not, namely, actors and actresses: "In what does an actor's talent consist? It is in the art of counterfeiting himself, of donning another character than his own, of appearing different from what he is, of pretending passion when he feels none, of saying something different from what he thinks just as naturally as if he really thought it, and, finally, of forgetting his own situation by dint of imitating that of others" (106). Actors are the incarnation of masquerade and nontransparency; acting is an art that makes a virtue of the human capacity to appear what one is not and is, therefore, the worst possible model for citizens in an ideal republic.

If one follows Slavoj Zizek's advice in the sphere of "the criticism of ideology"[29]—namely, to locate "the symptom" that explains the logic of enjoyment—one finds that the particular "symptom" which provides the clue to an understanding of Rousseau's ideological fantasizing is precisely the identification of the sciences and the arts, including preeminently "literature," with "corruption"; it is the sciences and the arts pursued as ends in themselves that in the First Discourse are represented as, to a significant degree, both cause and effect of the decadence of the modern European monarchies, as the locus of an inadmissible form of pleasure, and hence as obstacles to the making of a new society on sound moral and political principles.[30] Perhaps the most disturbing part of Rousseau's argument in his early writings, in fact, is the implication that a just and egalitarian republic can be created only on the basis of exclusions and the practice of censorship; its founding act includes the virtual expulsion of certain classes of people, such as writers, artists, thinkers, and performers, and the suppression of their works.[31] In the end, theater seems to function for Rousseau as a metaphor for all the arts, with the possible exception of music; from the point of view of civic virtue, art is synonymous with artfulness, with purely formal values, and with the externality of language itself.

Rousseau's ideal society is, in fact, associated crucially with homeostasis, and it is notable for having been inspired largely by the models furnished by classical antiquity, notably Sparta, and by classical writers from Plato to the second-century Roman statesman Cato the Elder. His goal was above all "to purify" contemporary manners and morals; and in order to achieve that, he was ready to eliminate from the social order a great many of the activities we normally associate with the advancement of enlightenment and "the public sphere" in Jürgen Habermas's sense,[32] along with those who, whether actively or passively, engage in them.

Moreover, the motivation both for the condemnation of certain classes of artists, writers, and thinkers in Rousseau's writings and for his own retreat from contamination by them is in many ways similar to that of antique Roman censor, traditional Church moralist, or modern party ideologue of the Left or the Right; they are all animated by the conviction that those they condemn (be they sophists and epicureans, dramatists, artists, and actors, aristocrats, bourgeois, or Jews) are an intolerable race of *jouisseurs* or voluptuaries—those whom Zizek, in his extension of a familiar Lacanian concept, has called "the subject(s) presumed to enjoy," and therefore those who should be saved from such scandalous enjoyment for their own sake as well as society's—even if it costs them their lives.

There are in this connection two important points to be made: one relates to the idea of "political will" and the other to "cultural revolution." First, over two hundred years before Mao Tse-tung, Rousseau was advocating putting "politics in command,"[33] at least in the form of the polis; with a highly influential reductionist move he subsumed both the practice of science and the arts to politics. Confirmation of this attitude is, in fact, to be found in one ringing sentence in the *Confessions*, at the point where Rousseau is discussing the themes of his projected work *Political Institutions*, of which *The Social Contract* was in the end to be the only substantial result: "I had understood that everything at bottom depended on politics *[tout tenait radicalement de la politique]* and that, however one approached the question, a given people would only ever be what the nature of its government made it" (*Confessions*, 480). Even if one makes allowance for the fact that Rousseau is specifically focusing on political institutions here, the formulation of the problem of moral virtue and human well-being in purely political terms is striking.

Furthermore, this is perhaps the most disturbing of the legacies he passed on to what, in retrospect, can be seen to be the first revolutionary party of the modern world—both in its doctrine and in the organizational techniques it devised for exercising power—the Jacobins. As François Furet puts it in connection with a discussion of Gracchus Babeuf, "[T]he Jacobin belief in the omnipotence of politics gives rise to the idea of the revolutionary party," a formation that Babeuf had already conceptualized by the 1790s as "a group of well-organized partisans who seize the central machinery of the state through a military putsch."[34]

There is, then, at the core of Rousseau's political theory a logic that elides the very notion of civil society and points to Jacobin revolutionary ideology at its most radical,[35] even if one finds in his works no theory of the party and no apology for revolutionary violence. It would be inaccurate as well as unfair to affirm a direct link between, say, Rousseau's Discourses and *The Social Contract*, on the one hand, and the Jacobin dictatorship at the time of the Terror, on the other, but he did prepare the discursive ground.[36]

Paraphrasing Furet in this connection, Lynn Hunt points to the dangerous confusion among the Jacobins that itself had its source in an antimodernist conception of politics at the heart of which was the unifying and coercive concept of the General Will: "The Terror was the logical consequence of the revolutionary distortion of the normal relationship between society and politics; politics was no longer the arena for the representation of competing social interests, but rather a terrorizing instrument for the reshaping of society."[37]

Along with a new conception of "political will," what Rousseau's Discourses and the *Letter to D'Alembert* also make explicit is that "to put the polis in command" is to subject civil society to the kind of total transformation of its values, institutions, and practices that we have come to call "cultural revolution"—a "cultural revolution" of the kind that we associate with almost all the major political revolutions of the modern world, starting with the French on down through the Bolshevik, Chinese, Vietnamese, and Cuban.[38]

In the Europe of the *ancien régime,* then, Rousseau was the first to argue so powerfully for the policing of the aesthetic in the cause of a new radical politics of individual and collective regeneration. It was culture, not war, that he identified as politics by another means. In the light of this, it is fully consistent with his developed political position that he should seek to replace the decadent, cosmopolitan theater of eighteenth-century European high culture with a kind of communitarian "people's theater." In lieu of alien forms of theater in his native Geneva, Rousseau argues for festivals based on the indigenous popular culture and for communal balls that have the great virtue of putting the contented and virtuous populace itself on display to itself; in place of the separation between active performer and passive spectator associated with theater, such spectacles, when properly supervised, would have the function of reaffirming the familial oneness of the collectivity: "These balls . . . would resemble less a public spectacle than the reunion of a great family, and from the midst of such joy and pleasure there would be born the preservation, unity, and prosperity of the Republic" (*Letter,* 176). One finds anticipated here the kind of mass public festivals that, first organized by the revolutionaries in the 1790s, were to become a central feature of the French republican tradition and to be taken up by the various twentieth-century revolutionary movements.

It is in his discussion of public festivals, in fact, that Rousseau evokes a Genevan at play and comes closest to presenting a portrait of his ideal happy, animated citizen in whom, unlike the actor, there is no gap between appearance and being: "He is lively, gay, warm; at such moments his heart is in his eyes as it is on his lips; he seeks to communicate his joy and his pleasures; he invites, he presses, he forces himself upon those who come by, he disputes their company. All the different circles become one; everything belongs to everyone" (170). In a passage such as this one recognizes the emergence of the politicizing of sentiment that at certain moments of high revolutionary fervor was to raise up the idea of "fraternity" to equal status with that of "liberty" and "equality."[39]

In any case, the kind of socially induced happiness Rousseau imagines in such collective popular events requires that modern Western civilization be "purified," or as we might say now in the wake of Bolshevism, "purged" of such divisive and subversive institutions as those of theater. And in such a cause, Rousseau has no qualms about wanting to impose the Spartan spirit of duty and self-sacrifice on his ideal republic. At the same time, he recognizes that, if he expects to be followed, a call for general denial must be preceded by his own example of self-denial. As his autobiography makes clear, his way of responding to the desire of the Other—which in his case is associated with the Calvinist God and the Republic of Geneva—is, on the one hand, to affirm the vanity of all those morally ambivalent achievements in the sciences and the arts celebrated by his contemporaries and, on the other, to explain how he came to see the error of his ways and find the path back to truth and the kind of "virile virtue"[40] that was to be another value he would pass on to the Jacobins and, through them, to revolutionary parties down into our own time.

Further, that Rousseau's suspicion of the aesthetic in general and literature in particular extended to all genres is confirmed by his famous comments on the novel and by his theory of pedagogy as laid out in *Emile, or On Education* (1762). When, in spite of his distrust of the novel, he did indulge himself by writing one (*Julie, or The New Héloïse*), it turned out to be a utopian and sentimental romance in letter form in which one correspondent ostensibly addresses his intimate thoughts directly to another. And even then, in the opening lines of his preface, the author finds it necessary to place the blame for his recourse to the genre on the immorality of his time: "Cities need theatrical performances and corrupt nations novels. I have observed the manners of my time and have published these letters. If only I had lived in an age when I should have thrown them into the fire."[41]

If *Emile* is significant in the context of the relationship between politics and aesthetics in Rousseau's oeuvre, it is because of his programmatic faith in "natural" or "negative" education, which dictates that through infancy and adolescence his Pupil be consciously isolated from virtually all contact with the wider and supposedly corrupt social world. The Tutor conducts his model education in a totally controlled environment remote from the corruptions of urban life—an environment, moreover, in which the exercise of power is all the more sinister because, although ubiquitous, it is also invisible:

> [L]et him [the Pupil] think he is always the master, but you will always be. There is no more perfect a form of subjection than that which gives the appearance of liberty; that way, you capture the will itself. . . . He will, of course, do only what he wants to; but he will only want to do what you want him to; he should not take a step without your having anticipated it; he should not open his mouth without your knowing what he is about to say.[42]

In light of the micropolitics of power outlined here, it is no wonder that Althusser observed a connection between Machiavelli and Rousseau. Among other things, *Emile* turns out to be a potent reminder that coercive reason was indeed a child of the Enlightenment along with emancipatory reason, and that "cultural revolution" was theorized before it was enacted. Pedagogy is clearly seen to resemble here those other "dubious sciences of man," like psychiatry, penology, and sexology, on which Michel Foucault exercised his remarkable critical intelligence. Rousseau seems to suffer no embarrassment in bragging that Emile is the object of a "perfect form of subjection" precisely because the power being exercised is wholly hidden. There are obvious echoes in the above passage of the theme of the Panopticon developed in Foucault's theories of the disciplinary society,[43] of the unseen seer, and of the opposition between the invisibility of the agent of power and the transparency of the objectified subject.

In any case, the course taken by Emile's education confirms that there is a significant cost in coercion in the making of a new man, just as there is in constructing new societies out of old. Some sense of the form that coercion took appears in the educational projects of those revolutionaries who were influenced by Rousseau's pedagogy, as is made clear by Mona Ozouf in the essay already referred to. His works and testimony could be cited both in support of those who believed that a rebirth of humanity might occur immediately and miraculously, like a religious conversion, and those who argued that it would involve organization, vigilance, discipline, and struggle over time, and it was the latter who proved to be his more influential disciples: "The first form [of regeneration] was carefree and spontaneous, the second meticulous and dirigiste—it is always associated with the figure of an invisible legislator or the hidden hand of a pedagogue, since in the second case the dirigiste connection that starts with laws and issues in morals is the only one imaginable."[44]

Dirigisme, in the case of Emile, finds expression above all in the determination to exercise total control over the Pupil's environment. As a result, in opposition to the practice of the age, Rousseau's Tutor delays teaching Emile to read for a long time and argues against giving him a literary education—including exposure in childhood to that "Professor of Cynicism," La Fontaine.[45] Until late adolescence at least, Emile is to be the student of one book, *Robinson Crusoe,* because it is the book that demonstrates the uselessness of books for a solitary, virtuous, and self-sufficient man living in what approximates to the state of nature. The great merit of Defoe's novel for Rousseau is that it teaches the lessons of nature and not of society. Rousseau's championing of *Robinson Crusoe* in *Emile,* coupled with the ban on virtually all other works of literature, is also a reminder that those who believe all wisdom and all essential knowledge is to be found in a single book—the Bible, the Koran, *The Communist Manifesto,* or Mao's "Little Red Book"—typically find no use for the creation and distribution of many competing books.

Taken together, the First Discourse and the *Letter to d'Alembert* are expressions of the "writerly" stance Rousseau adopted vis-à-vis the world; the author is not only willing to risk social ostracism in his determination to tell the truth as he sees it, he clearly enjoys the role (in the strong sense "enjoy" has recently reacquired from contamination by its French cognate). To be marginalized and persecuted by society at large is integral to his perception of the new identity he seeks to forge, since both in the Christian tradition (Christ and the Christian martyrs) as well as in the classical one (from Socrates through the great republican Roman tribunes) persecution is assumed to be the fate of the intransigent truth-tellers and moralists; the existence of powerful and worldly enemies confirms the fact that one is keeping the faith.

It is, in effect, as a recognition of this particular self-identification that one should read the short confessional preface of the First Discourse: "I foresee that I will not be easily pardoned for the position I have dared to take. Confronting directly everything that men currently admire, I can only look forward to universal condemnation *[blâme universel]*" (3). What is both striking and prophetic here is that the author self-consciously foregrounds his presence, invites the reader to consider first, not the work, but the man behind it. Moreover, the weight attached to the final noun/adjective combination of the passage in the French suggests a will to be in the public eye and to face martyrdom for the sake of an unpopular cause in which he believes.

In short, what the texts of the First and Second Discourses confirm, especially when coupled with the passages from the *Confessions* cited earlier, is that from early on Rousseau represents himself to himself as far more than a mere polemicist or one of those struggling *gens de lettres* described by Robert Darnton in *The Literary Underground of the Old Regime*.[46] He is not merely another of those who put their talent to use in the production of works in a number of literary genres in order to curry favor and pursue social advancement on some *ancien régime* Grub Street. In opposition to the worldly *philosophes*—"the wits and men of the world," "free thinkers and philosophers" referred to in the preface of the First Discourse—Rousseau sees himself as the stern moral conscience of the age and as potential Legislator with a capital L.

The self-styled patriot of the Republic of Geneva and son of a patriot was, after all, an avid reader of Plutarch.[47] The voice of his early essay is not yet from the wilderness nor from the mountain, though the epigraph from Ovid ("They take me for a barbarian because they do not understand me"), as well as the brief preface, already point to the pleasurable psychic investment found in a hypothesized martyrdom. The *Letters from the Mountain* (1764) is only the most resonant of Rousseau's titles in the way it illuminates the self-consciousness he brought to the role of a Moses-like lawgiver: as with Moses, a retreat from human society to the mountains is a necessary preliminary to commerce with divinity and a return to society with (re)founding documents.

Central to the new sociosymbolic identity that Rousseau was instrumental in forging is a commitment to place himself in the service of a cause and to convert others to it; like Saint Paul and Saint Augustine before him, the interpellated sinner becomes in his turn an interpellator relative to those who come after. Moreover, to glance forward to the twentieth century is to realize that what from the late forties on we have associated with the concept of *engagement* was integral to the idea of "the writer" from the beginning; and, as I shall suggest, from the beginning *engagement* was also not without its own fiercer pleasures.

In view of the crucial role in life Rousseau assigns to moral self-improvement as well as political reform, it is not surprising that he turned to the practice of "confession" and that it should come to constitute one of the most important elements of the singular legacy he left Western culture. Given the force of the mandate he took up to "purify" society, it is no surprise that he should first practice what he preached and begin with the practice of self-purification through confession. Moreover, Rousseau's example in this sphere both reinforces Saint Augustine's and diverts from it. He reinforces the Augustinian model, inasmuch as confession is consciously associated with self-abasement and auto-accusation; he diverts from it to the extent that he addresses his contemporaries rather than God, and does so in order to solicit their understanding for his integrity and his difficult life.

Saint Augustine clearly showed the way in another respect: in order to make a conversion convincing one has to confess one's own sins to the world; and the power of one's newfound faith is, in effect, measured both by the distance traveled—the greater the sinner, the more miraculous the conversion—and by one's capacity to identify the corruption within and announce it to the world—one proves one's spiritual worth by remaining always dissatisfied at not having gone far enough on the path of personal moral reform.[48] Like the Freudian superego, the Christian conscience grows more demanding the more one caters to it.

That Rousseau's *Confessions* will in many ways live up to the claim of uniqueness and candor made for them at the beginning is confirmed within the first two dozen pages. The notorious episode concerning young Jean-Jacques's discovery of the pleasure to be had from a spanking administered by the pastor Lambercier's thirty-year-old spinster sister is characteristic in ways that recall both alternatives in the game of Truth or Dare[49]—although one's respect for Rousseau's candor is at least slightly diminished when one learns he was not eight years old at the time, as he claims, but eleven.

One central function of the spanking episode is to explain the origin of highly personal erotic tastes that were to persist throughout the author's life. Another, especially in the context of his time, is to affirm right off his clear determination to reveal to all those aspects of a psychic life that no predecessor had dared make the subject of public disclosure. The episode is, in fact, revelatory of what the author will frequently refer to as the *"bizarrerie"* of his temperament and behavior. Striking throughout is, first, the absence of any recognition that, from a Christian point of view, he was engaging in the cardinal sin of lust; and, second, the nuanced understanding exhibited of the masochistic libidinal aim in question, its emergence in childhood, and its persistence into adulthood—a libidinal aim of a kind that by the late nineteenth century, with the rise of sexology, would come to be defined as a "perversion." The narrator is moved by an open-ended curiosity about himself and freely recognizes that pleasure is associated with the experience of punishment at the hands of a dominant woman, with exposure to a thrilling pain:

> The taste I first developed as a child, far from disappearing, became associated with the other [the sexual act] to such an extent that I was never able to separate it from the desires aroused by my senses, and that madness, when combined with my natural shyness, has always made me very reticent in the presence of women—since I couldn't tell or do all, the kind of sexual pleasure of which the other was only the final expression was never vanquished by him who desired it nor guessed at by her who could grant it. I have, therefore, spent my life desiring and remaining silent in the presence of those women whom I loved the most. Never daring to declare my taste, I at least titillated it through relationships that conserved it. To be on one's knees in the presence of an imperious mistress, to obey her orders, to beg her pardon, were for me the intensest of pleasures, and the more my vivid imagination stirred my blood, the more I resembled a bashful lover. (18)

The whole episode, with its halting, convoluted prose, has the richness and sharp particularity of the novel at its best or of an unusually illuminating psychoanalytic case history. Moreover, like a case history, it opens up the whole question of the idiosyncratic way in which, to our cost as well as for our pleasure, we fashion our erotic lives from childhood on and develop adult relations as a function of them. Rousseau locates in this early experience the source of a lifelong ambivalence in his relations with women that is expressed over time as awkwardness in their presence and as fantasized scenarios of the most pleasurable ways of making love to them. Following his lead, one might call what he describes "the schoolmistress complex." [50]

Further, the episode is important in the way it is self-consciously represented as important to a new conception of autobiography. It is the bold and wholly unprecedented opening move in a long, difficult, and disturbing process of self-exposure—not, as with Saint Augustine, to a God who presumably already knows, but to a world that obviously does not: "I have taken the first and most painful step in the dark and dirty [*fangeux*] labyrinth of my confessions (18)." The subterranean imagery of the sentence is particularly suggestive of Rousseau's conception of his psychic enterprise and recalls Diderot's praise of Samuel Richardson for having "carried the torch to the back of the cave." [51] There is something inherently modern in the idea of a subjectivity that is mazelike and unsavory in its complexity and not fully accessible to consciousness.

Reflecting on the episode, Rousseau goes on to make a point that opens up a dimension of autobiographical writing to which he was particularly sensitive and which was to have great importance for the subsequent history of work in the genre: "It is not criminal behavior that is the most difficult to recount but behavior that is ridiculous and shameful" (18). Some of the most memorable episodes of the *Confessions* are, in fact, characterized by either or both of those qualities, although it is the latter that in the end has carried the greater charge down into our time.

Ridiculous and shameful behavior have in common the feature of humiliation. The difference is that the former is frequently associated with the register of the comic, the latter with something far more painful. Shame, obviously, is a complex emotion; it concerns by definition forbidden behavior of a kind that, if brought to light, would make visible one's guilt and bring particular dishonor. Shame involves acts that we would most prefer to keep hidden from the world and that still have the power to make us blush years after the fact.

Yet if there is one defining characteristic of autobiography as practiced by Rousseau, it is that it gives peculiar emphasis to the narration of so-called shameful acts or, as in the case of the spanking episode, shameful pleasures. Thus the attention the mature narrator of the *Confessions* pays to the formation of "his way of sexual pleasure" *(sa manière de jouir)* is repeated in a number of subsequent episodes that shed a great deal of light on apparently ignoble aspects of his behavior or his secret psychic life. At the core of Rousseau's autobiographical project is a masochistic impulse similar to that exhibited in the spanking episode itself.

That truth-telling in maturity has its own libidinal rewards in addition to those of the narrative material on which it focuses is apparent, for example, in the famous anecdote in which the narrator describes the erotic charge he derived in adolescence from exposing part of his anatomy to young women. At a time when he claims he was still so ignorant of sex that women were for him the object of powerful but unfocused desire,[52] he found a form of satisfaction: "I sought out dark lanes or hidden corners where I could expose myself from afar to members of the opposite sex in the state I would have liked to be close up. What they saw, however, was not the obscene object—I never even thought of that—but the ridiculous object. The foolish pleasure I took in exposing it to their eyes cannot be described" (*Confessions*, 96–97).

The significance of this and the Mademoiselle Lambercier episode can hardly be exaggerated, from my point of view, because they proclaim, in effect, not only that in the *Confessions* there are to be no secrets but also that there are no longer such things as private parts—that is, in the language of Monty Python, after Rousseau even the private parts are public. At the same time, the narrator's way of naming and associating the opposition between the two "objects"—between buttocks and penis, between the passive organ of pleasure and the active one—is a way of disclosing a sexual ambivalence which seems to offer no alternative that is not ridiculous or obscene. The importance of the latter episode, however, also has to do with the recognition of its deviance relative to a presumed male heterosexual norm and, therefore, shameful by the standards of the world. On this occasion the masochism of the spanking scene is combined with a pronounced taste for exhibitionism. If there is a difference between the two episodes, it is that in the latter case the behavior is made to seem as ridiculous as it is shameful. Moreover, the subsequent humiliation to which the young Rousseau is subjected itself constitutes the kind of punishment his gesture seems unconsciously to invite, even though it takes a comic turn.

In short, both of these episodes, along with a number of others, confirm the way in which the art of confession as practiced by Rousseau combines exhibitionism with a masochism that invites the pleasures of censure and even chastisement at least as much as those of love and understanding. Although he ostensibly began his autobiography in the 1760s in order to set the record straight and to rescue his reputation from the calumny of his enemies and the misrepresentations of false friends, it is evident that the narrator found significant enjoyment in evoking intimate details of his life and loves, desires and transgressions that by no means always show him to advantage. There are occasions, such as the incident of the stolen ribbon, when his sense of guilt so many years after the fact is in excess of the occasion and seems, therefore, designed to be read as a sign of a rare sensibility and virtue. More interesting and more numerous, however, are episodes in which he discovers enjoyment in the power to shock even when it apparently redounds to his disadvantage.

Furthermore, to push the analysis a stage further is to realize that at the core of Rousseau's psyche is a martyr complex. The masochistic streak he himself identifies in his sexual being involves the victim furnishing much of the evidence required for his own public condemnation. Self-justification often seems to be less a purpose than a pretext that enables "the writer" to parade exhibitionistically before the world his weaknesses, idiosyncracies, deviances, and humiliations. The "aggressivity" that in the epigraph to this chapter Kundera associates with "the urge to violate another's privacy" may be turned inward as well as outward.[53]

Finally, the narrator does not simply take his pleasure from such acts of self-display; there is also a narcissistic reward to be found in the pride he takes in narrating them. The implied claim is that he has had the courage to reveal more of himself to the world, more of "the dark and dirty labyrinth" of his psychic and even his corporeal life, than anyone else before, and he finds a great deal of satisfaction in such pioneering candor. Given the multiple forms of pleasure it promotes, it is no wonder autobiography is so popular among writers and readers alike.

The whole discussion of his practice of masturbation confirms the lengths to which Rousseau was prepared to go on the path of confession and illustrates the depth as well as the limits of his self-understanding. The narrator evokes his first innocent emission of semen—"wholly involuntary"—and goes on to explain how he initially contracted the habit of masturbating during his stay in Italy. At the same time he condemns the "vice" in a curiously ambiguous language that also echoes the received wisdom of the day: "I was soon reassured and learned this dangerous substitute that eludes nature and saves young men of my temperament from frequent disorders at the price of their health, their energy, and sometimes their life" (119). He then goes on to exclaim how, because of the extraordinary character of his love for Madame de Warens and his remarkable powers of self-restraint, he ceased indulging in the practice at the precise moment when he might have been expected to be most tempted, namely, when he was living under the same roof with her and was constantly in her company, but had no physical relationship with her. On this occasion the purpose of the episode seems to be self-celebratory; the "bizarreness" of his temperament here is in his extraordinary capacity for virtuous self-restraint and for a form of love that transcends the flesh: "In a word, I was good because I loved her (119)."

Obviously, I am not claiming that episodes of this type are all there is to Rousseau's autobiography. The *Confessions* clearly cover a lot of ground. Among their chief concerns are the moral and emotional life of the author from infancy through childhood, youth, and manhood and into late middle age, and the toll so much living took on a fragile body and psyche. The work touches on loves, affections, seductions, friendships, enmities, triumphs, betrayals, wanderings, flight, and exile, search for a career and a place in society, the discovery of a vocation and the commitment to a moral-cum-sociopolitical cause. At the core of the *Confessions,* and the subject of many of the most brilliantly rendered anecdotes, however, is the narrative of the protagonist's complicated sentimental and sexual relations with women.

The episodes already referred to are examples of Rousseau's own preoccupation with the nature and source of his singular sexual taste. The range of erotic experience recorded, however, is itself much wider and much richer than they suggest. In a number of cases Rousseau associates his youthful self with a kind of innocence in such matters that has something in common with the appeal of Henry Fielding's fictional hero Tom Jones. In such episodes as his brief encounter with Madame Basile, for example, there is a kind of disarming candor in the telling: in spite of her encouragement, he remains frozen with timidity at her knees, unable even to touch her dress, in a state simultaneously "ridiculous and delicious," until interrupted by her husband's return. And there is a kind of happy exuberance in the description of his first experience of undiluted sexual pleasure with Madame de Larnage: "If what I felt for her was not exactly love; it was a very tender response to the love that she showed me; it was a sensual pleasure of such burning intensity, with such a sweet intimacy in our exchanges, that it had all the charm of passion without the delirium that sets one's head spinning and leaves one incapable of sexual climax" (293).

Moreover, although Rousseau expresses disgust at the idea of consorting with prostitutes, like many another male visitor to Venice before and after him, he is not above seeking out an encounter with one or more of its famous courtesans and of going on to tell the story of his *aventure galante* in the mode that Casanova was to adopt. The evening spent with Zulietta (377–79) is, in fact, represented as in many ways the culminating example of the author's commitment to truth and candor, the example in which he reveals what is perhaps the most secret touchstone of his "nature," the example that constitutes a test both for the author of the whole autobiographical project and for the reader alike: "The force with which I remember at this point the purpose of my book makes me scorn the false modesty that would prevent me from carrying it out. Whoever you are who wants to know a man, dare to read the two or three following pages; you will come to know J.-J. Rousseau fully."

Nowhere more than in this peremptory challenge to the reader, in which he poses in the third person, does Rousseau invite a reading of his work that is so consciously ad hominem; nowhere more than here does he insist on his singular daring in making narrator and reader go where no one has gone before. This is a case of "truth *and* dare" in which "the writer" self-consciously flags those moments when he is transgressing traditional limits. The theme is once again the protagonist's sexual functions and dysfunctions, and once again the bizarre scene evoked lives up to the advance billing.

Having examined carefully the astonishing beauty of the young woman who is his to dispose of, instead of taking pleasure in the spectacle, he finds himself suddenly sexually indisposed: "I tasted the prospect but there was no charm in it. I spoiled the pleasures, I willfully killed them off. No, nature did not make me for sexual pleasure." At first prepared to be swept away by the promise of so much voluptuous pleasure, he describes, in precise if imagistic language, the retreat of blood and the disconcerting loss of desire: "Suddenly instead of the flames that were devouring me, I felt a mortal chill run through my veins. . . ." It is at this point that he begins to explore the cause of his sudden impotence and to seek "the fault" in the sexual other, the hidden pathology that alone could explain the availability to him of such a rare woman. It turns out that the single mark of imperfection he does discover on that otherwise perfect body is a "téton borgne"—a "blind [i.e., nippleless] tit"—the perception of which has the force of a revelation: "I saw clear as day that I was holding in my arms not the most charming being I could possibly imagine but a kind of monster, an outcast of nature, of men and of love." This painterly episode deserves greater attention than I can give it here, but its quasi-allegorical meaning is clearly that of an anamorphosis: the passage from desire to disgust occurs with the perception of the mark of corruption on the erotic object; the beauty of the public woman is the baited trap of worldly depravity. In this case, Zulietta is monstrous because her visible lack is the sign both of the frigid woman and the nonmaternal woman. As a result, the narrator can evaluate his own sexual dysfunction in retrospect as a sign of his natural virtue, since it has its source in hers.[54]

In the end, it is the kind of sharply rendered limit-experiences described here that explain much of the fascination of Rousseau's *Confessions* and the enormous liberating influence they were to exercise.[55] Moreover, a great deal of that fascination derives from the combination of, on the one hand, the precise writing associated with the French *roman d'analyse* at its best and most provocative with, on the other, the apparently true story of a celebrity's complex erotic life. Although Rousseau condemned the novel for the corrupting influence on young lives of its seductive fictions, he, in fact, appropriates some of its techniques in the construction of many of the most successful episodes and scenes throughout the autobiography. However, he justifies his practice not on aesthetic grounds but on the ethical basis of truthfulness to life.

If an occasional episode reads as if it might have come from such a piquant and scabrous work as Diderot's *Bijoux Indiscrets*—"a blind tit" is of the same order as "a gossipy vagina" relative to what it suggests about women's sexuality—others are much closer to the eighteenth-century sentimental tradition. In fact, the longest, most sustained love affairs narrated in the *Confessions* are those that concern Madame de Warens and Madame d'Houdetot. They are significant in this context because they illustrate so well the kind of material and the approach to it that was to make Rousseau a cultural model for subsequent generations. Both love affairs effectively revealed to a wide public what it was that was so self-confessedly extraordinary as well as bizarre about the most intimate experiences in the life of a man who was already conscious of his fame—and who was to become even more famous as a result of his unprecedented disclosures.

In the case of Madame de Warens, there is the relationship of the young Rousseau (called here *petit*, or "little one") with a woman who was over ten years older and whom he addressed as "Maman." And here, once again, Rousseau provocatively anticipates a long line of psychoanalytic commentators, first, by emphasizing the strangeness of the affair—"I promised bizarre things in the story of my affection for her"—and, second, by referring explicitly to the incestuous character of their relationship: "For the first time I found myself in the arms of a woman, a woman I adored. Was I happy? No. I enjoyed the pleasure. Some uncontrollable sadness poisoned the charm. I felt as if I had committed incest." And he goes on to conclude this evocation of his first act of love by shifting from his own response to that of his lover: "Since she was not sensual and had not sought sexual pleasure, she did not enjoy its delights and suffered no regrets" (224–25). The secrets of the boudoir do not stop at his own guilty and/or pleasurable psychic or physiological reactions; the story of his prowess and discomforts in the bedroom is not complete without some reference to his partner's response, to the "bizarreness" of her erotic behavior, which in this case means her frigidity.

On the basis of this episode, as well as of all the others discussed, it is apparent that, from the point of view both of the experiences he reports and of his attitude toward them, Rousseau was the principal eighteenth-century pioneer of those investigations of human sexuality that proliferated beginning in the later nineteenth century, and were associated with such individuals as Jean-Martin Charcot, Richard von Krafft-Ebing, Leopold Sacher-Masoch, Havelock Ellis, and Sigmund Freud himself.

Rousseau's explicit reference to the incestuous character of his affair with Madame de Warens is a reminder of another whole area of human behavior that he largely opened up for exploration by future autobiographers, including the writers I am focusing on here, namely, the area of familial relations and, in particular, the relations between children and parents. Rousseau was, of course, the victim of what the romantics called "a fatal birth," that is, his mother died in the course of bringing him into the world. The most interesting aspect of Rousseau's handling of these issues, however, is that circumstance seems to have given him greater freedom than usual to offer his own version of the Freudian "family romance" by inventing the mother of his dreams. Moreover, he represents his parents' marriage as idyllic and draws a portrait of Rousseau senior as a good and loving father, in spite of the fact that the boy seems to have been virtually abandoned by his father quite early in life. In short, the urge to improve in fantasy on a given set of parents is there, along with significant insight into the fact that the first secret of an individual's psychic life and the form taken by his pursuit of happiness are located in infancy. Nowhere more than in this sphere does Rousseau's sensibility appear typically "modern."

In any case, his broader purpose in the Madame de Warens episode, as in many others, is to show the complexity and perpetual surprise, the exaltation and frequent perversity of human sexual relations, not as one might encounter them in a novel—distanced, aestheticized, drawn through the web of narrative and fictionalized characters—but unmediated, passed on, as it were, directly from writer to reader as the truth of an exceptional and in many ways exemplary life, that is, his own. Rousseau wants his reader to be fascinated and astonished by him, to understand him, to judge him as a man in the wholeness of his behavior, and in the end to love and admire him.

Rousseau was, in effect, the first writer to adopt so consciously and consistently the stance described by Philip Roth's fictional character Zuckerman in an ironic postscript to Roth's autobiography, whose provocative title is *The Facts: A Novelist's Autobiography*. Zuckerman explains Roth's motivation for his foray into the confessional genre as an urge to set the record straight in the face of his readers' confusions of Roth himself and the fictional characters of his novels:

> But because some get it wrong and don't have any idea of who or what you really are doesn't suggest to me that you have to straighten them out. Just the opposite—consider having tricked them into those beliefs a *success*; that's what fiction's *supposed* to do. The way things stand you're no worse off than most people, who, as you know, often are to be heard mumbling aloud, "Nobody understands me or knows my great worth—nobody knows what I'm really like underneath!" For a novelist, that predicament is to be cherished.[56]

But it is not to be cherished by "a writer" in the mold Rousseau was largely instrumental in creating. The difference between a modern novelist like Roth and an eighteenth-century moralist and antinovelist like Rousseau, in fact, appears clearly in such a passage; unlike the novelist, if Rousseau claims to eschew the trickery of fiction, it is because he wants his readers to know what he is "really like underneath."

Especially remarkable in the *Confessions,* then, are the range and variety of the erotic experiences claimed by a man who presents himself as in many ways an anti-Casanova, an overly sentimental lover who was submissive and awkward in the presence of women. Given all he has to say on the subject, it is not surprising if in the end he also casts himself in the role of heroic lover. The implied claim to have suffered a long and tortuous education in affairs of the heart and senses reaches its climax in the narration of the greatest love affair of his life, a love affair that he refers forward to a number of times before he reaches it and that he evokes with the kind of sentimental stylistic ripeness that characterizes so many of the love scenes of his sentimental novel, *Julie, or The New Héloïse.*

If with Madame de Warens he was a filial, tender lover, with Madame d'Houdetot he represents himself as a sublime, passionate, and ultimately unhappy one. The love of his life was to be only partially requited and certainly unconsummated. In the end it seems the only reward of so much passion and so much emotional pain was a hernia. Yet unlike some of his other experiences as lover, the denouement of his love affair with Madame d'Houdetot does not cast him in a ridiculous or humiliating light. Rousseau clearly did not want to complete his self-portrait without at least one episode that revealed his capacity for a grand passion, that showed the full, sublime range of himself as ecstatically sentient being in love.

In the end, however, the most radically new aspects of the *Confessions* are to found in those writerly recombinations of episodes from the author's private life that uncover heroism as well as a masochistic pleasure in the narration of personal shame. Although long stretches of the autobiography are celebratory in their representations of the great beauty and virtuous pleasures of life, of domestic bliss and the grand harmonies of nature, it is nevertheless true that many of the most famous episodes often go out of their way to shock or reveal their author in the least flattering of lights.

In addition to the encounters already discussed, the desire to shock is apparent in the scene in the charitable institution in Turin where the young Rousseau is sexually molested by an older man characterized as "a Moor." It is there, the narrator claims, that he witnessed an ejaculation for the first time in his life: "I saw something sticky and white fly up to the mantlepiece and fall to earth and it made me sick to my stomach" (72). The episode involves, of course, the familiar topos of "the loss of innocence" and is clearly intended to fall into the category of "the obscene." The narrator himself, however, is no longer innocent and knowingly heightens the impact through the device of estranging the act by not naming it.

The impulse to reveal ignoble aspects of the narrator's past behavior appears in a number of other episodes, including, for example, the nasty little incident of the Rue des Moineaux in which Rousseau, Friedrich-Melchior Grimm, and the protestant minister Emmanuel-Christoph Klüpfel are said to have taken turns in having sex with a girl collectively kept for such commerce.

Then there is, of course, the behavior that is usually seen as the most notorious of all in the *Confessions,* the most difficult to reconcile with the claim of having lived a good and virtuous life in conformity with his own principles, namely, Rousseau's refusal to exercise the paternal function and his insistence instead on giving up all the babies he had with Thérèse Le Vasseur to public care. It seems that the great eighteenth-century celebrant of family values and the innocence of childhood himself preferred to live in a childless household catered to by a female companion who also functioned as his servant. The fact that such an apparently scandalous and unnatural act had become public knowledge was, of course, the immediate pretext of undertaking the *Confessions* in the first place.

Finally, in Rousseau's telling, not the least of the dysfunctions and humiliations he suffered start with and return to his body. Even before he encountered some of the illnesses associated with middle age, part of his asocial behavior, if not of his temperament, is explained with reference to a lifelong problem he had with urine retention—a problem that caused him so much anxiety he took the unheard-of step of not honoring an invitation to appear at court. Further, there are frequent references to other more or less chronic indispositions that involved bouts of "languor" of a kind we would associate with depression, as well as kidney problems, a hernia, and a range of psychic and psychosomatic disorders he refers to in connection with his erotic life. If the fact that Rousseau's writerly practice is remote from the classical aesthetics of *le beau idéal* still needed emphasizing, it is clear once again from the frequent references to his own scandalous body.

The claim made in the opening lines of the *Confessions* of showing a man for the first time in human history "in the whole truth of his nature" is in many ways justified. Apart from all those things one learns about the author that speak to his genius and his virtue, there are at least as many that reveal a whole range of psychopathological behaviors, including not least his paranoia. It is central to the argument of this book, in fact, that the originality claimed appears above all in the practice of what might be called a heroic shamelessness; Rousseau is the first consciously to go out of his way to reveal so many secrets of his private life that shock conventional *pudeur* or common decency, secrets that form no part of the stated purpose of self-justification, since his enemies would have known nothing about them prior to his telling. It is difficult to explain the characteristic path taken by Rousseau's narcissism in the self-portrait of the *Confessions* other than by reference to masochism. Yet the public self-abasement in which he engages is also triumphalist; it seems designed to achieve a level of candor that leaves his enemies with nothing to add.

There is a sense in which Rousseau was the first writer of modern Europe to dissociate martyrdom from its religious context and make it sociopolitical, psychological, and disturbingly pleasurable—something the narratives of so many romantic and postromantic heroes, from the *poètes maudits* to their avatars in contemporary mass culture, also embrace. It is as if, after Rousseau, once a shameful act from one's personal life has been publicly narrated, it undergoes a sea change and resurfaces as a sign of "the writer's" self-testing and integrity. Success has increasingly come to mean a *succès de scandale*. In effect, the more ignoble the thought or the act by conventional standards, the greater the writerly heroism required to report it, as, for example, Marguerite Duras's more recent works confirm. By the late twentieth century, in fact, shame has become widely refigured as a bourgeois or petit bourgeois emotion associated with outmoded late Victorian ideas of decency. Moreover, showing the world one's "obscene object" as well as one's "ridiculous" one has for a long time been the emblematic gesture of a certain writerly and artistic modernity, at least until it descended to the mass-market level of a Madonna rock concert or a T.V. talk show. A kind of limit has clearly been reached when a contemporary performance artist like Annie Sprinkle spreads her legs on stage and invites spectators one by one to view her cervix.

In an important sense, the emergence of the figure of "the writer" that has been sketched is effectively summed up in two other important works of Rousseau's that I can only refer to here: the *Discourse on the Origin of Inequality* and the final, unfinished work, *The Reveries of a Solitary Walker*. The former is one of the most hard-hitting and original essays of political philosophy ever written, the latter the emotionally charged and highly eccentric journal-cum-memoir of someone living at the limit. In the *Reveries* outbursts of bitterness, strange episodes, and urban encounters, anticipating Charles Baudelaire's *Paris Spleen,* alternate with some of Rousseau's most effusive celebrations of nature and the enchanted world he associates with his youth and young manhood.

If the *Origin of Inequality* is so important, it is because, within the space of some sixty pages, it introduces many of the crucial themes that were to haunt Western political thought over the next two hundred and fifty years. In this Second Discourse Rousseau takes off from some of the positions he had already outlined in the First Discourse five years earlier, positions founded in part on a genealogical reading of human history and on the denunciation of high culture as not emancipatory but hegemonic. It is, of course, in the resonant prose of his Second Discourse that he purports to describe the path taken by humanity from an original state of nature characterized by freedom, independence, and equality to the contemporary condition of bondage, dependence, and gross inequality. He thus lays the groundwork for a long line of future critiques of human history and culture associated with such names as Kant, Hegel, Marx, Nietzsche, and Freud. Rousseau's general theme might well be characterized as "Civilization and Its Discontents," in fact, since he starts from the assumption of a quasi-universal dissatisfaction with what European civilization has wrought and the need to wipe the slate clean.

In the course of explaining the historical origins and the injustice of social inequality, he identifies a number of evils that led up to the eighteenth-century situation, and the astonishing originality of Rousseau's mind is no more evident than in the evils he identifies:[57] the emergence of conventional human language, which laid the basis for the formation of human societies and for social control; the foundation of private property, which instituted vast differences of wealth; the preindustrial modes of production and organization of work associated with the invention of agriculture and metallurgy, and the consequent division of labor and social stratification produced; the establishment of master/slave relations, which left both parties dependent and unfree; the stimulation of unnecessary needs or creature comforts, and a subsequent debilitating taste for luxury; and, finally, a sense of alienation. All these ideas have, of course, had a remarkably extended afterlife, but none, probably, has proved more influential than the concept of alienation.

In an important sense, one can say that for Rousseau the function of confession on the individual level is itself the overcoming of alienation on the model of the Christian tradition, where it is, of course, a way of expiating one's sins and thereby preparing oneself for the sacrament of Mass and reacceptance into the body of Christ. As far as the Second Discourse is concerned, alienation is referred to in two related but different contexts. The first is more purely political and familiar in the discourse of eighteenth-century liberal and revolutionary thought: it has to do with the idea of "the inalienability" of the individual's right to life and liberty (*Origin,* 184). The second is more startling, because it has to do with the form of alienation to which a human being is subject by the very fact of living in society: "The Savage lives in himself; social man, always outside himself, can live only in the opinion of others, and it is, therefore, from their judgment alone that he derives the sense of his own existence" (193).

The very choice of words here reminds us that this is the beginning of the long path leading to an existentialist conception of the self's relation to the other and Sartre's famous affirmation that "Hell is other people!" The obvious consequence of Rousseau's position is, in any case, that alienation of self from self, or an anguished feeling of loss of autonomy and dependence on the opinion of the other, is fatally endemic to man's existence as social being. The only way to avoid it is to live the solitary life of a "savage" or recluse.

Yet in spite of the apparent contradiction involved, the overcoming of alienation was central to Rousseau's broad project, on the personal level as well as on that of society as a whole. Such a project was also a crucial part of his legacy to several generations of revolutionary intellectuals and "writers." If, as Rousseau argued, man was not created alienated in the state of nature, but was made so in the course of human history, what was once made in history was potentially susceptible to being unmade there. Hence the utopian goal he set himself was to invent a social order in which the individual was as free and self-sufficient as original, solitary, natural man. Given eighteenth-century circumstances, such a social order would necessarily require a new beginning, although it could also be inspired by a putative past, including the period that Rousseau represents in the Second Discourse as coming closest to humanity's golden age, a period corresponding roughly to the Stone Age, that is, before humankind took its first steps along the fatal path that led to the evils referred to above.

The essentialism of such a position is evident; and it is an essentialism that has dogged Western revolutionary thought from the Jacobins down through Marx and into the Marxist humanism of the 1950s and 1960s. At the heart of the project of emancipation has been the desire to overcome an assumed condition of alienation. Thus one of the primary reasons given for wanting to remake society from the ground up on the basis of unity and equality has been the recovery in historical time of an original, prehistoric lost wholeness.[58]

Above and beyond everything else, what makes Rousseau's Discourses so persuasive is that they embody a kind of socioideological fantasy of a harmonious and egalitarian social order in which existing, fundamental antagonisms have been overcome—antagonisms that, in his reading, characterize all those societies, including even fifth-century Athens, which have evolved beyond the model furnished by Lycurgus's Sparta or republican Rome. The important point to note in this context is that Rousseau's whole project starts with the diagnosis of what he holds to be a contemporary sociopolitical disease, observable in the general degeneration of morals and manners and in the dissolution of social bonds. This diagnosis is followed by an argument for the establishment of a superior, alternative society and by the identification of certain beliefs, values, practices, groups, and individuals as the obstacles to the desired social change. One recognizes here some of the constants of an ideological discourse that is old as classical Greece and as recent as modern revolutionary thinking from the French Revolution itself down through communism and national socialism, even though with 1789 there emerged a radical new way of conceptualizing the political: in all cases there is the assumption of a form of decadence to be overcome (that of *ancien régime* monarchical and aristocratic corruption, for example, or of weak, atomized liberal bourgeois democracy), plots to be thwarted, and enemies within and without to be neutralized through struggle and sacrifice.[59] The way to nonalienated modes of living in a nonalienating, nonantagonistic society is perceived as either backward to original simplicity and communality or forward into an entirely new, utopian future.[60] The Second Discourse, then, is primarily a political document, ending with what is virtually a ringing call to revolt, if not to revolution, on the social level: "[I]t is manifestly against Nature's Law, however one defines it, that a child give orders to an old man or an imbecile instruct a wise man, or that a handful of people be laden with superfluity while a starving multitude lack the bare essentials" (194).

At the heart of the bitter commentary, bizarre anecdotes, and rapturous musings of the solitary walker of the *Reveries,* there is, on the one hand, a similar affirmation of the need to revolt—this time in order to pursue one's own impulses—and, on the other, evocations of the enchanted world of nature remote from contemporary social life. The reason Rousseau appears in retrospect to be such an original figure in his time is that he sought to reinvent both himself and society in a way that had not been attempted before. If he has proved so influential, it is because, among other things, he embodies a form of heroic intransigence that asserted the need for rupture with the European present and for a new beginning that would restore mankind's relationship to the elemental and the ineffable in nature. It is thus typical that, in describing how he determined by the age of forty to take leave of worldliness and a career as a man of letters, Rousseau strikes a pose that is exemplary of the figure I am calling "the writer": "I left the world and its pomp. I renounced all finery: no more sword, no more watch, no more white stockings, no gilt; just a simple wig, a good solid linen coat; and, better yet, I plucked from my heart all the cupidity and all the desire that attach value to what I was giving up. I quit the place where I was engaged, and for which I was not fitted, and I began to copy music at so much per page, an occupation for which I had always had a decided taste."[61] The asceticism to which Rousseau gives expression here is also the other face of his anti-aestheticism.

What he claimed to want to leave the social world for, and one of the reasons why he became a cult figure in the age of romanticism, was nature, or as close to nature as an eighteenth-century European could get. There are, of course, a great many scenes in the *Confessions* and in *Julie, or The New Héloïse* in which Rousseau evokes the splendors of the natural world. But none are more memorable or more magically suggestive than the famous Fifth Walk of the *Reveries,* in which he calls up his memories of the idyllic life he lived on the Ile de Saint-Pierre in the middle of Lake Bienne in Switzerland. The significance of the episode in this context is simply to serve as a reminder that the other pole of Rousseau's rejection of the arts and sciences and urban forms of sociality is the cult of nature. It is as if long before Max Weber, in the age of reason itself, Rousseau had recognized the process of disenchantment of the world that the project of Enlightenment had begun, and took it upon himself to prevent it while there was still time.

Finally, as far as styles and forms of writing are concerned, a stance of revolt combined with a determination to retreat into the still virtually pristine world of nature translates into a clear preference for polemical, philosophical writing, on the one hand, and autobiographical revelation, reverie, and self-accounting, on the other, rather than "literature" of a more formal kind. From the beginning the mandate of "the writer" paradoxically encompasses a suspicion of the worldliness associated with "literature," with *gens de lettres* and with the milieux that patronized them—a suspicion that was familiar enough in the ecclesiastical tradition but that initially came as a surprise in an eighteenth-century lay thinker who had been associated with the philosophes and who at one time hoped to make a living as composer and musician.

The surprise is diminished, however, if one remembers that during the decades immediately preceding the French Revolution, the moralistic fervor formerly associated with religious faith came to be increasingly attached to political action and to a rebirth of patriotism in a classical republican mold. The position implied virtually throughout Rousseau's works is that if "literature" is not honest self-disclosure and advocacy, if it does not contribute to reforming the self and the social world, then it is at best without raison d'être, and at worst productive of vice. This, as indicated earlier, explains the difficulty he had in justifying his decision to indulge himself in the writing of a novel, even such a morally improving one such as *Julie, or The New Héloïse,* centered on a threesome of almost unexampled virtue: "My great embarrassment was in the shame of contradicting myself so openly and so grandly. After the strict principles I had affirmed with so much noise, after the austere judgments I had so firmly preached, after the series of mordant invectives pronounced on the effeminate books that emanated love and soft ease, could one imagine anything more unexpected or more shocking than to see me inscribe myself among the authors of the books that I had so severely censored."[62] (*Julie,* 514–15). In any case, the fact that Rousseau found it necessary to justify at length his recourse to a purely literary genre has proved to be enormously influential in establishing the attitude toward art in general that is characteristic of the ideal cultural type "the writer."

With the hindsight of over two centuries, we can more easily see the dangerous archaizing tendencies in Rousseau's political thought at the core of which is a nostalgia for a lost world. His opposition was not simply to the politics and institutions of old-regime absolutism but also to the recognizably modernizing trends associated with the new literary, philosophical, and political culture of the eighteenth century. It is clear that had it been formulated in such terms in his time he would have disapproved of the Habermasian "public sphere" or "the ideal of communicative rationality among free and equal human beings" even as a normative idea, for reasons that Keith Baker helps make clear: "Participants in this modern public sphere were to be conceived not as citizens of an ancient polis assembling together to engage in the common exercise of political will but as the dispersed members of a 'society engaged in critical public debate' " ("Defining the Public Sphere," 183).

The problem for Rousseau would clearly be focused on that notion of "dispersal," for "dispersal" implies distance between members of a social formation, "mediacy" rather than immediacy, or what Jacques Derrida once famously called *différance*.[63] Given Rousseau's suspicion of indirection or re-presentation in the linguistic and artistic spheres as much as in politics, it is to be expected that the direct democracy of "classical republicanism" was his principal model. The circuits of correspondence and communication associated with enlightened salon society, "the republic of letters," publishing, and the print media in the middle decades of the eighteenth century in France were remote from the kind of direct, sentient exchange between (national) assemblies of the sovereign people of which he so nostalgically dreamed.[64]

Baker might well have Rousseau in mind, in fact, when he points out that the Habermasian idea of "the public sphere," whether as a discursive category or a once and future social reality, "is altogether antithetical to the classical republican conception of the public political realm as the domain in which independent citizens participate in the common exercise of a sovereign, political will" ("Defining the Public Sphere," 187). And this last phrase, "sovereign political will," reminds us, of course, that the modern political discourse of will has its origin in Rousseau's concept of the General Will to which, under any legitimate social contract, once entered into, all particular wills are subordinated.

In this respect, it is important to note that his *Social Contract* itself is characterized in part by what it lacks, namely, a Bill of Rights—including, of course, the right to freedom of speech and of the press. Rousseau apparently assumed that if the principle of the General Will were functioning properly in a state there would be no need to set down constitutionally guaranteed limits to a state's power over a citizen's life, as there apparently was in a nation like England with a merely representative form of government. The purpose of the work in which the General Will played such a key role was, after all, "To find a form of association that defends and protects with all its collective force the person and the possessions of each member, and, as a result of which, everyone being united with everyone else, only obeys himself and remains as free as he was before." [65]

As Rousseau puts it in a famous and disturbing formula that has come echoing down the centuries, in practice this means that the tacit commitment embodied in the social compact is that "whoever refuses to obey the General Will be obliged to do so by the social body; which means nothing less than that he will be forced to be free" (*Social Contract*, 364)—a formula that seems to leave precious little space for the expression of conflicting social interests or dissent, let alone for such practices as civil disobedience. It was, in any case, on the basis of the ideas expressed in such passages that Rousseau and his successors were to derive the idea of the inalienability of sovereignty, hostility to parliamentary or representative forms of government, and the belief in "la nation une et indivisible."

The reconstituted polis Rousseau had, in effect, always dreamed of seems, then, to elide the idea of civil society as something distinct from the polity; as such, it is resolutely "unmodern," if by modern one means, first, the kind of public sphere in which "private individuals dispersed throughout society . . . participated in the critical discussion leading to the formulation of a rational, consensual judgment" ("Defining the Public Sphere," 187), and, second, the kind of political culture Baker defines elsewhere as follows: "It [political culture] sees politics as about making claims; as the activity through which individuals and groups in any society articulate, negotiate, implement, and enforce the competing claims they make upon one another and upon the whole. Political culture is, in this sense, the set of discourses or symbolic practices by which these claims are made." [66] To function openly and to the relative satisfaction of all, such a political culture presupposes a form of Habermas's public sphere or at least a liberal free exchange of ideas, including potentially dangerous and destabilizing ideas. But when, at his most reductionist, Rousseau subsumes science and the arts beneath the political, that is clearly not what he has in mind for his polis. Nor was it what the great majority of champions of the Jacobin and socialist revolutions—who, however, indirectly, drew on him— had in mind over the two centuries since Rousseau published his works.

There are a number of reasons why the paradigm change that concerns me should have occurred in the mid-eighteenth century, why, with respect to the idea of "the writer" in France, one can speak of *before* and *after* Rousseau. Apart from the emergence of the whole "public sphere" in the form already discussed, there is, first, of course, the impact of Enlightenment thought itself: the systematic philosophical project that culminated in the publication of Diderot and d'Alembert's *Encyclopédie* in the decade before Rousseau began his *Confessions* assumed that everything under the sun and in the heavens was potentially open to critical analysis in the light of reason and experience, including the religious, political, and social beliefs and institutions of the *ancien régime* itself as well as morality and human sexuality. Second, along with the new critical thought and a new moral discourse, a variety of political and socioeconomic forces were contributing to the decline of the neoclassical aesthetic in France; a literary culture that was no longer wholly centered on the taste and patronage of the court and the academies, or even of aristocratic salons, permitted, among other things, a radical rethinking of the institution of literature, including the nature and social role of those who wrote. Third, and related to this, was the new prestige attached to philosophers, natural philosophers, and *gens de lettres* that Voltaire had been among the first to observe earlier in the century in his comments on the English cultural scene in his *Philosophical Letters* (1734); the writer (in the generic sense) was in the process of emancipating himself from a courtly and aristocratic patronage system that promoted his talent only on condition that he acknowledge his social subservience, and was becoming a celebrity at a different court, that of public opinion.

It is of obvious significance in this respect that in the *Philosophical Letters* Voltaire gives a new and politically subversive definition of human greatness. In response to the question "Who is the greatest man?" he dismisses figures such as Caesar, Alexander, and Cromwell in favor of Sir Isaac Newton,

> for if true greatness consists in having received a powerful genius from Heaven and of having used it to enlighten oneself and others, a man such as Newton, a man whose like one scarcely meets in the space of ten centuries, is truly the greatest man; and those politicians and those conquerors that one comes across in every century are no more than distinguished rascals. We owe our respect to him who dominates minds by the force of truth, not to those who enslave men through violence, to him who knows the Universe, not to those who disfigure it.[67]

There is not only a radical shift here in the idea of greatness and in the social categories of men to whom it comes to be applied; Voltaire is also contributing to the idea that men of genius are a proper object of public adulation. Thus one of the things that strikes him in England is the homage paid by the nation to its great men. In light of my argument in this book, of particular interest is, first, the fact that Voltaire observes images of Alexander Pope on display in private houses ("[T]he Prime Minister's portrait is on the mantlepiece of his own study but I saw Pope's in at least twenty different houses") and, second, that he remarks on the fact that the

English build memorials to literary and intellectual greatness in their national shrine: "Go into Westminster Abbey. It is not in order to admire the tombs of kings that one goes there but [to see] those monuments which a grateful nation has erected to the great men who have contributed to its glory" (130). The first passage remarks on the phenomenon of the reproduction and circulation of images of literary figures as an established practice of English cultural life. The second passage clearly points ahead to the moment almost sixty years later when the unfinished and appropriately neoclassical Église Sainte Geneviève would be transformed into the Pantheon by the Constituent Assembly and dedicated, in capital letters along its frieze, *Aux Grands Hommes la Patrie Reconnaissante* (To Its Great Men a Grateful Country).

In this respect, the example of England's literary and political culture was obviously important in the decades leading up to the revolution. Yet by the time Sainte Geneviève changed functions, the difference between the situation in France and that in England was also very apparent, as the little word *patrie* in the dedication implies.[68] The Pantheon was to be no Westminster Abbey: its purpose was not to underline continuity with the past and its institutions and beliefs, but to signal a rupture with it by celebrating the patriot-heroes of the revolution who had contributed to the overthrow of absolutism, prominent among whom were great men in Voltaire's sense.

It was, therefore, both fitting and just that he himself should be the first of the major eighteenth-century philosophes and only the third of the great men whose remains were installed there, after René Descartes and the revolutionary hero Honoré-Gabriel Riqueti Mirabeau, in July 1991. Voltaire's apotheosis took a similar form to that of Mirabeau, including a huge chariot at the top of which the body of Voltaire reposed on an antique bed and a long, solemn procession through the streets of Paris that lasted some seven hours and involved a number of "stations" with accompanying oratory and hymns at sites that were emblematic of his career.[69]

If the decision to enshrine Voltaire among the immortals seemed fitting in July 1991, at a point when the Revolution had not yet cut all links with the moderate and liberal traditions in Enlightenment thought, it seems equally appropriate that Rousseau's remains were transferred there during its most radical phase, in early October 1994. The temporary monumental mausoleum erected in the Tuileries gardens as a temporary rest on the passage from Ermenonville to the Pantheon is a sign of the veneration Jean-Jacques had come to enjoy, and not only among Jacobins and their sympathizers.

The elevation of the status of figures like Voltaire and Rousseau, who had no connection with the traditional figures of authority in *ancien régime* monarchies nor with the exercise of state power, to that of philosophical prophets and universal legislators of mankind was a consequence not just of the revolution itself—although the peculiar fervor of those years contributed to the religiosity of the ceremonial—but of those special conditions of French political life in the mid-eighteenth century that are so well evoked by François Furet in the wake of Tocqueville. As a result of the dearth of representative institutions of an English kind, as well as other intermediary bodies of civil society, under the form of absolutism associated with Louis XIV and his successors, French society came to look to its philosophes and writers in particular to play the kind of political role for which there was no precedent elsewhere, including England. The loss as well as the gain of a situation in which men of letters came to play a preeminent political role was captured in some celebrated words of Tocqueville:

> When one recalls that the same French nation that was such a stranger to its own affairs and so lacking in experience, so constrained by its institutions and so powerless to change them, was at the same time also among all the nations on earth the most cultivated *[lettrée]* and the most enamored of refinement and wit, it is easy to understand how writers became a political power there and ended up as the preeminent political power.[70]

Tocqueville is, of course, concerned with the aberration that this represents from the point of view of a nation's political life. The argument of this book is that there is a comparable aberration as far as literature itself is concerned.

It is this situation that Roger Chartier has characterized so well as one that involved not only the "politicization" of literature but also the "literarization" of politics—"The politicization of literature was thus at the same time a 'literarization' of politics transformed into an expectation of rupture and a dream of an 'ideal world' " (*Cultural Origins,* 12). Moreover, as far as such "literarization" is concerned, it is Rousseau far more obviously than Voltaire or any other prerevolutionary philosophe who was the first to engage in it. Almost all of Rousseau's works—from the first two Discourses down through *The New Héloïse, Emile,* and *The Social Contract,* as well as the *Confessions*—can be said to promote the "literarization" of politics as much as the "politicization" of literature. At different points and in different ways, they are all haunted by "an expectation of rupture and a dream of an ideal world"—something that is clearly not the case for someone such as Voltaire, imbued with the neoclassical aesthetic and a satirist to boot.[71] Voltaire is quite properly associated with the "politicization of literature" but not with the "literarization of politics" in Chartier's sense. The difference between Voltaire and Rousseau in this respect is, in fact, another way of thinking of the opposition between writer and "writer;" and it is perceptible to some extent in certain visual representations of them during the early years of the revolution.

The story of the iconography of the French Revolution is a long and complex one that I have neither the expertise nor the space to explore here,[72] and so, too, is that part of it which particularly interests me, namely, the choice and modes of representation of the revolution's "great men." One example will have to suffice to suggest the kind of cult to which Rousseau was subject and the theories and values with which he was specifically associated.

I have in mind a painting by Jeaurat de Berty, *Revolutionary Allegory*. Probably the most striking aspect of the work is the heterogeneity of the signs that are crowded awkwardly into a rectangular space roughly divided between a top half of sky and suspended artifacts, including a portrait of Rousseau, and a bottom half consisting of a more painterly scene characterized by a quite remarkable eclecticism. What the painting lacks in compositional force is clearly made up for in the comprehensive range of references that, whenever the artist's power of graphic representation seems to flag, is relayed by words and slogans designed to communicate revolutionary orthodoxy with a minimum of ambiguity.

Especially significant for my purpose is the fact that at the very top, where, in *ancien régime* iconography there stood a tutelary deity or its surrogate on earth, the monarch, Jeaurat locates the most radical of the philosophes. The fact that Rousseau is represented as austere and wizened is less remarkable than that the portrait is, in fact, a painting within a painting and—like the twin tricolors that hang below, inscribed "Love of Country" and "French Republic"—is attached to supports outside the picture's space.

What is not suspended from above nor anchored within the scene below is the single, slightly off-center, purely allegorical eye. It is that eye, in relative close-up, which gives the picture its singular and disturbing force. The eye as pictorial motif was not, of course, uncommon in the mid-eighteenth century, whether in Masonic iconography or as symbol of divinity or of the abstract idea of vigilance; and in Jeaurat's work, too, it clearly transmits the notion of a power that sees and judges all. Detached from Rousseau, yet closely associated with Rousseau by reason of its position immediately below, the eye constitutes a warning and a guarantee of the transparency of the realm it overlooks.

The bottom half of the painting over which Rousseau and the eye preside together is a kind of utopian landscape with architecture and figures. Its politically didactic function is to array the symbols of the revolution in a scene vaguely organized in three overlapping planes: in the distance there is the outline of a trim and modest red-roofed town; in the foreground a garlanded column rises up, stuffed with pikes and axes, inscribed with some of the key concepts of revolutionary ideology (Strength, Truth, Justice, Union) and surmounted by a classical wreath and a red Phrygian bonnet; immediately to the right of the column and tight up against it is a tree of liberty; farther removed and located in the second plane to the left is an obelisk of equality, which is balanced to the right by a truncated classical column proclaiming both the idea of "The Regeneration of Morals" and "The Rights of Man and of the Citizen." The figures represented include two virtuously robed women with their own tricolor garland who are seen shaking hands "fraternally"; a soldier-patriot who stands guard next to a cannon; a citizen in red bonnet and sash who gestures emotively as he seems to scatter earth or seed, and a sheep, a rooster, and a hen who go about their productive bucolic business while an adoring dog faithfully sits and waits. The scene represented, then is, an idealized and politicized landscape in which the effects of an achieved cultural revolution are visible everywhere and a regenerated citizenry is constantly interpellated by the symbols and monuments they move among.

The importance of this allegorical scene for my purposes is that it effectively offers contemporary testimony to the existence of the new, overlapping political and literary cultures referred to by Chartier in the passage quoted earlier, cultures over which Rousseau was to exercise such a crucial influence. Furthermore, it is not the man himself but his image that is consciously associated by the artist with the idea of "rupture" and with a painted scene that is itself "a dream of an ideal world." The final disturbing lesson of the painting, however, is that the ideal world represented below the portrait depends on vigilance exercised from above, on the power inherent in that impersonal, all-seeing eye.

Finally, Jeaurat's work is also significant in this context because it specifically associates Rousseau with a crucial aspect of the French Revolution that Tocqueville understood so well, namely, its religious character: "No previous political upheaval, however violent, had aroused such passionate enthusiasm, for the ideal the French Revolution set before it was not merely a change in the French social system but nothing short of a regeneration of the whole human race. It created an atmosphere of missionary fervor and, indeed, assumed all the aspects of a religious revival. . . ."[73] Moreover, no other prerevolutionary thinker came close to Rousseau in preparing the discursive ground for this redirection of religious feeling into politics.

This portrait of Rousseau is just one among a great many that were produced either from life or at a distance, including oil paintings, engravings, statues, and, of course, the traditional death mask. The engravings typically were used to illustrate and/or popularize his works, and their captions frequently identify him as the author of a specific work, such as the one that captures him in a contemplative pose, eyes to heaven, bewigged and in knee breeches, in a mountainous natural setting expressive of rococo taste, in the act of composing *Emile*. Probably the most famous portrait of all, however, is the one that David Ramsay painted for David Hume in 1766. What is striking here is the sobriety of the image. The subject's dress is characterized by a simplicity that eschews *ancien régime* wig and lace for the "naturalness" of a plain fur hat and collar. Against a neutral background that admits of no distractions, only part of the face, the bare neck, and left shoulder are illuminated so that the focus falls on the directness and intensity of Rousseau's gaze. Thus, the genius of the Ramsay portrait resides in the fact that it accumulates enough painterly signs of the idea of severe philosopher to enable a viewer to reduce the ambiguity of the image in his or her own way and to project onto it appropriate fond fantasies—which is what, of course, the following generations did.

To repeat, it is through his radical political theory, his suspicious attitude toward art and literature, the disclosures from his private life, and the stance he adopts toward his public and toward a sociopolitical world in need of moral renewal that Rousseau stages the emergence of a certain idea of "the writer" on the European scene from the middle decades of the eighteenth century on, an idea of "the writer" that will develop into a kind of ideal type. From the romantic movement down to the last decade of the twentieth century, for good or ill, we have not finally done with Rousseau's legacy yet. And this is the case not simply in France or even Europe; the tradition that Rousseau inaugurated has also exercised a powerful influence in the United States and in the third world.

Furthermore, it is clear that it is impossible to make such a claim for any of Rousseau's contemporaries. One cannot speak in the same way of Voltaire's nineteenth- and twentieth-century legacy, with the occasional exception of a now-marginalized figure such as Anatole France. Nor, until his return to critical favor in the mid-twentieth century, would one have got very far in attempting to trace Diderot's descendence between, say, Goethe's early tribute and Milan Kundera's championship of the ironic, essayistic play of his narratives. The rational and neoclassical ethos with which Voltaire was imbued was characterized by a critical worldliness and a taste for satire directed against dogmatic faiths, nonrepresentative political institutions, and inhumane judicial practices, but it expressed no faith in the regeneration of man and drew the line at exercises in autobiography. *J'accuse* remained uncoupled from *je me confesse*. For different reasons, the same is true of Diderot. He is only half "a writer" in the sense I am giving the word here. Although he was one of the eighteenth century's most challenging critical thinkers and polemicists, the author of many of its most teasing dialogues and self-reflexive fictions, and its best known theorist of the divided self, autobiography as such was alien to his whole mode of thinking. The dialogical imagination undercuts the linearity and continuity of retrospective narrative and distrusts the self's capacity for introspection. Indeed, the very idea of the self seems incompatible with experiment and the systematic practice of irony.

I do not, of course, intend to argue that all the writers who came after Rousseau necessarily conform to the idea of "the writer" subsequently associated with his name. From relatively early in the nineteenth century, for example, the cult of the dandy and the beginnings of the emergence of aesthetic modernism were associated with a literary sensibility very much at odds with self-revelation and sociopolitical critique. Since the age of art for art's sake and symbolism especially, poets in particular have often insisted on the autonomy of art, and there are many others working in other genres who have sought to detach their literature from their life. Yet, as the relative marginalization of poetry in our century confirms, they are clearly working against the expectations of a powerful cultural tradition. The model generated by Rousseau's combined sociopolitical and autobiographical project—in particular, the model of "the writer"—has in the twentieth century become the norm by which we measure the public persona of writers as well as their practice, performance, and function.

The proportion of autobiographical self-revelation to sociopolitical critique may vary a great deal. Indeed, not all of those who were subject directly or indirectly to Rousseau's influence offer both, although the dimension of critical witness of self and world is always there. Nevertheless, in the mainstream French tradition Rousseau's example—whether or not it was immediate or mediated, and whether or not those concerned were always conscious of it—has been a powerful one for writers as different as François-René de Chateaubriand, Stendhal, Victor Hugo, Alfred de Vigny, Alfred de Musset, George Sand, Charles Baudelaire, Maurice Barrès, André Gide, Marcel Proust, Louis-Ferdinand Céline, Jean-Paul Sartre, Simone de Beauvoir, Michel Leiris, Roland Barthes, Marguerite Duras, Louis Althusser, Michel Foucault, and even Philippe Sollers and Julia Kristeva.

This does not, of course, prevent them from also reacting strongly against Rousseau's example. In fact, as I hope to show in discussions of Stendhal and Baudelaire, the struggle between the legacy of "the writer" and what might be called "the anti-writer" that is staged in the works of such figures is a richly illuminating one. If Stendhal makes himself into one of the nineteenth century's great novelists and Baudelaire into its exemplary poet, it is in part as a consequence of their effort to absorb and overcome an idea of writing and "the writer" that was transmitted by the romantic movement from Rousseau. One could, of course, make a similar strong case for Proust.[74]

To sum up, in light of modern European cultural and political history one can argue that there is a fatal flaw in Rousseauism. It involves, first, turning one's back on the Enlightenment and on modernity, if by modernity one means the recognition of the autonomy and mutual interdependence of the separate modes of cognition that are scientific-technological rationality, moral-practical rationality, and aesthetic rationality. It also involves fusing morality in general with political morality—or in other words, subordinating ethics to politics. Some of the consequences of this have been summarized by François Furet in a discussion of revolutionary ideology: "First, that all individual problems, all moral or intellectual questions, have become political, and that there is not a single human misfortune that is not susceptible to a political solution. Next, that to the extent that everything is knowable and transformable, action is transparent to knowledge and to morality" ("La Révolution française est terminée," 49).

In light of all this, my immediate concern is to see how Henri Beyle reacted to the Rousseauist legacy in the years that followed the decades of revolution and empire. How, during the Restoration and the reign of Louis Philippe, did the future Stendhal come to terms with a practice of writing that combined preeminently a faith in autobiographical witness and a form of *engagement* with a distrust of art and literature? How, finally, did he deal with the new cultural phenomena of "the politicization of literature" and "the literarization of politics"?

CHAPTER 2

Stendhal:
Overpoliticization and the
Revenge of Literature

Youth was at the helm in that age of fervid enthusiasm, of proud and generous
aspirations, whose memory, despite its extravagances, men will forever cherish: a
phase of history that for many years to come will trouble the sleep of all who seek
to demoralize the nation and reduce it to a servile state.

ALEXIS DE TOCQUEVILLE

In the passage I quote in my introduction from Milan Kundera's definition
of the "Novelist,"[1] having established the opposition that in his reading
distinguishes "the novelist" from "the writer," Kundera goes on to cite
examples of authors belonging to one or other of the two categories. It is
surprising that Stendhal is not mentioned in either, although there is no
doubt in my mind as to where he fits. The name of the author of *The Red*
and the Black, Lucien Leuwen, The Charterhouse of Parma, and *Lamiel*
should rightly appear between Fielding and Sterne, on the one hand, and
Flaubert and Proust, on the other, in the chronological list of preeminent
"novelists" referred to by Kundera.

Yet if one thinks back for a moment over Stendhal's career and writings, the reality appears more complex. Wasn't the author of the celebrated novels also the writer of books on music and the history of painting, of travel books written with evident political bias, of a sympathetic
life of Napoleon, of a treatise *On Love,* of a polemical essay on romantic
theater, *Racine and Shakespeare,* of autobiographical works, *The Life of*
Henry Brulard, Memoirs of an Egotist, and a journal, not to speak of a
variety of literary and political pamphlets and occasional pieces? Wasn't
Stendhal, in other words, the author of a substantial body of writing before he published his first novel, *Armance,* in early middle age, and did he
not continue to do work in other genres even while he was writing his
best-known novels? Wasn't he, in short, "a writer" before he was "a novelist" and didn't he remain one in part long after he began to publish

71

Physionotrace portrait of Stendhal
(Coll. Jacques Félix-Faure)

fiction? In the light of Stendhal's example, it seems that Kundera's categories are perhaps a little too categorical.

What they fail to capture is the possibility of a substantial ambivalence
in one who writes and the attraction exercised by other forms or writing
at moments of high historical drama, revolutionary political change, or
artistic ferment. It may well be that the Stendhal we remember is Stendhal
"the novelist"; it is nevertheless true that in many ways Stendhal was also
a man of ideas who for a long time hesitated about the kind of writing
through which he wanted to impress himself upon the world. The titles
alone of his non-fiction works go a long way to suggest that, along with
his enthusiasm for art, music, and literature, as well as for Italian travel,
Stendhal was also an ideologue in the early-nineteenth-century French

Olaf Sœdermark, *Stendhal*
(Musée de Versailles. Photo R.M.N)

meaning of the term, a disciple of rationalism in philosophy, sensualism in psychology, and liberalism in politics—a man, in short, with an eighteenth-century philosophe's wide-ranging interests, and, like Rousseau, an autobiographer. Thus in certain of these works at least Stendhal does, in fact, behave like "a writer" whose work is, in Kundera's words, "marked by his thought, borne by his voice"; unlike "the novelist" as ideal type, he frequently makes "a great issue of his ideas."

Nevertheless, if one assumes that Rousseau was for Stendhal a powerful predecessor to be reckoned with, whether he was always fully aware
of it or not, one is forced to conclude that Stendhal also deviates substan-
tially from the Rousseauist model of "the writer" as I have defined the
figure. A practice of writing that gave preeminence to autobiography and
to sociopolitical critique was undoubtedly a seductive one during the opening years of the nineteenth century, when Henri Beyle came of intellectual
age. Yet although Stendhal was drawn to such a practice on personal as
well as ideological grounds, it turns out in the end to be a temptation he
also resisted. Moreover, he did so with the radically different practice of
novelists such as Cervantes, Henry Fielding, and Laurence Sterne very
much in mind. The passionate amateur of fine arts and music also came
to admire and practice the art of the novel as they had practiced it, an art
of the novel that, in his hands as well as theirs, proved to be a remarkable
corrective to Rousseauist writing.

That this is the case appears most clearly in the implicit critique to
which, throughout his career, Stendhal subjects the three important dimen-
sions of Rousseau's work that were discussed in the previous chapter,
namely, autobiography, political advocacy, and the censorship of art and
literature; and the principal vehicle of Stendhal's critique was precisely the
novel. If in the radically different world of Restoration France, he enlarged
the scope of that genre to the point of virtually reinventing it, this is in
large part because his extraordinary intelligence was so attuned to the in-
vasive ideologies and institutions of the age and to the novelty and complexity of its new political culture.

It is, then, with a brief discussion of Stendhal's fiction that I shall begin
and end this exploration of his relationship to the normative idea of "the
writer" inherited from the eighteenth century, but in between I shall turn
to the way in which his practice of autobiography both models itself on
and distances itself from Rousseau's *Confessions*.

Something of the novelty and the complexity of the historical situation in
which those who looked back on the decades of revolution and empire
found themselves is encapsulated in the way in which Stendhal and
Tocqueville choose in their writing to remember and memorialize two sets
of events associated with different years. Although the two men were not
of the same generation, and therefore did not share the same historical
experiences, their lives did overlap significantly, and down through the
reign of Louis Philippe they were both fundamentally attached to the liberal tradition in political thought associated with the European Enlightenment. Born in 1783, Stendhal belonged to the generation that came of age
under the Consulate and the Empire; and he participated in Napoleonic
campaigns in Italy and Russia. Tocqueville was born some eighteen years
later (1805) and was therefore still a boy at the time of Waterloo, but the
first volume of his major work, *Democracy in America,* appeared in 1835

and is based on observations gathered during his visit to the United States in the years 1831–32, that is, in the same decade in which Stendhal completed his most important novels.

The first of the two historical events that concern me is the subject of the epigraph to this chapter. The passage quoted comes from Tocqueville's *The Old Regime and the French Revolution,* a work published in 1856, when he was in his fifties. "The age of fervid enthusiasm" Tocqueville has in mind is what, from the beginning, has been taken to be the opening year of the French Revolution (1789). As he looks back over close to a century of French history, Tocqueville singles out that year and no other as his *annus mirabilis* because he finds there the rare confluence of two fundamental yet frequently oppositional forces in French history which he identifies in a famous passage toward the end of the same work. In that passage, Tocqueville interprets collective French behavior as dominated by "two ruling passions," the "more deeply rooted and long-standing" passion for equality and the "more recent and less deeply rooted" passion for liberty; and 1789 is the year in which, for the first and perhaps last time in his experience, these two passions came together in French national life in marvelous and creative fusion:

> When the Revolution started, they came in contact, joined forces, coalesced, and reinforced each other, fanning the revolutionary ardor of the nation to a blaze. This was in '89, that rapturous year of bright enthusiasm, heroic courage, lofty ideals—untempered, we must grant, by the reality of experience: a historic date of glorious memory to which the thoughts of men will turn with admiration and respect long after those who witnessed its achievement, and we ourselves, have passed away.[2]

As far as historical memory is concerned, it is suggestive to compare the two passages by Tocqueville in praise of 1789 with the lines in the opening chapter of Stendhal's last great novel, *The Charterhouse of Parma* (1839), in which the narrator evokes the mood of euphoria associated with the less famous year of 1796, the year in which a French army invaded a northern Italy under Austrian domination. The date is different but the nature of the enthusiasm expressed—if not its object and the reasons for it—is comparable to Tocqueville's: "On the 15th of May, 1796, general Bonaparte entered Milan at the head of the young army that had just crossed the bridge of Lodi and taught the world that after so many centuries Caesar and Alexander had a successor. The miracles of bravery and genius Italy witnessed in the next few months woke a somnolent people from its sleep."[3] There follow references to the youthfulness of the young general's army, and to an interlude of some two years characterized by a mood of gaiety, pleasure, and plenitude in which, in the absence of authoritarian husbands and fathers, Italian women consorted with carefree French soldiers and Italian sons were free to indulge their Oedipal fantasies. As I have noted elsewhere, the opening of *The Charterhouse of Parma* deploys the utopian fantasm of a land without fathers.[4]

Further, as the novelist memorializes 1796 some forty years after the event, he associates it specifically with the idea of the end of an old regime and the rebirth of forgotten ideals: "The departure of the final Austrian regiment marked the fall of old ideas: risking one's life became fashionable; it was understood that after centuries of jaded sensations one should learn to love one's country with a genuine love and seek out heroic action" (26).

In these passages, both Stendhal and Tocqueville memorialize years that were times of "fervid enthusiasm, of proud and generous aspirations," years in which "youth was at the helm." In both cases, it is important to note, they were heroic times, although the character of the heroism itself is different: whereas 1789 was a year of revolution that marked the end of a society of privilege, of orders and estates, and of the absence of rights and of representative institutions, 1796 may be said to have inaugurated the idea, if not of empire—that was to come a few years later—then at least of the export of the ideals of the French Revolution by force of arms along with a new idea of military glory—the word *patrie* (country) in Stendhal's sentence bears with it connotations established during the most radical phase of the revolution, and "heroic action" confirms the idea of a citizen's duties as well as his rights in a nation threatened by enemies at home and abroad.

The interesting thing about both passages in this context is that they express passionate allegiances for two different though relatively recent dates in French history and thereby confirm how, after 1815 and down through nineteenth-century France, French political life was haunted by two potent memories or legends, the memory of revolution and the memory of empire.[5] The two passions that Tocqueville identified as competing for dominance in the collective French psyche, equality and liberty, were overlaid by the memories of two radically different historical moments. Furthermore, if one adds to the mixture those whose passions and memories were none of the above, but who looked back beyond 1789 to the *ancien régime* as a historical point of reference, then the complexity of the situation in which both Stendhal and Tocqueville lived and wrote becomes even more obvious. Most significant from my point of view is the fact that the novelist, like the historian and political theorist, reflected long and hard on the new and confusing political culture of the decades of the Bourbon Restoration and the July Monarchy, and on its implications for human happiness.[6]

Given the works in which the passages under discussion occur—a novel of the late 1830s, on the one hand, and a work of political history of the mid-1850s, on the other—it seems that we have here examples of the politicization of literature and of the literarization of politics, respectively, in the sense Roger Chartier has attached to those terms. In the case of Stendhal's novel, the opening point of reference and the occasion of the enthusiasm is a successful military campaign with important political ramifications for modern European history; in the case of Tocqueville's work of historical interpretation, a cool-headed liberal who had learned to be suspicious of popular political fervor evokes the inaugural year of revolution in a language that is celebratory, passionate, and idealistic.

In Stendhal's case in particular, the fact that one can speak of the politicization of literature is confirmed by the novelist's habit of thinking in terms of dates. The foregrounding of dates in the narrative of national histories is, in many ways, especially characteristic of revolutionary regimes, of countries that mark a moment of birth or rebirth with reference to a more or less violent founding act of nationhood that is also an act of rupture with a preceding order. Moreover, as in the case of France since 1789, dates that signify glory or the triumph of revolutionary ideals are also typically remembered in opposition to dates of infamy, of reaction and defeat. Thus in *The Charterhouse of Parma* itself 1796 turns out to be no more than a prologue for a novel of life in an age of reaction, the transition to which is also associated with a date: with his characteristic narrative verve and economy, Stendhal erases the utopian promise of the earlier year by submitting his young Italian hero, Fabrice del Dongo, to the chastening experience of another, 1815, the year that ushered in a wave of monarchical restorations throughout continental Europe. In some of the most famous battle scenes in Western literature, Fabrice's attempt to live out the heroic idea of love of liberty and of country that Stendhal associated with 1796 founders in the mud and blood, cynicism and confusion of a Belgian plain in 1815. Moreover, as Stendhal's two unfinished works on Napoleon confirm, the former young general of genius is himself implicitly blamed for the withering of the youthful ideals of 1796 in the venal age of the Empire he had created even before the restoration of the Bourbon monarchy.[7]

His historical situation explains why Stendhal was potentially a novelist of postrevolution. What it does not explain is the fact that, in some of the most astonishing political novels ever written, he was the first to discover the rich potential of a major theme of modern literature, the theme of "after the revolution"—which in his case meant after a "failed" revolution, although we now know that the picture of life after a "successful" one may look even worse. Perhaps the most challenging and disturbing aspect of *The Charterhouse of Parma*, however, is that it is a political novel that brilliantly defines the limits of politics. As a result, like all of Stendhal's novels to a greater or lesser degree, it is also a meditation on the function of literature in the modern age that was inaugurated by the French Revolution, an age that he was one of the first to portray as fundamentally and disturbingly political.

There is a sense in which *The Charterhouse of Parma* is the most astonishing example in Stendhal's oeuvre of what one might call the revenge of literature—over politics, that is. Such, in any case, is a theme that I

shall return to at the end of this chapter, after a detour through some of
the novelist's other works, including especially his autobiography. Along
with the theme of the politicization of literature, the issues that specifically
concern me are Stendhal's understanding of the relationship between art
and politics, the function of the writer, and the relations between the private self and public life in the modern world.

What is probably the first, and certainly the most important, early example
of a political novel in Western literature, Stendhal's *The Red and the
Black*, appeared in 1830.[8] That thinking in dates became a virtual reflex
for Stendhal in his postrevolutionary times is confirmed by the novel's subtitle, *A Chronicle of 1830.*[9] It is ironic that Stendhal was, in effect, upstaged, as far as the significance of that particular year is concerned, by
the July Revolution that occurred when his novel was about to appear,
since it was a revolution that went a long way toward destroying the institutions and the political alignments, if not the ideologies, of the reign of
Charles X that he had sought to represent. One is even tempted to conclude that the historical events themselves threatened to illustrate what is
probably the most famous aphorism in the work, namely, that politics is
"like a pistol shot at a concert" or "a stone attached to the neck of literature, and in less than six months it drags it under."[10] That such turned
out not to be the fate of Stendhal's work has to do with an art of the
novel in which local political issues are put on display only to be transcended; the point of them is, so to speak, the critical distance from which
in they end they come to be seen.
    It is hard to imagine a more succinct and pointed summary of the per-
ceived nature of the new political culture and of the quality of French
provincial life at that specific moment than one finds in the opening chapters of the 1830 novel. With Balzac and Stendhal, of course, the historical
novel invented in Britain by Walter Scott to reanimate past ages was transformed in France into the historical novel of contemporary life. Historical
romance became modern romance or modern literary realism or, as with
Stendhal, modern romance and modern realism at the same time. In any
case, starting with an opening chapter whose ominous title is "A Small
Town," Stendhal goes on to evoke both the two passions and the two
memories referred to earlier and a great deal more besides, including what
we have come to call "interests" and an associated *esprit de parti.*
    The Red and the Black is far too familiar a work to require detailed
exegesis here. It is worth recalling, however, that through the realist representation of the provincial town of Verrières as a stratified social milieu
with multiple links to Paris and to national politics, Stendhal puts into
play the complex weave of the fears and ambitions, intrigues, suspicions
and aspirations of a postrevolutionary, postimperial world divided largely
along class and ideological lines. Through a variety of references and character sketches that, for the first time in fiction, explain human behavior

and human relationships in sociopolitical as well as psychological terms, the two passions of liberty and equality are very much in evidence, although on this occasion they are represented as antithetical rather than complementary. As for the two memories, they are mentioned specifically in the case of the retired Jacobinist/Bonapartist military surgeon, for whom 1796 is a significant point of historical reference, and in that of his protégé, the young hero of Stendhal's story, Julien Sorel himself. Those memories are also present as a pervasive anxiety among the provincial bourgeoisie and, later in the novel, much more spectacularly in the fearful, airless salons of a Parisian aristocracy returned from exile but still haunted by the idea of violent revolution.

Beyond an analysis on the level of passions and memories, Stendhal completes the famous somber picture of French small-town life by swift references to a series of tendentious oppositions of a kind that were to remain at the center of French literary, artistic, and intellectual life down through the nineteenth century and beyond—oppositions between nature and industry, beauty and utility, Paris and the provinces, men and women, youth and age, fathers and sons. However, the most fundamental oppositions, those producing the political patronage and the political surveillance that Stendhal observes, concern class interests and political allegiances—oppositions between bourgeois and peasants, bourgeois and aristocrats, priests and anticlericals, liberals and unregenerate royalists *(ultras)*, partisans of the Empire and enemies of the Empire.

Finally, the opposition that contains all the others is the one symbolized in the antithetical colors of the title, namely, the opposition between a celebrated recent past and an abhorred present, between an age of empire and military glory, associated with the splendor of military uniforms, and an age of boredom and mourning connoted by the habit of the priesthood. Not referred to in the title, however, is the color that actually dominates the opening part of the novel, set in Verrières, namely, grey: the sober grey of the mayor's clothes, the drab class and behavioral attitudes of a provincial, industrial bourgeoisie partly imbued with the Saint-Simonian cult of productivity but chiefly absorbed in the task of enriching itself.[11]

At the beginning of *The Red and the Black,* as elsewhere in Stendhal's fiction, the narrator is not shy to declare his sympathies or express his views energetically; and it is typical that in presenting his picture of provincial French life, he does so as if to a hypothetical urbane visitor from Paris. Thus the summarizing judgment with which Stendhal concludes the opening chapter is of particular significance because it takes an explicit political form that helps situate his thinking in relation to Rousseau as well as Tocqueville: "In fact, these good people [of Verrières] exercise the most boring of *despotisms*; it is on account of this ugly word that living in these small towns is unbearable for anyone who has lived in the great republic that we call Paris. The tyranny of public opinion—and what public opinion!—is quite as *stupid* in small French towns as in the United States of America" (*The Red and the Black,* 222).

Both the point of view as well as the categorical judgment expressed here underline Stendhal's distance from Rousseau and his relative closeness to Tocqueville.[12] The point is that for Stendhal, as for many French liberals of his generation, American democracy seems to represent almost as great a threat to those things he cherishes as does the idea of despotic government, and that far from being a force for emancipation and enlightened self-government, as the philosophes tended to assume, public opinion is a tyrannical and leveling force.[13] Finally, the metaphor equating Paris with a republic in which a person of culture should seek salvation provocatively reverses Rousseau's views of Paris and his idea of the virtuous republic as such.

Even more than in such direct expressions of opinion, however, the most obvious way in which Stendhal reflects on and challenges Rousseau's legacy in *The Red and the Black* is in the portrait of the first of his series of passionate young heroes and heroines, Julien Sorel. On the one hand, of the two memories referred to above, the adolescent peasant's son cherishes that of Napoleon and the Empire in a way that is, in fact, far less critical than his author. On the other hand, in the beginning at least, Julien is driven by the other of the two passions, the desire for equality. And in this it is Jean-Jacques himself who is his principal model.

Critics have, of course, frequently pointed to the significance of the three books that guide Julien in the conduct of his life, that is, Napoleon's *Memorial of Saint Helena* and the bulletins of his Grande Armée, and Rousseau's *Confessions*. But it is in the precise language Stendhal uses to explain his hero's choices that he makes clear his relationship to the tradition I am exploring here, including the fact that he had subjected the *Confessions* to a close reading:

> The horror he felt at the idea of eating with the servants was not something that came to Julien naturally; in seeking his fortune he would have done far more painful things than that. He derived that particular antipathy from Rousseau's *Confessions*. It was the only book through which his imagination represented the world to him. The collection of bulletins of the Grande Armée and the *Memorial of Saint Helena* completed his Koran. He would have faced death for these three works. He never believed in any other. As the result of something the old military surgeon had said, he regarded all other books in the world as full of lies, written by rascals for reasons of ambition. (235)

The most striking feature of the passage is the spirit of dogmatism it implies, a dogmatism that is comparable to the one advocated by Rousseau in his *Emile* insofar as it is founded on the idea of one or more sacred texts on which the true believer is to model his conduct—the metaphor of the Koran is clearly intended to signify a quasi-religious intolerance. For the education of his Pupil, Rousseau's Tutor had prescribed *Robinson Crusoe* alone; the master text in Julien's education, in turn, is Rousseau's *Confessions* itself, along with the apparently very different works relating to Napoleon. It is in any case no accident that, along with his Rousseauist dogmatism, Stendhal also attributes to his young hero a class background similar to Rousseau's, a similar resentment of class privilege, a similar paranoid attitude, similar success with an older provincial woman, and, finally, a similar love of mountain scenery and a desire to retreat from the world.

However, given the irony with which Stendhal represents the exploits of Julien Sorel, one can only speculate that Rousseau would have considered that he had committed the sin of sins. Although he never realized his ambition "to write comedies like Molière and to live with an actress," [14] Stendhal was, among so much else, a brilliant comic novelist, who frequently represents his naive hero as a comic as well as a sympathetic character. In a great many scenes up to the denouement, Stendhal does for the doctrinaire and hypocritical young Julien what Molière does for the misanthropic Alceste, that is, he makes him a figure of fun because the principles which command his conduct are in contradiction with his desire.

The Red and the Black has a classic narrative structure to the extent that it represents the principal phases of a young man's education in life: it follows his progress from ignorance to final insight, achieved on the basis of experience of the world and a maturing capacity for self-knowledge. Only when Julien is faced with death by execution does he complete his moral and sentimental education by shedding all worldliness and all ambition and understand that the most important thing is "the art of enjoying [*jouir*] life" (667). All of Stendhal's young heroes and heroines sooner or later become committed to the pursuit of happiness. That in the end they all fail has to do with Stendhal's fundamental belief that the nineteenth century was inimical to happiness; and in his view the principal reason for this is the greatly expanded role played by politics.

It is not surprising, then, that an important part of Julien's education concerns his political education in a thoroughly politicized Restoration France in which civil society as a whole is represented as very much on the defensive. Nowhere is this made more obvious in the novel than in the first chapter of Part 2, whose ironic title is "The Pleasures of Country Life." If I refer to it here, it is because it goes to the heart of Stendhal's contestation of that part of Rousseau's legacy which would "put the polis in command."

The chapter opens with Julien boarding the coach that will finally take him out of his province and send him on his way to Paris and to a situation in a noble family. His travelling companions are two old friends, the Bonapartist Falcoz and the worldly Saint-Giraud, who come upon each other again by chance. The astonished Julien overhears the latter's explanation of why he is returning to Paris, an explanation that develops the comments on the tyranny of public opinion with which the first chapter of Part 1 had begun. In part because of the way Saint-Giraud's comments are isolated in the text and in part because of the summarizing force they have in the context of the novel as a whole, their significance is out of all proportion to the minor role the character himself plays.

Saint-Giraud expresses his opinion of country life in the reign of Charles X as follows:

> "I am fleeing the abominable life people lead in the provinces. I like the cool of the woods and the peace of the country, as you know; you have often enough accused me of being a romantic. I have never been interested in politics, and it is politics that is driving me away."
>
> "But which party do you belong to?"
>
> "To none, and that's the source of my trouble. The only politics that interests me is the following: I love music and painting; a good book is an event in my life. I'm about to be forty-four. How much longer do I have to live? Fifteen, twenty, thirty years at the most?"
> . . . (435–36)

Saint-Giraud then goes on to narrate a series of bitter little anecdotes about the political divisions in French life on the eve of the July Revolution, the factionalism, suspicion and hate that abound on the local level in Restoration France and go a long way to poison civilized social relations or the *douceur de vivre* in general. Moreover, he distributes the blame widely, taking in different social classes as well as different parties, including monarchists, Bonapartists, and liberals alike. And, much to the consternation of Falcoz, he even condemns the dead Emperor, charging him especially with the return of the priests and the renewed power of the nobility.

Saint-Giraud is, in other words, an apolitical man and therefore, from Stendhal's point of view, a member of a besieged minority in French society in the opening decades of the nineteenth century. He is a belated incarnation of the *honnête homme* of *ancien régime* France with more than a touch of the Enlightenment philosophe, a man of taste and a lover of literature and the arts as well as of the beauties of nature; and he finds himself ostracized under the radically new conditions of the postrevolutionary, postimperial modern world. It is characteristic that in the end Saint-Giraud terminates his survey of country living in disturbingly new times with the ironically anti-Rousseauist observation that "I shall now seek solitude and the peace of country life in the only place where they still exist in France, in a fourth-floor apartment on the Champs-Elysées" (437). It is the theme of "the republic of Paris" once again.

In short, Saint-Giraud is represented as a sympathetic figure who argues for the defense of privacy and the individual's right to pursue happiness in his own way in a society that, as a result of decades of upheaval—the revolution, the Empire, and now the Restoration—had undergone a degree of politicization that was unprecedented. The upshot of Saint-Giraud's testimony is, in any case, that there are areas of human life and human relations that politics should not be allowed to reach into because they are, in effect, more important than politics.

The idea of a significant expansion of the sphere embraced by politics in the early nineteenth century had already been raised in the travel book Stendhal had written a dozen years earlier, *Rome, Naples, and Florence in 1817*, but it cohabits oddly in that occasional work with a concern for political liberty. In some respects, in fact, the travel book might be regarded as a somewhat lightweight companion volume to Tocqueville's *Democracy in America;* Stendhal's title could be "Despotism in Italy" and his work, like Tocqueville's, is written from the point of view of a half-critical, half-sympathetic French liberal. On the one hand, Stendhal finds himself obliged to pay attention to political realities in spite of himself—"We live under such a baleful star in this century that although the author only wanted to enjoy himself, he found himself forced to darken his painting with the melancholy tones of politics."[15]—and to recognize that Italian backwardness is due to lack of liberty in its public life.[16] On the other hand, he points to the human and cultural cost as well as the undoubted gains of the kind of political culture associated with representative institutions, a bicameral legislature, a constitution, and a relatively free press—all of which were crucial elements in the political program of early-nineteenth-century French liberalism.

The greatest surprise of the 1817 work, in fact, is not the picture painted of the negative impact of a lack of freedom on Italian manners and Italian creativity in the early years of antirevolutionary backlash, but the ironic asides made on the quality of life in those countries where liberal political institutions and practices already existed, namely, Britain and the United States. The fear expressed is that although Italy needs to be rescued from absolutist governments if its well-known creative energies are to be realized, the introduction of parliamentary and/or democratic politics is also likely to overwhelm Italian joie de vivre and the love of the arts. Like Tocqueville in volume 2 of *Democracy in America* (1840),[17] Stendhal comments on the artistic barrenness of the United States compared with the major European countries in spite of all its democratic freedoms.

Even more telling, however, are the misgivings expressed about the English model, given that Britain was still a society dominated by its aristocracy. The problem for Stendhal is that there, where political debate occupies a large proportion of the time and energy of a country's leisure classes, less time is devoted to the arts and ideas. "In the twentieth century," he notes regretfully, "all people will discuss politics and read the *Morning Chronicle* instead of going to applaud Marianne Corti" (51). Although he acknowledges it as inevitable and even necessary, he deplores the politicization of social life associated with liberal institutions because although those institutions may be a sine qua non for the happiness of a collectivity, they also divert interest from life's higher pleasures: "The charming Milanese will find that the time will come only too soon when they are seized by the political fever that makes one insensitive to the arts but that, thanks to feudalism, one has to go through if one is to achieve happiness" (312).

Thus *Rome, Naples, and Florence in 1817* as a whole is deeply ambivalent: it is both a plea for liberal institutions (including preeminently representative legislative bodies, elections, parties, interest groups, and a political press) and a lament at their likely influence on Italy, given that they imply the politicization of social life and the concomitant marginalization of the arts. In brief, as I have noted elsewhere, it "is a political pamphlet that ironically asserts the limits as well as the necessity of politics in the nineteenth century." [18]

The condition to which Stendhal refers in this work of 1817 and describes in far greater detail in the great novels of the 1830s is, then, what I would call "overpoliticization," that is, a condition under which a political interpretation of life and human relations gains ascendancy to the point of marginalizing all others. The most important reason why it is a crucial issue for Stendhal and goes unremarked by Rousseau is, in part, a historical one, the difference of their situations relative to the French Revolution, the difference between a "before" and an "after." It is also, in part, a difference between one who puts the passion for equality first and one whose primary commitment is to liberty. Thus it is doubtful whether, given his egalitarian temper, his Roman taste for civic virtue, his conception of citizenship, and his suspicion of literary art, Rousseau would ever have found Stendhal's critique congenial.

Stendhal shares the eighteenth-century liberal faith in representative institutions and the suspicion of power, but he combines it with an early-nineteenth-century aesthete's disdain for what we have only recently come to call the culture of politics and for those who absorb themselves in it. Thus the new freedom that Stendhal was one of the first in his time to demand is the freedom *from* politics. At its most immoderate, overpoliticization takes the form of the Maoist injunction referred to in the previous chapter to "put politics in command." When that stage is reached, what should at worst be justified only under extreme and temporary conditions comes to be the norm in a nation's life.

Overpoliticization, then, is the situation briefly described by Saint-Giraud. It is also one of the major themes of *The Red and the Black* as a whole. If the ambitious young peasant, Julien Sorel, takes the wrong path in life, it is not simply because Restoration France has blocked the revolutionary idea of *une carrière ouverte aux talents* but also because he, along with his countrymen as a whole, has learned to calculate and behave politically. Whereas the classic French *roman d'analyse* had universalized its psychological observations, *The Red and the Black* illuminates the historical and sociopolitical determinants in human behavior. Thus the aesthetico-moral lesson of the novel's denouement involves a form of transcendence of politics. Paradoxically, it is in the privacy of his elevated prison cell that Julien undergoes a virtual conversion and is liberated from a preoccupation with social ascension to that of the pursuit of happiness or, in other words, to the idea of living and loving fully during the few days before his execution, gladly isolated from the political interests and social ambitions of life in contemporary society—isolated from what one of Virginia Woolf's characters refers to in shorthand as "money and politics."[19] It is in episodes such as these that one sees Stendhal's romantic ethics and their relationship to his aesthetics most clearly. In this final idyllic space of his fiction the novelist happily fantasizes about the heroism of living at the outer limits of the pleasure principle.

If, because of his historical situation, Stendhal found himself obliged to come to terms with the legacy of Rousseau's political thought in his novels, this is even more obviously the case as far as autobiography is concerned. In the opening pages of his most sustained attempt to write his own, *The Life of Henry Brulard,* Stendhal evokes at some length the mood and circumstances that led him in the mid-1830s to follow the lead Rousseau took some seventy years earlier with the *Confessions.* He then goes on to tell the story of the childhood and education of the future writer, up to the age of seventeen, in a form that has some obvious similarities with Rousseau's: it includes episodes of happiness, misfortune, melancholy, infantile sexuality, persecution, and resistance, evocations of the awakening of a political consciousness, and celebrations of love, nature, and the various arts, along with occasional references to an unfolding talent. It is, however, typical that Stendhal avoids the sententiousness of phrases such as "the discovery of a vocation."

Yet the differences between the two autobiographies are more striking than the similarities. Probably the most interesting feature of *Henry Brulard,* and the source of its originality, is that it displays a remarkable self-consciousness about the genre, and therefore lays bare a number of ethical presuppositions and formal devices that underlie the genre as Rousseau reinvented it. With the example of the *Confessions* to hand, Stendhal was already aware of the crucial problem to which the fictional Zuckerman draws the attention of his creator, Philip Roth, in *The Facts: A Novelist's Autobiography:* "With autobiography there's always another text, a countertext, if you will, to the one presented. It's probably the most manipulative of literary forms."[20]

If one of the most striking features of the *Confessions* is the fullness of the images it projects, including especially its self-portrait, *Henry Brulard* turns out to be the work of someone who is a breaker as well as a maker of images, including self-images. This seems, in part, to derive from what

Stendhal himself diagnosed as his *pudeur*—a concept that in French combines the idea of "modesty" with that of "discretion"—and, in part, from a related taste for irony and the disruptive energies of the comic muse. It is for these reasons that *Henry Brulard* illuminates in a new way the interesting tension in French literary culture between what I am calling "the writer," on the one hand, and "the poet" or "the novelist," on the other. To compare *Henry Brulard* with Stendhal's novels is to understand better the difference within the culture between the artistic vocation of "the novelist," whose model later in the century was to be Flaubert with his insistence on impersonality and authorial distance, and the *engagement* of "the writer," who affirms a lived continuity between his life and his work, his work and society. Hermann Broch had the novelist in mind when he said of Musil, Kafka, and himself, "The three of us have no real biographies." [21]

According to Stendhal's account in *Henry Brulard*, it was at the approach of his fiftieth birthday that he finally succumbed to what might be called the "Rousseauist temptation" after a number of earlier false starts. It was then that he apparently decided he did have a biography, or rather that one should properly be set down as an exercise in self-accounting. Born in 1783, he had had a relatively eventful life—at least until his appointment as consul at Civitavecchia in 1831—that included an unhappy childhood in a very bourgeois family in Grenoble, the pain of the death of his mother, his years of soldiering with Napoleon's armies, his travels and extended sojourns in Italy, his social life in Paris, and above all his various love affairs in different continental cities. Yet a wealth of experience or richness of incident does not, of course, in itself justify or explain the autobiographical impulse.

By the moment in 1832 when he first had the idea of writing *Henry Brulard*, Stendhal was already the author of two novels and would complete a third before largely executing his idea in 1835–36. If he nevertheless found it important to tell the story of his life, and to tell it not just for himself but for a fantasized future readership, it was because the notion of autobiography had attained the status of a normative idea in the culture. After Rousseau and the romantic movement in general, a body of work in one or more of the traditional genres was not enough; at a certain point in his life a poet or novelist was henceforth likely to be tempted to take up the challenge of giving a full account of his life and achievements. "The writer" had become a public man (or woman—one thinks, for example, of Madame de Staël and George Sand) whose own story was felt to be at least as interesting as those of his or her fictions. Moreover, in a sentimental age that also unsentimentally enjoyed intrigue, this was especially true if an account of "the writer's" sufferings in the world and the discovery of a vocation were accompanied by details of love affairs and scandalous disclosures.

If Rousseau's *Confessions* was in many ways Stendhal's most important model in the decision to make a private life public, there are a number of reasons for this: first, autobiography was demonstrably a vehicle capable of satisfying the curiosity he had about himself; second, it enabled one to give expression to certain exemplary features of one's life as writer, including especially the position of marginality and opposition; and third, Rousseau's work also proved that there was a substantial and sympathetic audience for the revelations a writer had to offer about himself and his times.

Like the *Confessions, Henry Brulard* is centered on themes relating to the making of a writer as well as of a man, even if it only takes the story of its subject's life up to his seventeenth year before he had made any serious effort to put his talent to the test. *Henry Brulard* also follows Rousseau's lead in emphasizing the formative influences of the narrator's early years and especially of a given set of family dynamics in determining the form taken by the protagonists's erotic life and subsequent pursuit of happiness.[22] After Rousseau, in fact, and long before the age of psychoanalysis, it came to be routinely assumed that the secret to an understanding of the mature man lies buried in his infancy—"the child is father of the man"—which also explains the recourse to autobiography. Yet significant differences between Stendhal and Rousseau appear almost from the beginning in the way in which they narrate their relations with their parents.

Unlike Rousseau, whose mother died at the moment of his birth and whose father is remembered with proper filial piety, Stendhal evokes a classical Oedipal drama: "I wanted to cover my mother with kisses and did not want any clothes in the way. She loved me passionately and often embraced me; I returned her kisses with such fire that she was often obliged to leave. I hated my father when he came and interrupted us. I always wanted to kiss her on the breast. Be good enough to remember that I lost her in childbirth when I was barely seven years old" (*Henry Brulard*, 26). The passage is characteristic of Stendhal, and uncharacteristic of Rousseau, in its peculiar combination of directness and discretion. Not only does the mature narrator move rapidly over memories that remain highly personal and painful more than forty years after the event, his way of addressing the reader constitutes an appeal for understanding that at the same time stops exaggerated pathos. Intimate feelings in the form of incestuous desires are referred to but not represented in the kind of novelistic scene evoked by Rousseau in his affair with Madame de Warens. As a result, it takes Stendhal less than a page to evoke his memories of his mother and record her death in childbirth, when he was only seven, before he ends the episode with a typical elliptical comment: "That was the beginning of my moral life" (27).

The phrase seems to mean that his mother's death was an experience of loss of a kind that introduced him to the tragic dimension of human experience. But having said it, Stendhal quickly moves on. Thereafter, his life will involve him in one way or another in endlessly repeated efforts to recover the ecstatic sense of well-being he first enjoyed in his mother's presence. Yet it is ironic that nothing he subsequently writes about his relations with women will yield more intimate details than one finds here. There are no scenes in *Henry Brulard* that are in any way comparable to the episodes involving Mademoiselle Lambercier, Madame de Warens, or Zulietta in the *Confessions*.

The frequently interrupted story Stendhal does tell calls up other moments of happiness along with experiences of loss, indignation, isolation, and boredom, the pleasures of reverie, and the consolations of writing, all of which are summed up in a suggestive paragraph before Stendhal's narrative proper begins:

> The usual condition of my life has been that of an unhappy lover who loves music and painting or, in other words, enjoys the products of these arts but doesn't practice them badly. With an exquisite sensibility I sought out the spectacle of beautiful views; that is the only reason I have traveled. Landscapes are like a bow that played across my soul, and the prospects I saw had never been referred to by anyone. . . . I realize that reverie is what I have preferred above all else, even more than being considered a man of wit. (13–14)

The passage is interesting, first, because it suggests the kind of less-than-racy revelations Stendhal typically offers about himself and, second, because the range of sentiments concerned expresses both what Stendhal must have found most appealing in Rousseau's work and what makes him so different. Nowhere is this more obvious than in the final sentence: if in the end he prefers Rousseauist reverie, his attachment to un-Rousseauist wit, and to the critical worldliness wit implies, nevertheless remains almost equally strong, as Stendhal's novels make very clear. Sentiment in Stendhal is typically tempered with irony.

Furthermore, just as Stendhal and Rousseau alike claim that the form of their erotic life was set early, so, apparently, were their sociopolitical attitudes. But in this sphere the young Beyle seems to have been even more precocious than his great predecessor—a fact that can be explained both by their very different family circumstances and by their different historical moments. In effect, their familial situations were in one sense reversed; whereas, from the perspective of *ancien régime* France, Rousseau claims to have experienced his early home life with his artisan father as idyllic and associates it with the benevolent political institutions of the republic of Geneva, Stendhal remembers his bourgeois father's home at the very moment of the revolution as an example of an unenlightened despotism. The young Rousseau only began to experience directly the abuse of power when he became an apprentice, and the injustice of privilege when he left Geneva, but Stendhal already saw himself as a victim of oppression in his home and in his hometown of Grenoble. If his "moral life" began with the death of his mother, therefore, his "political life" started out as resistance to a domestic tyranny presided over by "two devils," namely, his father and his aunt Seraphie.

In other words, *Henry Brulard* seems to follow the exemplary lead of the *Confessions* in establishing the idea of "the writer" as someone who from an early age began his rebellion against arbitrary power and embraced the cause of truth and social justice. Yet, as will be clearer later, Stendhal goes on to diverge sharply from the path taken by Rousseau, not least because in his fiction the relationship between art and political advocacy is an antithetical one.

Nevertheless, *Henry Brulard* begins, like the *Confessions*, with brief references to boyhood escapades that are calculated to suggest turbulent, erotic energies. Where Rousseau recalls "pissing" in an elderly neighbor's saucepan, Stendhal evokes two pointed incidents with characteristic verve. In the first, apparently attracted by an irresistible combination of plumpness and redness, he bites the exquisitely named Madame Pison du Galland in the cheek. In the second, he accidentally drops a knife into the street, where it unfortunately lands close to a lady noted for her disagreeable character. Given the nature of the incident, it is a little disingenuous of Stendhal to accuse his aunt Seraphie of overreacting when she is angry with him. But the point of the episode is to allow him to explain the early emergence of an opposition to the arbitrary exercise of power with a memorable line: "I rebelled; I was about four years old" (25).

Moreover, the episode also prepares the explicit formation of a political consciousness that apparently occurred just a few years later. It was the outbreak of the revolution that enabled the young Beyle to equate explicitly the arbitrariness of absolute monarchy with the tyranny of paternity: "Soon there was politics. My family was one of the most aristocratic in town, which meant that I immediately identified myself as a fierce republican [*républicain enragé*]" (88–89). If there is still any doubt as to where the political sympathies of the adolescent Beyle lay and why, it is finally dissipated by the great pleasure he apparently felt, just before his tenth birthday and in opposition to his *ultra* family, at the execution of Louis XVI: "I experienced one of the sharpest moments of joy of my entire life" (99). The intensity of the pleasure taken in the regicide seems to confirm its character as a displaced parricide.

On the basis of such political attitudes, and in view of the fact that he undertook to write an autobiography at all, it might seem that a great deal in Stendhal's personal circumstances, convictions, and historical times destined him to become "a writer" in the Rousseauist mold. The fact that he ended up the most original novelist of early-nineteenth-century France instead is, in effect, the apparent paradox that interests me here. If no answer is likely to be fully satisfactory—one comes up against the mystery of the way taken by a psyche and a talent in a given familial and sociohistorical matrix—it obviously has to do in part with individual life experiences and the radically different political times that Stendhal lived through, compared with Rousseau, of which the regicide referred to is one of the earliest and most visible markers. In many ways the unprecedented nature of those times, in fact, became the dominant theme of Stendhal's great novels; and it was, in a turn the novel form that enabled him to describe brilliantly what was so unprecedented about them.

Evidence of the kind of important difference between Stendhal and Rousseau that, in the late 1820s and 1830s, was to take the former in the direction of the novel appears, on the one hand, in the different attitude toward art and literature already referred to, and, on the other, in a markedly new postrevolutionary attitude toward the bourgeoisie. For Rousseau, the *citoyen de Genève,* descended from the artisanal class of that city and ill at ease with the aristocratic ethos of French high culture in his time, bourgeois was an honorific state that was synonymous with burgher or emancipated citizen of a free, and preferably republican, city state. In the culture of French Restoration society, especially in the age of Louis Philippe, the word's meaning had, of course, undergone a radical change for the worse in advanced artistic and intellectual circles. The associations of the word for Stendhal are effectively summarized in the scorn he expressed for Grenoble and the Grenoblois, including especially the particular bourgeois male whose name he inherited and went on to erase through the choice of a variety of pseudonyms: "Everything that is low and base in bourgeois behavior reminds me of Grenoble; everything that reminds me of Grenoble horrifies me, no, *horror* is too noble a word, *sickens me.* As far as I am concerned, Grenoble is like the memory of an extreme case of indigestion; there is no danger, just an awful disgust" (86). The choice of imagery here confirms that this is no ordinary contempt, but a visceral hatred that goes a long way back and even causes the man in his fifties to register its impact in his body.

Further, Stendhal's feelings about Grenoble are an extension of his hostility toward his father, whom, in a symptomatic sentence, he associates with Rousseau's beloved Geneva itself: "My father, who was melancholy, shy, spiteful, and without charm, had the same character as Geneva (people add there but they never laugh) . . ." (82). It is, of course, a commonplace of literary and cultural history that from the romantic period down through the twentieth century, part of the self-representation of writer and artist involves the expression of profound opposition to the bourgeoisie, though it is an opposition that has increasingly come to be defined less as a moral and aesthetic disgust, as here, than as an issue of class. And Stendhal, as a contemporary of the first generation of romantics in France, came to define himself quite early as a dandy and an aesthete as well as a man of the world.

It is characteristic of his historical moment in this respect that when, as an adolescent, Henri Beyle planned his escape from home and from the equally despised home town of Grenoble, and fantasized alternative futures elsewhere, he hesitated between two paths. Emancipation seemed possible either through success at school in a curriculum centered on mathematics or as a man of letters living in Paris. Beyle's talent at math was, in fact, to lead him by means of the recently established centralized school system, with its competitive examinations, to a *grande école* in Paris, and potentially, in the age of Napoleon's *grande armée*, a career in the military; his relatively untested talent for writing offered the even more desirable prize of the independent and fêted life of the writer, also in the capital. Stendhal traces the first sign of literary ambition back to the age of seven, when, instead of reading Plutarch, like Rousseau, he first decided he would like "to write comedies like Molière" (85).

That Stendhal, a talented young provincial of his time, should be drawn to the idea of the literary life in Paris is not particularly surprising, given the fact that since the mid-eighteenth century the prestige of men of letters and philosophers had, indeed, in a few instances come to rival that of princes and generals, as Voltaire had hoped. Moreover, like Sartre at the beginning of the following century, Stendhal learned from his grandfather to celebrate the genius of certain great writers.

It is noteworthy in this context that for Stendhal's worldly and revered maternal grandfather Gagnon, Voltaire did, in fact, have the status of a household god, whose image was to be found in his study in the form of a little bust "as big as a fist and standing on an ebony base that was six inches high." The peculiar cult of writers (in the generic as well as in my special sense) that emerged in France, first with the high Enlightenment and then with the Revolution, is confirmed by the reverential attitude the mature narrator attributes to his youthful self: "This bust was placed at the front of the desk where he [grandfather Gagnon] used to write, his study being situated at the end of a large apartment that opened on to an elegant terrace planted with flowers. It was a rare favor for me to be admitted there, and an even greater one to see and touch the bust of Voltaire" (26).

In that laying on of hands one sees the kind of emotional investment associated with the identification of an ideal ego as well as the role played by preindustrial modes of mass reproduction of images in diffusing models of cultural idols. Although he did not realize it as a boy and was never himself a great admirer of Voltaire's literary work, Stendhal notes, in a highly charged comparison, that the philosophe was "the legislator and apostle of France, our Martin Luther" (26). The writer in the mold of Voltaire as well as "the writer" of whom Rousseau furnished the prototype had both come of cultural age.

Another indication of why in Stendhal's case the novelist outlasted the autobiographer and the political analyst appears toward the beginning of *Henry Brulard*, in the summarizing references to his experience of love and sex. With a flourish worthy of Tristram Shandy, the fifty-year-old narrator is represented standing on the banks of Lake Albano and inscribing in the dust with his stick the initials of the dozen or so women he had loved in the course of his life. The gesture is less a dismissive one than an expression of tenderness tempered with irony and discretion—the famous *pudeur*—for there will be almost no details of these affairs in the body of the work, no Rousseau-like references to unexpected pleasures or "secret vices," nothing on his own or his mistress's way of sexual pleasure, and not simply because Stendhal stops his narrative before reaching the appropriate stage of his life. It was a code of urbanity as well as a temperament that made it impossible for him to engage in the heroic shamelessness of the kind Rousseau invented—which perhaps explains why, in spite of a number of sharp vignettes and memorable lines, his autobiography is in many ways disappointing and certainly does not have anything like the stature of his novels.

The point of the enumeration of his loves is, in any case, to indicate how his life can be broken down into two parts: the first is constituted of his active life as lover or aspirant lover and the second of his life as a writer: "Most of these captivating beings never favored me with their charms, but they literally occupied my whole life. Only after them came my works" (16). If it was indeed one of his early ambitions to live and write in Paris (for the sake of the living at least as much as the writing), by the time he was composing his memoirs in Civitavecchia he found that the pleasures of the writer's life had largely passed him by and that the writing itself was his chief compensation: "I return to my administrative rut, remembering all the time the writer's life I lived on the third floor of the hotel de Valois, rue de Richelieu, in Paris" (15).

It is no surprise that, given what Rousseau had made of it, Stendhal first found the temptation of autobiography irresistible and then went on to discover why it was not, in fact, for him; there is, after all, something clearly paradoxical about an autobiographer who puts a high premium on privacy. In any case, on the one hand, he was alone in Italy and writing it afforded him the opportunity to daydream and, in his loneliness, to have diverting conversations with one of the most intelligent men he knew, that is, himself, on a subject that was especially close to him, his own past. On the other hand, he found himself temperamentally and ethically incapable of giving the kind of account of his intimate psychic life and sexual relationships that made the *Confessions* such a *succès de scandale*. Consequently, *Henry Brulard* is both autobiography and critique of autobiography; "the anti-writer" again and again cuts short the promise of intimacy and outbursts of "writerly" effusion.

It is true that, in light of a lack of enlightened interlocutors at Civitavecchia and his problematic relationship to his reading public in his homeland, Stendhal used the genre to attempt a dialogue with a fantasized community of readers. In that sense, for the time of the writing at least, Stendhal seems to have found the possibilities of autobiography rewarding ones. Yet from the beginning he remained skeptical of what could be truthfully represented. From the title and the various projected titles and subtitles on, as well as from the opening pages of the work proper, it is clear that in Stendhal's hands the genre was to be problematized not long after it had been first fully consecrated in France. And this is the case for ethical as well as aesthetic reasons. The ironic and/or mystificatory significance of Stendhal's many pseudonyms has been discussed in a number of places, and the substitution of the self-mocking "Brulard" for the hated patronym and the anglicization of his given name are suggestive of the effects Stendhal sought. Moreover, the most extravagant of the projected announcements of the work, with its reference to the murderer of the radical revolutionary leader Jean-Paul Marat, proclaims its character as hoax: "*Life of Henry Brulard.* To the Gentlemen of the Police. This is a novel imitated from *The Vicar of Wakefield.* The hero, Henry Brulard, tells his life after the death of his wife, the famous Charlotte Corday" (1).

The implication of this and other devices is that Stendhal found it impossible to tell the story of his life without at the same time playing the ironist and pointing up the deceptions and self-deceptions inherent in such narrativization. Part of the explanation of his discomfort with the Rousseauist model can be found in his taste for more spirited and less morally uplifting countermodels of autobiography, such as the *Life* of Benvenuto Cellini. Part of it, too, seems to derive from the pleasure he took from an early age in a tradition in the novel that began with Cervantes. According to *Henry Brulard* itself, it was the discovery of Cervantes's comic masterpiece that enabled him to escape from the peculiar unhappiness of his childhood and changed his life: "*Don Quixote* made me die of laughing. . . . Imagine the effect of *Don Quixote* in the midst of all that horrible sadness! The discovery of that book . . . is perhaps the greatest period of my life" (79–80).

It was clearly through Cervantes's work that Stendhal first experienced the exuberance and liberating energies of the novel at its best. Thus it is no accident if an eighteenth-century exemplar of the Cervantean tradition in fiction, Laurence Sterne, was to furnish Stendhal with a countermodel for the narrative of a life to that derived from Rousseau, a countermodel that prefers invention and the spirit of play to claims of truth. The satirico-sentimental struggle of Tristram Shandy to get a life told right presides over *Henry Brulard* at least as much as the *Confessions* does. But it also seems that in Stendhal's case the whole autobiographical project is undermined from the start because he finds it fundamentally uncongenial, not to say dishonest—a form of mystification that combines a sentimental narcissism with *emphase,* or overwriting.

In this respect, one of the most striking features of *Henry Brulard* is the number of highly schematic plans and sketches it contains. Sterne had already shown briefly the power of graphic figures to subvert the monotony and solemnity of the printed page. Thus, whatever their actual purpose in his mind, Stendhal's little sketches and matchstick figures in the text have the effect of introducing a spirit of play into the serious task of self-presentation. It is as if he were already critically positioned by the comic tradition in fiction to unmask the conventions of autobiography that Sartre and Barthes could only illuminate a century and a half later through the application of such twentieth century concepts as "bad faith" and "the imaginary."

Evidence of Stendhal's ironic critical distance from his autobiographical material is to be found scattered throughout *Henry Brulard,* but it is concentrated particularly at its beginning and its end. The opening chapter of the autobiography is characterized by a series of typically Shandyan movements. It takes Stendhal two chapters, for example, to get baby Henri into the world—"After all those generalizing thoughts I shall now be born" (23). And from the beginning there are the false starts, interruptions, digressions, various forms of doubt, and a preoccupation with whom he should entrust the manuscript to for the purpose of publication and with the nature of his future readers, if any. The focus of the writing throughout is often as much on Stendhal, the narrator, as on Brulard/Beyle, the young protagonist, as much on the present of enunciation as on the past of the enunciated, and at the beginning and end the discursive present of the writing overwhelms the narrative of the past. Consequently, the work for long stretches has the air of a conversation between the narrator and himself or of a frequently brilliant monologue before an audience in which he now and then steps out of his role to apologize and to warn that what he is doing cannot legitimately be done.

Stendhal claims in the opening pages that he first thought of the idea of writing his memoirs as an exercise in self-analysis: "I am about to be fifty; it's about time I got to know myself. What have I been, what I am, in truth I would be hard pressed to say" (6). It is characteristic that the idea comes upon him with an air of spontaneity and is presented as the fruit of idleness and curiosity about himself rather than as a need to set the record straight and justify his conduct before the world: "That evening as I was returning home, bored from an evening at the ambassador's, I said to myself that I ought to write my life; that way I would finally know, when it was finished two or three years later, what I have been, whether gay or sad, witty or stupid, brave or cowardly, and on the whole happy or unhappy—I could have Fiori read the manuscript" (8).

It is equally characteristic that he should in the very next paragraph cast doubt on the value of the exercise in a way that is important to my purpose: "I like the idea of it. Yes, but what about that awful quantity of 'I's' and 'Me's'! That's enough to put even the most generous of readers out of sorts. If one overlooks the difference in talent, 'I' and 'Me' recalls Mr. Chateaubriand, that king of egotists" (8). What worries Stendhal is apparently the fundamentally self-regarding and monologic character of a first-person genre centered on the author's self, a lack of reciprocity in the relation with another. One is also reminded by such passages that Barthes in *Roland Barthes* refers to "I" as "the pronoun of the imaginary."[23] How, in brief, does one avoid the famous narcissistic and illusory entrapment that is inherent in contemplating at length one's own image?

Finally, as far as Stendhal's opening self-critical skirmishes are concerned, less than half a dozen lines further on the text breaks off altogether, to be picked up three years later, in 1835, without any attempt at explanation.

Yet it is, in the end, the pleasure in the writing combined with the desire to be read that persuade the author to go on: "My *Confessions* will cease to exist thirty years after being published, if the 'I' and the 'Me' bore the readers to death; yet I shall have had the pleasure of the writing and of having undertaken a thorough examination of my conscience. Moreover, if it is a success, I run the risk of being read in 1900 by beings I love such as the Madame Rolands, the Melanie Guilberts, etc . . ." (10). It is in such passages that Stendhal illuminates his dilemma as that of a would-be public man in search of a public. As with Rousseau, autobiography is figured as an offer of intimacy to a reader in exchange for recognition. But given that, unlike Rousseau, he was no celebrity in his time, Stendhal in his early fifties was uncertain who, if any, his readers would be. Was anyone interested? In part as a result of such uncertainty, there was an absence of the effect of self-mirroring through another by means of which "a writer's" ego may be inordinately puffed up.

An important theme of Rousseau's *Confessions* had been the indignities the author suffered from the *ancien régime*'s patronage system and his struggles to remain independent in the face of incomprehension and hostile cabals. It is partly for such reasons that there is peculiar intensity in the appeal Rousseau makes to his readers. Yet with respect to his readers, Stendhal's marginal situation in Restoration Europe was much more complex—not only did he not live in his homeland most of the time, he was also faced with rapidly evolving taste, an expanded literary market, and shifting forms of censorship.

From the point of view of relationship with a reader, the attraction of autobiography was that it promised, for once, unmediated communication; in exchange for making oneself transparent to another, one was rewarded with sympathy and understanding. Not only could one come to know oneself, one could also be one's own advocate and make oneself known directly to the reader. That is why Stendhal apparently decided he would write *The Life of Henry Brulard* as if he were writing to a friend:

> Feeling good for nothing, not even for writing the official correspondence of my job, I have had the fire lighted and I am writing this, without lying, I hope, without deluding myself, and with pleasure, as if it were a letter to a friend. What ideas will that friend have in 1880? How different from ours! . . . This is something new for me: speaking to people of whose way of thinking, form of

education, prejudices, and religion one knows nothing! What an
incentive to be true, and nothing but *true*, that alone is worthwhile.
Benvenuto was *true*, and one reads him with pleasure, as if it had
been written yesterday. (11)

By his early fifties Stendhal had apparently already decided that his
best hope for a more sympathetic audience lay with posterity and not
among his contemporaries. That is why he hypothesizes a readership of
the years 1880, 1900, and 1935 in *Henry Brulard*. Yet the above passage
also reveals the risks of the exercise: the future, even more than the past,
is another country, and the image of oneself returned by such a distant
mirror is necessarily a blurred one. Thus once again Stendhal speculates
about problems that go unacknowledged in the *Confessions*, problems that
cast doubt on the value of his work. Here as elsewhere the conversation
with himself is pursued; Stendhal cannot resist chasing thoughts with af-
terthoughts.

Further, with respect to his declared determination to tell the truth,
Stendhal reveals how radically un-Rousseauist he was in a single sentence
of the paragraph immediately following the one just quoted: "But how
many precautions one has to take in order not to lie!" (11). The significance of this remark is that it defines truth-telling, like story-telling, as
neither natural nor spontaneous, as Rousseau had assumed. On the contrary, as Stendhal's practice in *Henry Brulard* makes clear, truth-telling
requires constant self-scrutiny and a readiness to interrupt the flow of
one's narrative; it requires not trust but distrust, not sentimental overwriting of a Rousseauist kind but a capacity for detachment, irony, and wit.
Already in the opening chapters, therefore, as Stendhal tries to outline the
different periods of his past, he adopts the strategy of playing the philosophe in order to classify his friends according to the phases of his life,
arranging them by genus "like a collection of plants" (23).

It is in the second chapter that Stendhal defines the problem of truth
for the autobiographer in visual terms. In order to escape from the spell
of a remembered image, he behaves like an early nineteenth-century ideologue and comes up with a strategy for breaking it that involves a distancing effect achieved by the ironic application of philosophical method to
the subject's emotional life: "So as to consider them [the women he loved]
as philosophically as possible and, therefore, to strip them of the aureole
that sets my eyes dancing, dazzles, and deprives me of the capacity to see
clearly, I will order these ladies (in the mathematical sense of the word)
with respect to their different qualities." The opposition between Stendhal
and Rousseau appears sharply in the choice of the adverb "philosophically" as well as in the goal he sets himself to try "to destroy the *dazzling*
of events by considering them in military terms. It is the only means I have
of reaching truth on a topic about which I am unable to converse with
anyone. With the modesty of a melancholy temperament (Cabanis), I have

always been in this respect of an unbelievable and insane discretion [*pudeur*]" (19). He is so discreet, in fact, that the only love affair he can bring himself to narrate in some detail is his love affair with his mother—although he will suffer from far fewer inhibitions in his fiction.

Stendhal, then, sees himself as a breaker of images, including self-images, but not in the same iconoclastic, satirical sense in which Flaubert, for example, is a breaker of images of romantic love. He still believes in the authenticity of past emotion but prefers understatement in the present. His un-Rousseauist goal is to disentangle the deceptive aura of memory from the reality of past experience and at the same to avoid being caught up in a retrospective narcissism. There will, therefore, be no portrait of himself as romantic lover, no intimate details, no descriptions of peculiar tastes, no account of psychopathologies or physical infirmities, and above all no scenes of heroic self-disclosure.

Symptoms of Stendhal's dilemma as autobiographer consequently occur in his efforts to narrate some of the emotional high points of his life. As anyone who has some familiarity with the works of Stendhal might expect, the episodes that mean the most to him are those that concern his early childhood, including especially the death of his beloved mother, his love affairs with a number of women, the pleasures of art, music, literature, and beautiful landscapes, and the freedom and happiness he associates with his early travels in Italy. Stendhal looks back at his life with an overwhelming sense of loss. As a result, he, more than anyone else before Proust, focuses on the drama of memory from the point of view of the present of the writing.[24] The process of recalling of his happiest moments, in particular, turns out to be peculiarly painful; emotion for him is recollected in turmoil. The difficulty he has in narrating those moments is the sign that there is something seriously wrong. And nowhere is this more evident than in the final two or three short chapters before the unfinished autobiography breaks off.

Just as he had trouble getting started, so by the end he finds it impossible to evoke adequately the ecstatic sensations he experienced, and he gives up. Symptoms of the trouble occur at Rolle, in Switzerland, on his way for the first time to Italy, and it is there that he specifically evokes Rousseau as negative model: "How could I represent the ecstacy of Rolle? I will perhaps have to reread and correct this passage in spite of myself, for fear of lying with artifice like J.-J. Rousseau" (391).

Then, on the following page, after having described the extraordinary moment when he observed the Swiss countryside from the church tower at Rolle ("That was, I believe, the closest I have ever come to *perfect happiness*. For such a moment as that, life is worth living"), with a characteristic gesture he refocuses immediately on the ethical question of the writing: "What can be said about such a moment without lying, without turning it into fiction [*roman*]? " (392). In spite of its ambiguity, the comment should not, I believe, be taken to imply that novel writing itself is a form of lying, but that genres should not be mixed and that autobiography is fatally flawed in this respect. The lesson of his great novels, on the other hand, is precisely that the surest approach to truth is through the detour of fiction.

What is perhaps most interesting about such episodes is that the emotion is by no means entirely that of the seventeen-year-old youth. Stendhal stages the drama of memory here by evoking the sensations of the middle-aged narrator alongside the inadequately rendered feelings of the youthful protagonist. Not only does the memory of past happiness signify present pain, the narrator also denies the existence of an art of language by means of which the aging man can reanimate the intensity of the boy's pleasure without some form of deceit: "My heart still beats thirty-six years later as I write this. I abandon my paper, I wander around my room, I start writing again. I prefer omitting some true feature rather than falling into the execrable error of declaiming in an all too familiar way" (392–93).

It is in a similar vein that he concludes his final chapter, on his first visit to Milan and his love affair with Angela Pietragrua. There, too, the sublime quality of his experiences is such that he finds it impossible to set them down in a coherent order. "What shall I do?" he asks. "How does one paint mad happiness?" Or, again, "As a reasonable man who hates to exaggerate, I don't know what to do." What he does do, of course, is give up. Half a page later, he signs off with a characteristic last word that is also a romantic conceit: "One destroys such tender feelings when one gives a detailed account of them" (414–15).

If one of the advantages of autobiography after Rousseau was presumed to be in the immediacy of an encounter with a reader, it turned out to have been a liability for Stendhal. Having struggled to represent episodes from the first seventeen years of his life, he seems to have reached the conclusion that autobiography was not only uncongenial for someone of his temperament, but that it was an impossible genre for a novelist for reasons that the fictional Zuckerman also explains to Philip Roth in his autobiography: "What one chooses to reveal in fiction is governed by a motive fundamentally aesthetic; we judge the author of a novel by how well he or she tells the story. But we judge morally the author of an autobiography, whose governing motive is primarily ethical as against aesthetic. How close is the narration to the truth?" (*The Facts*, 163). Unlike Rousseau, Stendhal was aware that that final question is one he could not answer to his own satisfaction.

Perhaps autobiography was a test he had to submit himself to in order to overcome his temptation to be "a writer" like Rousseau rather than a novelist like Cervantes or Sterne. In the end, it is clear that though the unfinished *Henry Brulard* is often a work of remarkable critical acuity and self-knowledge, it is not in the same class as the great novels of Stendhal's maturity. Only there, if anywhere, can it be said that he found a form that, in Kundera's words, met "the demands of his dream."

In sum, the difference between Stendhal and Rousseau relative to auto-biography might be briefly formulated as that between *pudeur* and shame-lessness, between a belief in the value of privacy—or in privacy as a value—and a will to transparency. The result, in any case, of the writing and abandonment of Stendhal's own "Confessions" in the years 1835–36 led him to a kind of reaffirmation of his faith in the novel and the comple-tion of his masterpiece, *The Charterhouse of Parma*, by the end of the decade; for if Stendhal can be said to have believed in anything, it is in imaginative literature of the most heroic and extravagant kind.

In *The Red and the Black* Stendhal's diagnosis of what I have called over-politicization is expressed in the famous similes referred to earlier, which the author interpolates into his narrative in a brief exchange with his fic-tional publisher: " 'Politics', the author continued, 'is a stone tied to the neck of literature, and in less than six months it drags it under. Politics, where the interests of the imagination are concerned, is like a pistol shot at a concert. The noise is strident but not energetic. It is out of tune with all the other instruments' " (*The Red and the Black*, 575–76).

The interest in these sentences is that they constitute one of the most succinct rejections of the idea of *littérature engagée* that has ever been formulated. It is no accident that the second of Stendhal's hyperbolic meta-phors concerns music, because not only was he a lover of music (opera in particular), but music, as the symbolists were to claim, is the purest of the arts, in the sense that it is the least easily adapted to programmatic pur-poses, although as modern history has taught us, it can be recuperated ex post facto. In any case, in their typically urbane way the above comments affirm the idea of the autonomy of art and literature. They are also an expression of the eighteenth-century liberal belief in the importance of the separation of powers, applied here to the aesthetic sphere, on the one hand, and the political, on the other. They constitute, finally, a warning about the fate of art and literature in the new political and politicized culture that emerged in the postrevolutionary decades.

The paradox is, of course, that their author virtually invented what has come to be called "the political novel" in the modern world—although in the case of *The Charterhouse of Parma* it might be more appropriate to speak of "political romance"—and it is this paradox that explains the striking originality of Stendhal's great works in the genre; that is, not only do they focus on the greatly expanded role of politics in social life, they also illuminate the threats to life and happiness politics constitutes and assert the importance of establishing limits to its reach, and not simply in the case of the reactionary regimes on which he explicitly focuses.

Among the most succinct expressions of Stendhal's view of the promise and the limits of politics is a short scene from the unfinished novel that attempted to do for the reign of Louis Philippe what *The Red and the Black* did for the age of Charles X, *Lucien Leuwen* (1834–35). The scene,

which in V. Del Litto's edition is relegated to the "Notes and Variants"
section, involves a discussion between the most reflective of Stendhal's
sympathetic young heroes, the eponymous Lucien himself, and Gaulthier,
the dedicated editor of Nancy's republican newspaper. That for those loyal
to the revolutionary tradition political faith had come to occupy the place
once associated with religious faith is made clear in the very words
Gaulthier uses in his attempt to persuade Lucien to put his trust in the
republican future. He compares the condition of republicans in the reign
of Louis Philippe to that of early Christians under the Roman Empire, but
it is an analogy Lucien rejects in terms that are deeply skeptical of the
contribution politics as such can make to the cause of human happiness:

> "But, my good friend," said Lucien in a discouraged voice, "the
> early Christians saw great happiness in heaven. But I do not feel
> that I will experience supreme happiness under a Republic. My sus-
> ceptibilities will not be shocked by hideous sights, preventive ar-
> rests, the massacre of Transnonain Street, etc., etc. But the absence
> of such evils does not mean I shall be happy. It seems to me that
> my happiness will always depend on my personal actions. First you
> must have a passion and then you must be able to satisfy it." [25]

In short, at best politics can merely establish the external conditions which
allow an essentially private individual to pursue happiness in his own passionate way.

In the end, *The Charterhouse of Parma* makes clear the extent to which
Stendhal believed literature should be not only autonomous but also oppositional relative to the political sphere as a whole. If any novel can be said
to have been conceived as literature taking revenge on politics, it is this
extravagant work of his late fifties. Stendhal's insights into the relations
between politics, on the one hand, and art and ethics, on the other, find
their most luminous and most poignant as well as their most disturbing
formulation here.

It is with *The Charterhouse of Parma* that Stendhal most obviously
reestablished the nineteenth-century novel's links with the genre's great
beginnings in *Don Quixote*. It is also Stendhal's *Tempest* or, given that in
an age of grand opera it is the most operatic of tragicomic novels, his
Magic Flute. Like *Don Quixote*, *The Tempest*, and *The Magic Flute*, *The
Charterhouse of Parma* offers an example of the liberating energies of the
creative imagination at work at the height of its author's powers in a genre
uniquely suited to his purposes.

The significance of Stendhal's novel here is that it offers an unusual
example of D. H. Lawrence's point in his well-known essay "Why the
Novel Matters": the work manages to combine criticism of life in his time
with the celebration of life's potential by means of a series of effects that
could not be achieved outside narrative literature in general and the novel
in particular. And its most stunning achievement, in the context of the

present book, is that it puts politics on display in order to suggest how important it is, for ethical as well as for aesthetic reasons, to delimit the sphere of its effects.

The political character of *The Charterhouse of Parma* derives, of course, from the fact that it focuses on the fate of a small group of sympathetic characters forced to live their lives and pursue happiness in a small autocratic state under the disabling conditions existing in early nineteenth-century Italy. Stendhal had no compunction about dividing up the world of his fictions between a majority of "ignoble souls" *(âmes basses)* and a distinct minority of "noble" ones *(âmes nobles)*—his famous "happy few"—and insisting on the latter's right to blaze their own passionate path through life, under circumstances that throw up all kinds of obstacles in their way, frequently at great cost to themselves and those around them. It is notable in this respect that the combination of *pudeur* and will to truth that inhibited him in his autobiographical writings is in many ways absent from his fiction. What is most scandalous in Stendhal is to be found in his novels, and nowhere more so than in the conduct of his extravagant characters, of which *The Charterhouse of Parma* has more than its share.

Stendhal endows them with a kind of heroic singlemindedness and fearlessness that makes many of them seem like figures out of another age. There are, of course, such extraordinary figures as Mathilde de la Mole *(The Red and the Black)*, who seeks to model her conduct on that of a sixteenth-century ancestor and dreams of embracing her executed lover's severed head on her lap; the duchesse de Sanseverina and Fabrice del Dongo *(The Charterhouse of Parma)*, both of whom appear to be out of the kind of Italian Renaissance chronicle that was the original source of the novel, the first taking spectacular revenge on the prince who blackmailed her into a sexual encounter by flooding a valley and accompanying it with a fireworks display in order to humiliate him, and the second returning to the prison from which he had escaped, and where his life is very much at risk, because of his love for the jailer's daughter; and perhaps the most flamboyant of all, the wild child/woman Lamiel *(Lamiel)*, who organizes her own deflowering early on out of unsentimental curiosity and was to have ended up the lover of a bandit chief before burning down the Palais de Justice.

As far as *The Charterhouse of Parma*, in particular, is concerned, the main characters there give the impression of having been drawn from the Renaissance world chronicled by one of Stendhal's favorite authors, Benvenuto Cellini, or even out of the romance of one of his favorite Renaissance poets, Ariosto *(The Charterhouse of Parma*, from some of its passages, might be retitled *Fabrizio Furioso)*.

Stendhal's most memorable and most endearing characters, then, are products of the fantasms of an early nineteenth-century man of the world, who, in his own life, had relatively little in common with them. As such, they are made the embodiment of antisocial yet heroic energies that cannot be contained by their age or by any other outside moments of revolutionary or patriotic fervor. Their exemplary status for Stendhal is in the fact that they transcend the petty passions of those around them—the pursuit of wealth and position and *l'esprit de parti*—with grand and obsessive ones that drive through the pleasure principle as well as the reality principle into a kind of sublime romantic *jouissance*.

Moreover, the small and autocratic state of Parma is experienced as a challenge to their energy and their ingenuity as well as their passions; Ernest IV's state is no more than a series of constraints to be circumvented or triumphantly overcome. Thus despotism, unlike liberal constitutional or democratic regimes, is paradoxically represented by Stendhal as a school for great souls. The most memorable characters of *The Charterhouse of Parma* are, in fact, defined to a large extent in terms of their distance from political life and those who engage in it: the indifference of Fabrice, the contempt of la Sanseverina, the ironic distance of Mosca, who compares politics to a game of whist that has to be played according to the rules and that he has learned to play like a connoisseur. Moreover, Fabrice and the duchesse de Sanseverina, in particular, speak in a postreligious age the transcendental languages of romantic love and of natural and artistic beauty.

It is thus typical of the romantic absolutism that characterizes Stendhal at least as much as his worldliness, that the denouement is a virtual hecatomb in which three of the four main characters die and the fourth survives almost in spite of himself. The survivor, Mosca, is, in fact, the most tragic character in the novel, the one who comes closest to the classic idea of a tragic hero in his clear complicity with his own downfall. Politics may be a game for him, but unlike the other main characters of *The Charterhouse of Parma*, it is a game in which he is finally entrapped. Mosca, the *honnête homme* with the tolerant and humane instincts of classic eighteenth-century, prerevolutionary liberalism, ends up contaminated by the repressive system he was trying to control; he becomes in part the kind of political animal that he despised, and he lives to regret it. Through the figure of Mosca, in fact, Stendhal is the first novelist to raise the troubling idea of political power in the modern world as a Faustian bargain. Thus, along with everything else, *The Charterhouse of Parma* is the tragedy of modern political man.

What is true of Stendhal's characters in his Italian novel is true of the work as a whole. He appeals throughout to registers that go beyond the social and the political. Nowhere is this more apparent than in the character of the work's fiction-making itself. Stendhal's great theme is not commitment to sociopolitical change but devotion to the utopian imagination or the reinvention of life in the interest of individual happiness; and his complex, sprawling tragic-comic romance turns out to be a wonderful vehicle for his purpose.

Stendhal claimed, as we know, to be temperamentally incapable of working from a plan, which is perhaps another reason why he found autobiography so uncongenial: it requires you, so to speak, "to follow an outline" with at best a minimum of selection and foreshadowing. Moreover, what is true of autobiography is also true in a different way of a political cause. *Engagement* in literature presupposes commitment to a programmatic idea of the collective future and therefore freezes the imagination. It is at best an art of persuasion; when it becomes salvationist, it becomes a mode of coercion.

What one finds in *The Charterhouse of Parma* is something very different, something that might be thought of not as *engagement* but as *désengagement*. The novel folds its overlapping love stories and its satirical commentary into a swashbuckling romance, *un roman de cape et d'épée*. Written in some fifty-five days, it achieves its purposes through sudden changes of pace, panoramic effects, the variety of its scenes and situations, a large and diverse cast of fictional characters, and wild twists in the plot. And Stendhal holds it all together through his mastery of a range of registers that shifts between wit, humor, passion, sentiment, fantasy, comedy, tragedy, satire, darkness and light, the romantic and the absurd. In other words, *The Charterhouse of Parma* as a whole is an example of the novel transcending itself; it is as ironic and inventive and liberating an exercise as one could hope for. Like Mozartian opera at its best, it is an unsurpassably exhilarating experience that is also specifically aesthetic in nature.

Stendhal's purposes, then, transcend the mere satire of life in a minor absolutist state in an age of reaction, although the result of his technique of miniaturization is to render absolutism absurd as well as barbaric. The effect of the work as a whole is to restore a balance in which "literature" takes its revenge over politics as such and not just over all that is most sordid, most cowardly and hypocritical in political life. *The Charterhouse of Parma* becomes a vehicle for throwing the reality principle to the winds and with it the pursuit of wealth, power, and social position, the spirit of caution, or calculation of interest, and even compromise.

That is not to say Stendhal was an adherent of the aesthetic movement, as it first came to be defined by his contemporary Théophile Gautier. As his cult of romantic love alone implies, Stendhal was not simply a believer in art for art's sake. That is why the art of the novel he developed included a broad range of nineteenth-century life, if only in order to put it to shame. Nevertheless, it is clear that if forced to choose he would have reversed the revolutionary line of descent that from Rousseau to Mao "put politics in command" and would have "put aesthetics in command" instead—that is, if such a phrase is not an oxymoron. In any case, Stendhal came to regard the aesthetic sphere as the one in which the most important values could be articulated and celebrated, the sphere in which new possibilities could be tried out and new ideas freely formulated. Moreover, the novel was especially congenial to his purpose, since it enabled him to suggest where in a desacralized universe one might come closest to transcendental experiences, that is, in romantic love and in the spectacle of natural or man-made beauty—art, music, and, of course, literature itself. Those moments of illumination to which certain privileged characters of Stendhal's novels are occasionally subject approximate what another great novelist, Virginia Woolf, in equally difficult historical times was to call "moments of being."[26]

That even such a level-headed analyst of sociopolitical life as Tocqueville was also not immune to movements of heroic enthusiasm is attested to by the epigraph to this chapter. The warning uttered there concerning 1789—"a phase of history that for many years to come will trouble the sleep of all who seek to demoralize the nation and reduce it to a servile state"—is the kind of warning that, along with so much hope and melancholy, is part of the ethos of *The Charterhouse of Parma.*

In another passage from the end of the same work, *The Old Regime and the Revolution,* Tocqueville goes on to describe the French national character in a way that both caters to the myth of *l'exception française* (the idea of French uniqueness) and goes a long way toward explaining Stendhal's attachment to the memory of 1796 as well as to the young heroes of his novels:

> The Frenchman can turn his hand to anything, but he excels in war alone and he prefers fighting against odds, preferring dazzling feats of arms and spectacular successes to achievements of the more solid kind. He is more prone to heroism than to humdrum virtue, apter for genius than for good sense, more inclined to think up grandiose schemes than to carry through great enterprises. Thus the French are the most brilliant and the most dangerous of all European nations. . . . (*The Old Regime*, 211)

The passage is valuable from my point of view because it helps identify what is disturbing as well as dazzling in Stendhal's fictions. Not only is there something knowingly anachronistic about the conduct and the values of his most passionate, proud, and energetic characters (what in *Henry Brulard* he refers to as *espagnolisme*), like Rousseau before him he turns his back on modernity, although the ideal country he sets in opposition to it is not Sparta or Republican Rome but Renaissance Italy. The kind of modern world associated with the idea of the public sphere discussed in the last chapter may have attracted him in his more sober moments but it was without the power to stir his imagination or his loyalty. Stendhal was a dandy, an aesthete, and an unabashed elitist as well as a liberal; he had little taste for the kind of political culture discussed in the previous chapter and described by Keith Baker as follows: "It [political culture] sees politics as about making claims; as the activity through which individuals and groups in any society articulate, negotiate, implement, and enforce the competing claims they make upon one another and upon the whole. Political culture is, in this sense, the set of discourses or symbolic practices by which these claims are made."[27]

Nevertheless, the challenge to the complacencies of our own modern world and its own overpoliticized culture represented by *The Charterhouse of Parma* is hard to overstate. One way to explain it is to use Gramsci against himself and suggest that Stendhal's great novels were the first literary works of the modern era to reflect on the loss that occurs when political discourse itself becomes hegemonic. For reasons similar to those that led him to trust the novel and distrust autobiography, Stendhal championed ethics and aesthetics over politics. Given the need in our present circumstances to restore the balance, it is fitting to refer to the first of my epigraphs at the beginning of his book and to give the last word on the topic to a former dissident poet and exile from Soviet communism, Joseph Brodsky.

Commenting on the generation of writers that came of age in the Soviet Union under Stalinism and post-Stalinism, he writes, "Books became the first and only reality, whereas reality itself was regarded as either nonsense or nuisance. Compared to others we were ostensibly flunking or faking our lives. But come to think of it, existence which ignores the standards professed in literature is inferior and unworthy of effort." Brodsky then goes on to imagine his fellow dissidents standing and grinning at each other in their dilapidated kitchens as they inquire, "*Liberté, égalité, fraternité.* . . . Why does nobody add Culture?"[28]

CHAPTER 3

Charles Baudelaire:
Portrait of the Poet
as Anti-Writer

The more man cultivates the arts, the less he gets a hard-on. There is an ever-increasing divorce between spirit and the brute. Only the brute really gets a hard-on; fucking is the lyricism of the people.

CHARLES BAUDELAIRE

Charles Baudelaire is a case apart in the context of this exploration of a legacy that, whether reaffirmed or contested, was of the greatest significance for French culture for over two hundred years. Baudelaire is the only poet on whom I focus. From the point of view of early- to mid-nineteenth-century French literary history, Rousseau has a great many obvious heirs, including the authors of the first-person, confessional *romans personnels*, such as Etienne Pivert de Sénancour or François-René de Chateaubriand, or poets such as Alphonse de Lamartine, Alfred de Musset, and Victor Hugo himself. Yet with the partial exception of the latter, none of them is "a writer" in the full sense I am giving the word here—although Hugo was the first to make a programmatic identification of the revolutionary tradition in politics with romanticism in literature, and later in his life he never ceased fulminating against the imperial regime of Louis-Napoleon from his place of exile on the Channel Islands.

If I choose to focus on Baudelaire, it is in part because in the literary and intellectual sphere the significance of a legacy often appears more clearly when it is contested than when it is simply taken up. This is particularly true when in the light of subsequent historical experience that legacy is experienced as a peculiarly bitter one; and for someone like Baudelaire, born in 1821 and therefore coming of age in the political culture that had established itself by the middle years of the reign of Louis-Philippe, such was clearly the case.

A more important reason why it is particularly rewarding to explore the significance of Baudelaire in this context is that since roughly the early part of this century, both in France and abroad, he has been taken to be

Gustave Courbet, *Portrait of Baudelaire*
(Musée Fabre, Montpellier)

the Poet of the French nineteenth century, with the occasional exception, as poetic taste has waxed and waned, of Mallarmé. For the educated reading public at large Baudelaire is above all famous for a single, not particularly long, volume of verse, *The Flowers of Evil,* for the idea of the autonomy of art, and for a certain conception of the poetic life that he came to embody—to some extent for his contemporaries but especially for all readers of Western poetry over the century or so since his death in 1867.

Thus in an important sense, given the way I have defined "the writer," Baudelaire might well be regarded as the very embodiment of "the antiwriter." Isn't the Poet, as he came to be perceived and represented in the postromantic decades down through the aesthetic movement and poetic symbolism, associated as he is with the idea of "poetic purity," in most respects an antithetical figure to "the writer" in whom a combination of sociopolitical commitment and confession is paramount? In other words, could one not say even more emphatically of the Poet what Kundera says of the Novelist in contrast to "the writer" in the passage quoted in my introduction? Distinguishing between them, Kundera notes that the latter "has original ideas and an inimitable voice. He may use any form (including the novel), and whatever he writes—being marked by his thought,

Etienne Carjat, Charles Baudelaire
(Photo Bibl. Nat.)

Etienne Carjat, Charles Baudelaire with engravings
(Photo Bibl. Nat.)

borne by his voice—is part of his work." The Novelist, on the other hand, "makes no great issue of his ideas. He is an explorer feeling his way in an effort to reveal some unknown aspect of existence. He is fascinated not by his voice but by a form he is seeking, and only those forms that meet the demands of his dream become part of his work."[1] At the very least one recognizes an affinity between Kundera's Novelist and the nineteenth-century poet in whose aesthetics both the discipline of form and the notion of dream were central, and who committed his life to exploring limit experiences and pursuing a new ideal of poetic beauty in the context of modern urban life.

Yet Baudelaire is not, of course, simply the author of *The Flowers of Evil*. His complete works constitute two fat volumes of densely printed pages in Claude Pichois's Pléiade edition, even if one discounts the extensive editorial notes. Apart from the verse, Baudelaire was also the author of an important volume of prose poems, *Paris Spleen:* of "private journals" (the *Journaux Intimes;*) of a short story, "La Fanfarlo"; of exploratory essays on drugs and alcohol; of literary criticism; of art criticism and theory, including the celebrated "Salons" and "The Painter of Modern Life"; of music criticism, including essay on the Richard Wagner; of aphoristic travel notes on Belgium; and of other occasional pieces of literary and even political journalism. Finally, he was also a translator of English and American poetry and prose, including important works by Edgar Allan Poe and Thomas De Quincey.

Moreover, in a great many of these writings, in one way or another, Baudelaire is focusing on important issues of his day, including particularly matters relating to the specificity and function of art and literature and their relation to politics, to social and moral questions, and to the meaning of progress and civilization in urban industrial society. Thus it could be said of at least some of this heterogeneous material what Kundera says of the work of "the writer," namely, that Baudelaire does make a "great issue of his ideas" and often speaks in "an inimitable voice."

The fact is, of course, that before he was transformed by posterity into the mythic figure of the Poet, he was in many ways very much a "man of letters" of a distinctly mid-nineteenth-century French kind, existing on the bohemian fringe of Parisian society, open to the plethora of new ideas and movements in science, industry, philosophy, politics, society, art, literature, and music that characterized the age, and obliged to make a living through his writing. He was thus aware of the new conditions of literary production, publishing, and distribution dominated by a market economy in an era that saw the invention of new technologies for collecting and propagating news, and the emergence of mass circulation journalism and the feuilleton alongside book publication and the periodical.[2] He knew from first-hand experience the world of publishers, editorial offices, theaters, and cafés, and the practice of literary politics in his time through which one either made or broke a career. He tried his hand at various forms of writing because he recognized the need to be flexible if he were to earn a living by his pen, as he notes in an article on his friend Pierre Dupont: "The poet must survive by himself; as Honoré de Balzac said, he must offer a commercial dimension *[une surface commerciale]*. His tools must feed him" (*Oeuvres* 2:30). Moreover, echoes of the bitter ambiguities inherent in such circumstances reverberate throughout his writings, including in particular the prose poems and the private journals, as well as in a poem such as "The Venal Muse" from *The Flowers of Evil,* where the selling of one's writings is characterized as a form of prostitution.

Baudelaire was no doubt preeminently a poet, but he also engaged in many of the kinds of writing associated with the figure of "the writer" as I have defined him, and was even briefly the coeditor of an ephemeral political journal at the height of the revolutionary euphoria associated with February 1848, although he wrote no significant works of political philosophy or even an autobiography as such. He was not, in any case, politically naive, one of those poetic "dreamers of dreams" associated with Lamartinian romanticism, symbolism, or an important strain in contemporary High Victorian poetry in England.[3]

It is significant, in this connection, that Walter Benjamin should open his celebrated study of the poet, *Charles Baudelaire: A Lyric Poet in the Era of High Capitalism,* with a section entitled "The *Bohème,*" in which he cites the authority of Karl Marx in order to emphasize the connections between mid-nineteenth-century literary and artistic bohemia and political conspirators, including most notably, Louis-Auguste Blanqui and Louis-Napoleon, the future second emperor himself. What is perhaps a surprise, coming from Benjamin, is the association he perceives between the latter and Baudelaire, presumably with the purpose of discrediting the poet's claim to have contributed anything valuable to the intellectual debate in his time outside his poetry: "During his emperorship Napoleon continued his conspiratory claims. Surprising proclamations and mystery-mongering, sudden sallies, and impenetrable irony were part of the *raison d'état* of the Second Empire. The same traits may be found in Baudelaire's theoretical writings. He usually presents his views apodictically. Discussion is not his style." Moreover, Benjamin is especially unequivocal in his view of Baudelaire's grasp of political issues: "Baudelaire's political insights do not go fundamentally beyond those of the professional conspirators."[4]

At first glance Baudelaire also seems to share a fundamental characteristic of the Rousseauist "writer" insofar as, unlike his contemporaries the Parnassians or the proponents of "l'art pour l'art," he by no means eschewed autobiographical references in his writing in various genres, most notably in the *The Flowers of Evil, Paris Spleen,* and the provocatively named "My Heart Laid Bare" (Mon Coeur mis à nu). If one excludes the critical and theoretical writings, in fact, it is clear that there is a half-submerged confessional dimension to his poetry and his prose poems as well as his journals. However, the confessional material is for the most part consciously distanced and transcended through artistic form and the assumption of a persona, in ways I shall discuss.

In general, as Walter Benjamin understood so well in spite of the demurrals just quoted, what is striking about Baudelaire's writings as a whole is that, on account of its range, his literary oeuvre more than any other's—including even the realist novelists—affords a remarkable education in nineteenth-century attitudes, aspirations, tastes, and ideas in the sociopolitical as well as the moral and aesthetic spheres. The subtitle of Benjamin's book, *A Lyric Poet in the Era of High Capitalism,* captures the enormously productive tension at the heart of Baudelaire's achievement, namely, the tension between the apparently antithetical categories of poetic lyricism and industrial capitalism.

Baudelaire's importance for me in this context is that he came to redefine the task of poetry and of the poet in the modern world, and he did so in opposition to both the romantic idea of the poet, on the one hand, and the Rousseauist idea of "the writer," on the other. Baudelaire was an energetic polemicist and champion of a new aestheticism as well as a poet. He inherited the romantic movement's contempt for Enlightenment rationalism and, in particular, for Voltaire, "the anti-poet." At the same time he recognized in Rousseau a more formidable adversary, the example of whose life and career was still very much alive in his time. Rousseau represented a temptation that Baudelaire was determined to resist, not least because Rousseau's suspicion of the whole aesthetic sphere and his subordination of all artistic activity to ends laid down by the polis constituted a potent attack on the autonomy of art and literature. It is no accident that the earliest significant reference to Rousseau in Baudelaire's extant writings should be a note that reads, "On Jean-Jacques—a sentimental and infamous writer" (*Oeuvres* 2:54).[5]

In many ways, for reasons I shall suggest, Baudelaire's understanding of the task of poetry might be summed up provisionally in three short sentences from the 1851 article on Pierre Dupont referred to earlier: "Poetry has a great destiny! Whether joyful or lamentable, it bears forever within it a divine utopian character. It never fails to contradict fact, under penalty of ceasing to be [*à peine de ne plus être*]" (*Oeuvres* 2:35). However, the meaning Baudelaire gives to such an abstract and apparently neoromantic idea of poetry and of art in general only appears progressively in his rich and complex poetic practice and his theoretical formulations from the beginning to the end of his career.

What I would emphasize for the moment is first, an idea of poetry as simultaneously critique and transcendence that, as I shall suggest in my epilogue, overlaps in interesting ways with Michel Foucault's conception of the philosopher's task, and second, the portrait Baudelaire paints of the Poet as type, a portrait that takes off from the one associated with the French romantics but that develops into something significantly more interesting, in which articles of aesthetic belief are combined with the formulation of a code of conduct and an ethics of the self. It is, in any case, on Baudelaire's portrait of the Poet and on his conception of the task of poetry that I shall concentrate here.

His understanding of that task is articulated principally in his writings on aesthetics, in his critical essays and his "Salons," and to a lesser extent in his poetry and prose poetry. His evolving portrait of the Poet appears in some early poems of the *The Flowers of Evil,* such as "Benediction," "Beacons," and "The Albatross," as well as later, more important poems from the same volume; in the aesthetic writings on poets and painters; in certain prose poems of *Paris Spleen;* and in the late journals.

In any case, what makes Baudelaire so interesting in this context is the way in which the kind of autobiographical material that since Rousseau had issued in "confessions" is typically depersonalized by Baudelaire and associated with the condition of the Poet in general. Thus, from the level of individual love and spleen poems to that of "the secret architecture" of *The Flowers of Evil* as a whole, personal experience achieves a formulation that associates it allegorically with the spiritual drama of the poetic life in the modern age. Even when Baudelaire seems closest to succumbing to the Rousseauist temptation of autobiography, in "My Heart Laid Bare," in the fragmentariness, range, irony, and directness of address of the work he manages instead to anticipate a twentieth-century work such as Barthes's *Roland Barthes.* As a result, Baudelaire self-consciously paints one of the nineteenth century's most memorable and most influential portraits of the Poet as hero in opposition to "the writer." His point of departure was the life and works of another poet, Edgar Allan Poe, in whom he claimed to find uncanny anticipations of ideas and attitudes he had assumed to be his own.[6]

Finally, a number of his more discriminating and distinguished contemporaries recognized precisely in Baudelaire the incarnation of a specifically poetic heroism; and by way of conclusion I will refer to the portraits painted of Baudelaire by such major figures as Courbet and Manet as well as those by some of nineteenth-century France's most famous photographers. The diffusion of images of Poet, Artist, and Composer, as well as of "the writer," was, of course, an increasingly important phenomenon of nineteenth-century European cultural life from the Romantic movement on.

Michel Foucault formulated the task of the philosopher in a way relevant to my purpose in a relatively late essay on Kant that suggests the turn his own thought was taking in the years before his death. Taking his title from the Kant essay ("What Is Enlightenment?") discussed in my first chapter, Foucault was inspired by the German philosopher's example to pose for his own time the question "What is modern philosophy?" And if one were to ask "What is modern poetry?" one might do worse than answer by substituting "poetry" for "philosophy" in Foucault's response, as follows: "Modern poetry is the poetry that is attempting to answer the question raised so imprudently two centuries ago: *Was ist Aufklärung?*"[7]

Given the reputation of the Age of Reason as inimical to poetry as it came to be understood from the romantics on, that answer may surprise. The point is not, however, that Enlightenment thought itself had anything particularly illuminating to say about the poetic muse but that, as Foucault puts it—following in this a specifically German and philosophical conflation of Enlightenment and modernity—the Enlightenment, first, exhorted mankind to emerge from its "self-incurred immaturity" and to recognize the sole sovereignty of reason in the realm of public debate, and, second, it broke down a religious and/or metaphysical mode of understanding into three autonomous spheres of knowledge: scientific reason, moral-practical reason, and aesthetic reason. Art, literature, and music were apparently henceforth to stand on their own feet and to derive their raison d'être from their own values and practice. And one corollary of this was that aesthetics itself also first emerged as a separate branch of philosophical investigation.[8]

It is because the Enlightenment posited the autonomy of art and literature that the question "What is modern poetry?" might well be posed in connection with it. Given that the arts had ostensibly been detached from issues of religious faith as well as from scientific cognition and even morality and practical affairs, what, after all, was the function of poetry? The romantics, of course, gave a variety of answers that centered on a rejection of their historical present and a nostalgia for a lost age of faith, on the exploration of new modes of spiritual experience or states of the soul, on the trust not in reason but in the reasons of the heart, on the rehabilitation of nature and the simple life, or on the cult of energy, passion, and the imagination. By the 1840s in France at the latest such answers were already beginning to appear dated or at the very least in serious need of reformulation.

It is, in effect, in answer to questions such as these that Foucault declares Baudelaire himself to be "an almost indispensable example" ("Enlightenment," 39). For Foucault, as for so many others, it is Baudelaire who articulates so brilliantly the direction taken by aesthetic modernism under the conditions first established in the eighteenth century by cultural modernity. Baudelaire is the one who provides the fullest and most satisfyingly complex answers to questions such as "What is the meaning of the so-called autonomy of art in the middle decades of his turbulent, increasingly urbanized and politicized century?" "What might Kant's famous injunction "Dare to know" ("Aude sapere") mean in art, music, literature, and above all poetry at that time?"

Foucault summarizes Baudelaire's relationship to modernity not simply as a will to acknowledge the fleeting, ephemeral, contingent character of the historical present, but in an attitude that "consists in recapturing something eternal that is not beyond the present instant, nor behind it, but within it." And it this attitude that leads to the "heroization" of the present. Then, in commenting on "The Painter of Modern Life," Foucault locates the meaning of that present in the idea of a painter, Constantin Guys: "[W]hen the whole world is falling asleep, he begins to work, and he transfigures that world. His transfiguration does not entail an annulling of reality, but a difficult interplay between the truth of what is real and the exercise of freedom."

Finally, Baudelaire is characterized by Foucault as, in effect, possessing the most advanced consciousness of modernity, inasmuch as his poetry is itself at once a critique and a transcendence of his age. It is at this point that the task of poetry comes to appear as virtually synonymous with that of critical philosophy: "For the attitude of modernity, the high value of the present is indissociable from a desperate eagerness to imagine it, to imagine it other than it is, and to transform it not by destroying it but by grasping it in what it is. Baudelairean modernity is an exercise in which extreme attention to what is real is confronted with the practice of a liberty that simultaneously respects this reality and violates it."

Surprising as it may be, then, Foucault seems to discover in Baudelaire's response to his age not only a specific "type of philosophical interrogation," but one that is rooted in the Enlightenment. That is to say, one "that simultaneously problematizes man's relation to the present, man's historical mode of being, and the constitution of the self as autonomous subject" ("Enlightenment," 41–42). In the light of this, it is also surprising that Foucault hardly refers to the character of Baudelaire's aesthetic quest, since poetic and artistic beauty came for the nineteenth-century poet to constitute the very ground on which the critique of contemporary life and humanity at large was to be conducted.

What *aude sapere* might mean in the context of nineteenth-century poetry appears in the most original of Baudelaire's early formulation of his aesthetics. The radical newness of a poetic sensibility that represents a rupture both with the practice and self-understanding of "the writer" and of the romantic poet finds expression early in two memorable ideas from his "Salon of 1846," which Michael Fried has called "one of the most brilliant and intellectually ambitious essays in art criticism ever written."[9] The first idea states: "Experiencing pleasure is a science" (*Jouir est une science*). The second idea affirms: "A painting is a machine all of whose systems are intelligible to an experienced eye."[10] The first quotation focuses on the understanding and disciplined mastery of sensations and comes, in fact, from a short introduction to the "Salon" that appears under the heading "To the Bourgeois." The second formulates a disturbingly new conception of art and is from a section that is attempting to explain wherein resides the genius and originality of Delacroix.

In the context of early-nineteenth-century moral and aesthetic values, both ideas have significant shock value, although neither is entirely original. If not precisely antonymic in character, both knowingly confuse categories that had long been felt to belong to different realms of human experience, namely, pleasure and science, in one case, and art and technology, in the other. Yet the first occurs in the context of an apparently ironic appeal to the bourgeoisie of Baudelaire's age to learn to appreciate art, though it is nonetheless serious despite its irony; and the second is clearly to be taken at face value, since, in the process of defending Delacroix, Baudelaire refutes the idea that chance plays a role in artistic creation. Moreover, he compounds the provocation, in effect, by first declaring, "Chance plays no greater role in art than it does in mechanics." We are, it seems, a long way from an early nineteenth-century romantic aesthetics centered on the concepts of poetic genius and inspiration, although, as is well known, Baudelaire in many respects believed in some of the central tenets of an Anglo-German romanticism of which Edgar Allan Poe was only in part an intermediary.

The second quotation, "A painting is a machine all of whose systems are intelligible to an experienced eye," confirms the first relative to the analyzability of art objects, and seems almost to be anticipating Le Corbusier's high-modernist credo that "a house is a machine for living in"— although Baudelaire does not, of course, go so far as to say "form follows function," since that formula privileges "function" in a manner that was antithetical to Baudelaire's aesthetic faith. At the same time his apparently mechanistic conception of artistic fabrication is far removed from romantic notions of art as somehow natural and effortless, and is certainly derived in part from the brilliant insights of Poe's "Philosophy of Composition."

In such formulas Baudelaire is, in effect, redefining the task of art and poetry in negative terms at least as much as in positive ones, for in describing pleasure and painting as learned and disciplined activities, he is also denying that they are subordinated to the affirmation of faith or the expression of metaphysical truths. The Poet is once again conceived not as a Hugolian mage, seer, or prophet but as a maker; not as a teacher, moralist, or social theorist but as a fabricator of sensations and beautiful objects that induce a specifically aesthetic pleasure. At the same time art is already by implication a mode of cognition for which there is no substitute, a mode of cognition, moreover, that involves critique and self-discipline, a new conception of lyrical intensity, and the pursuit of transcendence and self-transcendence.

Although brief, Baudelaire's opening address to his contemporaries of the bourgeoisie is also significant in a number of ways that are relevant to the idea of "the writer." In the first place, this address belongs to a long line of essays by writers, poets, artists and philosophers—from, say, Friedrich Schiller to Matthew Arnold, the Frankfurt school in general, and Jürgen Habermas—that attempt to explain how important it is for laymen engaged in the practical affairs of the world to receive an aesthetic education. Second, from the first lines of his introduction Baudelaire makes clear that he is no poetic innocent, that he is fully cognizant of the sociopolitical realities of the mid-nineteenth-century world in which he lived—that, in the terminology of Bourdieu, the field of literary culture is in a dominated position within the field of power: "You [the bourgeois] are the majority— in number and intelligence; thus you are power—that is to say, justice" ("Salon of 1846," 415). Yet, in spite of the elliptical irony of this, Baude- laire does seem to mean what he says in the following two pages.

Mentioning different categories of bourgeois by name, from scholars and landlords to shopkeepers, politicians, and merchants, he warns them that they have been badly advised by certain contemporary zealots; having spent three-quarters of their day pursuing business and public affairs, they have a right to their leisure, a right to feel and to enjoy. Moreover, their leisure should consist of more or less intense forms of discriminating plea- sure, which for Baudelaire means they must have access to art.

The troubling and ingenious paradox of Baudelaire's argument, how- ever, is that enjoyment is assumed not to be natural but something that has to be taught, as the statement of his thesis affirms; it is a science that one can only learn through exposure to art: "Experiencing pleasure is a science; exercising the five senses requires a special initiation that occurs only with good will and need. That is why you need art." The whole short piece is, in fact, a tissue of ironically coded references in which many of the assumed discursive oppositions of the age are undone in a purposely bland anticipation of utopian harmony. Thus not only does science oper- ate in the cause of pleasure, with art and technology appearing as one, but the aesthetic sphere as a whole is claimed to have its own utilitarian func- tion, and society's wealthy are reconciled with its artists on the basis of mutual need. The goal in the end is to affirm the truth of an apparent paradox, namely, the *necessity* of art

Finally, in a pastiche of a romantic peroration that suggests Baudelaire is indeed writing his own *Aesthetic Education of Mankind,* though in the ironic mode, he affirms: "When you have given society your science, your industry, your work, your money, you demand payment in the pleasures of your body, your reason, and your imagination. If you recover the quan- tity of pleasure necessary to establish balance in all the parts of your being, you will be happy, fulfilled, and benevolent, just as society will be fulfilled, happy and benevolent when it has found its general and absolute balance" ("Salon of 1846, 415–17).

With its insistence on the utopian goal of feeling "happy, fulfilled, and benevolent," and its reference to "the pleasures of your body" and to a "general and absolute balance," this sounds closer to a parody of Herbert Marcuse's Marxian appropriation of Freud in the 1960s than to Schiller's understanding of an aesthetic education. Nevertheless, in the light of all that has been said on Baudelaire and his relation to the early aesthetic movement, it is interesting to note that in spite of his tongue-in-cheek style he ends up sounding not unlike Schiller; he affirms the belief that for the production of morally responsible, fully sentient human beings the education of the senses through the experience of art is crucial, in order to balance a scientific mode of cognition and an absorption in the practical affairs of the world. What is more, the new harmony between faculties on the level of the individual is assumed to prepare a new harmony between different groups in society at large. In brief, two short years before the revolution of 1848 Baudelaire is expressing an emancipatory social function as well as a broadly humanizing function for art and literature that has a great deal in common with some of the strands in nineteenth-century French utopian thought. But he typically does so in a manner also designed to *épater le bourgeois*.

The difference between the Baudelaire of the "Salon of 1846" and the Schiller of the *Aesthetic Education* is, of course, the absence of any reference to reason as such, or of an idea of art that is a reconciliation between the sensuous and the particular, on the one hand, and the spiritual and the universal, on the other. Not the least modernist aspect of Baudelaire's short text is, in fact, the provocative emphasis on the sheer sensuality of the sensuous: "Art is infinitely precious, a refreshing and warming brew that reestablishes both stomach and spirit in the natural balance of the ideal" (415–16). As his projected preface for *The Flowers of Evil* reminds us, the originality of Baudelaire in the age of art for art's sake was not in his assertion of analogies between poetry and painting or music, but between poetry and cooking or cosmetics.

We are, in any case, a long way from a classical German conception of *Bildung* and the role of the aesthetic in that coupling in a single sentence of a "stomach" and "the ideal." If the tone of the piece reminds us of anything, it is of the new bohemian counterculture that emerged in Paris from the 1820s on, of Théophile Gautier and Gérard de Nerval, and of the will to shock of the so-called *petits romantiques* of the 1830s and 1840s. It is also a confirmation of how long before the midcentury the familiar modernist opposition between artist and bourgeois, art and life, had hardened into mythic categories as part of the instantly recognizable physiognomy of the new age of industrial capital, with its class antagonisms and its increasingly democratic political culture.

The "Salon of 1846" is interesting for what it has to say about the social necessity of art and the importance of the artist's role, but it is less explicit than the "Salon of 1859" on what constitutes the specificity of art, on art and literature as a privileged and unique mode of cognition. In an important sense the most interesting part of the essay of 1859 contradicts the hope expressed in that of 1846 in the possibility of the harmony of the different faculties and the implied affinities between science and industry, on the one hand, and art, on the other. If the earlier "Salon" may be said, in a lighthearted moment, to raise the utopian possibility of a future society in which the bourgeois cohabits with the artist on terms of reciprocal need and respect, the "Salon of 1859" draws a firm line between art and industry or poetry and progress. This comes as no surprise, given the thirteen years that separate the two "Salons"—years that included what were for Baudelaire, as for so many others, the politically climactic moments of February and June 1848 and Louis-Napoleon's coup d'état of 1851. From the beginning of his literary career, in the reign of Louis Philippe, Baudelaire found himself on the defensive for art's sake on several fronts at the same time, and things, were if anything, to grow only more complicated under the Second Empire.[11]

This is particularly apparent in a section of the "Salon of 1859" entitled "The Modern Public and Photography," for it is there that Baudelaire makes very clear the extent to which the invention of photography in the 1830s had forced a radical reevaluation of aesthetic values. The section is also relevant to my purpose because he focuses on the new mass narcissism of the emerging age of mechanical image making and instant self-portraiture—a narcissism to which "writers" and even poets were to be scarcely more immune than the public at large.

It is no accident that it was a Parisian and a poet who was the first major theorist of aesthetic modernism. In addition to experiencing the effects of dual revolutions in one of Europe's great cities—the sociopolitical one of 1789 and the profound politicization of French life that was its consequence, and the economic one of the Industrial Revolution, with its equally significant impact on social relations, the material environment, and urban life—it was also in Paris that the remarkable potential of the new medium of photography was most rapidly apparent when viewed against the background of the extraordinary creativity of the Parisian art world.[12] It was, in fact, in response to that new medium, as well as to the changing material environment of urban life and the social and political culture, that Baudelaire elaborated his new and highly influential modernist aesthetics. Consequently, as I shall make clearer later, if one can, in fact, speak of the idea of "the autonomy of art" in connection with him, it is in a very different sense from the one that obtained in the eighteenth-century aesthetics associated with Kant.

The invention of photography in the 1820s and the rapid development of its possibilities did, of course, precipitate a fresh debate by the middle decades of the century on the nature and ends of art that engaged the attention of painters as different as Ingres, Delacroix, and Courbet, and of poets and critics from Lamartine to Francis Wey and Hippolyte Taine. Baudelaire was by no means alone in realizing that photography raised in a new way the question of the specificity of the work of art.

Central to Baudelaire's understanding of that specifity is the belief that art is not the imitation of nature, neither in the time-honored sense of the theory of mimesis that is at least as old as Aristotle nor in the relatively new sense the French realists were giving the phrase in the 1840s.[13] Art,

Baudelaire argues, in the "Salon of 1859," is about wonder and astonishment in a special sense that relates it to the creation of beauty. Thus, having declared that "the desire to astonish and to be astonished is a very legitimate" goal of art, even mistranslating Poe slightly for his purpose,[14] he goes on to assert that there are, nevertheless, ways of astonishing that have nothing to do with art. It is at this point that he turns to photography and to the popular philistinism of the public at large, insofar as it assumes the essence of art to be in an exact as possible imitation of nature.

He summarizes the popular credo as follows: "I believe in nature and in nothing but nature. . . . Thus the industry that would give us a result identical to nature would be absolute art." And he concludes sardonically: "A vengeful God has granted the wishes of the multitude. Daguerre was his Messiah. And that multitude said to itself, 'Since photography gives us every desirable guarantee of exactitude—for that's what those foolish people believe—art is photography.' It was from that moment on that obscene society rushed forward like a single Narcissus to contemplate its trivial image on a metal plate" ("Salon of 1859," 617). Such are the terms in which the Poet establishes his distance from the aesthetic naivety and narcissism of those who enjoy faithfully reproduced images of themselves.

In denying photography the status of art Baudelaire once again follows Poe and resorts to what is perhaps the central concept of Anglo-German romanticism, namely, the imagination. In a famous passage he goes on to refer to it as the *faculté maîtresse,* the powerful recombinatory faculty that produces brilliant and illuminating new syntheses out of the material of the given world and generates strange new beauties. It is by means of the imagination that one is able "to astonish and to be astonished" in ways that Baudelaire makes most apparent in a variety of ways in a great many poems of the *The Flowers of Evil.*

One of the most remarkable and unexpected qualities of that volume of verse is, in fact, the way in which it magically transposes the raw materials of nineteenth-century life into something rarer and finer, thus fulfilling the goal Baudelaire affirmed in "Rockets"(Fusées): "Language and writing as magical operations, as an evocative sorcery."[15] It is as if Baudelaire were consciously taking up the challenge implied by Max Weber's subsequent diagnosis of the central experience of rationalized, urban modernity as "disenchantment" or "demythification"; the function of art, particularly poetry, for the French poet was precisely to rediscover "enchantment," as poems such as "Invitation to a Voyage," "Evening Harmony," and "The Balcony" among others triumphantly confirm.

In this connection, it is once again Valéry who sums up so succinctly and so well the originality of *The Flowers of Evil* under the influence of Poe and the consequent distance between that volume and French romantic poetry: "*The Flowers of Evil* contains neither history poems nor legends, nothing that depends on a narrative. One finds no philosophical tirades there. Politics does not put in an appearance. Descriptions are rare and always *meaningful*. However, everything is enchantment *[charme]*, music, and a powerful and abstract sensuality. . . . *Luxe, calme et volupté*" ("Situation de Baudelaire," 609–10).

Although Valéry is pointing to Baudelaire's great significance for the theory of "pure poetry," it is also important to recognize the difference between Baudelaire and aestheticism with respect to the range of material from contemporary life that is incorporated into his poetry. As has long been recognized, though it is occasionally forgotten, Baudelaire does not disengage art from social life, from the urban environment, the material world of the changing city or even the lives of its poor and disenfranchised. On the contrary, an insistence on the autonomy of art cohabits with the incorporation of such subject matter into his poetry, as the "Parisian Tableaux" section of *The Flowers of Evil* and many of the prose poems of *Paris Spleen* make particularly clear.

Baudelaire's most sustained discussion of the task of poetry and the role of the poet in his time is to be found in what is also the nineteenth-century's single most important manifesto of aesthetic modernism, namely, "The Painter of Modern Life." In spite of the work's familiarity, it is necessary to refer to it here because it sketches the outlines of a modernist ethics as well as an aesthetics and presents a portrait of the artist or poet as hero, that is, a figure who in most respects is the antithesis of the Rousseauist "writer."

Surprise has often been expressed that the French poet who invented modern poetry for the West virtually single-handed, and who was a friend or companion of some of the most famous avant-garde painters of his day—including, notably, Courbet and Manet—should seem late in his career to celebrate above all the work of a relatively minor artist, Constantin Guys. It would have been illuminating to have had Baudelaire's extended evaluation of Manet's work, of the kind that he carried out earlier on Delacroix, instead of little more than a passing reference to it.

The fact is, however, that at the time Baudelaire wrote the essay on Guys, Manet was only beginning to come into his own as probably the most original artist of a generation that did not lack originality. "The Painter of Modern Life" was published in late 1863, a few months before Baudelaire left France for Brussels, where he was to spend his remaining years of unhappy exile and rapidly declining health until his death in 1867. Baudelaire and Manet were, of course, good friends and implicated each other in specific works. The prose poem "The Rope" is dedicated to Manet as the source of the macabre incident evoked, and Baudelaire is a member of the crowd in Manet's *Musique aux Tuileries* (1861), a painting whose subject matter is very close to that of a familiar Baudelairean prose poem, "Widows." Manet also painted a portrait of Baudelaire's mistress, Jeanne Duval, probably in early 1862. However, it was not until 1863 that Manet's work became a cause célèbre in the art world with the public exhibition of *Le Déjeuner sur l'herbe*—a painting that, like the *Olympia* of two years later, could almost have inspired, or been inspired, by Baudelaire's observations on the need, when painting modern courtesans, to transcend the grand manner and the models furnished by Titian and Raphael in order to represent them with all the signs of a provocative contemporaneity.[16]

It is also true that in some ways, in order to bring out the apparent contradictions at the heart of his modernist aesthetics, Baudelaire needed a fashionable artist like Guys, who was notably prolific and preoccupied above all with representing the taste and look of his time, with capturing its essential transience *sur le vif* in the form of "engravings of fashions" or "sketches of manners." The "divine utopian character" that Baudelaire claimed for art in the Dupont essay, its way of denying "fact," appears all the more paradoxical in the work of an artist so attached to representing for a commission "the floating world" of fashionable, mid-nineteenth-century Parisian life.

It has, in any case, been clear for a long time that, whether in spite of or because of Guys, in an age that first saw the proliferation of literary and artistic manifestos, "The Painter of Modern Life" is an important manifesto of aesthetic modernism that in many respects takes off from Théophile Gautier's brilliant and provocative apology for aestheticism in the preface to *Mademoiselle de Maupin* of 1835. In this connection, another reason why "The Painter of Modern Life" is important in this context is that it is also by implication a great anti-Rousseauist manifesto in which Rousseau's celebration of nature and natural simplicity and his attack on civilization and the whole aesthetic sphere, on luxury, refinement, and decoration, are taken up and systematically reversed. Baudelaire's treatise, in effect, responds in the most provocative of terms to the challenge of the negative view of art expressed in the *Discourse On the Sciences and the Arts* and the *Letter to D'Alembert on Theater*.

As a result, to read "The Painter of Modern Life" is to discover the outlines of a very different conception of literature and a very different notion of the writer from that of "the writer" in the Rousseauist mold. It is on these aspects of the essay that I shall concentrate here, although it is helpful to recall in passing some of its famous propositions relative to the dual character of beauty, the historicity of the present, the peculiarly passionate sensibility of the great artist, the artist's relationship to crowds and to the modern big city, Baudelaire's evocation of the artist at work, and the celebrations of the dandy, of women, and of makeup.

It tells us a great deal about ourselves and our contemporary situation, as well as about Baudelaire, that a lot of this material has once again recovered the capacity to offend that it had largely lost in the age of high modernism, although not for the same reasons. There is little sympathy for dandies in a democratic and highly politicized public culture such as ours, and this is especially the case when the figure of the dandy is associated with a self-mastery that masks feeling; the undisguised misogyny of many of Baudelaire's more energetic pronouncements on women does not sit well in a society whose literary taste has been thoroughly sensitized by feminist thought; and, finally, the idea of the autonomy of art that has traditionally been looked on with suspicion in the United States in particular currently finds few champions either within the academy or outside.[17]

Much of the significance of Baudelaire from a late-twentieth-century cultural point of view that is imbued with the assumptions of the German philosophical tradition resides in his understanding of history. And the key to that understanding is to be found in the very word that is at the heart of the essay on Guys, "modernité." The fact is that Baudelaire's "modernity" is not the same as Max Weber's, Jürgen Habermas's,[18] or even Walter Benjamin's, which is the main reason why I have attempted to avoid confusion by using the expression "aesthetic modernism" with reference to Baudelaire. When he uses "modernité," he does not necessarily do so with negative implications relative to its impact on the possibilities for human freedom. Nor does he do so as if it referred to the world that was inaugurated by the Enlightenment under the banner of the autonomy of reason. Finally, he does not use the word with historicist associations either, whether those of a merely evolutionary or developmental kind, as is associated with French thought from Condorcet through Comte, or of a dialectical kind, as in Hegel and Marx.

"Modernity" for Baudelaire is associated with the idea of the recognition of human existence as always lived in historical time, with the perception of the present as history—with all that implies, including the need in every age to conduct a kind of artistic and poetic inventory of its unique and unrepeatable characteristics—and, finally, with the thrill of the new. In short, "modernity" is not merely the latest expression of some hidden historical dynamic or inner necessity of reason; it is not simply a stage to be gone through only to be sublated in its turn; it is a historical moment to be embraced like any other because in spite of its apparent facticity and boundedness, it potentially opens directly onto eternal truths.

That is why the role of the artist is to represent the modern world in its relativity and newness on its own terms, both for what it is and for that which within it also transcends it. Things are not necessarily getting worse, as Rousseau's genealogy of the human race and its emergence out of the innocence of prehistory in the *Discourse on the Origin of Inequality* would have us believe; nor are they getting better, as the more or less naive celebrants of progress in Baudelaire's time claimed. Things, so to speak, have always been that bad, which is also why one should make the most of what is always potentially there.

Furthermore, it is on account of such a position that Baudelaire places art, and not a salvationary politics or even the polis, at the center of human experience; in a postreligious age, the mode of transcendence in which he believes is neither moral nor spiritual as such, but aesthetic. In any case, it has nothing to do with a return to a simpler and nobler past, nor with the establishment of a future utopian society on earth, but is associated centrally with what he calls "the immortal appetite for beauty." For Baudelaire, art remains the sign of man's spiritual nature at a time when it has already been acknowledged that God is dead.[19]

That this is the case appears first in Baudelaire's famous relativist and dualist conception of beauty, the idea that every era has its own form of beauty by means of which it may have access to a transcendent reality: "Beauty is composed of an eternal, invariable element, whose quantity is excessively difficult to determine, and of a relative, contingent element, which is, if you like, either by turns or all at once, a period, fashion, morality, or passion" ("Painter," 684–85). A point to note in passing, and to which I shall return later, is that it is in response to this definition of beauty that Benjamin observes, "One cannot say that this is a profound analysis" (*Charles Baudelaire,* 82). And that is, of course, true if one is committed to a materialist and a dialectical understanding of history as Benjamin was.

Nevertheless, for Baudelaire it is precisely the task of poet or artist to discover the secret of the beauty that characterizes his historical moment. Following Poe's lead, Baudelaire attributes to the artist an attitude of naive wonder in the face of the world in which he finds himself that is in marked contrast to the stance of suspicion characteristic of "the writer." Baudelaire compares the artist's openness of spirit and senses to the hero of Poe's tale "The Man of the Crowd," who is recovering from a serious illness. The artist is he who has the capacity to live life as if he were in a state of permanent convalescence or, in a metaphor familiar from English romanticism, like a child for whom everything is fresh. "Genius," Baudelaire notes in a famous sentence, "is childhood recovered at will."

The originality of Baudelaire's aesthetics is to be found in the fact that he takes over this romantic notion of artistic expression as deriving, in the first place, from naive wonder and transfers it from the natural world to that of contemporary urban life. Baudelaire's modernism is founded on an enthusiasm for the spectacle of the ever-changing, man-made present in its variety, facticity, and artificiality: "It is to such a deep and joyful curiosity that one should attribute the fixed look and animal ecstacy of children faced with something new *[le nouveau],* whatever it may be—a face or a landscape, light, gilt, colors, iridescent fabrics, or the enchantment of beauty embellished by makeup ("Painter," 690).

The provocative element of Baudelaire's modernism appears here both in the idea of beauty as a pure function of artifice and in the relative indifference of the object that calls forth such aesthetic absorption. But the key word is "enchantment"; in an age in which the realists were representing the banality and tawdriness of average life, Baudelaire was rediscovering its brilliance—which, among so much else, explains why even his famous "spleen" poems turn out to be so exhilarating.[20]

He goes on to comment on how an artist friend was fascinated when still a boy by the forms, shades, light, and colors of his father's body as he washed: "The spectacle of the exterior world already filled him with respect and seized hold of his brain" (690–91). The attitude expressed is typical of aesthetic modernism to the extent that the subject is unimportant; the principle invoked is that of the pure gaze. In this case the key word characterizing an attitude toward the attraction of a world of natural and non-natural things in their materiality and newness is "respect." Together with "enchantment," "respect" is a reminder that for Baudelaire art is a form of celebration in which soul and senses seem to participate equally; it has nothing to do with mere mimesis or with the levelling of perception, amounting to a form of denigration, that he himself associates with literary realism. Furthermore, even the rapidly changing, raggedly industrializing capital[21] that his Poet encounters as he wanders its streets is far from that "disenchanted world" Weber associated with the processes of "rationalization," initiated in the seventeenth and eighteenth centuries and accelerated in the course of the nineteenth.

Baudelaire's position is probably nowhere more apparent than in his famous definition of modernity in art—a definition that, with its reference to "the eternal," does not always sit too well with a twentieth-century understanding of modernism—and in his description of the artist's task in the new, crowded urban world. "Modernity," he affirms, "is the transitory, the fugitive, the contingent half of art, the other half of which is the eternal and the immutable." Thus, unlike the passive flaneur, who is content simply to enjoy the changing spectacle, the artist energetically seeks out a spiritual dimension, frequently in objects of the most material and apparently futile kind: "He sets out to separate out [dégager] from fashion the element of the poetic contained in the historical, to bring forth [tirer] the eternal from the transitory." It is a question of transforming matter by purifying it, as the metallurgical metaphor of "extraction" suggests: "[S]o that *modernity* is worthy of becoming antiquity, it is necessary that the mysterious beauty human life unconsciously invests in it be extracted from it" ("Painter," 694–95). As the crucial verbs here confirm, the artist's task is made to appear an active one that has an alchemical aspect of transmutation to it—in Baudelaire's famous shorthand, "flowers *from* evil."

Moreover, Baudelaire not only evokes with some precision the goal of artistic creativity in his time, in "The Painter of Modern Life," the "Parisian Tableaux" section of *The Flowers of Evil* itself, and in certain of the prose poems in *Paris Spleen* he also gives a detailed description of the modern artist/poet at work. Preeminent here is the idea of the restless, questing spirit who goes everywhere and explores all aspects of the contemporary metropolis with an open-minded attitude that is beyond good and evil; he is the last to take his leave of the nocturnal streets and cafés and return home to write his verse. In the imagery of one of the characteristically sardonic prose poems, the poet is also someone who has "lost his halo" in the mud while crossing a street.

Finally, the work of creation itself, is undertaken while others sleep, involves memory, recapitulation, and recombination—a work of imaginative transfiguration by means of which the given world is transcended in art. In what is probably his most complete evocation of what he means by "the divine utopian character" of poetry, Baudelaire writes, "And things are reborn on paper, natural and more than natural, beautiful and more than beautiful, strange and endowed with an enthusiastic life, like the soul of their author. A phantasmagoria has been extracted from nature. All the materials that have accumulated in the memory are classed, ordered, and harmonized and undergo the idea of forced idealization that is the result of a *childlike* perception, that is to say, the sharpest of perceptions, and magical by dint of ingenuity" ("Painter," 693–94).

In an age that specialized in "physiologies" of social types and of urban scenes, in the process of articulating his critical aesthetics Baudelaire, of course, gave a new meaning to the character and historical destiny of the dandy alongside his portraits of the flaneur and the artist.[22] Although all three have certain characteristics in common, it is the figure of the flaneur that has proved the most influential in the long run, inasmuch as it helped generate a whole new conception of the modern city as the milieu of choice for adventurous spirits on account of the brilliance and variety of its spectacle. Like Poe's "man of the crowd," Baudelaire's flaneur discovers pleasure of a new order by plunging into the urban crowd: "His passion and his profession is *to marry the crowd*. To set up home in numbers, in the ever-shifting, in movement, in the fugitive and the infinite, is the intensest of pleasures *[une immense jouissance]* for the perfect flaneur, for the passionate observer" (691–92).[23]

The dandy, on the other hand, keeps his distance. Yet in one respect, at least, he is closer to the artist than is the flaneur. Whereas the latter is content merely to enjoy the spectacle of the new urban world as it unfolds before him in the course of his peregrination, the dandy is committed to transforming the merely given world into something that brilliantly surpasses it. The difference between dandy and artist is, of course, that the dandy becomes his own art object. The dandy belongs to the new and ephemeral aristocracy of an age of transition in which the traditional aristocracy has disappeared and the democratic idea has not yet been fully (and, from Baudelaire's point of view, fatefully) established. The paradox of Baudelaire's position, however, resides in the assertion that with the modern dandy narcissism is raised to the level of asceticism. The cult of the self that the dandy exemplifies is no mere self-indulgence but the practice of a discipline, an exercise in self-surpassing that Baudelaire compares, on the one hand, to the rules of a monastic order and, on the other, to a form of spiritualism or stoicism. In short, Baudelaire attributes to the dandy in his time the kind of practices of self-mastery that came to interest

Foucault a great deal in the last two volumes of *The History of Sexuality*.[24]

The significance of the figure of the dandy in Baudelaire's critical writings is the explicit association of aestheticism in life, as in art, with an ethics. Moreover, the ethics concerned has the character of a counterethics relative to what might be called "confessionalism." The dandy is a non-confessing animal who, far from believing in transparency, always wears a mask. It is this that Foucault, in effect, identifies as fundamental to Baudelaire's notion of aesthetic modernism in "What Is Enlightenment?": "Modern man, for Baudelaire, is not the man who goes off to discover himself, his secrets and his hidden truth; he is the man who tries to invent himself. This modernity does not 'liberate man in his own being'; it compels him to face the task of producing himself" (41–42). In short, Foucault connects his reading of Baudelaire and the idea of the dandy with his own late moral philosophy. As I shall suggest in my epilogue, Foucault's Baudelairean "aesthetics of existence" stands in marked contrast to the Rousseauist "confessionalism" of Louis Althusser.

The flaneur, the dandy, and the poet or artist have in common the fact that they all exist within what Bourdieu calls the sub-field of the avant-garde, which he defines as "an anti-economic economy"—one that rejects the values of the marketplace in favor of the higher values articulated in literature and art. The flaneur lives for the sake of pure spectatorship. The dandy is an example of autonomous man who exists in order to produce himself for himself and for the small elite in democratic mass society that shares his tastes. At the top of the hierarchy in the nineteenth-century French literary field—and therefore above both novelists and dramatists, who at least have some commercial potential—the Baudelairean poet celebrates his own autonomy as producer of rarefield aesthetic artifacts for other producers and for the minority of readers who enjoy works of a difficult and esoteric formal beauty for their own sake.

The section of "The Painter of Modern Life" in which Baudelaire establishes his distance from Rousseau and from romanticism and affirms his association with the aesthetic movement is the notorious "In Praise of Makeup," which follows the sections on "The Dandy" and "Woman." One of its most celebrated and provocative passages is worth quoting again in this context because of the way in which Baudelaire distinguishes the sensibility of his time from that of the eighteenth century and the culture that had generated the figure of "the writer" in the first place: "Most of the errors relative to the beautiful are born of the eighteenth century's false conception of morality. Nature was taken at that time to be the base, source, and type of every possible idea of good or beauty. The negation of original sin contributed more than a little to the general blindness of that period" (715).

He then goes into one of the frequent perorations against nature that are scattered throughout his occasional writings and that contain distinct echoes of the Marquis de Sade as well as of Joseph de Maistre:

> [N]ature teaches nothing, or almost nothing; that is, it *forces* man to sleep, to drink, to eat and to protect himself, as best he can, against the rigors of nature. It is also nature that forces man to kill his fellow men or to eat, imprison and torture him. . . . Reflect for a moment on everything natural, analyze all the actions and desires of pure natural man: you will find nothing but horrors. Everything beautiful and noble is the result of reason and calculation. Crime, the taste for which the human animal develops at his mother's breast, is originally natural. Virtue, on the other hand, is *artificial,* supernatural. . . ." (715).

As the last three sentences of this passage remind us, Baudelaire's talent for sloganeering is at least the equal of Rousseau's and he frequently seems to direct it programmatically in opposition to values the latter cherished.

A case in point is the way in which the word "depravity" is used in "The Painter of Modern Life," once in adjectival form and once as a noun, in contexts that indicate clearly the mid-nineteenth-century poet is using the word consciously in opposition to Rousseau's notorious use of it in the *Discourse on the Origin of Inequality* ("I almost dare say that the state of reflection is a state against nature and that the man who meditates is a depraved animal" [25]). On the second occasion, Baudelaire turns Rousseau's proposition right around: "Cursed be he who like, Louis XV, takes depravity to the point of having no taste for anything except *simple nature.*" Moreover, after this Baudelaire pushes paradox to the point of identifying fashion which has typically been considered the height of frivolity and even decadence, as an expression of humanity's quest for spiritual truths: "Fashion should thus be considered to be a symptom of the taste for the ideal that rises in the human brain above everything crude, terrestrial and disgusting that natural life accumulates there, like a sublime deformation of nature, and like a permanent and repeated attempt at the reformation of nature" (716). It would be hard to encapsulate more effectively the extent to which Baudelaire distances himself from Rousseau than in the idea that fashion is "a sublime deformation of nature" or that nature is in need of "reformation" by human artifice.

Furthermore, there is a comparable distance between Baudelaire's celebration of fashion and the view of it expressed by one of the poet's most important twentieth-century champions, Walter Benjamin. In her summary of the German thinker's attitude to fashion in *The Dialectics of Seeing: Walter Benjamin and the Arcades Project,* Susan Buck-Morss describes fashion as a symptom of the pathology of "capitalist modernity." She glosses Benjamin as equating it with a mere craving for novelty, as a mode of reification in which the human capacity for innovation and change is alienated in commodities. In short, in Benjamin's own words, "Fashion prescribed the ritual by which the fetish commodity wished to be worshiped" (97–99). It is in response to a social phenomenon such as fashion, then, that one is made aware of how unsympathetic to Baudelaire's own kind of aesthetic idealism the historical materialist Benjamin was. "Alienation," "reification," and "commodity fetishism" are powerful concepts of a hegemonic political discourse of truth, in opposition to which Baudelaire himself affirmed the autonomy of art and literature.

To sum up, it is as if in his portraits of the dandy and the modern poet or artist Baudelaire consciously, term for term, reverses the characteristics associated with the model of "the writer" derived from Rousseau. The artist is most at home not in nature, but in the streets of the modern capital city that Rousseau claimed to despise; he seeks the embrace of the crowd, not the path of solitary meditation; he has affiliations with the flaneur, and the dandy, not with the hard-working and virtuous citizen; he puts his faith not in politics, social change, or revolution but in an art that no longer takes nature as its norm and measure; finally, in the sphere of personal morality, a form of aestheticism and a commitment to the reinvention of the self replace confessionalism, or a belief in guilty secrets and in the salutary power of their disclosure.

In spite of its familiarity, "The Painter of Modern Life" has lost little of its polemical force. Indeed, as suggested above, given a contemporary American literary culture strongly influenced by a humanitarian morality, democratic politics, and feminism, its power to offend is perhaps once again as great as it ever was. Whatever one thinks of the judgments expressed, however, there is no doubt that Baudelaire the critic and critical theorist of culture was in many respects the equal of Baudelaire the poet. Moreover, given that his most celebrated pamphlet brilliantly counters the arguments of the *Discourse on the Sciences and the Arts* and the *Letter to D'Alembert on Theater,* Baudelaire can be said to have proved at least Rousseau's equal at his own "writerly" game.

In the end, the works that best suggest the way in which Baudelaire's kind of aesthetic modernism marks a decisive new break with the tradition I derive from Rousseau are the relatively late *Paris Spleen* and "My Heart Laid Bare." In spite of their titles, these works turn out to be both more and less than confessional. That is, they frequently draw on autobiographical material, but they do so in ways that self-consciously establish a distance between the material and the form in which it is given expression. At the same time, inasmuch as they range widely over questions of religious belief, morality, nature, politics, and society, as well as art and literature, they are also part of a campaign to combat the influence of eighteenth-century thought in general and Rousseauism in particular.

Moreover, it is in his two final works, if anywhere, that Baudelaire comes closest to operating like the literary artist with the technique of a putschist that Benjamin, in effect, claims he was—a poetic double of Blanqui or Louis-Napoleon who was given to "surprising proclamations and mystery-mongering, sudden sallies, and impenetrable irony. He [Baudelaire] usually presents his views apodictically. Discussion is not his style . . ." (*Charles Baudelaire*, 12). It is not, of course, clear whether Baudelaire himself would have recognized such a characterization of his work as a whole, although one can think of examples from different phases of Baudelaire's career that might be said to justify Benjamin's identification of the poet as a Blanquist proponent of unpredictable, spontaneous insurrection. There is, for example, the notorious passage from the "Salon of 1846" in which he evokes the pleasure experienced at witnessing a member of the guard striking a republican with his rifle butt, since the object of the assault is, after all, "an enemy of roses and perfumes, a fanatic of utensils" (490). There are prose poems such as "The Bad Glazier" and "Beat Up on the Poor" in which the poet/protagonist himself engages in gratuitous acts of violence and assaults his innocent victims along with humanitarian ideology itself. A similar mixture of perverse violence and irony are to be found, for example, in the calculatedly fierce diatribes against women and humanity in general in "My Heart Laid Bare."

Baudelaire's ambition for *Paris Spleen* seems to have rivaled that for *The Flowers of Evil;* that is, he regarded the volume as a "pendant" to his volume of verse in its size, scope, originality, and achievement. He apparently began writing the prose poems, a relatively new and experimental genre, in the mid- to late 1850s and completed them over a period of several years. His enthusiasm for a genre that, in Kundera's words, seems effectively to have met "the demands of his dream" is expressed in the famous dedication to Arsène Houssaye in terms of a new content and a new form. After some pointedly witty opening sentences, he points out that he saw the possibility of applying the technique of the prose poem Aloysius Bertrand had applied in *Gaspard de la Nuit* "to the depiction of ancient life, which is so strangely picturesque," to "modern life, or rather to *a* modern and more abstract life." At this point Baudelaire fantasizes about the extraordinary expressive potential of the new genre, like Kundera, in terms of "a dream" to be realized: "Which of us has not, when he was feeling ambitious, dreamed of the miracle of a poetic prose that is musical without rhythm and without rhyme, flexible enough and energetic enough to adapt itself to the lyrical surges of the soul, the undulating movements of revery and the disturbances [*soubresauts*] of consciousness?" The famous sentence is as fine an example of a poet thinking through the possibilities of a new poetic form as one could hope for. Only a new, fine-grained, more supple language and a less rigid form can hope to register the fugitive sensations, aspirations, and disturbances of what Baudelaire goes on to define as a specifically modern consciousness. He conceives the prose poem as the genre that will enable him to articulate the experience of contemporary urban life: "It is above all from the experience of huge cities, from the exchange inherent in their multiple relationships that this obsessive ideal is born." [26]

Furthermore, collected in volume form the prose poems give rise to what Umberto Eco has called "an open work," that is, a work without the "secret architecture" of cycles and sections that give the *The Flowers of Evil* the character of a spiritual journey, a work that, as the author himself indicates, may be opened at random and read as the mood takes one, a work without "head or tail."

The parallels and precedents of the prose poems are often less literary than painterly. There are some similarities of subject matter between them and the work of Constantin Guys, as Baudelaire represents it in "The Painter of Modern Life," but in many ways they are closer to the art of Manet as it developed in the 1860s. Like Manet, Baudelaire may be said to have abandoned the "grand manner" of the academic tradition, which in his case were those traditional poetic forms that constitute the core of *The Flowers of Evil*—even if he had already invested them with a disturbing and decidedly unheroic new content and with an unprecedented moral ambiguity—for a technique that was both more intimate and more minimalist, closer to the *croquis de moeurs*—the street scene or anecdote from life.

The verse poems of *The Flowers of Evil* that come closest to the prose poems are the relatively late ones from the "Parisian Tableaux" section. For the most part they proceed from the same kind of modernist aesthetic that presided over the creation of paintings such as Manet's *Musique aux Tuileries* and *"The Universal Exhibition of 1867,* along with many of the other paintings discussed by T. J. Clark in "The View from Notre-Dame" and "The Environs of Paris" sections of *The Painting of Modern Life*. One finds a variety of scenes from contemporary Parisian life, scenes from fashionable and unfashionable streets, forgotten corners of the city, boulevards, cafés, places of entertainment, and public gardens, in which the influences from Poe and from the Balzacian novel along with other literary, quasi-sociological and artistic catalogers of modern life overlap and reinforce each other.

For the most part Baudelaire gives up the satisfactions of the beautiful and the self-consciously well wrought for that which suggests swiftness of execution and incisiveness. Thus when he is not creating poems that attempt experimentally to rewrite in prose some of the most rhapsodic and beautiful verse of *The Flowers of Evil*, the form is typically anecdotal and enigmatic with echoes of E. T. A. Hoffmann as well as Poe, although everything is characteristically pared down and concise and the focus is on the present and on the poetic subject's intense relationship to it.

The point of view typically adopted in the prose poem as Baudelaire developed it is that of the artist as flaneur, and he frequently locates such a figure as protagonist within the world he represents. The stance is that of an open-minded yet passionate and critical observer of the urban scene and the behavior of its human fauna. He is one who sets out daily in pursuit of adventures and chance encounters and who, when others have gone to bed, seeks out the verbal form that will render the day's experiences in their variety and their brilliant or disturbing specificity. The task of the poet is to observe, represent, comment, and pass on.

The tone is by turns compassionate, reflective, celebratory or witty, ironic, mystificatory, mocking, bitter. The most singular and strident chord sounded, however, is that which, in the wake of Poe, may be said to proceed from "the imp of the perverse." However, this does not preclude a wide range in the prose poems in terms of mood as well as subject matter. As far as the latter is concerned, one finds evocations of strange, marvelous and/or disturbing encounters, anecdotes, impressions, reveries or fantasies, all of which in one way or another constitute reflections on modern life and the poet's troubled relationship to it.

Some of the most interesting prose poems are, in fact, those that appear to be most personal, such as "One O'Clock in the Morning" which reads like a diary entry. The narrative movement of this poem is exemplary, inasmuch as it represents the poet engaged in a kind of ethico-aesthetic stocktaking of his experiences of the day. The poem begins with the poet gratefully embracing his solitude and lamenting his life ("Horrible life! Horrible city!") as he recalls a series of unsavory encounters with colleagues from the world of letters, publishing, and the theater, and as he recognizes the complicity and perversity of his own behavior. The final movement, however, takes the form of a prayer that he might rise above all pettiness and lies: "Lord God, grant me your grace so that I may create a few beautiful lines of verse which prove to me that I am not the worst of men, that I am not inferior to those I despise" (*Paris Spleen*, 287–88).

What is characteristic of this poem is, first, the fact that an ethic of self-improvement finds its justification in the sphere of aesthetics and, second, that the "I" of the poem is not identified with Baudelaire as such but with the Poet. In this connection, it is notable that another prose poem, which proclaims in its title its character as confession, "The Confiteor of the Artist," also connects that confession not to the man who sins and suffers in the world but to the artist who struggles to fulfill his task; once again, the "I" who confesses is the Poet, and the principal theme of the poem is the postromantic artist in his vain struggle to meet the standards set by the remote and indifferent natural beauty of sea and sky: "The pursuit of beauty is a duel in which the artist cries out with fear before he is overwhelmed" (*Paris Spleen*, 278–79). In brief, confession of such an order has little to do with the meaning Rousseau invested in the term; it is, rather, the expression of the will to transcend human messiness as soon as possible for beauty's sake.

If *Paris Spleen* is imbued with the dream of a new and more expressive poetic form that will encompass the variety, heterogeneity, fragmentariness, and bizarreness of modern life, "My Heart Laid Bare" tends toward aphorism and maxim; it is, to use Benjamin's word, apodictic. Thus it is no accident that it opens with a reference to the eighteenth-century *moraliste* Vauvenargues, for of all Baudelaire's works it comes closest to that classic French tradition of disabused and elliptical commentary on human behavior, although the tone throughout is of an unprecedented fierceness.

Nowhere, in fact, are Baudelaire's fundamentally un-Rousseauist beliefs more apparent than in those short passages and notations that have been collected by Baudelaire's editors under the general rubric *Intimate Journals,* among which "My Heart Laid Bare" has the most resonant and, in this context, the most relevant title. Both titles are in many ways misnomers, although the second was Baudelaire's own, because in spite of what they suggest, there is relatively little that is specifically autobiographical or confessional about the *Journals* in the sense of forming the coherent narrative of a life or at least of some of its more crucial episodes. Written relatively late in his life, they constitute instead something like an inventory of his hates and beliefs, observations and opinions, and exhortations to himself to work and pray of a kind that never found explicit expression in his more formal writings and that were recorded from day to day in journal form.

It is significant from the perspective of this book that with the first mention of the title of his work in a letter dated 1861 to his mother, Baudelaire identifies Rousseau as a model, if only as a negative one to go beyond. He refers to "a big book I have been dreaming about for two years, *My Heart Laid Bare,* in which I collect all the targets of my rage. Ah! if it ever sees the light of day, Jean-Jacques's *Confessions* will appear pale." Later in the same year, in another letter to his mother, he summarizes his future projects as follows: "In short, twenty topics for novels, two topics for plays, and a big book on *myself,* my *Confessions.*"[27]

Yet the material we have is far from resembling Rousseau's great work either in form, content, or importance. Even though Baudelaire makes an elliptical assertion of, "Absolute frankness, a means of originality" in the section entitled "Rocket,"[28] there is no equivalent to the frankness Rousseau deploys in narrating scandalous and/or humiliating anecdotes from his own life in the *Confessions.* Apart from a few references to his mother and to expressions of remorse, the most moving and most personal statement of the private journals concerns the sudden realization that he was on the point of losing his mind: "I cultivated my hysteria with intense pleasure and terror. Now I am never without vertigo, and today, the 23rd of January 1862, I felt pass over me *the wind of the wing of insanity.*"[29] Yet the notation is characteristic and characteristically different from Rousseau insofar as it is imbued with a specifically poetic sensibility that places a high value on concision and that employs a metaphor, in lieu of anecdote, in order to render brilliantly the terror of the experience as sensation.

The material published in the private journals is, in fact, drawn from a collection of more or less brief comments and observations that were found on sheets of paper under a variety of headings, including "Rockets," "Rockets-Suggestions" and—particularly suggestive perhaps of his determination to live a disciplined life and remake himself—"Hygiene," as well as "My Heart Laid Bare." Apparently written for the most part over the years 1855 to 1865, the observations are contemporary with the major poetic and critical work of almost the last decade of Baudelaire's life. What they amount to is an odd assortment of fragments, comments, opinions, judgments, prejudices, and personal feelings about a whole range of issues from the most private to the most public. If they deserve the title *Intimate Journals* at all, it is because they offer a Baudelaire apparently with his hair down, a Baudelaire in a sense as anti-dandy, a Baudelaire who does not, for once, master his emotions or transmute them into verse or prose poems but who expresses himself passionately, fiercely, bitterly, often alternating praise and invective, spiritual or aesthetic illumination and carnal loathing. Both in a general attitude of defiance and in a habit of turning all his thoughts into incisive and well-turned, albeit elliptical, phrases, the private journals also end up, in fact, being in many ways the opposite of "confessions."

Yet here, if anywhere, Baudelaire comes closest to resembling "the writer" at work. He speaks directly in the first person. He is above all preoccupied with the expression of ideas and is free with his opinions without having to submit them to the constraints of poetic form. Further, he touches in passing on a whole variety of themes that preoccupied him, commenting, frequently in a phrase, on religion and original sin; on morality and spiritual hygiene; on politics and social issues; on art and aesthetics; on the nature and function of the artist and poet; on the dandy; on the nature of woman; on prostitution, love, and pleasure; on travel; and on a number of his contemporaries, including, notoriously, George Sand.

The key to understanding the fierce originality of Baudelaire's observations and their power to shock both in his time and ours is what might be called his antihumanism. The most succinct expression of the general attitude is to be found, written in English, in a typically elliptical note: "Self-purification and antihumanity" ("Rockets," 659). Both concepts are of crucial importance and they are closely related. As Baudelaire came to define him in the course of his writings, the Poet is fundamentally an anti-humanist who rejects the self-congratulatory stance adopted by the human animal toward his species in his time. What this means, of course, is that all higher achievements are taken to be the result of a victory achieved in the first place over one's self and one's natural inclinations, a victory of "self-purification."

Nowhere is this antihumanism more apparent than in his judgments on love and politics, and given that love and politics relate most directly to the issues that preoccupied "the writer" from Rousseau on, I will limit myself to commenting on these topics here. The most revealing anecdotes of the *Confessions,* it will be remembered, concern Rousseau's sexual life; and the majority of his other important writings are either political or concern the relationship between art and politics.

It is interesting in this respect that whereas in *The Flowers of Evil* there is a variety of love poetry that runs the gamut from the sensual and cruel to the celebratory and ethereal, the private journals largely limit themselves to expressing a chastened and bitter view of human erotic relations that begins with their origins in human anatomy: "We are, in fact, reduced to making love with the excremental organs" ("My Heart," 688). As a result, it is not surprising if the physical expression of human love is represented as remote from the conception of it associated with romantic poetry: "There is in the act of love a striking resemblance to torture or to a surgical operation" ("Rockets," 659). One can only assume that it is on the basis of personal experience that the conclusion he reaches is a Sadean one: "I say that the unique and supreme pleasure in love resides in the certainty of causing pain *[le mal].* Both man and woman know from birth that all sexual pleasure is to be found in pain" ("Rockets," 652). In short, as far as human erotic relations are concerned, the private journals remind the reader not of such celebratory poems as "Evening Harmony" or "Invitation to a Voyage" from *The Flowers of Evil,* but of the ferocity deployed in "To One Who Is Too Gay" or "The Duel." If love is denounced, it is also in part because it signifies weakness or the expression of an emotional need; it displays a lack of the kind of self-mastery and self-sufficiency deployed by the dandy.

The observations in the journals on politics and on the possibilities for social life are no less harsh than those on love. Unlike Tocqueville or Stendhal, Baudelaire late in his life was moved by no memory of a year of promise, by no equivalent of their 1789 or 1796, respectively. The generation that came of age in the early 1840s had little opportunity to experience politics as heroic, at least until 1848 itself. But as with his exact contemporary Gustave Flaubert, a decade or so after 1848 most of his crucial pronouncements on that year concern the naivety of the various faiths associated with it—the faith in human progress, in democracy, and in "the people" on which belief in democracy rests.

In discussing the homologies between the cultural field and the fields of power and class relations, Bourdieu discusses in a number of places the misrecoginition that, from the mid-nineteenth century on, frequently led the literary and artistic avant-garde to express sympathy and solidarity with the working classes, on the grounds that both groups found themselves in the position of the dominated and their common enemy seemed to be the same dominating bourgeoisie. The disenchantment recorded by poets and novelists with 1848 and its aftermath may, therefore, be explained in part by the discovery that they in fact despised the bourgeoisie as a class for very different reasons from those of urban workers and artisans, and that they did not much admire the latter's fiercely egalitarian principles, democratic political culture, or taste.

In any case, looking back as well as forward in his journals, Baudelaire affirms the inevitable failure of the dream of revolution in the light of humanity's natural—that is to say, animalistic—origins. Moreover, Baudelaire's disabused comments on the year of revolution concern himself as well as his contemporaries. He refers to his state of "drunkenness in 1848" and goes on to ask, "What kind of drunkenness was it?" The elliptical answer, which seems to embrace his fellow citizens as well as himself, is, "The taste for revenge. The *natural* pleasure in destruction. A literary drunkenness, involving a memory of things read." And he continues in the same vein to affirm "The horrors of June. The madness of the people and of the bourgeoisie. The natural love of crime." His litany of complaints ends with "My fury at the coup d'état. How many shots I was exposed to. Another Bonaparte! The shame of it!" He concludes that "1848 was only fun because everyone constructed his utopia like so many castles in the air" ("My Heart," 679).

On the one hand, the meaning of these fragments of an unwritten political theory seem to suggest that in politics, as in love, the artist should behave like a dandy and keep himself for himself; on the other, there is here an anticipation of Benjamin's attempt to find a theory for the emergence of a specifically nineteenth-century form of boredom, at least as it relates to a revolutionary style of politics. Whereas in February 1848 Baudelaire seems to have reacted like Benjamin's revolutionary, for whom "boredom is the threshold of great deeds," from at least the mid-1850s on it is as if, long before the late twentieth century, he had discovered "the truly infernal horror of modern times," namely, that through repetition revolution itself had already become boring—"condemned to repeat itself, and condemned to fail: 1789, 1830, 1848, 1871."[30]

It is in the light of such judgments on love and politics, as on so much else, that I believe one should understand the isolated assertion that "[t]he man of letters is the enemy of the world" ("My Heart," 695). It is of particular relevance here, for it is a crucial element in Baudelaire's self-representations and explains his understanding of the Poet's task. The world referred to is the human or social world, the world of economic activity, social interaction, politics, and ideology. Moreover, it is another example of the way in which Baudelaire reverses Rousseau's position on an issue, since, as I indicated in an earlier chapter, in the polemics he conducted against his fellow philosophes Rousseau had, in effect, declared himself "the enemy of the man of letters." As formulated by his theory and practice, the task of "the writer" was in part to save the world from the *gens de lettres*. In a word, "the writer" is "useful"—what else does Sartrean *engagement* mean but being politically and socially "useful"?— and Baudelaire seems to have had as high an opinion of "a useful man" as Théophile Gautier had of a toilet: "Being a useful man has always struck me as something hideous" ("My Heart," 679).

One could say that the reason George Sand among all Baudelaire's contemporaries is singled out for his harshest comments is that she attempted to be "useful" or that she presented herself as a "friend" rather than an "enemy of the world." In her writing and in her life, as well as in the causes she embraced, she was in many respects the most influential representative of the Rousseauist tradition in literature in the mid–nineteenth century, and she was a woman to boot—which is to say, in Baudelaire's language, "natural," or "the opposite of the dandy." Referring to George Sand unambiguously as a "latrine," "a dumb creature," "a stupid cow," Baudelaire justifies his contempt on the grounds of her sentimental faith in God ("The Sand woman is for 'the God of nice people,' the God of the concierge and thieving servants"), her love of the workers, her faith in her good heart and good sense, and her moralizing: "She has always been a moralist. Only she used to be into counter-morality. Therefore, she has never been an artist" ("My Heart," 686–87). If everything else were not enough, the case against her becomes conclusive because of the way she confuses art with morality. The judgment also confirms that in Baudelaire's case aesthetic modernism is also a modernist aestheticism.[31]

I will conclude this sketch of the Poet as Baudelaire came to represent and celebrate him with two quotations that sum up the way he interpreted the task of poetry in his time as that of critique and transcendence. The first quotation concerns the relations between art and politics, and the potential disaster for aesthetics of the triumph of the democratic ideal. In it the poet turns in an aphoristic mode to a topic he refers to later, in "My Heart Laid Bare," as "the people's hatred of beauty" (691): "Why democrats do not like cats is easy to explain. Cats are beautiful; they awaken ideas of luxury, cleanliness, sensuousness, etc." ("Rockets," 662).

The second quotation, which I have used as the epigraph to this chapter, raises the question of the relationship between art and civilization, on the one hand, and sexual desire, on the other, and implies a Freudian theory of sublimation before the fact: "The more man cultivates the arts, the less he gets a hard-on. There is an ever-increasing divorce between spirit and the brute. Only the brute really gets a hard-on; fucking is the lyricism of the people" ("My Heart," 702). In these three brief sentences, Baudelaire makes short shrift of Rousseauist "natural man" in order to celebrate the spiritual qualities of his antithesis, the amateur of artificial beauty. "Fucking" is not for those superior beings, like the dandy and the artist, who disdain to seek satisfaction in merely human relations outside themselves.

Taken together, the two quotations to some extent confirm Benjamin's view of Baudelaire as a provocateur or literary putschist. They have the directness and disruptive energy of slogans designed to shock established opinions and force attention. At the same time, they affirm once again Baudelaire's belief that all higher human accomplishments are achieved against nature and not because of it. On the one hand, the critique implied in the spheres of politics and sex goes beyond that of sentimental humanitarianism and embraces humanism itself. On the other hand, the transcendence affirmed in a postreligious age is of an aesthetic order; humanity learns to recognize its creatural limitations and aspires to something higher through the pursuit of artistic beauty. The mirror of self-perfection is the mirror of art.

In the light of pronouncements of such an order it is not surprising that Benjamin is forced to conclude, toward the end of the first essay in his book *Charles Baudelaire*, that from the point of view of a twentieth-century Marxist Baudelaire is in many respects a disappointment. As its title ("The Paris of the Second Empire in Baudelaire") indicates, the focus of that essay is not so much Baudelaire the poet or critic, nor his poetry as such but the new urban world of industrial capitalism as represented in his work. Nevertheless, in the course of reflecting on how his own society's "progressive cadres" should approach Baudelaire, Benjamin finds himself reluctantly obliged to conclude, in a particularly illuminating footnote, that "[t]here is little point in trying to include Baudelaire in the fabric of the most advanced position in mankind's struggle for liberation. From the outset it seems more promising to investigate his machinations where he undoubtedly is at home—in the enemy camp. Very rarely are they a blessing for the opposite side. Baudelaire was a secret agent—an agent of the secret discontent of his class with its own rule" (104).

It may seem odd that virtually the highest praise Benjamin is able to come up with for the nineteenth century's most important poet is that he was a "secret agent" in the class war—particularly in light of the associations of that phrase in English with Joseph Conrad's bitterly antirevolutionary novel. Nevertheless, the designation does enable Benjamin to force Baudelaire into the category of "the writer" in spite of himself. Although he was a declared enemy of democracy and of class-based politics, he did, according to Benjamin, make a contribution to human emancipation by conducting his own sardonic critique of bourgeois society from within. The aesthetic modernist was also in practice the subtlest of moles, who through his representations of the phantasmagoria of urban capitalist society helped demythify his historical present and prepare "the awakening" that would lead to future "social redemption."[32]

In a similar vein, Sartre once also accused Baudelaire of "turning his back on the future" and choosing "to live his life backwards. He lived in a period which had just invented the future. . . . For the sociologists, the humanists and the manufacturers who discovered the power of capital, for the proletariat which was becoming conscious of itself, for Marx and for Flora Tristan, for Michelet, for Proudhon and for George Sand, the future existed and gave the present its meaning." Thus, according to Sartre, it required great willpower to oppose such a movement and the belief "in the Becoming of humanity and [the celebration of] Progress" (*Baudelaire*, 165–66). Yet Baudelaire was apparently perverse enough to bring it off.

Neither Benjamin nor Sartre accept the eighteenth-century tripartite division of reason to which Habermas referred in the essay quoted earlier, a division that sought "to develop objective science, universal morality and law, and autonomous art *according to their inner logic.*"[33] They do not put much faith in art and poetry as such to effect a critique of human life from a point of view beyond politics, although the poet who was so important to them both clearly did. Against the philosophers of suspicion he categorically affirmed the autonomy of art and the independence of the artist: not only should the artist not belong to a political party, as Baudelaire put it in a projected preface to *The Flowers of Evil*, he should also refuse to submit art to the worldly logic of sociopolitical ends or to accept political discourse as the discourse of final truths.

A modern poet who is clearly in sympathy with Baudelaire's understanding of the task of poetry, inasmuch as he, too, views "aesthetics" as "the mother of ethics," is Joseph Brodsky. In response to a British interviewer's question about the "moral seriousness and moral urgency" with which he regarded poetry, Brodsky replied, "It's not moral seriousness. Well, it is moral seriousness, moral urgency in the end, but essentially aesthetic seriousness, aesthetic urgency—which is more important. Aesthetics is the mother of ethics, as far as I am concerned." And Brodsky concludes in a phrase that suggests an unexpected filiation with Baudelaire's dandy: "The net result of wrong moral choice is vulgarity. Evil is vulgar."[34]

A final example illustrates Baudelaire's aesthetic-ethical stand on these issues. Among the short reflections and exhortations under the heading "Hygiene, Morality, Conduct" (which Sartre characterized as "puerile"), there is a late note that reads, "Wisdom in brief. Appearance *(toilette)*, prayer, work," ("Hygiene," 671). That "appearance" should be associated with "prayer" and "work" is, of course, vintage Baudelairean provocation. Yet the attitude expressed here, implying calculated self-presentation, the discipline of art, and an attitude of humility relative to a transcendent order is probably what Foucault had in mind when he defined Baudelaire's conception of "modern man" as "the man who tries to invent himself." That is, Baudelaire was committed to the idea of perfection and self-surpassing in and through art, somewhat like Nietzsche's Superman. Thus far from being a political progressive, his Poet is not even a humanist; man—and even less woman—is not the measure but a creature to go beyond. The difference between two critical thinkers like Benjamin and Sartre and the nineteenth-century poet is that whereas they reason in terms of the pathology of modern industrial capitalist life and assume the possibility of a future cure, he locates the source of the pathology in human life itself. That is the fundamental reason Baudelaire rejected a politics of liberation in favor of a poetics of invention.[35]

One important aspect of Baudelaire's historical moment is that the climax of his career as poet in the 1850's coincided with the emergence of the first generation of "artist-photographers" who came to explore the potential of the new medium in the field of portraiture. The most celebrated of these, Félix Nadar, was almost an exact contemporary of Baudelaire's and belonged to the same marginal world of Parisian artists, poets, writers, and composers. He opened his first photographic studio on the rue Saint-Lazare in 1853 and within a few years achieved fame, in part as a portrait photographer of those painters, poets, writers, and composers. Apart from Baudelaire himself, Delacroix, Sainte-Beuve, Champfleury, and Meyerbeer were the subjects of his work.[36]

The beginning of the process of the democratization and mechanization of portraiture, of course, preceded Niépce's invention of photography in 1824. As Gisèle Freund, for example, points out, during the second half of the eighteenth century the growing popularity of miniature oil portraits was followed by the perfecting of the much simpler technique of the silhouette; a further development, the physionotrace—a mechanically drawn portrait that combined elements of the silhouette and the engraving—became particularly fashionable during the period of the French Revolution and the Empire. By the late 1850s, however, rapidly evolving photographic technology had already expanded beyond what Nadar and his immediate contemporaries had been able to achieve in terms of speed and cheapness of production, and with Eugène Disdéri photography entered the age of the mass media and a clientele that embraced large sections of the lower-middle classes.[37]

Given his views on photography, it may seem that the most familiar images of Baudelaire posterity has inherited are probably those made by Nadar and by Etienne Carjat, but it is not, in the end, so ironic. The fact is, in spite of Baudelaire's refusal to recognize photography as an art, there is a sense in which in the 1850s it was briefly an avant-garde art before it seemed to succumb to being a middle-class one in the closing decades of the same century, and he was fortunate enough to have posed for "artist-photographers" of talent when it was. Freund points out the bathos that resulted when a photgrapher like Disdéri set out to represent cultural types such as "The Operatic Tenor," "The Writer," "The Painter," and "The Scholar" with the aid of props and a stylized register of gestures. But the portraits of Baudelaire are much more interesting.

In any case, as a friend or acquaintance of many of the most famous painters and photgraphers of his time, it is not surprising that as his reputation grew from the late 1840s on he was frequently painted, sketched, caricatured, and photographed.[38] To some extent, the quality of these representations constitutes a fitting confirmation of the genius of his poetry and his exemplary avant-garde life, which gave rise to the modernist idea and image of the Poet.

In the most familiar photographic portraits, Baudelaire tends to look straight out and down at his observer; his body is self-consciously posed within the frame and his right hand is often thrust resolutely yet debonairly into his cape at the chest; his clothes are casually elegant, as befits the modern poet, and include, along with the dark cape, a cravat and a white collar; his striking face is typically partly in shadow, his mouth fixed in a severe line, and he wears an expression of quiet hauteur that makes no concessions to a potential interlocutor. Little changes over the years: the hairline recedes; and the locks at the back of his head grow longer. In short, in a cultivated look that gives nothing away, as well as in the special quality of the photographic image making of his age, he becomes the representative not of a class but of an elite caste of nineteenth-century European men.

Along with Félix Nadar's relatively youthful (1855) portrait, probably the most widely reproduced images of the poet are Etienne Carjat's remarkable 1861 photograph (which in the lines on the emaciated face and the severity and directness of the look seems especially designed to project the qualities of a troubled life as well as a refined sensibility and the secret knowledge associated with it) and his 1863 portrait of Baudelaire as connoisseur and dandy. It is as if in complicity with the first generation of artistic photographers Baudelaire had found the art of overcoming the supposed "naturalness" of the medium and produced a kind of mirror image, after Poe himself, of a somber genius that also satisfied the dandy's taste for self-mastery and self-invention. With the passage of time it was this look that came to be associated with the look of the Poet, with a capital P.

Of all Baudelaire's portraitists, Courbet is probably the one who went furthest in interpreting for posterity the idea of the Poet that Baudelaire came to represent and in translating that idea into a brilliant image that is quasi-allegorical in character. Both in the original *Portrait of Baudelaire* of 1847 and in the version that appears in the large allegorical painting of 1855 entitled *The Painter's Studio*, Baudelaire is represented with his head shaven and in deep shadow, wholly withdrawn from the world around him and absorbed in the reading of a book. In *The Painter's Studio*, the poet's isolation and self-absorption in the scene are suggested by the way in which his head and torso barely enter the frame of the picture, at the extreme bottom right; he is at the margin of the crowd, not of it, and definitely not marrying it. In the 1847 portrait the sense of the intensity of an inner life and of secrets to be deciphered and transmitted is enhanced by virtue of the fact that the poet is seated on a bed or divan set against a bare wall and has before him the simple tools of his trade: a table to write on, a pen and inkwell, writing material, and another book. At the same time, unlike the polished photographs, the figure, his clothes, and the objects in the painting have the honest, rough-hewn quality of Courbet's painterly realism. The effect is of an *Ecce Homo Poeticus.*

Sartre might well have had both Courbet's and the photographic portraits in mind, along with Baudelaire's own works, when he diagnoses the particular form of "bad faith" to which he succumbed qua Poet:

> A hundred, a thousand times in his writings he [Baudelaire] speaks of 'the poet' and 'the artist.' He managed to have himself justified and consecrated by the writers of the past. He even went further than this by forming a friendship with a dead poet. The real purpose of his long liaison with Edgar Poe was to procure his elevation to the mystic order. . . . Once he was dead, however, his portrait assumed its final form and its features became clear. It was perfectly natural to describe him as poet and martyr; his existence had become a destiny." (*Baudelaire*, 142–43).

The central purpose of Sartre's short book is to demonstrate that that "destiny" was a fabrication—was, in fact, of the poet's own choosing. Be that as it may, Sartre is no doubt right in recognizing that the Baudelairean idea of the Poet for a long time exercised an enormous fascination over French literary life, although from the early decades of this century that figure, too, has been in significant eclipse. Where Sartre is far less perspicacious is in his failure to identify and describe the lineage of "the writer" to which he himself belonged, or the very different look he cultivated despite appearances to the contrary.

CHAPTER 4

Jean-Paul Sartre: Writer, Militant, Graphomaniac

Above all,—and this is something I have said on a number of occasions,—Sartre was our Jean-Jacques Rousseau. He always made me think of Marx's sentence on Rousseau, which I quote from memory: "In spite of all his divagations that man remained wholly intransigent and refused all compromise with the powers that be."

LOUIS ALTHUSSER

In *Past Imperfect,* his study of French intellectuals during the decade following World War II, Tony Judt follows Tocqueville in tracing the typical relationship between intellectuals and political power in France back to the last decades of the *ancien régime:*

> The intellectual Enlightenment in France can be thought of as a mostly one-sided conversation between philosophers, journalists, and others on the one part and the royal power on the other. Replacing the Church as the counterweight to the secular authority, writers and others discovered their public identity in the act of criticism, representing the interests of the people, of humanity, or simply of reason to a government reluctant to listen or understand. From early on, therefore, French thinkers were accustomed to address themselves to the state and to see themselves as intermediaries between the latter and the rest of humanity.[1]

In other words, that position of defiant marginality, of vigilance and solidarity among French intellectuals that found its focus in salons, clubs, *sociétés de pensée,* and collective publishing enterprises in the eighteenth century waxed and waned during the years of revolution and reaction of the nineteenth century until it became a mode of institutionalized cultural behavior under the Third Republic. As Judt goes on to remind us, with the Dreyfus Affair the idea of the engaged intellectual of the left emerged in the recognizably modern form that Emile Durkheim was one of the first

143

Jean-Paul Sartre
(Photo J. Robert. © Gallimard)

Jean-Paul Sartre
(Photo Rapho)

to articulate forcefully as a combination of commitment *and* detachment. That is, it came to be expected of intellectuals that they should participate in public life, but only qua intellectuals, refusing to "suborn their actions and writings to the needs of the moment or party politics. What they had to offer, in other words, was not merely assistance to the cause of justice or support for the defenders of the Republic but a vision of society, of the ways in which the inadequate present might be rendered into a better future." Judt adds, "Even for those who did not share Durkheim's critique of modern society, with his dream of seeing contemporary anomie overcome in a fully 'integrated,' conflict-free world, the image of the engaged intellectual bringing to the community a wholly articulated moral countervision was very attractive" (*Past Imperfect,* 251).

In the context of his peculiarly complex times in the middle decades of our own century, Jean-Paul Sartre came to rearticulate in his own existentialist/Marxist discourse a comparable view of the intellectual; but he did so in ways that also reestablished the continuity over the centuries with the prerevolutionary thinker whose legacy in the sphere of literature as well as politics was still very much alive. The great interest and challenge of Sartre for me here is that in his career as novelist, playwright, philosopher, political theorist, essayist, critic, scriptwriter, journalist, biographer, and autobiographer the French tradition of "the writer" I trace back to Rousseau achieves a brilliant climax before going into an apparent eclipse. Also of interest is the fact that no one has written more provocatively and more disparagingly than Sartre himself on the antithetical role of the writer (in the generic sense,) in historical perspective, the writer as man of letters, and on the urgency in our time of demystifying that role.

In this connection Sartre's experience of war—at a prisoner-of-war camp, and German occupation during the years 1939–45—was crucial, as he himself acknowledged. After what was for him, by his own admission, the individualistic and apolitical decade of the 1930s, when he achieved recognition as a novelist (with *Nausea*) and short-story writer (with "The Wall"), the war years left Sartre forever preoccupied with his own situation and with the ambitions and responsibilities of writers and intellectuals in a powerful national culture that celebrated its literature and lionized its famous authors. From the mid-forties on, no one argued more forcefully than he against the fetishization of literature and the special fame (or *gloire*) that accrued in France to those who created it.

The position he reached in his maturity relative to a certain late-nineteenth-century French notion of the career of the man of letters is summed up with characteristic sardonic wit in a comment in "Self-Portrait at Seventy." Looking back from the vantage point of his seventieth year, Sartre evokes his youthful understanding of the proper relationship between a famous author and sociopolitical action, only to mock it. His assumption had been that "a writer spends his time writing until he's fifty, then once he reaches fifty, he does his *J'accuse,* like Zola, or he goes off

to Chad, like Gide, and comes back to announce: Colonialism is rotten."
Then, after a political sabbatical of a year or so, he gets back to the proper
business of writing his novels or his poems. The mature Sartre came to
affirm that political commitment should be integral to how one lives one's
life and writes one's books.[2] The difference is important, inasmuch as it
brings into sharp focus the distinction between the man of letters, including one whose political sympathies are progressive, and "the writer."

In their different ways even Sartre's major works of philosophy, *Being
and Nothingness* and *The Critique of Dialectical Reason*, address the question. They have important implications relative to the freedom and social
responsibility of the writer; and the latter work in particular may be said
to argue specifically for the transformation of the writer in the generic
sense into "the writer" as I have defined the figure. But it is above all to
Sartre's shorter works of literary and philosophical theory, to his critical
biographies, and to his autobiographical works that one has to go for his
principal discussions of the issues.

There are, on the one hand, the important manifestos, the "Presentation" of *Les Temps Modernes* (1945), *Existentialism is a Humanism*
(1946),[3] *What Is Literature?* (1947), and *Search for a Method (Question
de Méthode)* (1960); and, on the other, the series of biographies that
spanned the greater part of his career, from the *Baudelaire* of 1946 to the
monumental but unfinished three-volume work on Flaubert that he was
still working on when he went blind in 1973, and including the works
on Genêt and Mallarmé.[4] Finally, there is the autobiographical material,
including the autobiography proper, *Words* (1964), which was intended
to be a provocative farewell to literature, but which almost from the moment of its first publication became a literary "classic" in spite of itself,
the film directed by Alexandre Astruc and Michel Contat, *Sartre: un film*
and the interview conducted by Michel Contat, "Self-Portrait at Seventy."
Moreover, Simone de Beauvoir's extensive accounts of her life and their
relationship as a couple came to be increasingly confused with Sartre's
own commentary, from the publication of the first volume of her autobiographical trilogy, *Memoirs of a Dutiful Daughter,* in 1958, down through
the *Conversations with Sartre* of the mid-seventies to her public act of
leave-taking, *The Ceremony of Farewell* (1981), which appeared shortly
after his death.[5]

It is enough to recall the extraordinary range of Sartre's writings in a
variety of fields and a number of literary genres, as well as the radical
sociopolitical causes he embraced, to be aware that if there is one figure in
twentieth-century France who is a worthy successor to Rousseau in the
eighteenth it is Sartre—Rousseau, it should be noted, rather than Voltaire,
with whom Sartre was occasionally compared in his lifetime on account
of his international stature, his critical distance from establishment culture
in his time, and his readiness to challenge publicly specific acts of injustice
practiced by the French state.[6] It is enough to refer to some of the most

central and enduring concepts of Sartrean thought, such as "freedom," "responsibility," "opposition" *(contestation)*, "alienation," and above all "transparency" and "authenticity," to perceive the continuity with the Rousseauist tradition, whether or not Sartre specifically acknowledged it. In spite of the political courage Voltaire displayed in challenging the state institutions of the *ancien régime,* there is no equivalent in that large oeuvre to the important works of radical political theory associated with both Rousseau and Sartre, nor did the last of the great neoclassicists engage in autobiography. Sartre's specific French intellectual lineage is implicitly confirmed in the subtitle he gave to *Situations, X: Politique et Autobiographie.* This late work is divided into two parts, "Political Texts" and "Conversations Concerning Myself." In this connection, in her biography entitled *Sartre: A Life,* Annie Cohen-Solal reminds us of the sheer "writerly" variety and abundance of Sartre's work during the years 1946–49— a period when he was at the height of his fame—a variety and abundance that gave a new and heroic aura to the idea of the French literary intellectual in the postwar decades: "The genres included lectures, essays, plays, articles, introductions, radio broadcasts, biographies, philosophical speculations, screenplays, songs, novels, reports. The themes ranged from esthetics, literature, ethics, politics, and philosophy to travel, art, and music" (280).

As far as political and social commitment are concerned, there was no sudden dramatic conversion in Sartre's case comparable to the "illumination de Vincennes," as a result of which Rousseau claimed to have understood his critical moral and social task in life. Nevertheless, the isolated subject or "man alone" *(l'homme seul),* as Sartre refers to himself,[7] who down through the 1930s was in revolt against his class and was always ready to challenge established values and play the role of provocateur, in his behavior as well as in his writing, was a very different figure from the man who emerged from captivity and occupation in the early forties. The brief experience of the prisoner-of-war camp, in particular, democratized Sartre, and he first became politically active with the attempt to organize the "Socialism and Freedom" movement in 1941.[8] From that moment on he took to expressing his solidarity with what he took to be the progressive sociopolitical movements of his time, although he always remained an intellectual and mostly stayed at a distance from the activities of a political party, including especially the French Communist Party. However, this did not prevent him from proclaiming himself "a fellow traveler" during the years 1952–56, and from the postwar era on he never ceased to identify himself as a Marxist as well as an existentialist.

There is, in fact, an interesting convergence between Rousseau's ambitious attempts to integrate an understanding of self and society, of autobiography and grand political theory, with the existentialist's attention to subjective experience and the specificity of individual lives, on the one hand (something that explains Sartre's fascination as a lycée student with

Bergson's descriptions of the operations of consciousness and his mature interest in opposition to doctrinaire Marxism in the whole sphere of "the micro-social"), and with his sociopolitical thought, on the other. The gap between *Words* and *The Critique of Dialectical Reason* is perhaps not as wide as that between, say, the *Confessions* and *The Social Contract,* but in both cases the author seems to be just as committed to bearing witness to the intimate events of a private life as to theorizing on the course taken by universal history and on the exploitative character of the social and political institutions that have mostly emerged from such history. The last major philosophical theorist of alienation in the French tradition echoes the first in a variety of ways. Centered as it is on how to effect a transition to a just and egalitarian society in a world of "scarcity" and "need," *The Critique of Dialectical Reason,* in particular, has the character of a work of historical anthropology that combines elements of a *Discourse on the Origin of Inequality* with a *Social Contract.*

Furthermore, the convergence between Rousseau and Sartre is also confirmed by the fact that although both wrote distinguished works of imaginative literature, they nevertheless shared a suspicion of the aesthetic sphere on political grounds; in their maturity both insisted on the primacy of the political and of man as a political animal.

One could, of course, argue that the major influences on Sartre, after Husserl and Heidegger, were Hegel and Marx, but none of these German thinkers wrote novels or autobiographies, nor did they make a crucial issue of "transparency" or collapse the traditional distinctions between private and public life, as both Sartre and Rousseau attempted to do in their different ways. Moreover, none of them lived in a manner that consciously defied accepted codes of behavior in their time and provoked the charge of scandal. That is to say, none were "writers" in the sense that interests me here and in the way that, some two hundred years after Rousseau, Sartre preeminently was.

In this connection, summarizing the life Simone de Beauvoir and Sartre lived as a couple in the late thirties, Cohen-Solal notes, "Together they hunted down news items and worshiped transparency: 'My least feelings and thoughts were public from birth,' he [Sartre] wrote in 1939. 'Until the present war I *lived publicly.*" She goes on to add, "Two intellectuals in revolt against society and the provinces, they will invent, in defiance of the society in which they refuse to participate, a set of customs, norms, codes, and new models that later will earn them a tremendous following" (*Sartre: A Life* 86). It was on the basis of such attitudes that the myth of existentialist Saint-Germain as a new *vie de Bohème* was propagated by the French and international media in the years immediately after World War II.

A conclusive sign of the different and highly public cultural role played by Sartre, in contrast to the German philosophers just mentioned, is to be found in the final image with which Cohen-Solal chooses to illustrate her biography. It is a photograph of her subject's funeral procession and shows a bird's-eye view of a Parisian boulevard dense from top to bottom with little black and white dots representing people swarming around trees and among stationary cars. Sartre's was the kind of funeral more usually associated in our time with royalty, heads of state, sports heroes, and film and rock stars, not with philosophers or men of letters of a traditional type—although in France, at least, there have been notable precedents going back to the ceremonial entombments referred to in chapter 1 of both Voltaire and Rousseau in the Pantheon in the 1790s and including the national funeral given to the immensely popular Victor Hugo in 1885.

The point about the size of Sartre's funeral cortege, however, is that it can be attributed to a celebrity status that was not merely a function of Sartre's written works or even his theater but was also due to the influence of a life lived in full view of the mass media, which had reported him and reported on him and had diffused his image over some forty years, not only throughout France but throughout the world. It is therefore no accident that Sartre's last significant major statements, made shortly before and after he went blind, are found in a series of tape-recorded interviews, some of which were also captured on film. In this connection, the fact that he was to complete the highly literary autobiography of his early years with an oral account of his subsequent life and career is fully consistent with his sense of his role as advocate and witness and of the importance of the media for his purposes.

The interview is a genre that can hardly be said to have existed as such before the age of the mass media and the possibility of the mechanical reproduction of sound and images,[9] but by the late twentieth century it has achieved a kind of ubiquity, as a result of which visual images and the spoken word have usurped many of the functions of the written word. The subject of an interview is typically a "celebrity" of one kind or another. Its purpose is ostensibly informational but it is also typically popularizing, promotional, and self-promotional. Moreover, in an important sense an interview offers itself as an ideal act of communication. It typically involves two people, a speaker and a listener—interviewer and interviewee (although there may, of course, be more than one of each)—in a one-on-one exchange that is concentrated and focused in ways average conversations rarely are. At the same time, if, as is the case with Sartre, the declared aim is to be as direct and as "transparent" as possible, the interview seems to afford a special opportunity for autobiographical revelations and unmediated access to the truth of a life and its works. And it is this situation of contrived intimacy that the listener to a taped interview "overhears." Further, in the case of a filmed interview, the third-party spectator enjoys the surplus pleasure associated with observing the subject/object of his or her absorption. The seduction of the image of an ideal ego relays the attraction of voice.

As far as revelations are concerned, nowhere does Sartre sound more

Rousseauist than when he explains to Michel Contat in "Self-Portrait at Seventy" the reason he has no objection to answering personal questions: "I think that transparency should everywhere replace secrets, and I can imagine the day when two men will have no more secrets from each other because they will have none from anyone, because subjective life as well as objective life will be offered in its totality, given." And he adds, in a set of observations that recall Rousseau's nostalgic meditations on the idea of an original natural language and total communication, "If we truly wanted to exist for each other, exist as a body, a body that can always be stripped bare—even if it never happens—ideas ought to appear to the other as if they proceeded from the body. The words spoken are perceived as articulated by a tongue in a mouth" (141–42).[10] Even in Rousseau it is hard to find a more utopian conception of the lost transparency of human communication or of speech as natural, unmediated, and corporeal.

Moreover—again as with Rousseau—the goal here and throughout might be summed up as the overcoming of alienation. It is a characteristic mark of Sartre's oeuvre, as of his eighteenth-century predecessor's, that in pursuit of this goal, both within a work and between works, he will constantly shift from the objective to the subjective and back, from self to world, politics to psyche, or from confession to *engagement*.

Given the space limitations imposed by the format of this book, in what follows I can look at only some of the relevant shorter works of theory that illustrate these fundamental attitudes before turning to a discussion of the autobiographical works in book and film form. My relatively narrow focus remains the way in which Sartre can be said to have updated Rousseau's "writerly" legacy in the middle decades of our own century, and why, in the light of recent political history in particular, for good or ill that legacy seems to have expended itself.

At the age of seventy, Sartre summarized the literary program of his prewar years as follows: "To tell the truth about existence and to demystify bourgeois lies was one and the same thing, and that was what I had to do to fulfill my destiny as a man, since I had been born to write" ("Self-Portrait," 177). From the point of view of the immediate postwar period, the limits of the social isolationism implied in that passage, the idea of "man alone" and of an individual author's "destiny," had become obvious to him; as a result, he set out in collaboration with others to rethink for his time the whole institution of literature and the function of the writer.

Engagement, as Sartre clearly notes in the *Sartre* film, derived from the situation in which he and others found themselves during the occupation of France when they united in the task of fighting against the Nazis: "[T]here was a commitment to that precise task, a recognition of the value of the communist group, a need to write on the questions that concerned us, and also if necessary to defend the group with which we were associated." He goes on to explain his understanding of the concept of *engage-*

ment and the relationship it implied to the left-wing political parties in the situation immediately after the war: "At that time *engagement* meant for me what a left-wing intellectual did when he didn't belong to a party."[11]

It was, of course, in *What is Literature?* that Sartre first laid out in detail the theory of *engagement* in the sphere of literature, a theory that was to prove so influential down through the middle decades of the twentieth century in France and throughout the Western world. In a section entitled "For Whom Does One Write?" one also finds a critical survey of the changing function of the writer down through French history. That survey is followed by a final section, "Situation of the Writer in 1947," defining the writer's role in the apparently extreme circumstances of the immediate postwar period in France. It is in these concluding sections especially that Sartre might also be said to give his own account of the emergence and persistence over some two hundred years of the figure I have been calling "the writer"; in the process he effectively acknowledges his own filiation with that figure and its origins in the French Enlightenment period.

From the point of view I have adopted in these pages, it is notable that it was precisely while reflecting on *What Is Literature?* that Kundera commented on the way Sartre invariably speaks of "writer" and "prose writer" *(prosateur)*, never of "novelist" or "dramatist," as if issues of genre or of literary form were of relatively little significance.[12] Moreover, Sartre excludes poetry from consideration from the beginning by placing the activity of the poet in another category of language use altogether: whereas the poet relates to words as "things," the "prose writer" regards them as "signs" to be manipulated. Prose is thus defined as "utilitarian by essence," even when it is employed in works of imaginative literature. It is disturbingly symptomatic that Sartre could assume in the 1940s that it was possible to answer the question of what "literature" is without reference to poetry or even a discussion of the connotative play of language or of the formal issues specific to imaginative literature in general. The effect of Sartre's opening gesture is to misrepresent the relational complexity of the literary field as Bourdieu defines it by lopping off an important dimension of it. Sartre places off-limits what Bourdieu calls the autonomous pole of the field—the restricted sphere poetry has occupied since symbolism, in which poets write chiefly for other poets and success is measured in noneconomic terms—as opposed to the most heteronomous pole—for example, mass-market fiction, where one's audience is measured in hundreds of thousands and to succeed is to be a best-seller.[13]

The reason Sartre represents such a formidable challenge in the context of this book is not simply because he was the most complete and influential embodiment of the idea of "the writer" in our time, but also because he himself applied his extraordinary intelligence to analyzing his function and his relationship to a literary tradition that he found problematic. Although since the mid-sixties at the latest his reputation has been in decline, it is a serious mistake to underestimate his capacity throughout his career to illuminate those questions of cultural and institutional history on which he focused, as anyone who still takes the trouble to read his works knows. Is it necessary in the early 1990s to recall that there was a good reason why Sartre dominated the intellectual and literary life of his age through the range and power of his writing? No one else enjoyed the respect of his professional peers, as well as of a broad section of the educated public, and in such a variety of fields, as he did in the role of philosopher, political theorist, novelist, dramatist, short-story writer, and critic. There is no doubt that his many readings of writers and their changing social role still has the capacity to illuminate in spite of their clear limitations.

What changes our perspective on such questions is something he could hardly have anticipated, namely, the collapse of the idea of revolution that reached a climax in the late 1980s—although for those who were attentive to the realities of life throughout the communist world, east and west, clear signs of deep moral and sociopolitical malaise went back a very long way indeed. In Sartre's case, it is as if the last major political event with sufficient power to reorient his thinking in an important way was May 1968, when he was in his early sixties. The few years of active thought left to him after that were almost entirely taken up with absorbing the lessons and the promise of those few weeks when it seemed that a new social order was on the point of emerging in France on the heels of a revolution of a wholly unanticipated type. The fact is, however, that less than a decade after his death the bicentenntial year of 1989 I referred to in the introduction, which had been planned to celebrate a tradition of revolution, ended up burying it instead. It is this radically new postrevolutionary historical perspective that enables us to see Sartre differently from the way he saw himself and to locate him at the end of the tradition of "the writer."

To appreciate Sartre's own self-understanding of his situation and the critical French literary tradition with which he associated himself from the early forties on, it is still useful to begin with *What Is Literature?* What, for example, does that work have to say, not so much about literature as about the institution of literature and the makers of literature, that is, about its writers and the social conditions under which they wrote? More particularly, what does it say about "the writer" that enables us to see how much the world of literature has changed between the half-century that extends from the mid-forties into the mid-nineties?

In response to the question that constitutes the title of the second section of his book, "For Whom Does One Write?," Sartre provides a broadly Marxist reading of the French literary past, which he divides into three phases, the last of which is itself broken down into two. His narrative history of the French literary institution is collapsed into that of the class struggle in France, which Marx himself had analyzed in two celebrated pamphlets,[14] and includes the evolving relationship of writers to the changing class publics. In the first phase, from the Middle Ages down through the seventeenth century, Sartre affirms the existence of a solidarity between writers and ruling-class ideology, as a consequence of which the reading public is unified and limited to the aristocracy. With the eighteenth century there emerges a split in the reading public between an increasingly self-assertive bourgeoisie and the aristocracy, between a rising class whose class interests are temporarily those of humanity at large and a class in decline. It is with the Age of Enlightenment, therefore, that literature for Sartre ceases to be merely conservative and *moraliste* in order to take on a "negative" character relative to its present; that is, it becomes synonymous with critique and doubt. Also, for the first time ever, literature comes to be regarded by its writers as no longer simply a means but an end in itself, or what Sartre himself calls "autonomous." [15]

Third, as far as the nineteenth century is concerned, following Marx and others, Sartre locates a division in the crucial middle years of 1848–51. Whereas the writers of the French romantic movement had for the most part turned nostalgically away from their bourgeois public to the restored aristocracy, the period from 1850 to 1914 is characterized by what he calls "the great refusal," which derives from a complete divorce between the temporal and spiritual spheres; aware of the deep contradiction between the demands of literature and bourgeois ideology, French writers reject all forms of social utility, turn to the cult of art for art's sake, and constitute themselves as an aesthetic priesthood or new aristocracy. Moreover, this "great refusal" takes place in the second half of a century that also sees the appearance of a new *public virtuel* for the writer, namely, that of the working masses, whose emergent class consciousness causes a breakdown of the earlier, all-encompassing concept of "the People."

As far as the avant-garde literature of the early twentieth century is concerned, Sartre largely assimilates it to surrealism, which he characterizes as a form of antiliterature defined by a spirit of mere negation and irresponsibility; the avant-garde writer is in secret complicity with bourgeois society, he is "a house writer" who is "a rebel and not a revolutionary." [16] In Sartre's reading it is not until the shattering experience of war and occupation between 1939 and 1945 that the era of the socially responsible, politically self-conscious, historically situated writer dawns, the kind of writer—or "writer"—that Sartre himself was determined to be.

It is in this context that Sartre gives a definition of the *engagement* with which he was to be associated throughout the rest of his life. *Engagement* begins with recognition of the fact that, whether one likes it or not, one is situated in a concrete social context within a historical continuum: "I would say that a writer is committed [*engagé*] when he takes up the task of becoming as lucidly and as fully conscious as possible of the fact that he is embarked; that is to say, when both for himself and for others he transforms his commitment from that of a spontaneous reaction to a state of reflection" (124).

In this connection, of particular interest for my argument is the way in which Sartre connects his theory of *engagement* with the break he locates in the middle decades of the nineteenth century. Moreover, it is here that he refers specifically to Rousseau and compares him, on account of his politically progressive attitudes and his "two publics," to Richard Wright in the contemporary United States:

> At the time of the Encyclopedists, it is no longer a question of sim-
> ply liberating the *honnête homme* from his passions by showing
> them to him without evasion, but of contributing by means of his
> pen to the political liberation of man as a whole. The appeal the
> writer addresses to his bourgeois public is, whether he likes or not,
> an incitement to revolt; that which he addresses at the same time
> to the ruling class is an invitation to lucidity, to the critical exami-
> nation of the self, to the relinquishing of his privileges. Rousseau's
> situation very much resembles that of Richard Wright, who wrote
> both for enlightened Blacks and for Whites: as far as the nobility is
> concerned, he *bears witness*, and at the same time he invites his
> fellow commoners to become conscious of themselves. His writings,
> as well as Diderot's and Condorcet's, not only prepared ahead of
> time the storming of the Bastille but also the night of the fourth of
> August. (152–53)

If Sartre singles out Rousseau's role as exemplary here, it is because of a new view of the function of writing he attributes to him and because of Rousseau's indirect association with the political events of the French Revolution. The mention of the night of the fourth of August along with that of the storming of the Bastille is of particular significance because Sartre thereby connects the popular insurrectionary moment with a legisla-tive session that invoked principles of equality and brotherhood of a kind that Rousseau's writings had prepared. The night in question, of course, is famous for the mood of revolutionary euphoria in which the National Assembly witnessed the renunciation of various forms of privilege by members of the different estates and effectively approved the end of the feudal order of the *ancien régime*. In the reference to Rousseau, in any case, one recognizes Sartre's own acknowledgment of a continuity between the eighteenth-century philosopher's conception of "the writer's" task and his own. Sartre identifies in Rousseau the emergence of an idea of writing as a form of action that is consciously political and emancipatory in its own right.

Although it would be a decade or so before Sartre would attempt a comprehensive theoretical effort to fuse his earlier existentialism with Marxism in *The Critique of Dialectical Reason*, which appeared in 1960,

What Is Literature? bears witness throughout to the mutually supportive relationship he assumed to exist between the two bodies of theory, or what in the early years of the Second World War were summed up in the slogan "Socialism and Freedom." The idea of the social responsibility of the writer who, as a human subject, is free to choose the way he lives and writes, though not under circumstances of his own choosing, is the single most important theme of the work.

What is Literature? is, in fact, unusually rich in resonant slogans that exhort the writer to commit himself to the cause of humanity, that is, to be fully cognizant of his historical situation and his social task, whatever the circumstances. Literature is, in effect, defined allegorically as an institution whose finality is universal human freedom. "To write," Sartre declares, "is, therefore, both to reveal the world and to offer it as a task to the generosity of the reader" (109). The writer represents the world "so that free men who face it experience their freedom." A work of art is defined as "an act of confidence in men's freedom" (111). The final goal of art is "to recuperate this world by making it visible as it is, as if its origin were to be found in human liberty" (106). Moreover, the idea of the aesthetic itself is associated almost exclusively with the perception of liberty. In one of the more Heideggerian moments of *What Is Literature?* Sartre even declares that "aesthetic joy" is nothing other than the sudden consciousness I have of a capacity to recuperate and interiorize the nonself; the world becomes a "task" that I freely accept insofar as I commit myself to bear witness to its being (108).

It is thus characteristic of Sartre's updating of the idea of "the writer" in light of his existentialism and his Marxism that he should also represent literature in terms of a relationship between two free human subjects—a writer who by my definition is also "a writer," and a reader whom I am also tempted to call "a reader," inasmuch as he, too, is expected to be as historically self-conscious and as politically committed to the project of human freedom as "the writer" himself: "[T]he writer, a free man, addressing free men, has only one subject: human liberty" (112). Furthermore—and this is where Marxist political theory relays Sartre's existentialist ethics—in the mid-twentieth century both "writer" and "reader" are expected to be aware of the fact that the project of human freedom also implies a commitment to the cause of proletarian revolution and the universality of a future classless society. No man is entirely free—and before the age of the new feminism "man" is itself taken to be a universal—unless all men are free from repression and exploitation.

To emphasize how far we have come since the 1940s, it is worth quoting from the series of perorations with which the section "For Whom Does One Write?" ends. In the characteristically maximalist discourse of manifestos, they evoke the utopian goal to which Sartre declares himself committed as twentieth-century man and "writer": "The writer will take it [the world] as it is *[tel quel]*, in all its rawness, its sweat, its stench, and its ordinariness in order to offer it up on the foundation of one liberty to the liberties of others." Moreover, the new literature Sartre celebrates is the synthesis of a form of "negativity," which frees one from the hold of a given reality, and a "project," which sketches the outline of a future social order. Literature is a "Festival, a mirror of flame that burns everything it reflects, and an act of generosity, that is to say, free invention, a gift" (196). By the end, however, the demand that literature always have human liberty as its end turns out to be a decidedly illiberal one.

In sum, the idea of literature to which Sartre subscribes implies a belief in the establishment of "the concrete universal": it is universal because it embraces the whole of humanity and concrete because it is grounded in an understanding of history. Only then can literature itself be seen to have overcome its own alienated condition and realize itself as "in its essence, the subjectivity of a society in a state of permanent revolution. In such a society it would overcome the opposition between speech and action" (196).

What I would like to highlight here is, first, the idea of literature as related "in its essence" to revolution and, second, the belief in a future utopian moment in which speech has the immediacy of action. Both the idea and the belief can be said to have their distant source in the writings of Rousseau. The idea implies that the fundamental raison d'être of literature is political, that if it does not actively promote the emergence of a future egalitarian society it cannot be justified. The belief echoes passages from the *Discourse on the Sciences and the Arts,* the *Discourse on the Origin of Inequality,* and the *Letter to D'Alembert on Theater* in which Rousseau asserts his faith in the possibility of a restored transparency in human relations and the idea of an original "natural" speech. Not to recognize this fact in the modern era is to fail to be aware of the essential autonomy of literature in Sartre's sense and to remain mired in a specific mode of alienation as a result of which the literary work of art takes itself as a means and not as an end.

Sartre's focus on a writer as always "situated," not only socially and historically but also with respect both to a given public and a given cultural tradition, enables him to be particularly alert to literature as institution: "One cannot write without a public and without a myth—without a *certain* public that historical circumstances have produced, without a *certain* myth of literature that depends to a great extent on the demands of the public. In a word, the author is situated *[en situation],* like all men. But as with every human project, his writings contain, define, and transcend that situation . . ." (188).

It is in light of this analysis that Sartre defines his own task as that of choosing a new and broader public and of changing the myth of literature. He identifies himself with Rousseau in eighteenth-century France and with Richard Wright in the 1930s and 1940s in the United States, insofar as Sartre, too, claims to be writing for two publics simultaneously: an oppressed class and those elements in the oppressing one who are ready to acknowledge the injustice of their privileges. Whereas for Rousseau that had meant writing for the bourgeoisie, on the one hand, and the enlightened members of the *ancien régime* aristocracy, on the other, and for Wright it meant addressing America's blacks along with nonracist whites, Sartre assumes that the writer in his time and country should seek his audience in the working class as well as among those open-minded bourgeois who recognize the fact of class oppression.

In light of what precedes, the final section of the work, "Situation of the Writer in 1947," says nothing that surprises. It remains interesting because Sartre attempts to take stock there of the situation in which he and his peers found themselves in a France that from a moral and cultural, as well as a material and political, point of view seemed to have failed. What indeed is "literature" if it is incapable of dealing with the issues that led to the most destructive war in world history? And what is its responsibility for ensuring that such conflicts are avoided in the future?

Having characterized French writers as irredeemably bourgeois—"we are the most bourgeois writers in the world" (204)—in a long opening discussion Sartre goes on to evoke the two generations of writers that had preceded the one which came of age during the late thirties and early forties, namely, Sartre's own. In spite of the obvious differences between those who began their literary careers in the opening decade of the twentieth century—Gide, Proust, Claudel, Mauriac, and Giraudoux, among others—and those who started to publish in the decade or so after the First World War—Cocteau and the surrealists are named—both generations are characterized as idealist: "In a word, from pure poetry to automatic writing, the literary climate tends to the Platonic" (240).

On the other hand, those who as young men and women had experienced economic depression and social conflict, the rise of fascism, war, and occupation were the first French writers to discover "historicity." It was consequently their fate to find themselves "forced to create a literature out of historicity" (245). Unlike previous generations, who had been content to relate "being" to "possessing" in their writings, the task of postwar writers was to bring out the connection between "being" and "doing." What was called for was "a literature of production" and not "a literature of consumption"—what Sartre also calls "a literature of praxis"—that is, a literature in which the function of social and cultural negation is allied with the function of construction with the intention of "making history" (265).

It is, of course, notable that *What Is Literature?* poses the question of its title in historical terms and lays out its argument with reference to many of the climactic dates of French history, beginning with the French Revolution, in ways that remind us of both Tocqueville's and Stendhal's affective relationship to specific dates and their associated memories. In the context of dates such as 1789, 1830, 1848–51, 1870–71, however, the year 1947, to which Sartre explicitly addresses himself in his final section, has something anticlimactic about it. The fact that he chooses to highlight the year of composition is, however, significant for a number of reasons.

One of the principal themes of *What Is Literature?* is the duty of intellectuals in general and writers in particular to rise to the historical occasion. Certain dates in history are, so to speak, rendezvous with destiny that one either heroically seizes or, as a result of bad faith, fails to seize. It is at such moments that the truth of a life and the value of an oeuvre are revealed. Such, for example, was 1848–51 for Baudelaire and Flaubert, and both failed the test history set for them. And although this remains merely implicit in Sartre's work, such also were presumably the years 1939–44 for the author and his contemporaries. Sartre does not, in fact, address directly the question of how well, in light of his theoretically high standards, he and his friends lived during the years of the occupation; there is no expression of guilt nor anything else that is particularly illuminating on the role played by France, the French people, French politicians, or French intellectuals. Whether animated by guilt or not, there is no doubt that a lot of the polemical energy of *What Is Literature?* derives from the author's determination not to miss his second chance, the rendezvous with history represented by the beginning of the Cold War.

It is in light of this that one should read Sartre's statement that in the late 1940s French writers and intellectuals should keep their distance both from "the Anglo-Saxon bloc," on the one hand, and Soviet-style communism and the dogmatism of the French Communist Party, on the other. Given the complexity of the French situation, in which the natural ally of the working class, the Communist Party, was failing in its mission, it was, moreover, the duty of the writer to take up the historical role of witness of the oppressed that he had briefly performed for the bourgeoisie in 1789 and had failed to perform for the proletariat in 1850. Thus the purpose of aesthetic experience was limited to "historializing" the consciousness of the reader that man could be eventually treated as an end and not as a means: "[W]e must transform his [the reader's] formal good will into a concrete and material will to change *this world* by appropriate means so as to contribute to the future establishment of the concrete society of ends" (297).

Such considerations relative to the constitution and expansion of a public lead Sartre naturally to reflect on the new importance of what he himself calls the mass media. It was, as Annie Cohen-Solal reminds us, as a consequence of the theatrical production he put on in his prisoner-of-war camp in December 1940 that Sartre became interested in theater and in engaging the attention of an audience directly. But by the time of his 1947 manifesto on literary *engagement* he had broadened that interest to include cinema and radio as well as mass circulation journalism. If what he calls *"le public virtuel"* of the working masses is to be transformed into a real public, then the writer will have to learn to go beyond the book. Conceding that "the book is the noblest and oldest form," he goes on to affirm that there is nevertheless "a *literary* art of wireless and of film, of the editorial and of the newspaper article" (291).

As he confirms in *Words,* Sartre's enthusiasm for cinema—the twentieth-century art form born ten years before his own birth in 1895— goes back to his youth in Paris and his visits to movie theaters with his mother. His biographer has reminded us that when called upon to give an address to an assembly of teachers, students, and parents as a freshly appointed teacher of philosophy at the annual prize-giving in his lycée in Le Havre, he exhorted the students to familiarize themselves with the new art of their time, the art of film.

Along with the desire to increase the size and social composition of his public by writing for those media to which mass audiences were drawn, Sartre is clearly also concerned with the most effective forms of witness and advocacy at a time when the importance of his public role had become clear. He also seems to have realized that the effective promotion of a cause presupposes self-promotion. That is why, among other things, he rejects Julien Benda's warnings to an earlier generation that writers and thinkers should remain detached from public affairs.[17]

Such a general attitude explains Sartre's readiness to try out a wide variety of forms of expression, from the traditionally literary, such as the short story, the novel, drama, and the critical essay, to speeches, lectures, political journalism, and the interview, and in middle and old age film and the videotaped interview. It is nevertheless interesting to note that even at that stage of the development of the media in France, before the age of television, Sartre was conscious of what he calls "literary inflation." In a remarkably percipient passage that anticipates the Foucault observation I quote in my introduction, he comments on the cost as well as the need of seeking out a mass audience: "In reaching out to a wider public, an author makes a less profound impression on it; he recognizes himself less in the influence he exercises; his thoughts escape his control, become cruder and more popularized; they are received with greater indifference or even skepticism by bored or harassed souls who, because they are not addressed in their 'native language,' continue to consider literature mere entertainment. All that remains are formulas attached to a name" (270). There is, in short, in the process of spreading the word, a point beyond which the writer devalues the word and discovers that he is functioning as the propagandist of a cause.

By the time *What Is Literature?* was published, in 1947, Sartre had already established himself as a major figure even by the standards of the French literary and intellectual past. Although his denigrators were probably at least as numerous as his admirers, he was widely acknowledged to be one of the leading novelists and playwrights to appear in France since the late thirties; and he was also the country's most influential younger philosopher, the one most directly associated with a radical new movement in philosophy that threatened to undermine all traditional French beliefs, including the rationalism of the French philosophical establishment itself.

It was apparently at his Paris lycée that Sartre first came under the spell of philosophy as a result of reading Henri Bergson's accounts of human psychic experience, but it was not until his years at the Ecole Normale Supérieure that he decided to make his primary commitment to philosophy, in large part thanks to Descartes's example; it was the "revolutionary thought of that "explosive thinker" which made the young *normalien* appreciate the kind of potent critical weapon philosophy might be.[18]

The significance of such an attitude toward philosophy for his mature thought was to become increasingly clear in subsequent decades. In 1960 he formulated his position in *Search for a Method,* a short work that has the character of a manifesto and that serves as a preface to the magnum opus of his middleage, *The Critique of Dialectical Reason.* If I refer to *Search for a Method* here it is because it illustrates the way in which "the writer" typically regards his work as a single project encompassing different fields as well as different media and different genres. After a gap of a dozen or so years—and in the very different historical context of post-1956, following the Soviet suppression of the Hungarian democratic movement—*Search for a Method* takes up with reference to philosophy many of the issues raised in *What is Literature?* relative to aesthetics.

An alternative title might well, in fact, have been *What Is Philosophy?* inasmuch as the work outlines what in Sartre's view philosophy in reality is, although it does so on this occasion in the context of exploring the limitations of Marxist theory and the need to complement that theory with the critical and concrete investigations Sartre associates with existentialism. Thus, in a short preface to *Search for a Method,* he affirms unequivocally that "I consider Marxism the one philosophy of our time which we cannot go beyond," only to go on to say, somewhat more equivocally, that "I hold the ideology of existence and its 'comprehensive' method to be an enclave inside Marxism, which simultaneously engenders it and rejects it."[19]

That Sartre regarded himself as a *philosophe de combat* equally as much as an *écrivain de combat* is made clear in an opening chapter that asserts, with characteristic panache, "In our view *Philosophy* does not exist"—an assertion he immediately modifies by describing it as "the particular way in which the 'rising' class becomes conscious of itself" (3–4). Philosophy is, in short, redefined downward as an ideology or mode of class self-awareness and therefore to be regarded as essentially "practical," in the sense of being derived from and related to praxis; its "method is a social and political weapon." Finally, the historical task of philosophy in our time is to impreg-

nate the consciousness of the masses so as to become "a collective instrument of emancipation" (5–6). In such and similar statements one recognizes
a continuity with the tradition of the philosopher as antiphilosopher that in
the modern world goes back to Rousseau, although in Sartre's case it is, of
course, mediated by Marx's materialist philosophy of praxis.

At the center of Sartre's argument in *Search for a Method* is the question he himself puts: "Why, then, are we not simply Marxists?" His answer to that question constitutes the core of the work, and it hinges on
the assertion of the abstract, a priori character of classical Marxism and
its failure to take account of the experience of "real men" in the specifity
of their lives and their overlapping relations. In the context of a discussion
of Paul Valéry, he sums up the problem with the comment that "Marxism
lacks any hierarchy of mediations which would permit it to grasp the process which produces the person and his product inside a class and within
a given society at a given historical moment" (56).[20] It is as a response
to that lack that he will go on to elaborate his own theory of "the
progressive-regressive method," which is also his theory of biography and
is something I will return to in connection with his autobiography.

In spite of Sartre's recognition of the indispensable power of Marxist
theory to totalize universal history, he is equally adamant in insisting that
without existentialism it risks degenerating into a crude economic determinism which is incapable of accounting for the variety of human behavior and the human potential for self-determined purposive action. Even
after accepting as his own the lessons of the dialectical philosophy of history, Sartre is still at pains to assert the existence of a space of freedom.
At the heart of the *Search for a Method* there remains a celebration of the
role of human agency in historical development.

The method he is searching for—what he calls his "heuristic"
method—is, in fact, that of "dialectical totalization." And what he means
by that phrase is made clear in a passionate peroration that effectively
summarizes the task of the committed philosopher:

> The object of existentialism—due to the default of the Marxists—
> is the particular man in the social field, in his class, in an environ-
> ment of collective objects and of particular men. It is the individual,
> alienated, reified, mystified, as he had been made to be by the divi-
> sion of labor and by exploitation, but struggling against alienation
> with the help of distorting instruments and, despite everything, pa-
> tiently gaining ground. The dialectical totalization must include
> acts, passions, work, and need as well as economic categories; it
> must at once place the agent or the event back into the historical
> setting, define him in relation to the orientation of becoming, and
> determine exactly the meaning of the present as such. (133)

The significance of the passage from my point of view is twofold. First,
it outlines a method that in opposition to Marxism asserts the relative

freedom of the human subject to transcend the local historical conditions in which he happens to be located: man is a self-surpassing animal, potentially capable of transcendence even under the most adverse conditions. Second, against Engels and what he refers to as "lazy Marxism," the passage implicitly raises the question of the importance of reducing the opaqueness of social reality and the role attributed to chance in human affairs. American "micro-sociology" and psychoanalysis are two of the major bodies of theory he advocates as valuable supplements in exploring mediations between the way individual lives are actually lived and the ultimate determinants, which are their relation to the means of production.

Sartre's own mature philosophy of praxis is centered on the concept of "the project," that is to say, in a belief in humanity's orientation toward the future or in its capacity for self-surpassing whose point of departure is existing conditions. "The project" is, so to speak, the form taken by human creativity at all levels; it is a process of mediation between a present that is to be negated and a future that is to be positively embraced—although Sartre's understanding of the dialectic implies that once a subjective project has been objectified it will itself constitute a further mode of alienation to be surpassed in its turn. In brief, Sartre's "philosopher" is at one with "the writer" to the extent that in their writings in a variety of modes they are both engaged in the task of overcoming "alienation" and "reification" with a view to universal human emancipation. The end of philosophy, like that of literature, is not in itself but in its impact on a world that must be changed.

If *Search for a Method* is valuable in defining with some precision Sartre's view of philosophy and the function of the philosopher in our time, it is also helpful in understanding his theory of biography, including the kind of biography in which an author chooses himself as subject. Between the books on Baudelaire, Mallarmé, and Genêt, on the one hand, and Flaubert, on the other, Sartre produced *Words*, which was written mostly in the years 1953–54, although it was not published until 1964.

Apart from his numerous works in the genre, some idea of the importance of biography in Sartre's *oeuvre* can be gathered from the frequency and centrality of his references to biographical investigations in *Search for a Method*. Moreover, it is important to realize that his biographical writings were in no sense peripheral, not something he engaged in as a relaxation from the demanding work of philosophy, of political theory, or of the writing of novels and plays. It is, in fact, in biography that the power of existentialist theory to restore a lost concreteness to Marxism is made manifest; biographical studies illustrate Sartre's mature philosophical method in action.[21]

It is in the context of refuting Engels' way of reducing all human particularity beyond the economically determined to the effect of chance that Sartre indicates how high the stakes are for him. He calls Engels wrong in declaring, with reference to the historical figure of Napoleon, that if "such a man, and precisely this man, arises at a determined period and in a given country," it "is naturally pure chance" (*Search*, 56). The "practical" task Sartre sets himself, the task of his so-called progressive-regressive method, is to prove that chance has nothing do with it. By means of a series of cross-references between a given subject's present and his past and between objective conditions and subjective reaction, Sartre seeks to demonstrate how such a subject negotiates—sometimes in good faith but more often in bad—the web of circumstances into which he is inserted from the moment of his birth: "Existentialism refuses to abandon the real life to the unthinkable chances of birth. . . . It intends, without being unfaithful to Marxist principles, to find mediations which allow the individual concrete—the particular life, the real and dated conflict, the person—to emerge from the background of the *general* contradiction of productive forces and relations of production" (57).

Sartre then goes on to cite briefly the case history of Flaubert in order to conclude that it is only through the analysis of that novelist's early life and familial dynamics, along with his class belonging, that one can understand the beliefs, the practices, and even the literary work of his maturity: "[E]verything," Sartre emphatically concludes, "took place in *childhood*" (59–60). Then, in two remarkable sentences that go to the heart of his own project in *Words*, he comments that the trouble with the Marxists is that "[t]hey have forgotten their own childhoods. As we read them, everything seems to happen as if men experienced their alienation and their reification *first in their own work*, whereas in actuality each one lives it *first*, as a child, *in one's parents's work*" (62).

On the evidence of Rousseau's *Confessions*, the difference between Rousseau and Sartre in this respect is that whereas both insist on the importance of childhood, the former, like the English romantics, tends to perceive it as a period of innocence that predates alienation, the latter insists, on the other hand, that alienation is a condition of sociality into which up to this point at least the human child is born. *Words* is thus in an important sense Sartre's personal testimony to the way in which in his case, too, "everything took place in childhood"—with the important proviso that it is also Sartre's conviction that childhood is a mystified condition that is to be surpassed as soon as possible. But I will return to that topic later. In the meantime, it is important to realize that *Words* is significant in the context of this book in a number of other ways as well.

In his published works, from *Imagination* in 1936 to the appearance of *Words* in 1964, Sartre maintained a rough balance in his writings between the more purely literary—short stories, novels, plays, literary criticism—and philosophical, political, or general theoretical works. But with the publication of the account of his childhood and adolescence, he also announced his break with that past. On one level, *Words* was to be a farewell to literature whose central target was the French literary tradition itself, as well as the institutions and value systems that supported it. Along with *What is Literature?* it is Sartre's most extended piece of writing on the writer as man of letters and is therefore of special significance here.

In this connection it is worth also recalling that Sartre published no short stories after his brilliant first collection, *The Wall*, of 1939. The third volume of the *Roads to Freedom* trilogy, *Troubled Sleep*, was his last novel and appeared in 1949. His last play, *The Condemned of Altona*, was written at the end of the 1950s. This means that he stopped writing fiction altogether by his mid-forties and drama by his mid-fifties, and that for the final twenty-odd years of his life he effectively ceased to be a writer, in the sense of literary artist, altogether. On the other hand, he remained "a writer" in spite of his blindness and other infirmities virtually down to the moment of his death. It is symptomatic in retrospect that what is now seen as his major work of critical philosophy, *The Critique of Dialectical Reason*, should have appeared immediately following his last work of literature.

Given that *Words* was more or less completed in the early fifties, one can say that from 1959 at the latest he returned to his original commitment to philosophy, for from then on he wrote solely as a critical philosopher, political theorist, polemicist, and propagandist. Although it may seem paradoxical that, over a period of some fifteen years, he also devoted himself to the study of one of the great canonical figures of mid-nineteenth-century French literature, namely Flaubert, who had lived the kind of ivory-tower artist's existence that Sartre claimed to despise, the reasons for this are already laid out in *Search for a Method;* and they are less literary than critical and philosophical.

With *Words* Sartre may be have said to have reached in his late forties the point where Rousseau began his career as "writer" in the *Discourse on the Sciences and the Arts:* a major function of Sartre's autobiography is to illuminate the complicity of literature as traditionally conceived in the perpetuation of an exploitative cultural hegemony and social inequality. *What is Literature?* had already offered a demystifying historical survey of the French literary past and its writers, but with *Words* Sartre also implicates himself in the promotion of the traditional French myth of literature.

The work may be said to be "confessional," in the Augustinian as well as the Rousseauist sense, to the extent that it is written from a point of view subsequent to a conversion. Its author is at pains to express his contrition for the sins of his childhood and adolescence, sins that in this case are not of the body but of the mind; in the eyes of the censorious autobiographer, young Poulou was guilty above all of a characteristic form of bourgeois "bad faith." Although, unlike Rousseau, he recounts no specific incidents that at the time provoked a sense of shame—no equivalent to Rousseau's scene of exhibitionism or tale of the stolen ribbon—the autobiographer throughout does look back in contrition. At the moment of the writing the guilt he seems to live with is that of having once been a pseudo-child called Poulou. Consequently, here, too, the classic French intellectual's *j'accuse* is accompanied by the *je me confesse* that I have identified as one of the major identifying signs of "the writer."

Even more than most autobiographies by writers, Sartre's *Words* focuses on literature and the education that prepared its author for his vocation as writer. Unlike the majority of such autobiographies, however, the education in question is interpreted as an alienation and a mispreparation. That the aspects of his life evoked relate largely to the childhood of a writer is confirmed by the title itself, as well as the titles of the two parts it is divided into, "Reading" and "Writing." The implication is that Poulou's formative years were dominated by mere words—as the choice in the French of the word "mots" rather than "paroles" suggests—that is, written words as opposed to the spoken ones that imply direct communication and social exchange.

Further, the title also implies an opposition between "words" and "acts," which in the Western tradition is as old as the Bible but which in Sartre's lexicon might be better formulated as "words" and "praxis."

Words, then, may be described as a work of contestation and demystification in a vein that since the early twentieth century at least we have come to recognize as characteristic of French literary intellectuals. Moreover, it takes the form of a satirical anti-autobiography that knowingly distances itself from the tradition of autobiography initiated by Rousseau, although there is a similar will to bear public witness to private behavior in the interest of more truthful communication among people.

There are three major targets of the critical work of demystification. The first two are obvious, the third somewhat less so. The first target is the institution of the bourgeois family and bourgeois childhood; the second, the institution of literature and the cult of the literary life; the third has to do with the genre of autobiography itself, which is also the vehicle of Sartre's retrospective critique.

To take up the last target first, there are, it turns out, at least two paradoxes in Sartre's relationship to the genre. To begin with, it is by now a commonplace that to write an autobiography is traditionally "to tell the story" of a life, with all that that implies relative to literary fabrication. Moreover, as the narrator of *Nausea* had made clear a quarter of a century earlier, Sartre belonged to the age of suspicion that culminated in the *nouveau roman* and was baptized as such by Natalie Sarraute, an age which, among other things, distrusted the process of narration itself. From the viewpoint of Sartre's prewar existentialist novel, the trouble with traditional narrative was that it conferred retrospective order and the appearance of a destiny on the multiple contingencies of day-to-day living. Narratives imply continuities after the fact, logical-temporal chains of events, a kind of organic unfolding in chronological time, even a destiny, whereas Sartre, as he notes toward the end of *Words*, celebrates instead rupture and discontinuity of a kind that achieved its fullest expression in the idea of permanent revolution.

The second paradox has to do with the fact that autobiography is a form of stocktaking that typically embodies elements of narcissism as well as nostalgia for a lost world and those who people it, including a more innocent former self. Yet unlike Rousseau, Sartre proclaims himself indifferent to the past and, by implication at least, committed to the future. The self he reanimates is just as unlovable as almost all of those who nurtured and educated him. And he claims to look back with no special tenderness on the great majority of the intimate spaces from which, as an infant, he first looked out and explored the flavors and contours, sights and sounds of the material world. He apparently regards nostalgia in particular as a singularly dishonest emotion; consequently one finds no equivalent of Colette's Saint Sauveur, Proust's Combray or even Roland Barthes's Bayonne in Sartre's schematic references to the provincial milieux of either his father's Dordogne or his mother's Alsace. If Sartre is atypical in the French tradition, it is because he is a quintessentially urban writer even by the standards of what is usually taken to be a highly urban literary tradition; he is someone whose senses and imagination never seem to have been exercised by the natural or the provincial world. He thus writes about his past simply in order to disassociate himself from it and denounce it, together with the autobiographical genre that traditionally sustained its myths.

Words is thus characterized by an apparent distaste for most of the features that have constituted the typical appeal of autobiography since Rousseau, for author and reader alike. One of the consequences of Sartre's stance is that there are substantial omissions, strict limits in time—the work only covers its subject from infancy into early adolescence—and a programmatic determination by its mature narrator to analyze and judge negatively almost every thought and act of his young subject. The chief pleasure the narrator seems to take in representing his past is, in fact, in finding combinations of words precise enough or wittily sardonic enough to show up his own boyhood monstrousness or the monstrousness of those who made him. Sartre never seems happier than in those flashes of stylish writing that encapsulate the insights of a fierce and politicized moralist in rebellion against the inheritance of a culture, a family, and a class.

If, among other things, *Words* presents itself as a farewell to literature, or at the very least a certain idea of literature, therefore, it is disingenuous, for it turns out to be in contradiction with itself. From its publication, the work has been generally regarded as a self-consciously literary tour de force that had the ironic effect of Sartre's being awarded the Nobel Prize, which, of course, he declined to accept.

In the light of all this, it comes as no surprise that, along with the genre of autobiography, a second major target of the writer's backward gaze is the bourgeois family and childhood itself. One would not have expected a

French left-wing intellectual writing in the early fifties to sound a celebratory note on that subject. From Stendhal down through Baudelaire and on to Gide, there is no dearth of major French writers for whom the bourgeois family was the target of their irony and their anger. Ménalque's affirmation in Gide's *Immoralist*, "Families, I hate you," is merely the most memorable formulation of the attitude. But by Sartre's time the hostility of literary and artistic circles to the family had been reinforced by the identification of it as the primary institution of social reproduction in class society. This is not, of course, surprising when one recalls that, from the late nineteenth century down through the Vichy regime and beyond, the family as social and ideological unit had also been enlisted in the nationalist cause: the political right had made common cause with the Church in affirming that strong family structures and rapid repopulation were a patriotic duty in the campaign for national renewal. In any case, *Words* starts and ends with the affirmation of the culpability of the French bourgeois family and the myth of childhood it promotes.

In his brief references to the need for detailed biographical studies in *Search for a Method*, Sartre makes it clear that as far as he is concerned alienation begins at home, long before an individual encounters a workplace. Alienation is experienced first of all in the family; to an existentialist Marxist that means through the father's work as well as through the family's class position.[22] It is in light of this that one should understand the narrator's decision to begin *Words* with an evocation of the family of his maternal grandfather, Charles Schweitzer, the man who occupied the place in Poulou's life of the father who had died when the boy was only fifteen months old.

The book's opening lines recall nothing so much as the evocation, by the novelist Sartre knew better than any other, of the early life of another Charles, Charles Bovary, both in their satirical tone and in their stylistic polish: "In Alsace in the 1850s a schoolteacher heavily burdened with children agreed to become a grocer. This defrocked pedagogue sought compensation: since he was obliged to give up forming minds, one of his sons would form souls. There would be a pastor in the family and it would be Charles. Charles fled in haste, preferring to try his luck with a horsewoman. His portrait was turned to face the wall and henceforth no one was to speak his name."[23] The literary heritage on which Sartre seems self-consciously to have drawn is clear: the satirical distance established in narrating the earlier lives of Sartre's grandparents and progenitors belongs to what in his typology of "modes" in *The Anatomy of Criticism* Northrop Frye once called "the low mimetic mode," that is, the mode of less than average human life and of the grotesque.

Although Sartre's target, along with childhood, is the institution of bourgeois marriage in general, he gives particular emphasis to paternity and to the form of paternity that looked to him like a grotesque enlargement of it, grandpaternity. If maternity alone is represented in a somewhat more flattering light, it is apparently because his relationship with his mother was in many respects an atypical one, at least until her second marriage when he was eleven years old. Since up to that point she was forced by her first husband's death to live under her parents' roof with her son, she is perceived as in many ways more as an elder sister than a mother.

In any case, with his "I hate my childhood" (*Words*, 137), Sartre may be said to have taken up over fifty years later where Gide had left off. After Freud it was perhaps no longer necessary to distance oneself from the romantics' view of childhood as a kind of paradise lost of the heart and senses and to insist on its non-innocence, on the fact that human beings are appetitive and sexed subjects from birth; but Sartre contributes in addition the idea of the child as monster, that is, as fundamentally unnatural and alienated. Indeed, given that the autobiography represents Poulou as in many respects a young, bourgeois prig, Sartre might well have adapted the title from one of his memorable early stories of a fascist youth, "Childhood of a Leader," and called *Words* "Childhood of a Man of Letters."

Childhood is for Sartre the primary experience of alienation because one is not born a child but is socially constructed to become one. Moreover, insofar as you learn virtually from the beginning to see yourself as others see you, you may be said to serve an apprenticeship in what in *Being and Nothingness* Sartre called the sphere of the *en soi*. The adult's look objectifies the child, and the child struggles to conform his behavior to that objectification, and thereby alienates himself from his own subjectivity. He acts out a series of prescribed behaviors that have only the appearance of spontaneity. Thus a child typically learns to play the role chosen for him in the fantasmatic drama of those who brought him into the world and raise him. Family life is "family theater" (75).

In short, the story Sartre tells of his childhood is a story of "bad faith" at a time when he had not yet developed the critical distance to take responsibility for what he was: "The truth of my being, my character, and my name were in the hands of grownups. I had learned to see myself with their eyes. I was a child, one of those monsters they make with their dissatisfactions" (66).

Thus childhood in *Words* is theorized in the straightforward existentialist terms that had first been made explicit roughly two decades earlier in *Being and Nothingness*. To escape from the alienating objectifications of the other's look and to discover one's destiny as a free and responsible subject or *pour-soi* is part of the complex and difficult work of maturation. As a result, at best autobiography bears witness to the effort of exorcism necessary for the unlearning of a learned role and the surpassing of one's childhood. It is also central to the purpose of *Words* to show that what is true of the category of "child" is also true of the categories of "mother" and "father," and "grandparents" within the family, and of "man of letters" in the world beyond. By the time of *The Critique of Dialectical Reason* Sartre will use the concept of "extero-conditioning" to explain in a more general way how a whole set of ideological representations are interiorized, including that of one's own place in the scheme of things.

As noted earlier, an important theme of *Search for a Method* is the need to supplement Marxism with bodies of theory that illuminate the mediations which condition individual conduct within the broad framework of class society. As far as childhood is concerned, Sartre refers to psychoanalysis as an indispensable tool. It has to said, however, that once he has explained an important dimension of his own psychic disposition on the basis of the Oedipus complex, he does not find much use for it and virtually ignores what might be called the founding concept of psychoanalysis, the unconscious. In fact, Sartre concludes rather simplistically that because he never experienced directly the rivalry of a father for the possession of his mother, he was spared direct Oedipal conflict altogether and emerged happily free of a superego. Eliding entirely the role played by his grandfather in this respect, he draws the conclusion that his special relationship to the world, what he calls "his incredible lightness" (13), is the result of never having suffered from the presence of a father.

The first problem with such a position is that from the point of view of psychoanalysis, the whole process of socialization involves submission to the paternal Law as such and the formation of an unconscious that necessarily includes a superego. The second and more serious problem is that it enables Sartre to affirm his own strange innocence because he had never had to work through the Oedipus complex. If there is any explicit self-praise in *Words*, it is to be found in this claim that because he was "nobody's son," he was in the happy possession of a disposition that never had to learn to obey and consequently to command: "I am not a leader, and I don't aspire to become one. Commanding and obeying are one and the same thing. The most authoritarian of men commands in the name of another, a sacred parasite, namely, his father; he passes on the abstract acts of violence he first underwent" (13).[24] In short, Sartre interprets the happy accident of his father's early death as largely the reason for the exemplarity of his own life.

Apparent fatherlessness is clearly intended to explain his lifelong anti-authoritarianism and his taste for anarchism, yet it is also an example of a blindness that is itself a form of "bad faith," given the very real power he exercised in French political and cultural life, and in many ways throughout the world, in the middle decades of the twentieth century. It is the abuse of that power by Sartre and other French intellectuals that is the main theme of Tony Judt's *Past Imperfect*. It may well be true that Sartre largely succeeded in living outside the hierarchies of political and social life, but the hollowness of his claim to the innocence of powerlessness is made very clear in light of the concept of "symbolic power" deployed by

Bourdieu in a work like *Distinction*. Sartre was, after all, a *normalien*, a lycée professor of philosophy at a time when that was a prestigious position, and eventually the most visible writer/intellectual of his generation in a country where, if anywhere, the power of the intellectual was institutionalized. It is no accident that by the end of his career, as De Gaulle among others recognized, he was untouchable by the French state.

As for the paternal role, Sartre's judgment on it is characteristically dogmatic, for all its air of objectivity: "There is no such thing as a good father; that's the rule. But one shouldn't blame men for this; it is the paternal relation that is rotten" (11). The problem, as Jacques Lacan was explaining in his *Seminars* at about the same time, was structural; paternity is the site of a necessary negation that gives rise to the formation of the unconscious—although just how, in light of this, Sartre explains his continuing existentialist faith in a subject's capacity for self-transcendence through thought and action is never explained.[25]

By midlife, then, Sartre is happy to identify in his youthful self the origin of his sense that he was "the master of no one and nothing belonged to him" (70). The fact that he lived without a father in his maternal grandparents' rented apartment also meant that he was without the self-evident assurance of the property owner, to whom "the things of this world reflect what he is. Those things revealed to me instead what I was not: *I had no* consistency or permanence. *I was not* the future guardian of the paternal assets; *I was not* necessary for the production of steel. In a word, I had no soul" (71). In other words, the young Sartre saw himself as relatively freer than most to become a literary intellectual because he was outside the male generational chain of command. The discovery of essential contingency was part of his birthright, an essential contingency that he was aware of when very young but which he managed to hide from himself during his years of impostorship.[26] Sartre represents his intermittent awareness of his contingency in the recurring image of himself as "a traveler without a ticket."

His critical analysis of the bourgeois family, of childhood, and of his own sense of having emerged relatively unscathed from infancy is also connected to the third principal target of *Words*, the institution of literature and the mythic figure of man of letters. If, from the point of view of the critical autobiographer, the task of the son and heir is to surpass his childhood and to submit the paternal inheritance to a critical analysis, this is even truer for a young writer relative to the literary tradition in which he is historically situated. In this respect, Sartre concludes that young Poulou was not so free; Charles Schweitzer saw to that.

The specific argument of *Words* on this topic is that the heir to a long and powerful literary tradition is necessarily engaged in a critical debate not so much with the literature of the past as with its creators. That is, as Sartre's literary biographies as well as his autobiography make clear, it is a debate to be conducted ad hominem.

The impostorship and alienation he associates with childhood, and with the other roles assumed by the members of a family, are to be found with equal obviousness in the transmitted image of the man of letters: like the child, he, too, is "a monster," an unnatural and alienated creature who is unaware of his own unnaturalness and his own alienation. The man of letters is, in fact, the product of a collective "grand illusion" that Poulou interiorized both through the influence of his grandfather and through the elevated site from which he looked down on the world from his grandparents' apartment in the Latin Quarter: "Mine was a sixth-floor apartment in Paris with a view across the rooftops." It was there that he breathed "the rarefied air of belles lettres. The Universe appeared in layers at my feet and everything there humbly solicited a name; to give it one was both to create it and to take possession of it. Without that grand illusion I would never have been a writer" (47).

It was not only the view from on high that determined the young Sartre's future choice of vocation, although that view functions as a kind of metaphor of the Poet's task as conceived by the French romantic poets, including especially Victor Hugo himself. The choice of vocation derived much more concretely from the role played in Sartre's life by his grandfather. If, as he affirms in *Search for a Method,* a child's primary alienation occurs through the work of the father, then Poulou's was brought about by the petit bourgeois teacher of German language and literature who stood in the place of his father, the only person who worked outside the home in the four-person family that shared the apartment on the rue Le Goff, grandfather Schweitzer. The cult of literature and of its creators that was at the origin of Sartre's choice of career was founded on a culturally transmitted myth on which Poulou's grandfather depended for a living.

From the point of view of Bourdieu's conception of the literary field, the idea of "the man of letters" was one of those preexisting positions that an aspirant producer of literary works might covet, come to regard as a vocation, or see as "an impossible destination, an unacceptable destiny or one that is acceptable as a temporary refuge or a secondary accessory position" ("Field of Cultural Production," 64). Having first coveted the position, Sartre then went on to consider it "a grand illusion" in a literal sense, since, as he will go on to make very clear, like the category "child" that of "man of letters" has a great deal to do with looking and being looked at. It is in response to the images circulating in the milieu in which one grows up that one constitutes one's self-image. And nowhere, perhaps, is Sartre more interesting in *Words* than in the implications of his remarks on photography's role in imagemaking in the late nineteenth and early twentieth century.

The "grand illusion" of the man of letters in the modern world depends a great deal on the invention of photography. But, in the first place, what Sartre has to say also concerns the connection between photography and middle-class family life, on the one hand, and between photography, social reproduction, and the transmission of cultural values, on the other. In all cases there is an implied relationship between the alienating look of the Other, in general, and the camera, which is a particularly potent version of that look: the camera fixes and objectifies a subject once and for all in a mechanically frozen look. If, as Sartre claims in *Search for a Method,* a literary work of art is itself "the alienated objectification of self" (147), this is doubly the case when one is the object of someone else's art, as in portraiture, including photographic portraiture.

Through the references to the place of photographs in his own family, Sartre implicitly reminds us of how, from the mid-nineteenth century on, photographic imagery increasingly pervaded social life at all levels. Photography disseminated images of great men and women, kings, queens, and emperors, presidents and prime ministers, as well as celebrities from the world of sport, culture, art, literature, theater, music and, of course, eventually cinema itself. Thus the entry of such images into middle-class homes and the effect they had there as icons and ideal egos is part of the story Sartre has to tell about his own childhood and his early assumption of a vocation.

Apart from everything else, photography became crucial to celebration and self-celebration from the national and international to that most local of levels that is the family. By the closing decades of the nineteenth century middle-class families of relatively modest means could afford to cover walls, mantlepieces, bureaus and the pages of family albums with edifying portraits or scenes from domestic life—then, as now, unflattering images tended, of course, to be destroyed.

If one attempts to draw out some of the implications of Sartre's observations, it is clear that from the point of view of existentialism the camera itself is the look of the Other that objectifies and alienates in the most radical of ways. The invention of the camera reinforced the habit of seeing oneself as the alienated other others see; that is, in the domestic sphere one becomes the unnatural child, mother, father, grandparent, hero or heroine, sage or mascot of hearth and home.

A final effect of photographic portraiture in the middle-class family was to change the character of memory in ways that Sartre again implicitly deplored. Lives are made even more mythic because less fleeting or, to use a crucial Sartrean concept, less contingent. With photography, albums and group portraits of weddings, births, and birthdays increased the sense of family unity, continuity, and even destiny over time. Parents and grandparents, children and grandchildren could be seen to join hands across the generations. And the hierarchy of relationships, of dependence and independence, was typically reflected in the compositional structures centered on a patriarch and/or matriarch.

As far as the man of letters is concerned, the connection Sartre makes between the figure of his grandfather and photography is addressed in a wickedly suggestive passage:

> In truth, he [Charles Schweitzer] went too far in the direction of the
> sublime; he was a nineteenth-century man who, like many others,
> including Victor Hugo, mistook himself for Victor Hugo. That
> handsome man with his flowing beard, who was always to be
> found between two theatrical poses, like an alcoholic between two
> drinks, was, in my opinion, the victim of two recently invented
> techniques, namely, the art of photography and the art of being a
> grandfather. He had the good fortune and the bad to be photogenic
> and his photographs filled the house. (*Words*, 15)

In other words, Charles Schweitzer, like Victor Hugo before him, was the
incarnation of inauthenticity who lived his life as a series of *tableaux vi-
vants*. He had learned to see himself as an image on the basis of another's
image in a kind of infinite recession of images. Charles Schweitzer was
always about to freeze into a fresh pose for the benefit of some uncandid
camera. Finally, the metaphor of the alcoholic confirms how addictive the
self-representation inspired by photographic portraiture is.

The force of Sartre's insight relative to the two "new arts" of photography and grandpaternity concerns more than his grandfather, then, and the
peculiar monstrousness, after Victor Hugo, of that particular patriarchal
role. Charles Schweitzer reproduced in his own life the images of father,
grandfather, patriot, republican, and pedagogue that he found in the representations and self-representations of a great writer. In the matter of "inauthenticity," nineteenth-century France's great national popular poet had
a lot to answer for.

In connecting Victor Hugo with his quintessentially Third Republic,
anticlerical, teacher grandfather, Sartre was drawing attention to the influence of a poet and author who remained accessible to a lay public and
morally uplifting down through the age of the *poètes maudits* and early
hermeticism. Sartre is also reminding his readers that the reason Hugo
became a household deity was because the artist, visionary, and keeper of
the republican faith were combined in his old age with the patriarchal
guardian of a national moral life centered on the family. By the end of
the nineteenth century, dozens of different representations of the grizzled
patriarch in a variety of media had the effect of confirming that unstable
romantic genius could be recuperated and domesticated. Along with the
photographic images that preceded them in certain editions, verses like
those collected in Victor Hugo's *On the Art of Being a Grandfather* (1877)
spoke to the dignity and higher purposefulness of ordinary middle-class
family life.

In light of the popular cult of Victor Hugo in the Third Republic, it is
difficult to avoid the conclusion that his reassuring grandpaternal image
was not without influence on the choice of another peculiarly photogenic
patriarch at a moment of national demoralization in 1940, namely, Mar-

shall Pétain. And although his physique left a lot to be desired, Charles De Gaulle, too, had the necessary look of Hugolian greatness and authority in a France on the verge of civil war in 1958.

In the opening decades of the twentieth century, in any case, in that sixth-floor apartment just off the Boulevard Saint Michel on the rue Le Goff, literature was taken to be a matter for great universal geniuses who bore witness, in their lives as much as in their works, to the traditional values of civilization, progress, and the moral life, to family, republic, and nation. There was, it seemed, no higher mandate than that of the creator of works of literature and no more certain way of assuring one's own fame and immortality. It is therefore no accident that one of the children's books that the mature Sartre looks back on with particular antipathy was entitled *The Lives of Famous Men*. Nowhere more than in the destinies recorded there does the middle-aged Sartre identify the "bad faith" that he saw as endemic to a hegemonic bourgeois culture that assumed its own universality.

In short, after Gide and the surrealists, among others, Sartre lays a substantial portion of the blame for a traditionalist idea of the writer in modern French cultural life on the endlessly reproduced image of Victor Hugo. Yet, as I shall argue later, Sartre himself was not as immune from the influence of such an image as the dymystifying affirmations of *Words* would have us believe. He did, after all, choose to attack the myth of the great writer in a work of autobiography that put a decade of his own life on display. He also contributed massively in his own time to the perpetuation of a two-hundred-year-old counter-myth, that of "the writer." The ugly duckling that he took himself to be in his early years turned out to be almost as photogenic in his maturity as his grandfather, once the art of photography had done its work. He became in his own way just as much "a victim" of it as his grandfather. In any case, the ubiquity of Sartre's image at a certain historical moment might be said to have possessed a power to distort and alienate comparable to that of the monstrous Hugo himself. Certain photographs and films from his late-middle and old age suggest that Sartre, too, came to take himself for Jean-Paul Sartre.

As noted above, it is no accident that Sartre abandoned the idea of writing a sequel to *Words* but consented instead to continue the narrative of his life and career in the form of filmed and other interviews, even before his blindness made it impossible for him to achieve the kind of precision and stylistic polish he associated with the practice of writing itself.[27] In spite of the regret he obviously felt at not being able to continue what had been a daily habit for the greater part of his life, it was quite consistent with his earlier position that he was more than willing to pursue his sociopolitical commitments by reaching out through recorded interviews to audiences who would not have sought out his written works. In the years after 1968, in particular, "communication" became a crucial Sartrean buzzword and the *Sartre* film itself, both in its popular documentary form and in the subjects it addresses is an expression of his will to "communicate."

On the other hand, his sense of the relative futility of the career of the traditional "man of letters" is suggested by his description of the situation of the French writer prior to the Second World War compared with that in the new mass-media age of the seventies. According to Sartre, given that an author considered himself successful before the war if he reached an audience of five to ten thousand people, his work was necessarily "elitist" in character. A decade or so later this was no longer the case: "Literature underwent an enormous transformation after 1945 because of the transformation of the means of communication due to the war." Henceforth, one could think in terms of "a total public"; and access to this "total public" was through the mass media (*Sartre*, 79). Along with journalism, radio and film were initially the means of communication adopted by all those who took seriously their social responsibilities as intellectuals and "writers." [28]

Thus both the film *Sartre* and the interview "Self-Portrait at Seventy" are logical extensions of the determination that goes back to his earliest plays and *What Is Literature?* to reach as wide an audience as possible. As far as the institution of literature and the opposition "writer"/man of letters is concerned, there is a clear continuity between the film, in particular, and *Words*. *Sartre* takes up and repeats certain crucial themes of the (anti)literary autobiography, including notably the story of how Sartre was spontaneously cured in the early fifties of the "neurosis" of literature that had afflicted him since childhood—a "neurosis" that derived from an inherited faith in the idea of the "mission" of the writer (in the generic sense), a belief that he personally was "ordained" to write, and a desire for the fame and immortality *(les immortels)* associated with the successful accomplishment of the mission. To be a writer in a postreligious age had, paradoxically and inadmissably, once seemed to the young Sartre a way of feeling "recruited by God" (*Sartre*, 27).

Going beyond *Words*, however, *Sartre* elaborates on its subject's subsequent discovery of forms of social communication that were also the beginnings of his reflections on the limits of "literature" and the necessity of demystifying it. He repeats here the fact that the crucial experience was that of the German prisoner-of-war camp. It was in the camp, he claims, that he discovered the unsuspected pleasure of emerging from the elite status in which he had always previously found himself in order to communicate with a wide variety of individual men on a daily basis: "There was a seamless communication *(une communication sans trou)*, day and night; we saw each other, we spoke to each other directly and between equals. The toilets were communal, you see. And when you use them with a lot of other people, your elite status disappears."

The fact that he found evacuation to be a great leveler fits into a generalized belief in the salutary role of the body as a whole in the promotion of equality and transparency between human beings. Throughout the work of Sartre's maturity the origins of sociality are perceived as less symbolic— as a structuralist anthropologist such as Levi-Strauss might have argued— than corporeal. Nowhere is this more apparent than in the body's importance for Sartre in any proper act of communication: life in the prison camp is described as "perpetually body to body"; that is to say, "you were perpetually communicating" (*Sartre,* 67).

It is nevertheless a fact that in spite of the determination expressed, for example, in "Self-Portrait at Seventy" that "transparency should always replace secrecy" (141), he retains the right not to give an account of his intimate relations with women or even of the significance of sex in his own life. Like Rousseau before him, he is more than willing to recount the various infirmities that afflicted his own aging body, and even to reflect on the significance for him of his ugliness;[29] unlike Rousseau, he reserves the right to remain silent on his experience of love and on how he took his sexual pleasure: "I haven't, for example, described the sexual and erotic relationships of my life. Moreover, I see no reason for doing so except in a different society in which everyone would put his cards on the table" ("Self-Portrait," 146).

In any case, it was as a result of wartime experiences, in and after the prison camp, of a fundamental human solidarity across class lines and in opposition to a common enemy that Sartre went on to construct models of a social ideal of full and unmediated communication in a classless society. Moreover, his awareness of the resistance movement confirmed the insights he had gained in the camp; it was these experiences, reinforced by his readings on the French Revolution, that culminated in a central concept of *The Critique of Dialectical Reason,* "the group in fusion," in which group consciousness is mediated by the threat of external force and a violent revolutionary response to it.

The intense excitement and heightened sense of solidarity associated with participation in collective resistance to a threat, the open confrontation of violence with violence, is the catalyst that transforms the atomized relations of a series into the reciprocal, mutually supportive relations of a group—a form of resistance that Sartre himself witnessed in the streets during the insurrectionary moment that was the liberation of Paris in August 1944[30] and that he observed from a relative distance in May 1968. The society he dreamed of was the libertarian kind that he refers to airily in a talk given for the B.B.C. immediately after the Liberation, part of which is quoted in the 1972 film, namely, "a republic without institutions, without an army and without a police" (*Sartre,* 74).

In the film itself, however, Sartre limits himself to drawing the generalizing—and typically dogmatic—conclusion about human language that "silence is reactionary," whereas "communication necessarily implies truth and progress"; communication is an expression of the "trust" one places

in language as the vehicle of truth.[31] This reference to "trust" in language
is a reminder that Sartre seems to have virtually ignored the skeptical implications, from the late 1950s on, of structuralist theory and poststructuralism for any theory of communication. Moreover, that by the early 1960s
he was out of touch with some of the most influential intellectual movements of his time is confirmed by the fact that, like Rousseau before him,
from a Derridean perspective he laid himself open to the charges of "logo-
centrism" and "a metaphysics of presence."[32]

Indeed, as far as the different media are concerned, the logical consequence of Sartre's attitude is that the greater the apparent presence of human bodies and the greater the immediacy of voice, the more effective is
the act of communication that takes place. As a result, a hierarchy of media and genres might well be established on the basis of which drama
would appear to be superior to fiction, film to literature, and a speech to
a book.

Beyond Sartre's utopian idea of unmediated communication in a transparent society, there is a further disturbing fallacy that relates to his critique of the institution of literature and to the way in which he updates
the Rousseauist model of "the writer." From the mid-forties on, Sartre
consistently elevated an extreme situation into a norm as a result of which
he was ready to politicize every aspect of human life. The particular
French experience of war and occupation became for him a metaphor for
"the human condition" in general: "The frequently horrible circumstances
of our struggle [during the German occupation] enabled us to live the cruel
and unbearable situation we call the human condition without pretense
and without a veil. The exile, captivity, or above all death that we mask
in happier times were the constant object of our concerns; we learned that
they are not avoidable accidents or even continuing, external threats, but
that we should recognize in them our fate, our destiny, the deep source of
our human reality itself" (*Sartre*, 71–72).[33]

A telling example of the potentially grotesque consequence of taking
such an extreme situation for the norm is to be found in a statement Sartre
made at the beginning of the BBC talk: "We [the French] were never as
free as under the German occupation" (*Sartre*, 71). Even if one acknowledges the special meaning attached to "freedom" at a time when existentialism was in its triumphalist phase, against the background of the approximately fifty million deaths of the Second World War, including the
six million victims of the Holocaust, such hyperbole remains a problem.
To confuse a metaphysical interpretation of the human condition with the
daily terror experienced by ordinary people in a police state is to seem
either callous or hopelessly out of touch.[34]

It is also, by implication, a reminder of the situation of relative privilege in which non-Jewish French intellectuals mostly found themselves
even under the German occupation—something that Simone de Beauvoir's
account of the war years in the second volume of her autobiographical

trilogy, *Force of Circumstances,* rather innocently confirms. Sartre's unfortunate phrase is, in any case, an example of the way in which "the classic intellectual" presumed to speak on behalf of others and interpret their situation for them from a (safe) distance; it implies the kind of intellectual isolationism that under the influence of 1968 he came to denounce.

Like so much else that was written during the immediate postwar period, in journals like *Combat, Les Lettres Françaises, Les Temps Modernes* and elsewhere, the BBC talk has the character of a short manifesto. On the basis of the recent experience of a cruel reality and the failures and betrayals of traditional French social institutions, it points to the necessity of a radical revolution along socialist lines. At the same time, it is a reminder that we all live under the threat of imminent death with no other reason for existing than the one we individually and collectively decree, and no other recourse than our own action.

However plausible from the point of view of existentialist philosophy, the consequence of this absolutist position in the sociopolitical sphere is to look upon people, whether they know it or not, as enlisted in a cause; to live the critically self-conscious life is to be in a permanent state of mobilization. In short, Sartrean existentialism evolved increasingly in the direction of a philosophy of praxis that posits the necessity of the radical politicization of daily life in society; the slogan implied by the name of a celebrated underground paper in occupied France, *Combat,* spoke to the way individual lives were henceforth to be lived and, in the case of literary intellectuals, works they were to write. The kind of overpoliticization of social life that Stendhal objected to in the decades of the Restoration in the early nineteenth century had come to be represented as a desirable norm.

It was, then, as a result of his wartime experiences that Sartre came to recognize the limits of individual freedom, the significance of history, and the importance of the group. If *Being and Nothingness* can be seen as in many ways the culmination of the prewar philosophy of the individual, of "man alone," his most important postwar work of critical philosophy, *The Critique of Dialectical Reason,* elaborates a theory of the group as it develops dialectically in history. The important point to note, however, is that the promise Sartre discovered in the French resistance movement and, in particular, in its communist members led him to project the idea of resistance as project onto postwar France. Resistance is related to the heroic image of revolution and to the iconography of the barricades that goes back to 1789; for Sartre, it characterized the kind of militant political action to which he remained committed throughout the rest of his life.

The path he took from existentialism to Marxism is, in fact, best understood against this background. Having defined the bourgeoisie without qualification as *salauds* ("sons of bitches") in his prewar writings, it was not difficult for him to go on to adopt a Marxist philosophy of history in which the enemy was no longer the Nazis but the bourgeoisie. From the mid-1940s on, it was the bourgeoisie that he identified as the obstacle to necessary historical change and the inevitable progress toward a free, just, and egalitarian society in which people are no longer exploited by other people. The transition from the war against Nazism to the war against capitalism was an apparently natural one, especially against the background of the Cold War.

The problem of transforming an extreme situation of war and occupation into a norm, however, is that it gives rise to a form of reductionism that Sartre practiced throughout his career from the end of the 1930s and that is at the basis of his theory of *engagement,* namely, the reductionism associated with Mao Tse-tung's injunction to "put politics in command." As far as literature is concerned, this meant that Sartre never ceased to affirm in one way or another over four decades that "all writing is political" or that "writers are always trying to deny the idea that literature is political" (*Sartre,* 82). In short, there are no spaces in the human world that are outside politics; overpoliticization is an oxymoron.

What is missing here, as from almost all Sartre's pronouncements on literature from *What is Literature?* on, is a recognition that at the very least one has also to acknowledge the existence of a sphere of aesthetic values, of the autonomy of form, of literary conventions and genre characteristics. Here, as elsewhere, there is a characteristic failure to make the kind of discriminations that Sartre accused doctrinaire Marxists of failing to make. One might even rewrite a famous comment he once made on Valéry—"Valéry is a petit bourgeois intellectual, no doubt about it. But not every petit bourgeois intellectual is Valéry" (*Search,* 56)—and say against him that "all literature is political but not all political writings are literature."

The most interesting aspect of the Astruc/Contat film *Sartre* in the present context—and, to a lesser degree, the interviews with Simone de Beauvoir and Michel Contat—is the way they follow the progress of the iconoclastic novelist and philosopher of the late thirties into "the writer" and, by the end, to a position that is even beyond "the writer." Sartre is of special interest here because in his own career as well as in his own self-representations he recapitulates the tensions and oppositions within French literary culture that I have discussed in previous chapters; by the early 1970s he reaches a point beyond literature in which the figure he cuts is that of "the militant." It is this side of Sartre that Althusser apparently had in mind when he paid him the signal homage, on that April day in 1980 when he was buried in the Montparnasse cemetery, of describing him as "our Jean-Jacques Rousseau." [35] Down into the 1980s, for France's intellectual clerisy, intransigence was the supreme heroic virtue and moral purity consisted in the refusal to compromise high principle for political efficacity.

The evolution I am describing in Sartre's public persona is particularly evident in the succession of images of him projected by the Sartre film and by the discursive as well as the imagistic context in which they are located. But before looking more closely at the significance for the theme of this book of the images concerned, it is important to realize what kind of film is involved.

It has to be said right off that although *Sartre,* like the interviews, is relatively informative, it is far from possessing in its medium the brilliance of *Words.* The interviews with Contat and Beauvoir were not, of course, designed to be much more than works of recapitulation and witness, although one is aware from time to time of Sartre's talent for rising to the occasion, of his remarkable intelligence, and of his formidable polemical style. The Astruc/Contat film, however, does have some pretensions to being, if not "a work of art," [36] then at least a significant piece of documentary filmmaking, although it never manages to reach that level. *Sartre* seems to have been conceived, in fact, as an exercise in illustrated oral history. It takes the form of a group interview in familiar surroundings—Sartre's own or Simone de Beauvoir's apartment—conducted by the companions, friends, and colleagues of a lifetime. The questions and answers are interrupted from time to time by voice-over commentaries or statements of position, accompanied by images of Sartre, with or without others, or by newsreel footage. Questions and responses are roughly chronological once the historical present of the group interview has been established with an opening sequence of Sartre lecturing in 1972, a reference to the Pompidou presidency, and a shot of the Montparnasse tower under construction that is designed to function as "symbol of a regime." From that point the film backtracks to photographs of the Schweitzer family and briefly evokes Sartre's childhood before moving down through the thirties and the rise of fascism, World War II and the Nazi occupation, and on into the periods of the Algerian War, the Vietnam War and the Russell Tribunal, the events of 1968, and the activism of Sartre's final phase before the onset of blindness in 1973.

There is from the beginning an implied contrast with *Words,* inasmuch as the project of the film is described not as (auto)biography but as "an intellectual itinerary." Whatever the filmmakers' intentions, however, the result is the portrait in historical time of an intellectual hero, who is represented as having been a courageous actor in some of the most momentous events of twentieth-century history. The effect of the crosscutting to newsreel footage or to images of Sartre addressing assemblies, demonstrating in the streets, or meeting with heads of state and revolutionary leaders might be described as creating a cult of intellectual personality. If Sartre was not actually always there as actor or even as witness, the newsreel footage implicitly puts him there by juxtaposing his commentary and/or image with the scenes represented.

In spite of the apparently open format of group questioning, the image presented is in patent contradiction with the stated view of the intellectual's role Sartre claimed to hold at the time of the film's making. As a result, *Sartre* paradoxically ends up resembling one of those "lives of great men" of which young Poulou had once been enamored and for which the mature narrator of *Words* castigated him retrospectively. Sometimes together with Simone de Beauvoir and sometimes alone, Sartre is transformed into one of the *monstres sacrés* of French cultural life, the signs of whose greatness are tracked from infancy to old age.

The unintended merit of the film, from my point of view, is that it underlines in its own way the opposition between writer and "writer" that is at the core of this book. Although it is undoubtedly true that Sartre did escape the mystification of the traditional writer of having been "recruited by God," he may be said to have contributed powerfully to an equally disabling countermystification, that of having been "recruited by History"—by a Hegelian and Marxist History with a capital H, that is. One "grand illusion" is replaced by another. Like Rousseau after his experience on the road to Vincennes, Sartre was the recipient of a mandate after all.

A work *on* Sartre is not, of course, the same thing as a work *by* Sartre; nevertheless, it is impossible not to notice the significant falling off in intellectual energy and aesthetic quality between the written autobiography and the film in which he was apparently more than happy to participate.[37] The result is no more than a workmanlike piece of documentary journalism that is in no sense an equivalent of the tour de force that is *Words*. There are, for example, no equivalents in the film of the stylistic brilliance or the ironic turns of the knife by means of which the narrator demythifies the values and institutions of Poulou's middle-class French childhood. The film is at its worst, in fact, when it is establishing historical background. What it offers is not so much history as the familiar signs of history— Nazi book burnings, German soldiers marching down the Champs Elysées, scenes of Saint-Germain in the late 1940s, the street demonstrations of 1968—in which the use of the technique of imagistic synecdoche is inadequate to render anything like the complexity of twentieth-century sociopolitical or cultural life. A straightforward interview would clearly have been less mystificatory.

It is nevertheless the case that the medium of documentary film clearly fitted Sartre's determination at the time to play witness to a century and to advocate a cause. With the help of his collaborators, the film enabled him to narrate "an intellectual itinerary" that also has the character of a heroic and exemplary life; and the function of the sequences of images selected is to illustrate that Sartrean narrative for posterity.

A further interesting dimension of the film for my purpose is the way in which the narrative presents two decisive turning points in Sartre's commitments and self-understanding of his role. The first has to do with his rejection of the life of the man of letters and the second his impatience with the role of "the classic intellectual." If *Words* can be said to bear witness in an Augustinian way to an early life of (bourgeois) blindness and sinfulness from the point of view of someone who has undergone a conversion to a Marxian existentialism, *Sartre* repeats that witness and goes on to report on a second conversion, this time to what French intellectuals of the period in their parochial way called "Maoism."[38]

Moreover, one of the functions of the film is to illustrate these "conversions" as crucial to the subject's intellectual itinerary. Thus where the images of Sartre from the late thirties and forties suggest the established man of letters still behaving more or less in the polished style of Gide, those of the early seventies project the image of "the militant" or new "popular intellectual." The final significant newsreel photographs of the man show him in his windbreaker in the streets distributing the Maoist newspaper *La Cause du Peuple*, of which he was the nominal editor, or represent him addressing a crowd of workers at the gate of a factory.

By 1972, then, not only had Sartre distanced himself from the "art" of the written word, it was also his ambition to cease to be merely an intellectual in the classic sense, that is, one whose real intellectual work is centered elsewhere but who takes public positions on issues, signs manifestos, and even demonstrates, only to return afterward to his well-regulated bourgeois life at some distance from the masses and to pursue his work in the comfortable solitude of his study. Although Sartre urged a younger generation of French intellectuals to become one with the masses by participating with them in their life and work, he had to admit that, at his age, it was not for him, even if he was ready to look the part. By that point in his life, not only was he no longer a man of letters, he was scarcely even "a writer" anymore. He remained, however, "a militant."

A final aspect of *Sartre* that is also relevant to the themes of this book, but that can be mentioned only in passing, has to do with the discussion of its subject's long and complex relationship to the question of morals. I am tempted to say, in fact, that the film briefly tries to do for morality what *Words* had done for aesthetics. Whereas the 1964 book constituted an adroit demystification of "literature" and, by implication, of the idea of an autonomous aesthetic sphere untouched by politics and class relations, a decade later the film affirms the notion that the discussion of moral questions makes sense only in relation to political ones.[39]

It is perhaps typical that Sartre makes no mention of Antonio Gramsci or of the theory of cultural hegemony, even though *Words* clearly implies that aesthetics is politics by another means. A similar view is expressed concerning morality in *Sartre*, although the horror stories of twentieth-century political history clearly left Sartre troubled in spite of himself (after 1956) at the idea of simply conflating morality with politics.

The way he formulates his responses to the relevant questions in the film suggests he was seeking a kind of third way between the "political realism" of militant communism—for which the single criterion of the rightness or wrongness of an action was its efficacy in the historical context—and the traditional morality of the Western philosophical tradition whose weakness from Sartre's point of view was that it failed to recognize itself as a dimension of the superstructure in a class society.

He breaks down his own long-standing philosophical interest in ethical questions into three distinct phases. The first of these preceded the Second World War, when he attempted to pose the issues in traditional abstract, ahistorical terms; the second coincided with the early to late fifties, when he embraced a form of "political realism"; and the third is associated with the sixties and after, when he sought, apparently unsuccessfully, to achieve a kind of new synthesis: "[T]he problem for me has always been whether one had to choose between politics or morality or whether politics and morality were one and the same" (*Sartre*, 102). In spite of the misgivings expressed in the film and elsewhere, the testimony of his most significant writings from the early forties on is unfortunately that they are indeed "one and the same."

Yet when all is said and done, Sartre was in an important sense a "moralist," though a "moralist" of a particularly disturbing type. That is to say he was not so much a moral philosopher as someone who insists that one assume one's freedom and that one act always so as to respect the freedom of others. The result, in any case, is that his ethics appears to be as rigorous and demanding in its own way as Kant's—with the concept of "authenticity" occupying the place of the categorical imperative. What, after all, could be more exacting than the standard of conduct he affirms in his (in)famous 1945 lecture, *Existentialism is a Humanism:* "Everything happens to every man as though the whole human race had its eyes fixed upon what he is doing and regulated its conduct accordingly."[40]

From early in his career he assumes that human subjectivity is typically an alienated subjectivity that manifests itself most obviously in behavior characterized by "bad faith." Yet at the same time "bad faith" is perceived as that which may be overcome, although only at the cost of a lifetime of vigilance and self-critique. In short, if, as *No Exit* famously affirmed, "Hell is other people!" that is because one is always subjected to the look of the Other and is therefore transformed into an object. In the existential terminology of *Being and Nothingness* this means that one exists merely *en soi*, in a state of thingness; and the best one can hope to achieve is to make visible to the other one's hidden existence as a *pour soi*, that is to say, as a free, self-conscious, and self-regulating being. But as the fate of the trio in his 1944 play implies, the task is an endlessly frustrating one that presupposes relentless self-surveillance and self-discipline. *No Exit* is an unusually fierce morality play which affirms that those who are not up to the task deserve to share the fate of Sartre's imaginary characters. Probably the most horrifying feature of his theatrical existentialist hell is that one is forever under observation by a third person and the lights are always on. Yet in the normative moral universe he imagines for the social world outside the theater, that is also the case.

Under the circumstances, it is no wonder that Foucault associated Sartre's moral philosophy with the idea of "terrorism."[41] "Authenticity" is a demanding moral standard to set, not least because it depends on "transparency," or uninterrupted visibility of self to self as well as to others. Sartre has no patience with secrecy—as the lines quoted earlier from "Self-Portrait at Seventy" confirm—and seems to regard privacy as a typical bourgeois indulgence. There is no reference in his works to privacy in the liberal political sense. One might even regard Foucault's *Discipline and Punish*, in fact, as a kind of response to Sartre, inasmuch as the younger thinker explores the totalitarian potential of the institutionalization of the look in modern history in the form of the panopticon.

In sum, in the wake of the Second World War Sartre outlined an attitude toward morality that was similar to, though less developed than, his attitude toward aesthetics. Though it was not articulated in such terms, it is as if the theory of *engagement* developed in the sphere of art and literature was carried over into a morality that was an ethics of praxis. That is, his ethics, like his aesthetics, was effectively politicized because he shared until the end of his life historical materialism's suspicion of all human activities that were relegated to the level of the superstructure in a class society.

Rousseau's Discourses had already prepared the ground. But it was only post facto and in the wake of Hegel and Marx that the three autonomous discourses of Enlightenment philosophy corresponding to Kant's three critiques lost their autonomy. That is why, although he seems to have had second thoughts late in his life, Sartre for a long time assumed that in the modern age only one critique was necessary, *The Critique of Dialectical Reason*. Pure and practical reason, as well as aesthetic judgment, were subsumed under the dialectical philosophy of history.

There is, then, more than just a generational gap in the way Foucault distances himself from Sartre. On the one hand, for a long time his profoundest admiration went to those thinkers and artists who, like his mentor at the Ecole Normale, Jean Hyppolite, practiced "the systematic effacement of [their] subjectivity."[42] On the other hand, the importance to Foucault of such posthumanist thinkers as Nietzsche and the late Heidegger clearly signals his break with the French "writerly" tradition that emerged with Rousseau and of which Sartre was a belated avatar. Not only was the latter's existentialism "a humanism," as the famous, popularizing lecture affirmed, much to Foucault's disgust, so also was his Marxism.

From the Foucauldian perspective, what is missing in Sartre is a sense of openness, of doubt, and of the limits of a subject position. The theory of *engagement* assumes that one is potentially the master of truth and of universal history, and that one should participate in the struggle to implement that truth and to assume that history. More specifically, *engagement* is also a denial of the autonomy of the aesthetic sphere and of the importance of a space of experimentation and play. Absent from Sartre's work is a recognition of the fact that there is a realm of the unthought, the unexplored, the demonic, that transcends the categories of his Marxism or even his brand of existentialism. Moreover, the questions of pleasure or of an aesthetics as well as an ethics of the self, as Foucault formulates them, are not even raised.

That Sartre represented the end of something significant for the French intellectual tradition is confirmed finally by the judgments of two of his somewhat younger contemporaries, Louis Althusser and Jean-François Lyotard. The first makes a direct judgment on Sartre's contribution; the second, in the context of a discussion of postmodernism, rejects a long philosophical tradition of which Sartre was the most potent representative in his time.

In his posthumous autobiography, *The Future Lasts a Long Time,* Althusser writes dismissively of Sartre's major philosophical works: "I always thought that Sartre, who had such a brilliant mind and was the author of prodigious 'philosophical novels' such as *Being and Nothingness* and the *Critique of Dialectical Reason,* never understood a thing about Hegel or Marx or, of course, Freud. I saw in him at best one of the post-Cartesian, post-Hegelian 'philosophers of history' that Marx detested." [43]

With that reference to "philosophical novels," it is as if Althusser were taking up the major theme of Lyotard's *Postmodern Condition,* at least as far as Sartre is concerned. At the center of Lyotard's effort to describe the distinctive character of late-twentieth-century thought and postmodern modes of the philosophical legitimation of knowledge is the notion of "the crisis of narratives" *(la crise des récits).* Unlike "modernity," "postmodernity" in his reading has ceased to believe in the great master narratives or philosophies of history that first emerged in the Enlightenment to explain the progressive development of the human world.

As far as Sartre and the idea of "the writer" are concerned, Lyotard's argument is important because it describes our contemporary state of affairs as one characterized by an attitude of "incredulity as far as metanarratives are concerned." And in a sentence that has a special relevance for Sartre, he goes on to add; "The narrative function loses its functionaries *[foncteurs],* that is to say, the great hero, the great threats, the great journeys, and the great goal." [44] Not only does this proclaim the end of all totalizing historicisms in general, it is also another way of affirming that "the French Revolution is over" and along with it the heroic myth of revolution. So, too, in my reading, is the two-hundred-year career of "the writer" as hero. Perhaps the final image Sartre leaves us with, an image that manages to be both moving and disturbing in equal proportions, is that of a stubbornly intransigent, blind seer of a failed cause.

In the wake of the death of Sartre at the beginning of the 1980s and the collapse of faith in the idea of revolution at its end, the historical boundedness of "the writer" has become clear in ways that were difficult to see before. Nevertheless, a century and a half ago, Tocqueville had already characterized the specifically French cultural and institutional matrix in which "the writer," like the intellectual and the revolutionary, was first formed:

> Our revolutionaries had the same fondness for broad generalizations, cut-and-dried legislative systems, and a pedantic symmetry; the same contempt for hard facts; the same taste for reshaping institutions on novel, ingenious, original lines; the same desire to reconstruct the entire constitution according to the rules of logic and a preconceived system instead of trying to rectify its faulty parts. The result was nothing short of disastrous; for what is a merit in the writer may well be a vice in the statesman and the very qualities which go to make great literature can lead to catastrophic revolutions.[45]

In spite of all those French intellectuals who dreamed of it in the years immediately following the Second World War, there was fortunately no communist-style revolution in mid-twentieth-century France. By an irony of history, however, there was instead a division of intellectual-political labor such that "the catastrophic revolutions" occurred elsewhere around the world while "the great literature" was made in Paris.

Rarely, in fact, has French intellectual life appeared so brilliant and literary productivity been so high as in the middle decades of this century, at a time of virtual consensus among intellectuals at the left of the political spectrum. Under the circumstances, given the character of so much of that production, one is reminded of the peculiar malady that can afflict writers and intellectuals in periods of high intellectual ferment, the disorder Milan Kundera has called "graphomania":

> GRAPHOMANIA: "Not a mania to write letters, or family chronicles (to write for oneself or one's immediate family)" but "a mania to write books (to have a public of unknown readers)" *(The Book of Laughter and Forgetting).* The mania not to create a form but to impose one's self on others. The most grotesque version of the will to power.[46]

If Kundera's final sentences appear so incisive, it is because they contest the idea of the innocence of writing for a public outside one of the consecrated literary genres, an innocence that was a fundamental assumption of the theory of *engagement;* in the reference to "the will to power," they also challenge the associated idea of the disinterest and purity of the intellectual who maintains his distance from the practice and rewards of political power.

To some extent Sartre suffered from graphomania throughout his life as writer, although it was balanced at the beginning of his career by an

interest in aesthetic questions and by a critical awareness of the significance of form and the value of the artful detour. As he noted on more
than one occasion, from relatively early in his life part of virtually every
day was to be devoted to the production of its quota of written pages. But
once he gave up writing fiction, by the late 1940s, and plays, by the late
1950s, he became a victim of graphomania in a peculiarly acute form, as
both the bulky *Critique of Dialectical Reason* and the three long volumes
on Flaubert attest.

Perhaps the most remarkable aspects of these late works, apart from
their length, is that they seem not underedited but practically unedited,
either by the author himself or anyone else. In their original versions their
apparent formlessness is reinforced by the virtual absence of tables of contents, notes, or references to any other works in the field except canonical
texts by thinkers such as Marx or Freud. Far from being works conceived
in a dialogic mode dedicated to the free and open communication between
writer and reader that one might have expected of Sartre in light of his
theory, they are disturbingly solipsistic in character and make no concessions to a potential reader. Given their monstrously monologic nature that
seems designed to subdue rather than persuade a reader, it is not surprising
that there are probably no more than a few dozen people around the
world who have read the Flaubert volumes from beginning to end. In the
context of this book, however, they do have a kind of allegorical significance: they constitute a limit case that suggests what can happen when
"the writer" who despises formal values achieves cult status.

CHAPTER 5

The Cultural Twilight
of Roland Barthes

I daresay there isn't a single adolescent today who has the fantasm of being a writer.

ROLAND BARTHES

The epigraph, taken from Barthes's poststructuralist autobiography *Roland Barthes*,[1] is significant here because it is clear from the context that he does not mean writer in the sense that Sartre was a writer, or Rousseau before him—that is, "a writer"—but in the generic sense in which the word is sometimes a synonym for "man of letters." The regret that Barthes came to express by the year of publication of *Roland Barthes*, 1975, was of the disappearance from French culture of the very desire to live and write in the way that, earlier in the century, two writers who were very important to him, André Gide and Marcel Proust, had lived and written.

Given Barthes's popular reputation as a brilliantly provocative critic, scourge of French academic criticism in his time, and champion of high theory through the decades of structuralism, poststructuralism, and psychoanalysis, such a regret may come as a surprise. At least as much as anyone in Parisian literary and intellectual circles from the late fifties through the seventies, Barthes was associated with speculative new ideas and the glamour of successive, tough-minded bodies of critical theory that undermined long-cherished French cultural values and attitudes. The expression of regret for a way of life associated with an older and more traditional France is, therefore, certainly not something one would have expected from him earlier in his career. There was, in fact, a distinct turn in his thinking about his own writing and his role relatively late in his life, although there are signs almost from the beginning that he never really embraced the theory of *engagement* and, unlike Sartre, was always attuned to the specificity of literature and to the poetic play of language. What interests me here, in particular, is the apology to be found in his late work for the life and values of "the man of letters," on the one hand, and the

189

Roland Barthes
(Archives Seuil. *Roland Barthes par Roland Barthes*, 1975)

Roland Barthes
(Archives Seuil. *Roland Barthes par Roland Barthes*, 1975)

implicit critique he expresses of "the writer" and his tradition, on the other.

At first sight Barthes does appear to be preeminently "a writer" in the Rousseauist mold; although he would probably have been horrified at the thought, there are aspects of his work and practice that remind us of Rousseau's legacy. In Kundera's words, he does have "original ideas and an inimitable voice" and "whatever he writes—being marked by his thought, borne by his voice—is part of his work." However, unlike Kundera's novelist, Barthes by his own admission never sought, let alone found, a literary form that met "the demands of his dream"[2]—unless one considers the critical essay, the encyclopedia, or the fragment such a form. Barthes's ideas were important to him even as they evolved swiftly in response to the changing bodies of theory to which he was also a principal contributor. Moreover, in the writers he championed, the intellectual allegiances he expressed, and his critiques of French bourgeois society, he was broadly sympathetic with the left-wing sociopolitical agenda of his peers. Finally, he, too, was tempted to try his hand at autobiography, even if the resulting work took a very different form from the tradition of "confession" or even from Sartre's satirical model.

Though he never achieved the international or even national stature of "writers" from the previous generation like Sartre and Beauvoir, Barthes became a recognized public figure in his own right and was at the center of the Parisian literary scene for well over two decades. He also partly shared with his generation of French literary intellectuals a suspicion of the traditional genres of poetry, fiction, and drama, a suspicion that in his case was informed in the beginning by the theories of Brecht and that led away from a conventional understanding of literature toward the critique of ideology and to the practice of writing—or from "work" to "text" and "the death of the author." The earliest of his writings to come to the attention of a broader public were sharply written critical exercises in the unmasking of French popular ideology and cultural phenomena and were subsequently published in volume form as *Mythologies* in 1957. He went on to become a major contributor to the unprecedented expansion of French literary criticism and theory from the Marxist and existentialist moment of the post-war decade down through the heydays of structuralism, poststructuralism, and psychoanalysis.

In the last ten years or so of his life, however, he turned increasingly to fragmentary, meditative texts that, among other things, updated such marginal genres as travel and autobiographical sketches and the journal; and, like Stendhal before him, he wrote his book on love, the very title of which, *Fragments of a Lover's Discourse*, is expressive of his critical, meditative aesthetic. By the end, in any case, totalizing theory was out, replaced by exploratory, local exercises in cultural critique and autoanalysis that amounted to a kind of guilty return to literature and to the life of "the man of letters." He had in some respects come full circle, going back to the kind of ruminative fine writing, centered on the self, that he associated with the Gidean journal in his earliest published article: "On the final horizon, nothing other perhaps than the initial text" (*Roland Barthes*, 99).

A suggestive confirmation of this reorientation of his thinking is to be found in the expression of a more personal regret than the one on the rising generation to be found in my epigraph. In a late essay on Proust, "Longtemps je me suis couché de bonne heure" (For a long time I went to bed early), he expresses sorrow at never having tried his hand at a form of self-reflexive narrative fiction of the kind he associated with *Remembrance of Things Past*.[3] The theorist and essayist was drawn to the art of the novelist; aesthetic satisfactions had come to seem more rewarding than ideological critique or theory. Thus Barthes's return to his literary origins was an expression both of dissatisfaction with what he had accomplished and a sense of his own belatedness.

One is tempted to conclude that the reason for Barthes's volte-face was at least in part generational; but the fact is he was born in 1915 and was, therefore, only ten years younger than Sartre. There is a an important difference, however, in their relationship to the climactic years of their generation's historical experience, the Second World War. Although Barthes reached intellectual maturity in the mid-1930s and was almost twenty-five at the outbreak of the war, he never had to undergo the mobilization, fighting and prisoner-of-war camps that so marked Sartre and a whole generation of young Frenchmen, including Louis Althusser, as I shall point out in my epilogue. He never shared that salutary levelling on which both Sartre and Althusser report, in which a collectivity of disparate men learned to live together and to unite in the face of a common enemy. Nor, apparently, was he exposed to the tensions and anguish that was part of Marguerite Duras's experience of the war years. He was exempted from military service on account of the tuberculosis that was first diagnosed in 1934 and that was to recur a number of times down through the Second World War and would require long periods of treatment, including protracted stays in sanatoria. Because he was to a great extent marginalized by his illness, unlike many French intellectuals of his generation he was largely isolated from direct experience of the Occupation, and he also seems not to have shared in the heady experience of the Liberation in the way Sartre, for example, did.

If I bring up these facts of Barthes's life here, it is because one does not find in his writings references to the kind of heroic politics associated with moments of collective revolutionary fervor, idealistic military campaigns, popular insurrection, or national liberation invoked by Tocqueville, Stendhal, and Baudelaire, for example, not to speak of Sartre. It is, in other words, symptomatic that Barthes appears not to have been stirred by any of the great dates of the French revolutionary tradition from 1789 down through 1968, whether he experienced those moments directly or indirectly, as part of the collective cultural memory. In particular, he does not seem to have shared Sartre's anxiety about the importance of making one's rendezvous with history count for something, as Sartre attempted to do in 1944, 1947, and 1968. Barthes's writing is consistently less politicized, to the extent that he expresses no longing, on the basis of a historical or a personal memory of euphoric group fusion, for a future republic of virtue and equality. Although there is for a long time significant ambivalence, by the end the primacy of the aesthetic over the political becomes explicit.

The works in which Barthes thinks through these issues in brilliantly suggestive ways date from the last decade of his life, when he was making a form of self-reflexive literature out of some of his most intimate feelings and experiences, including his erotic experiences. They include the travel book *The Empire of Signs* (1970), the critical essay *The Pleasure of the Text* (1973), *Roland Barthes by Roland Barthes* (1975), *Fragments of a Lover's Discourse* (1975), and the posthumously published reflections on his final years, *Incidents* (1987). It is, however, on *Roland Barthes* that I shall concentrate here, although I will also briefly explore *Incidents* at the end, both because it is there that Barthes comes as close as anywhere to the mode of Rousseau's *Confessions* and because it has the character of a brief but suggestive final testament that focuses on the issues raised by this book.

Like Sartre before him, Barthes's turn to autobiography is accompanied by a critique of the role he has assumed; unlike Sartre, however, Barthes takes a nostalgic pleasure in returning to the beginnings of a career in which the young writer had not yet been tempted to transmute himself into "a writer." In order to understand the difference of orientation between Sartre and Barthes in this respect, it is helpful to remember at least two things: first, in Barthes's case, the Rousseauist legacy is mediated by Gide, and, second, Barthes was also from early on under the spell of the great anti-Rousseauist of the modern French novel, Proust.

In any case, I take *Roland Barthes* to be a rich cultural document of our time; it is there that its author comes closest to writing about himself in a way that illuminates his own ambivalent relationship to the Rousseauist lineage of sociopolitical *engagement* and of "confession." The autobiographical work stages the encounter between the Rousseauism that had survived in Sartre and poststructuralism.

Typically, Barthes provides in his autobiography a provocative opening for reflecting on the gap between the one who writes and the idea of writing that is also relevant to the issues that concern me. He formulates the problem as one in which an act of identification with an admired predecessor takes precedence over the act of writing itself. In a section named after the German word "Abgrund" (abyss), a section that also has to do with Gide's importance for him, he asks, "Can one—or could one formerly, at least—begin writing without taking oneself for someone else? The history of sources should give way to the history of figures: the origin of a work

is not the original influence, the first pose is; one copies a role, then metonymically an art: I begin to produce by reproducing the one who I want
to be" (*Roland Barthes*, 103). The originality of Barthes's insight here appears above all in the concept of a "history of figures," which to my
knowledge has never been attempted, although the present book touches
on some of the issues it would raise.

Barthes's claim is that one first writes in order to imitate someone who
has written, in other words, that writing begins with an image and the
desire of an-other (*for* an-other) in which one is happily alienated from
one's subjectivity: "[H]ow could he [Barthes] not have recognized himself,
desired himself in that writer [Gide]?" (103). The surprise here is in the
affirmation that the writer is in the first place a role-player. Writing is
what one does in order to remake oneself in another's image, to become
visibly desirable.

Furthermore, in the habits of a lifetime no major writer of his generation more than Barthes adopted the style of life of the French "man of
letters" in the turn-of-the-century mode; the settled life, centered on his
study in an apartment shared with his mother and punctuated by annual
vacations in the Southwest of France, alternated with nocturnal sorties
into the streets and cafés of Paris often associated with different forms of
gay sexuality. Thus in his sexual orientation and to some extent in the
habits of a double life, as well as chronologically, Barthes's life overlapped
with those of Gide and Proust: "When I was beginning to walk," he comments with evident satisfaction opposite a photo of himself as toddler,
"Proust was still alive and finishing *Remembrance of Things Past*" (27).
The nostalgia expressed is for a lost age as well as for a great novelist.

Barthes's own exercise in poststructuralist autobiography is interesting,
then, not least for the way in which it suggests how the supposedly avant-
garde theorist and critic of established values also enjoyed a wonderfully
old-fashioned writer's life that has a special affinity with his closet existence as homosexual. "The man of letters," unlike "the writer," was one
who observed while keeping at least part of his life unobserved; before the
age of gay liberation, a high value was placed on privacy.

Among the frequent occasions on which Barthes affirms that his persona and his sensibility are out of date, the most striking is probably the
section entitled "The Writer as Fantasm," from which this chapter's epigraph is drawn. Having commented there that no adolescent today in-
dulges in the "fantasm," or consciously fantasized scenario, of being a
writer (without quotation marks, that is), he goes on: "Of which contemporary would one want to copy not the works, but the practices, the gestures, a whole way of strolling through the world with a notebook in one's
pocket and a sentence in one's head (that is how I imagined Gide traveling
from Russia to the Congo, reading his classics and writing in his note-
books in the restaurant cars of trains as he waited to be served)?" (81).
Not Sartre or Beauvoir, presumably, or anyone else from the existentialist

generation that dominated Parisian intellectual life when he was first beginning to publish, nor anyone, apparently, from his own generational cohort.

What the fantasm Barthes refers to did for him, and apparently no
longer does, is impose the image and idea of "the writer minus his works"
(81). At issue is a whole way of being in the social world that is not that
of "the writer" as public individual or celebrity, but of the disengaged
aesthetic observer who remains partly in the shadow, a Baudelairean flaneur who travels in style with a notebook in hand. Like Proust and Gide
(the younger Gide, at least), Barthes prefers to keep his distance. Thus the
perception of the difference between a man of his generation and contemporary literary and intellectual youth is enough for Barthes to define himself to himself as someone living between two cultures, as a survivor from
the lost, pre–Second World War age.

It is characteristic of late Barthes that such questions are raised in the kind
of work which traditionally focuses on the unfolding of a life. What more
than autobiography offered opportunities of the kind he despised to put
oneself heroically on display and offer a retrospective narrative of a self
triumphant over obstacles and time? If Barthes allowed himself to take up
the challenge of what he knew to be one of the most mystified of genres,
therefore, it was because it enabled him once again to engage in unmasking the hidden work of "naturalization"—that form of ideological
representation that attributed to nature what is, in fact, the work of a
political culture—this time in the sphere of those cultural practices associated with writing itself.

Perhaps Barthes would not have dared take up the challenge at all if
the opportunity had not presented itself of adopting the format of Le
Seuil's well-known popularizing series, Ecrivains de Toujours (Writers for
All Ages). To appear in a series that features the canonical authors of
the Western literary tradition, from Homer to Sartre himself, provided an
opportunity for the kind of ironic self-distancing and interrogation of the
autobiographical genre that clearly appealed to him. As he notes, the titles
of the series take the form of X *by Himself.* Moreover, the books are
divided into two parts, the first of which is a copiously illustrated presentation of the writer's life and work by a modern critic, the second a selection
from his writings.

Barthes undertook the task of presenting himself in a format that was
apparently against his own critical and theoretical grain but that also
promised a variety of pleasures in the play between discretion and indiscre-
tion. He clearly enjoyed the risk he was taking of putting himself on display in the arena of contemporary Parisian intellectual life. Not the least
of the enjoyment he seems to have derived from the exercise is that of the
tightrope walker: the potential for disaster enhances the public triumph if
the act is elegantly brought off.

Barthes, of course, takes every opportunity to show that he himself is not taken in by his project. A variety of distancing techniques in *Roland Barthes* prevent a descent into the confessional mode; the Sartrean irony relative to the family and the institution of literature is updated by means of some of the devices of poststructuralism. Against the general mystification of a series format that requires him to treat himself as a canonical figure is the note in the author's own hand inside the front cover that invites the reader right off not to identify author and narrator too closely: "The whole thing is to be considered as told by a character in a novel." Thus does Barthes dispose of Stendhal's concern about the plethora of "I's" and "me's" in autobiography, and of what he himself calls "the pronoun of the imaginary" (62).

Further, the play of ironic allusions is pursued from the beginning in ways that invite the reader to take, and not to take, seriously the images the author reproduces for the occasion. There is, for example, frequent irony in the choice of particular photos, in the elliptical comments about them, in the formulation of captions with psychoanalytic associations ("The Demand for Love," "The Family Romance," "The Mirror Stage"), or in the symmetrical layout of images ("The Two Grandfathers," "The Two Grandmothers"). One should note, however, that, in spite of the denials, one also finds a distinctly non-Sartrean, virtually Proustian nostalgia for the lost provincial world of old Bayonne and the Southwest in general, and for a certain kind of bourgeois family life—what in one caption he sums up as "Family without Familyism."

The specific nature of the challenge Barthes faced in *Roland Barthes* is made clear in the way he chose to organize the work. Unlike other books in the Le Seuil series, in which photographs are distributed throughout a first part of critical presentation, Barthes groups all his images in the first forty pages or so and, after a couple of pages of introduction, restricts himself to captions and brief commentary. Moreover, in the second part, where selections from an author's works usually appear, he chooses not to cite passages from his previously published works but offers instead an alphabetized series of short reflections on a variety of topics.

In his first part then, Barthes confronts head-on the issues that Sartre had raised in passing in *Words,* those relating to photography and the family, on the one hand, and to photography and the writer, on the other. By offering a selection of photographic images of the kind one finds in most people's family albums, Barthes thematizes the impact of photography on family life and self-perception as well as on the writer's role. In this respect, he was, of course, not only different from Sartre—who was apparently more than content to leave the troubling deployment of family photos to a posthumous biographer like Annie Cohen-Solal—his work was also virtually without precedent. In the French tradition, at least, I know of no previous work of literary autobiography that makes a comparable use of photos of the writer, family, and friends.

The full irony of Barthes's situation is clear if one remembers that he was writing at the high point of Lacan's influence on French intellectual life, when the concepts of the imaginary, the symbolic, and the real were considered potent tools for the understanding of human behavior. As he reminds his reader, a volume that takes the format of *X by Himself* calls forth psychoanalytic associations: "[M]e by me? But that's the very project of the imaginary" (156). It was, after all, assumed that the theory of the mirror stage helped release us from illusory capture by our own image, freed us from the misperception of the self as oneness and continuity, precisely because it substituted the concept of the split subject for that of the unitary self. One of Barthes's principal goals is, in effect, to attempt to put his own imaginary on display: "The vital purpose of this book is to stage an imaginary" (109).

It is thus paradoxical, though not surprising, that on the first page of the second part of his book, just opposite the last of the many photos of the author, Barthes should note, referring to himself in the third person, "He does not like images of himself, he suffers when he is named. He considers that human relations are perfect when there is a void of images: abolish the *adjectives* between selves" (47). It is similarly paradoxical, though less surprising, that on the following page, under the heading "The Demon of Analogy," Barthes goes on to express his distaste for the very arts of the image, photography and cinema, one of which he is also exploiting. In this respect one sees how far Barthes leaves Sartre behind. From the point of view of the poststructuralist, photographic images are stricken with the original sin of "analogy": unlike writing, they imply a natural and not a conventional relationship with a model in nature. They also constitute the crucial core of those media that diffuse the image and idea of "the writer" in our contemporary mass culture.

Why, then, if there is an antithetical relationship between the "natural" illusionism of photography and the "conventional" signs of writing, did Barthes start off with a series of photos? What, so to speak, was in it for him?

In the first place, Barthes's selection of images from the family album, laid out in roughly chronological order, allows him to tell the story of his life without the potential embarrassment, at that poststructuralist moment, of using words. As Susan Sontag, among others, has pointed out, it is in the nature of photographic images to be ambiguous: they acquire a specificity of meaning only through contextualization, and this, in practice, means when they are located in a sequence or given captions.[4] Barthes produces the meanings he wants by adopting both strategies. On the one hand, images of grandparents precede images of parents which are followed in turn by snapshots of little Roland, Roland as adolescent, and Barthes as writer and lecturer; on the other hand, brief evocative commentaries or ironic one-liners draw out a meaning from what are frequently banal images.

It is probable, however, that family photographs exercised an even greater appeal over Barthes precisely because, as Sontag also says, they are in all our lives the focus of a peculiarly unnerving pathos: "It is a nostalgic time right now, and photographs actively promote nostalgia. Photography is an elegiac art, a twilight art. Most subjects photographed are, just by virtue of being photographed, touched with pathos." And she concludes, in a couple of sentences that have a particular aptness for Barthes at the moment of his writing *Roland Barthes*: "All photographs are memento mori. To take a photograph is to participate in another person's (or thing's) mortality, vulnerability, mutability" (*On Photography*, 15). She might also, of course, have added "or one's own." Thus the dead and future dead, along with the lost material worlds they inhabited, dominate the opening pages of *Roland Barthes*.

Although Sontag seems to be referring to photography as "a twilight art" primarily in the obvious sense that it records the former physical states of our intimates and familiars, as well as ourselves, the very phrase she chooses suggests another meaning that has a special significance for Barthes. Most commentators on photography as art have been too preoccupied with underlining its connections to the emergence of modernism to notice that there is a sense in which it, too, along with those things and people it represents, belongs to a now lost past at least as much as to our present. There is a sense in which photography can have a look that is as old-fashioned as oil painting, and with its sepia tones, standardized compositions, period poses, gestures, fashions and locales, this is especially true of photographic portraiture. As the elderly bachelor who narrates *Roland Barthes* sifts through the still lives of the family album, therefore, he knowingly generates a mood of *fin d'époque* as well as of *fin de race*. The heroic age of middle–class photographic representation, in its stillness and dated mise en scène, is as remote as his dead progenitors and the boy he once was. Thus the autobiographical work in which they appear amounts to a double act of homage: it pays loving tribute to a lost style of mechanical image making as well as to lost forebears.

The only explicit explanation Barthes himself offers of the inclusion of the photographs has to do with their peculiar hold over him. The opportunity they give him as author to interrogate private images of himself and his immediate world has its own reward; and in that respect, at least, he is more than prepared to make his private feelings public.

Even though they come first in the book, the images are introduced as the pleasure he granted himself once he had finished writing his text, a pleasure whose sources remain in many ways mysterious to him. He justifies his choice of particular images as opposed to others available to him on the grounds that they address him at levels that he does not control— what he calls "punctum" in his book on photography, *Camera Lucida*. They typically elicit "a state of troubling familiarity: I *see* the split in the subject (about which it cannot itself speak)" (*Roland Barthes*, 5–6); they remind him of repressed representations of his body ("le 'ça' de mon corps").

Apart from everything I noted above, therefore, the photos are also Barthes's own royal road to his unconscious; they enable him to pursue the exploration of his own psychic life, which, as is clear from the second, textual part of the book, is what at that stage interested him most. It is, in fact, this uncovering of the secret life of his body and psyche, of unsuspected desires and resistances, that connects the two parts of the book. In this respect Barthes is for once closer to Rousseau's *Confessions* than to Sartre's *Words,* although to the extent that he draws on psychoanalysis to explore the effects of his own unconscious, he can be said to have gone further than either.

By claiming to choose his photos not for their documentary value but because they "fascinate" him, then, Barthes is not distancing himself from the self-revelatory, confessional mode, but developing it further. He shares with his reader insights into the play of an unconscious desire, including his "perversions" (his word), that an analysand typically reserves for the dialogue with his analyst. Apart from everything else, *Roland Barthes* bears witness to the hold of psychoanalytic theory over French literary culture in the sixties and seventies.

One of the sections in the textual half of the book where the reader observes most clearly the way in which Barthes stalks the play of resistance and desire is the one entitled "I Like, I Don't Like" (*J'aime, je n'aime pas.*). In the apparently unmotivated alternation of likes and dislikes relative to a random sampling of the world's objects ("I like: lettuce, cinnamon, cheese, peppers . . . I don't like: white Pomeranian dogs, women in pants, geraniums, strawberries"), the subject that I am, and am not, reveals hidden consistences, an irreducibility that is its own: "[I]n the anarchic foam of my likes and dislikes, a kind of absent-minded hatching, the outline of a corporeal enigma emerges that calls forth [from another] complicity or annoyance" (120).

From Barthes's point of view, the foregrounding of his own family photos also offered the advantage of greater textual heterogeneity; in one sense both parts of the book constitute a single "text." As we have known since *Tristram Shandy,* and as Stendhal's *Life of Henry Brulard* reminds us, text and images may interfere with each other in playfully comic or ironically disturbing ways. Moreover, Barthes not only brings together lines of print and photos in a way that is potentially disconcerting for literariness, he also deploys a variety of other graphisms in his work—from sentences and a page or two of manuscript in his own hand to doodles to a medical chart.

Thus the parade of images at the beginning, which at first glance looks like an unpardonable act of self-indulgence, in effect does multiple duty: they allow him to raise again Sartre's questions about photography and the family (directly) and photography and the writer (indirectly); they permit him to call up nostalgically a familial and a cultural past; they enable him to pursue his exercises in autoanalysis through a different medium; and, finally, they become an integral part of his pursuit of an art of autobiography that subverts the traditional presuppositions of the genre. Although Rousseau's masterwork is his text of reference, like Sartre and others before him, he searches for ways to go beyond it.

In this respect, Barthes's purpose is clear. It is to replace autobiography—given all that that implies about narrative, unitary selfhood, and the relations between a life and a writing—with what, adapting one of Barthes's own neologisms, might be called poly-bio-graphy. Under the heading "The Work as Polygraphy," he writes, "I imagine an antistructuralist criticism; it would seek not the order but the disorder of a work; in order to do so, it would only have to look upon a given work as an encyclopedia. . . . As an encyclopedia, the work deploys a list of heteroclite objects, and this list is the work's antistructure, its mad and obscure polygraphy" (151). That is in the end the way in which Barthes attempts to reconstitute not the "order" of a life but the "disorder" of a living.

Polybiography, then, is the profoundly un-Rousseauist text of one's subjectivity as encyclopedia; it posits the self as "antistructure." In Barthes's model it implies an organization by fragment—one item after the other—and by alphabetical order—contiguity is an accident. That is why in *Roland Barthes* and throughout his writings from at least *S/Z* on, Barthes celebrates textual polyvalence and what might be called the aesthetics of the fragment: "In short, I proceed by addition, not by a sketch; I have a given (primary) taste for the detail, for the fragment, for the rush, and no talent for bringing it altogether in a 'composition' " (97)—although, as he notes in the following section, "The Fragment as an Illusion," even the technique of interrupting the flow of one's discourse will not in the end preserve one from "the bed of the imaginary" (99).

To adopt that most random of orders, the alphabetical, is also to believe in the pattern-breaking energies of disorder and the sense of liberation it affords. The advantages for Barthes of the alphabet are, therefore, not only that it effaces the possibility of locating the site of an origin—"Where did he begin?"—but that the salvaged fragments of a former self or present work remain fragments: "[T]he important point is that these little networks [of associations] are not joined together, that they do not combine in a single, large network that would constitute the structure and meaning of the work" (151).

In sum, *Roland Barthes* is indeed designed to be that unprecedented, monstrous thing I am calling polybiography. That is, it is a kind of *biographie non-événementielle* that struggles knowingly to be plural—"The whole thing is to be considered as told by a character in a novel—or rather, by several" (123)—and that undoes the myth that one can ever exit from the present of enunciation or outlive one's past. Polybiography offers no climactic episodes, no threshold experiences, no scenes of revelation in which the secret of a sexual being is uncovered, no sequence of cause and effect, no discovery of a vocation, no ascent in stages from childhood to adolescence to a triumphant maturity as famous writer—in short, no imaginary summum of the kind Sartre mocked and Lacan denounced as central to the illusionism of ego psychology.

Polybiography offers instead simultaneity for continuity and a heterogeneity of moments: reflections, brief memories, tastes, attitudes, opinions, bêtes noires, passions, hopes, doubts, and regrets; the auscultation of a body's contacts with the world; and those intermittent resurfacings that testify to the persistence of unconscious desire. It is, therefore, characteristic that, just as the work opens with a handwritten comment inside the front cover, it closes with another that answers affirmatively the question whether or not "he" will be able to go on writing once *Roland Barthes* is done: "One writes with one's desire, and I have not yet done with desiring."

If it was Barthes's paradoxical goal to start with the image in order to invent a form of self-representation that is liberated from the dominance of the imaginary in the Lacanian sense, he both succeeded and failed—inevitably. The kind of success he had in mind is suggested in the section called "Coincidence," which begins with him reflecting on what he discovers in recordings of himself playing the piano: "The (biographical or textual) fact is abolished in the signifier, because it coincides immediately with it: by writing myself . . . I am my own symbol, I am the story that happens to me . . . the symbolic becomes literally *immediate*." And he goes on to note that it is tantamount to abolishing one's subjectivity, as in a suicide (61–62).

That Barthes is at the same time condemned not to escape from imaginary self-capture is, however, unavoidable, as he acknowledges more than once in the process of interrogating the images of his former selves: "[N]evertheless, especially for your own body, you are condemned to the imaginary register" (40)—that is, to see yourself erroneously as an achieved whole. The strategy he adopts to problematize the French tradition of autobiography going back to Rousseau and to distance himself from his images is to alternate between the visual/imaginary and the textual/symbolic elements of the work, to introduce a play between "a me" and "the impossibility of a me." Thus, for example, a picture of him as a baby on his mother's lap has the caption, "That's you." Yet the context is such that the caption, in effect, ironically undermines what it asserts; it suggests rather Magritte's stunning denial of the "pipeness" of his famous, painted pipe, that is, "This is not me." Even a realistic image of a pipe is not, of course, a pipe, anymore than a photograph is a person.

Yet in spite of all the ironic distancing techniques Barthes deploys, the photographs at the beginning nevertheless manage to combine the immensely seductive power of images with the equally seductive power of narrative, because those photographs are reproduced in chronological sequence. Whatever Barthes attempts to accomplish in his subsequent text, the reader encounters first the story of a writer's life in pictures. Consequently, the distinction John Berger makes between "the private use" and "the public use" of photographs is collapsed, as is typically the case where images of celebrities are concerned. We are able to appreciate and read Barthes's private family photos as if they were our own, that is, "in a context which is continuous with that from which the camera removed" them. At the same time, although these photographic images are offered for public consumption, they are not "public photos" in Berger's sense, precisely because "the information" they offer is not "severed from lived experience."[5] Barthes's pictorial narrative sees to that.

The result, in any case, is that the reader finds himself faced with a series of images that point to the mysterious unfolding of literary genius toward a triumphant maturity; however ironic the captions, one is invited to be "star-struck" once again by the mystery of the emergence of greatness. At what point, one wonders—in that toddler in rompers or that elongated youth draped over his mother's body—did "the great writer" first appear? In brief, Barthes nowhere fulfills more obviously the role of "great writer" in our time than at those points in his self-representations when he appears to be mocking the image making on which that role is culturally dependent.

Thus, although there are moments when, in the act of writing, Barthes manages, so to speak, to slip the moorings of his ego and experiences a kind of utopian abolition of the self, it is at best an evanescent mode of being. Nowhere does his whole enterprise seem to founder more obviously, in fact, than on the very photo which is at the book's characteristically eccentric center, and which marks the break between the two parts, between pictures and text. It is a full-page image of the writer that, Januslike, concludes Part 1 while it faces Part 2. It is the equivalent of a medium shot in the language of cinema and shows the author's head and upper body against a neutral background occupying three-quarters of the available space. The caption says simply "Lefty" *(Gaucher)* and it is obvious why: the author's right hand is in his pocket and his left is thrust upward and forward in the process of lighting a cigarette. The power of the photo derives from the fact that it manages to combine a metonymical figure of deviance with the fullness of the image of "the writer." It seems to proclaim that Barthes was born "on the left" even before he consciously located himself there. In this larger-than-life picture, the myth of "the writer" in France as oppositional literary intellectual can be seen to have survived into the age of poststructuralism.

"What does it mean to be left-handed?" Barthes asks later in his text in a section with the same title as the photograph. "You eat against the placement of your knife and fork; you find the telephone has been put back the wrong way round when a right-handed person has used it before you; scissors are not made to take your thumb. As a child at school, you had to struggle to normalize your body, in that little lycée world you had to make an offering of the right hand . . . a modest, not very important, and socially tolerated exclusion gave your adolescent years a slight but persistent bent: you got used to it all and carried on." (102). One recognizes here the strategies of someone who learned early to negotiate and resist the processes of normalization, someone who also took an ironic pleasure in the masquerade inherent in what Eve Kosofsky Sedgwick has called "the epistemology of the closet."[6] "The slight but persistent bent" learned in adolescence comes to be translated into the habits of a lifetime.

In Barthes's case, moreover, the closet is a peculiarly complex one. That is why left-handedness, as both photo and text confirm, was a signifier of deviance that is directly associated by him with his status as a man of the political left, with his Protestant background in predominantly Catholic France, and with his homosexuality in an overwhelmingly heterosexual society. It is also indirectly associated with his status as "writer" and intellectual. Finally, I would note in passing something he does not to my knowledge specifically address, namely, the perceived deviance of the seriously ill or formerly ill in a social world designed by and for the healthy; as noted above, Barthes endured a number of long bouts with tuberculosis in his early manhood, and he seems to have turned that experience into a lifelong habit of monitoring his body and its sensations.

In a variety of ways, then, Barthes remained attached to a writerly tradition inaugurated by Rousseau, although he would probably have hated the idea, and did so in spite of the fact that he also distanced himself from the ethics and aesthetics of confessionalism. And nowhere does he project the image of "the writer" more obviously than in that photo which shows him lighting a cigarette with his left hand. Even the three pictures that come just before and show him at a desk or a table in three different locations—surrounded by the implements of the writer's trade (old-fashioned implements, of course: no typewriter, let alone a computer) and apparently caught in "the act of writing"—do not project the aura of "the writer" in the same way. There is something about the left-hander's indifferent clothes, his long refined face, the cigarette and the lighter, the absorption in the pleasurable act of lighting up, the look that ignores the camera and, of course, the provocative left hand, that tells us this is a man who is set apart, someone who transgresses on principle. This is, in short, the French "writer" triumphant. Moreover, the seductive power of the image implies a narcissism that is collective as well as personal; it concerns an identifiable, self-confident ideal type as well as a man.

What Barthes says, in a section called "The Idea as *Jouissance*," about the hostility "common sense" shows for the language of intellectuals, is particularly relevant here. In this case it is specifically as literary intellectual that he claims to find himself excluded: "You don't talk as I talk, so I exclude you." And by means of a comment of Michelet's on "the infrasexuality" of intellectuals, Barthes connects such hostility to homo-phobia, concluding that *"because of his language"* an intellectual is "de-sexualized, that is, devirilized: anti-intellectualism is unmasked as a protest on behalf of virility" (107). Thus Barthes's precise and delicate language, like his left-handedness, his left-wing politics, his homosexuality, his cul-tural Protestantism, or his sickness, becomes the mark of a member of an excluded caste, and for that reason alone he undertakes to cultivate it against the world.

Moreover, in this respect one can observe a notable difference between his autobiography and Rousseau's, for Barthes clearly addresses himself exclusively to a cultivated audience of like-minded readers. He is con-sciously speaking to the converted; a community of moral and aesthetic values is assumed along with a common and highly literary language that is at once fastidious, precise, sensuous, and abstract. Thus although, as with Rousseau, his later writings are characterized by an unusual intensity of focus on himself, the stance adopted is a very different one. Barthes does not claim to offer his reader the truest possible self-portrait in the egalitarian spirit of a man among men, but instead offers discriminating pleasures centered on a highly individual sensibility and the adventures of a body in the world. The rewards are there for the reader, but they, too, are highly literate and discriminating ones.

Perhaps the most notable difference between Barthes and the tradition of "the writer" appears in relation to the concept of privacy. Although Barthes is willing to disclose certain of his most intimate thoughts and feelings, he does so selectively and often indirectly; the goal of transpar-ency to which Sartre subscribed as much as Rousseau is not something Barthes pursues. This is apparent in what he indicates relative to the sphere of "the private" in his time. As noted earlier, the concept is, of course, historically and culturally specific, and Barthes himself claims that it is also ideological, a question of a political "doxa." Thus he comments that privacy for the conservative is chiefly a matter of sexual privacy, whereas in received opinion on the political left, "sexual exposure is in no sense transgressive: in the light of this doxa I expose myself less in af-firming a perversion than in expressing a taste—passion, friendship, ten-derness, sentimentality, or the pleasure of writing turn out to be the un-statable propositions" (85). In short, the idea of "the private," like that of "the scandalous" to which it is in some ways related, is an ideological variable.

In light of the position he had reached by early old age, it is perhaps not too surprising that "the scandal" he puts ironically on display in *Ro-land Barthes* is the scandal of his taste for bourgeois pleasures and the rites of bourgeois life. Some of the most "shocking" aspects of what Barthes has to tell concern not his sexual orientation and erotic adventures but the culpable ordinariness of many of the passions and avocations asso-ciated with a long despised class. It turns out that the narrator's darkest secrets have to do not with his sexuality but with his life in avant-garde intellectual circles as what I am inclined to call "a closet bourgeois."

Barthes's attitude is partly summed up in a section entitled *Ease (Aise)*, a word that in French combines the idea of "comfort" with "relaxation." It is in this section that Barthes acknowledges his fundamentally hedonistic disposition: "A hedonist (for so he believes himself to be), he seeks a condition that is, in brief, one of comfort; . . . a comfort that he arranges, constructs for himself." But what is perhaps most crucial about *Aise* is that it also embodies an ethic, namely, "the willing loss of all heroism, even in the sphere of *jouissance*" (48).

The renunciation of a heroic ethic in any form is certainly rare among major French writers since the late eighteenth century and clearly distances Barthes from all the "writers" discussed in this book as well as the "anti-writers" such as Stendhal and Baudelaire. That Barthes also turns his back on heroism in the realm of sexual pleasure as well as in the moral and political spheres is perhaps most surprising, given the fascination expressed for erotic excess by such contemporaries as Georges Bataille, Jacques Lacan and Michel Foucault, among others. It is no wonder that the author of *Roland Barthes* represents himself as out of touch, and, given the drift of the culture, sees the admired model of "the man of letters" as obsolete. A philosophy of life that is centered on an unheroic hedonism is remote indeed from the moral and political combativeness of Rousseau's *Confessions,* from Sartre's philosophy of action, and from the taboo-breaking energies of the literary and intellectual avant-garde, including Foucault, as I shall suggest in my epilogue.[7] It therefore points decisively to Barthes's "disengagement," to his break not only with the postwar generation of Sartre and Beauvoir but also with theory in all its forms—with Marxism, structuralism, and, by the end, even psychoanalysis and poststructuralism. Barthes's avowed purpose becomes not saving the world but savoring it, and savoring it especially through his writing. He was, after all, the subtlest theorist of pleasure of our time, one of whose works, *The Pleasure of the Text*, decisively reoriented critical theory at a certain moment. In that respect, he is of the lineage of Stendhal and Baudelaire. The latter's "Experiencing pleasure is a science" formulates succinctly a belief that was very important to Barthes.[8]

The reason *Roland Barthes* turns out to be such an important document for my purposes is that it is centrally concerned with the question of the representation and self-representation of "the writer," and with illuminating the fundamental opposition that exists between "the writer" and a fin de siècle idea of "the man of letters." Barthes consciously attempts to "stage an imaginary," to put on display the illusory image of himself as mastery and wholeness, as I noted above. What he also succeeds in doing, though perhaps with less self-consciousness, is stage what might be called the "cultural imaginary," inasmuch as that imaginary has transmitted an image of "the writer" across two centuries. At the same time, he makes visible his entrapment in it. Unlike the Sartre of *Words,* the author of *Roland Barthes* is preoccupied with escaping from the very condition of "writer" that Sartre had embraced in his own quarrel with the institution of literature in France.

On the one hand, as we have seen, Barthes deploys the various devices of poststructural writing to distance and problematize the material of his personal narrative; on the other, he casts a number of nostalgic glances in the direction of "the man of letters." Unlike Sartre, who always affirmed his orientation toward the future, Barthes took increasing pleasure in trafficking with the past. Toward the end of our own century, we find Barthes looking backward to a literary model that emerged at the end of the previous century. This is not simply a case of the kind of generational change that Bourdieu describes, in which the consecrated avant-garde finds itself under assault from a rising avant-garde, although Barthes does express some impatience with new trends and attitudes that have no interest for him. On the other hand, there is a definite longing for the familiar stabilities of a lost family life and its cultural routines. There may also be an undeclared regret for the external conditions that made such a life possible, namely, a private income. In any case, the fact that he came to celebrate this figure and not "the writer" in the Rousseauist mold is, in effect, his way of acknowledging his own belatedness, his way of seeing himself as a phenomenon of the twilight of a certain literary culture.

Perhaps the paradox of paradoxes of Barthes's polybiography is the disjuncture between the experimental form of *Roland Barthes* and the nostalgia it intermittently evokes for a way of life that is at least a century old. The fact that Barthes enjoyed living like Gide, however, implies less a reflex of reaction than a form of transgression in the second degree. It is comparable to the pleasure he took in engaging in accomplishments typical of nineteen-century bourgeois girls (classical piano playing and watercolor painting) or to his idea of reintroducing a new sentimentality into the sphere of contemporary sexual politics. In short, in his hostility to the doxa in all its forms—behavioral as well as discursive—Barthes found it necessary to practice against the culture of his age what he himself calls "the transgression of transgression" (70). That is also why he may be said to have remained *gaucher,* of the left, in the sense of deviant, even when he can hardly be regarded to still being on the political left.

It is such an attitude that led him, for example, to recognize that he was, after all, "a political bad character" *(mauvais sujet politique)* (172). Moreover, he behaves badly, not only in the political sphere, in the sense of failing to respect the social norms and discursive regularities of left-wing as well as right-wing opinion, but in a great many other spheres as well. And this is the most abiding impression transmitted by the authorial persona that inhabits *Roland Barthes*. If he longs to lead the life of "the man of letters," it is for reasons that are critical and reactive vis-à-vis "the writer."

In my view, Barthes seems to have understood that, along with so many of his contemporaries, he had written himself into a corner. The literary representation of the self (or subject) and the commitment to ideas, independent of a given literary genre, leave the writer without a form in Kundera's sense, a form that transcends "voice" and "ideas" and enables a man or a woman to be more intelligent than he or she is in the world. Thus even though Barthes experimented with autobiography—pluralized, fragmented, and fictionalized it and substituted the concept of the subject for the self—he did not manage to reduce the writerly cult of personality or promote the cause of literature—to his own satisfaction, at least. He problematized and refined the practice of writing to the point at which he could write memorable sentences or even paragraph-length essays on his tastes and feelings, but he did not come close to achieving the magnificent impersonality of, say, *Remembrance of Things Past,* probably the work he most admired, in which critique, celebration, subjectivity, and transcendence of subjectivity brilliantly coincide. And in spite of his gestures toward fiction, he apparently found it impossible to use the novel form to think with or to rise to the level of what Kundera calls "the suprapersonal." In spite of all he had in common with them, he never discovered a way of emulating Proust or even Gide.

Thus, in spite of all Barthes's self-consciousness, polybiography remains to some extent an expression of graphomania or "writerly" will to power in Kundera's sense.[9] The critic and theorist turned hedonist reveals what it means in the late twentieth century to have the habits of "a man of letters" without the craft disciplines of the poet, the dramatist or novelist. With "the writer's" complicity, the different media continue to diffuse the image of an exemplary life, but the writing itself has become an appendage to a cult. Even poststructuralist autobiography sustains the illusion that we are learning important truths about an author, whereas, as Joseph Brodsky has reminded us and Barthes himself was aware, "A poet's biography is in his vowels and sibilants, in his meters, rhymes, and metaphors."[10] In a manner that is more critical and more self-conscious than that of his predecessors discussed here, Barthes leaves us with a new and disturbing notion of "the writer minus his works."

I will give the last word on the twilight of Roland Barthes to his own last word, the posthumously published *Incidents,* because that work manages to encapsulate in a single short volume the reason why in his case the idea of "the writer" comes to be eclipsed by that of the writer as "man of letters" or author of purely literary works. *Incidents* is the work of Barthes that in some ways is most similar to Rousseau's *Confessions,* but it is a pale reflection indeed of the great master text of French autobiographical writing. Although its final section, "Paris Soirées," comes as close as Barthes ever does to offering revelations about his sex life, it is written with a self-conscious flatness that mirrors the mood of desolation it describes.

The section narrates briefly, in the manner of a journal, how the narrator spent some two dozen evenings in August and September 1979, after returning from his annual vacation in the Southwest. He went out to dinner at friends' homes or fashionable restaurants, went to movie theaters alone, cruised, picked up "gigolos" (his word) in cafés or on the street, returned home to his apartment—sometimes with a companion or lover, but more frequently by himself—and invariably ended up alone in bed with a classic work of the French literary tradition, such as Chateaubriand's autobiography, *Memories from Beyond the Grave,* or Pascal's *Pensées.* There are a few references to well-known figures in the Parisian intellectual and literary circles in which he moved, as well as to friends and lovers; and the faded worldliness of Barthes's nocturnal Paris is suggested by the famous names of the cafés, brasseries, and restaurants of which he was a habitué, from the *Café de Flore* and the *Deux Magots* to *Le Select, La Rotonde, La Coupole,* and *Bofinger.*

Yet in the end Barthes maintains his characteristic reserve and offers few intimate details on his own emotions and sensations, the sex acts he engaged in, or even what it had meant for him to be a homosexual in a predominantly heterosexual culture in the middle decades of this century. He does occasionally "talk dirty," but without managing to dissipate the impression that the great stylist is somehow slumming. There is nothing comparable to the illuminating scenes or brilliant set pieces in which Rousseau reveals the secrets of his sexual being; nor does one find the kind of "scandalous" revelations in which, as I indicate in my epilogue, Louis Althusser will engage. In part, this has to do with "that slight but persistent bent" that he acquired early in order to pass unnoticed when it was important to him. In part, the absence of such material in *Incidents* is, as the narrator so perceptibly notes in *Roland Barthes,* due to the fact that in the late twentieth century sexual transgression is no longer perceived as transgression, at least in progressive circles. Through repetition it has lost its power to shock. Confessions have become a bore, have become the stuff of television talk shows.

Incidents might, in fact, be described as a work of "gossip and cruising" were it not for certain somber notations that punctuate the text, notations that concern the mood of a man in his sixties who has still not recovered from the death of his mother[11] and who is in the process of discovering that the erotic fantasies and habits of a lifetime are also coming to an end. If, as I believe, it makes sense to speak of the cultural twilight of Roland Barthes, it is one that comes to be overlaid with a personal twilight that had to do with the experience of death and of aging. *Incidents* is Barthes's saddest book because he seems to have lost interest

in experience, in the intellectual life, and in his own future. It is thus significant that the most achieved piece of writing, the piece in which the old
verve, the old verbal precision and suggestivity are to be found is the short
opening section on "The Light of the Southwest."

If the characteristic flair of "The Light of the Southwest," written in
1977, has gone from the "Paris Soirées" of two years later, that seems to
be related to what can only be described as a state of depression. This
finds expression, on the one hand, in an irritation at disturbing and unfa-
miliar trends in French society and French culture and, on the other, in his
sense of himself as a changed man. He had concluded *Roland Barthes* on
an upbeat note, proclaiming, "One writes with one's desire, and I have
not yet done with desiring." That still seems to be the case at the time of
writing "Paris Soirées"; the problem he identifies is that he himself is no
longer desirable, no longer the potential object of youthful male desire.

Reading the personal advertisements in *Libération* and *Le Nouvel Ob-
servateur,* he notes that they offer "nothing really interesting, nothing for
'old men' " (*Incidents,* 92). Finally, the failed encounter in the last "Soi-
rée" on which he reports ends with the melancholy observation that a
whole long period of his adult life, integral to his way of being in the
world, is over: "A kind of despair seized me. I wanted to cry. I saw evidence of the fact that I would have to give up boys because there was no
desire from them to me, and I am too scrupulous or too awkward to
impose my own. Such was the uncontrovertible truth, manifested by all
my attempts at flirting, that I lead a sad life, that finally I am bored, and
that I have to eliminate that interest or hope from my life" (115–16). It is
no accident that in his last work Barthes seems to be haunted above all by
Proust, even noticing at one point that he is in a street in the quartier
Saint-Denis where the Baron Charlus once found himself in *Remembrance
of Things Past.* The point of view of "Paris Soirées" is in many respects
that of an aging Charlus. As Barthes himself seems to acknowledge, he has
become a pathetic, perhaps even a tragic figure.[12] In any case, the example
of Proust and of the art of fiction proves in the end to be more enduring
than that of Rousseau, of politics and confession.

That this is the case is confirmed finally in the opening section of *Incidents,* "The Light of the Southwest." Barthes returns briefly there to his
own Combray, to the provincial and bourgeois world of his early years in
Bayonne, and to themes already explored in *Roland Barthes*: to childhood
and its relationship to a *pays* or region, to the body and its perceptions of
a special quality of the smells, the sights, and the light in a familiar place,
and to memory. Like Proust, the elderly Barthes is interested in the *insig-
nificances* of his Southwest, what from a global and analytical point of
view are its small, unimportant yet unique qualities. At the same time, the
short piece turns out to be his last, brief dismissive word on "theory," for
in it he raises the issue of the limits of "sociological and political analysis
that functions as a coarse sieve and fails to capture the 'subtleties' of the

social dialectic." And he goes on to celebrate literature's superiority over sociological and political understanding in its capacity to record precise local knowledges, locating the writer, in the traditional literary sense of that word, in a place that precedes and transcends constituted bodies of theory: "To 'read' a region is first of all to perceive it through one's body and one's memory, through the memory of one's body. I think that it is to this vestibule of knowledge and analysis that the writer is assigned: he is conscious rather than competent, conscious of the very interstices of competence" (18–20). Barthes, in the end, was the celebrant of life's "interstices." Literature had become for him the charmed sphere of the post-theoretical as well as of the postpolitical.

CHAPTER 6

Marguerite Duras:
Autobiographical Acts,
Celebrity Status

For seventeen days the sight of that shit didn't change. It was inhuman. It sepa-
rated him from us more than his fever, more than his thinness, more than his
nailless fingers, or the marks of SS beatings. We gave him golden yellow pap,
infant's pap, and it reemerged from his body dark green like mud from a marsh.

MARGUERITE DURAS

The story of "the writer" in France, which, in my telling, begins in the
mid-eighteenth century with Jean-Jacques Rousseau, draws to an end in
the closing decades of the twentieth century with Marguerite Duras. It is
possible that some other living French writers belong as obviously, in certain aspects of their work, to the "writerly" tradition inaugurated by
Rousseau, but none in my view gives us a fuller, richer, and, at the same
time, more disturbing sense than Duras of what it might meant to be "a
writer" toward the end of our century. For the time being, in any case,
precisely because of her remarkable talent and single-mindedness, her
work and career illuminate both the possibilities and the limits inherent in
a certain cultural understanding of writing and "the writer's" function.

Unlike Sartre, she has not sought to assume all aspects of the Rousseauist legacy equally, but from the late 1960s in particular she has developed it in a new and feminist direction that does not necessarily sit well
with mainstream feminists. On one level, Duras's credentials as activist
and militant appear to be superior to those of Sartre; she was active in the
French resistance during the Occupation and was even a member of the
French Communist Party for a number of years in the late forties and early
fifties. Yet her written work is not marked by the theory of *engagement* in
the same way that Sartre's clearly is from the mid-forties on. Nor, like
Sartre—or Simone de Beauvoir, for that matter—did she attempt to write
works of political theory or social critique. Finally, for a long time she
was known almost exclusively as a novelist or screenwriter who was not
particularly given to public pronouncements or self-representation.

Marguerite Duras
(Photo G. Schachmes. Sygma)

However, although Marguerite Duras was born only a year before Roland Barthes, in 1914, from the perspective of the late twentieth century it
is as if she belonged to a younger, resolutely avant-garde generation that
embraced the modernist aesthetic in art and literature, including the
French New Novel, and went on to embrace important aspects of feminist
theory in the late 1960s. It was a generation that also, until very recently,
rarely questioned its faith in the idea of renewal through revolution and
its broadly Marxist interpretation of world history and social change—
although Duras' relationship to all these movements has to be qualified in
a variety of ways. It is, in any case, impossible to find in Duras's writing
any Barthean nostalgia for a lost *vieille France* or for the fin de siècle
literary culture from which both Gide and Proust emerged. The idea of
"literature" that they embodied in their time is, in fact, for the most part
the object of her suspicion rather than her admiration, as it was for Sartre
and for Rousseau before him.

One has only to recall two of the concepts dear to Barthes referred to
in the previous chapter, "ease" and "privacy," to perceive the very different sensibility and moral climate of the two bodies of work. To enter
Duras's fictional world is to encounter pain and risk, solipsism and fantasm; what interests her are extreme experiences, often associated with
personal sacrifice and with modern, "writerly" forms of heroism. We are
once again confronted with a special heroic ethic in action.

A short passage from the published screenplay of *Hiroshima mon
amour,* the filmed version of which was, of course, directed by Alain Resnais and released in 1959, confirms Duras's characteristic understanding
of writing as resistance and provocation: "I have the honor of having been
dishonored. When the open razor moves across your head, you have an
extraordinary understanding of human stupidity. . . . I desire to have
lived such a moment. Such an incomparable moment."[1]

The words are spoken by the French actress and heroine of the film's
haunted love affair who, as the opening synopsis indicates, is in Hiroshima
in order to act in "an edifying film on Peace" (*Hiroshima,* 14). In the film
itself, however, all except the last two sentences of this piece of dialogue
were cut. Yet the attitude expressed is symptomatic of a core of convictions that are articulated and rearticulated in various guises throughout
Duras's fictions and films. The experience referred to in those omitted sentences is one that is familiar from some of the most disturbing images to
have survived from the Liberation of France in 1944, namely, images of
those women who were submitted to the public humiliation of having their
heads shaved on suspicion of having consorted with German soldiers during the Occupation, the so-called *femmes tondues.*

In representing the experience from the point of view of one of the
victims, Duras interprets it as a case of forbidden love, the shame of which
is in the end joyfully assumed. The short passage of dialogue captures, in
fact, what proves to be a characteristic combination of attitudes in Dura-

sian women, namely, a defiant indifference to the norms and values of society coupled with a readiness to go to the end of one's desire, in the Lacanian sense, whatever the cost to the self-preserving ego. Moreover, in this case as in others, the experience evoked is lent a quasi-sacred character; it shares the quality of the ecstatic sacrifice of self associated with the lives of women saints.

That this is the case—from Duras's point of view, if not necessarily from Resnais'—is confirmed by a sentence from an appendix to the screenplay in which Duras evokes her character's traumatic experience of the end of the war in her hometown of Nevers: "She practically stretches her neck out toward the scissors" (139). Suggested here is the peculiar *jouissance* of a martyrdom, which in this case is in the cause of those forces within that care nothing for self-preservation or the social law.

Further, the heroism in question is implicitly defined as specifically feminine to the extent that it combines a form of passive-aggressive witness and an extraordinary stoicism in the face of pain, suffering, and death: "To give an outward sign of one's pain would be to degrade that pain" (133). In the light of this, it is obviously no accident that an important volume of Duras's stories, to which I shall turn later, is called *Pain (La Douleur)*—although the American edition unfortunately goes under the name *The War*[2]—because the willingness to seek out and face down the shattering insights yielded by the experience of extreme pain/pleasure has been an abiding characteristic of Duras's writing throughout her life. What Kristeva says about one of her most haunting heroines, Anne-Marie Stretter, is broadly true of almost all of them: "Sorrow is her sex, the focal point of her eroticism" ("The Pain of Sorrow," 145).

Thus, in spite of many things they have in common, there are fundamental differences of attitude between Barthes and Duras on such issues as the practice of autobiography and the extent to which one puts oneself on display, visual representation, the vocation of "writer," and the nature and value of "literature" as opposed to "writing." It is these and related issues that I shall explore in this chapter.

To begin with, in Duras's works one finds none of the equivocations about autobiography that characterize *Roland Barthes*, although for most of her career when it is used, autobiographical material is often fictionalized and, therefore, distanced. The importance of that material in her work is apparent from the familial situations represented in her very first novels, *The Impudent Ones* (1943) and *The Quiet Life* (1944), and becomes even more apparent with the story of a family very similar to her own and its experience of life in French Indochina in the 1930s in *Sea Wall (Un Barrage contre le Pacifique)* (1950). And it is this same material that has re-emerged and been given far greater prominence in the overtly autobiographical works of Duras's old age, *The Lover* (1984) and *Pain* (1985).

Second, from early on, Duras seems to have been at home in our contemporary image-culture in ways that Barthes never managed to be in spite of his book on photography and his interest at one point in his life in a programmatic semiology. Although she first became known as a novelist, among contemporary French writers she is preeminently the one who has moved easily from novel writing to the writing of plays and film scripts, and even to the directing of films. Late in her career she has also lent herself far more than most to the exercise of the videotaped interview.

Finally, as far as the vocation of "writer" is concerned, the metamorphosis of Barthes from committed cultural critic and avant-garde theorist into "man of letters," at least in his fond self-representations, finds no equivalent in Duras. She embraces the role of "the writer," as I have been defining it here, in a number of ways, and nowhere more so than in her determination to prove an uncompromising witness to the disturbing movements of her own desire and behavior as well as to those of contemporary women and men during some peculiarly cruel decades of European history. Bearing witness is the form that "commitment" has principally taken in her work, but it is only in the last decade that it has involved the conscious choice of "making a public spectacle of herself." And it is for these and related reasons that, in recent years at least, she has become a celebrity of a kind that Barthes never was.

Since my particular focus in tracing the tradition of "the writer" has been on different modes of confessional writing or fictionalized autobiography, I will not attempt here to discuss Duras's work for the theater or cinema.[3] Further, in order to avoid repetition I will concentrate on two of her most recent and popular, as well as most controversial, works, *The Lover* and *Pain*. It is my view that those two books effectively express the significance of Duras's life and work as cultural phenomenon. That is, they illuminate in a striking way the continuity for over two centuries of the idea of "the writer" I am exploring here. No one in France over the past couple of decades has practiced the art of self-representation as self-disclosure and image making more consciously or more consistently than Marguerite Duras. At the same time, no other literary figure of the post-Sartre/Beauvoir generation has achieved her celebrity status.

Yet *The Lover* and *Pain* do pose a problem of genre definition that has not occurred up to this point, a problem that is symptomatic of the uses to which Duras has put her writing. Although I am claiming that they are recent contributions to a tradition of confessional writing that goes back to Rousseau, they are not works of autobiography in the obvious sense. It is, in fact, typical of Duras's strategy as writer to promote a deliberate play of ambiguity in this respect: she draws without apology on material from her own personal and family life, yet even in works that invite an identification between the "I" of the narrator and the author, she also intermittently distances that material with a variety of fictional techniques, beginning with the frequent avoidance of what Barthes called "the pronoun of the imaginary," the first person.[4]

On the one hand, taken together *The Lover* and *Pain* evoke certain climactic moments of Duras's life, from her birth in 1914 in Indochina down through her repatriation to France in the early 1930s and the four years of the Occupation. On the other hand, those same works can in theory be read in their own right as fictions whose interest is independent of the apparent identity between author and chief protagonist. Nevertheless, the success of both *The Lover* and *Pain* has been, in part at least, a *succès de scandale*, because they were, understandably, read as frequently disturbing revelations from the life of their celebrated author.

It is by now clear that Duras's method consists in obsessively working and reworking the same material over the years. The effect is of a return of the repressed, not in a single work, but across a body of work in which different permutations are tried out, different and increasingly more explicit revelations of the forbidden directions taken by her desire are adumbrated, although at a level where nothing final and definitive is asserted. The paradoxical result is often that, in the process of the reworking, material that started out as highly personal and specific to the author ends up seeming virtually anonymous and transpersonal.

In any case, the singular appropriateness for Duras's purposes of the strategic use of material from her life is confirmed in at least two ways: first, it enables her to avoid the disclaimers and the coyness that, as we have seen, typically accompany the opening justificatory remarks of modern literary autobiography; second, the play of me/not me seems to have given her the minimal distance she apparently needed to narrate certain intensely personal and painful experiences that come closer to matching elements of Rousseau's *Confessions* than any other work discussed in this book.

Consequently, there is an almost total lack of the irony or of the self-deprecatory gestures that characterize, say, Stendhal's *Life of Henry Brulard*, Sartre's *Words*, and Barthes's *Roland Barthes*. Duras focuses unambiguously on more or less extreme experiences of suffering, scandal, and dolorous ecstacy in which she has been implicated in the course of a long life. But she does so in such a way that her partly fictionalized surrogates have the disembodied and mysteriously driven quality of the personae of dreams. With the frequently nameless "she's" of her writings, Duras seems to be reaching for anonymous yet gendered figures who are engaged in primordial dramas that are endlessly reenacted in historical time.

The Lover is important to the argument of this book both because it is Duras's most overtly autobiographical work and because it is her greatest popular success. Of all her novels it is the one that most clearly crosses over from the sphere of Bourdieu's first principle of hierarchy in the literary field to the second, that is to say, from the autonomous principle of post-symbolist poetry or experimental writing—in which to lose economically or with respect to the size of one's audience is to win in terms of prestige—to the heteronomous principle, in which success is measured in terms of the number of works sold. Not only did it win the Goncourt Prize in the year of publication, it was also made into an execrable English-language movie that emphasized all the wrong features of what is, after all, on one level a romantic story of first love with nude sex scenes, set in an exotic locale from the French colonial past, and steeped in nostalgia for an adolescent girl who no longer exists. If one adds to such apparently made-in-Hollywood material the fact that the book is also a particularly well-written example of "her story," the source of its popularity is clear—although one can only assume that a great many of those who read the work got both more and less than they had bargained for.

It is also a particularly interesting work to read after the works discussed in my chapters on Sartre and Barthes because, along with the general theme of a writer's and/or "writer's" vocation that is common to all, it focuses once again on the questions of self-disclosure, image making, and the relationship of subjectivity to family in a given sociopolitical context at a given historical moment that, to anyone who has read this far, have become very familiar.

To begin with, if there were any doubt about the continuity of Duras's preoccupation with the image and with image making, outside of her work in film proper, *The Lover* puts it to rest. There is some irony in the fact that the point is made immediately obvious by the American edition of the work, but not by the French. Unlike the austere, featureless cover of *L'Amant*—an austerity that, when combined with the imprint *Editions de Minuit*, remains in Paris the signifier of high literary art—the American edition has two different photographic images of the author as a girl, one on its front cover and the other on its back. It is as if the editors at Harper and Row had gone out of their way to justify Susan Sontag's suggestive remarks of almost twenty years ago concerning the "aesthetic consumerism" peculiar to our time: "Needing to have reality confirmed and experience enhanced by photographs is an aesthetic consumerism to which everyone is now addicted. Industrial societies turn their citizens into image-junkies; it is the most irresistible form of image pollution."[5]

Yet if the American edition of *The Lover's* confirms Sontag's point about "image pollution," it is, in effect, with the full complicity of the French author. This is not a case of the kind of editorial hucksterism that for publicity purposes ironically refuses to put its trust in the printed word alone, since the cover of the American edition is on the whole truer to the spirit of Marguerite Duras's work than is that of the French edition. The white minimalism of the *Editions de Minuit* designers belies that image-culture in which Duras is so at home and in which her most popular novel is effectively plunged from the beginning in a variety of ways.

As the opening couple of paragraphs of *The Lover* make clear, for the elderly Duras looking back from the moment of her writing across a long life, the point of departure of her fictionalized memoir is an image of herself—or, to be more precise, two images. The work begins with the report of a stranger's judgment on her old woman's face and a commentary on a photograph of her youthful self that was never taken. The looking glass of her memory finds itself obliged to confront an image from the past that exists only in her mind's eye with one reflected in the eyes of an observer in the present. The latter image is that of the face she possesses more or less at the time of writing, that is, when she was close to seventy years old; the former is that of the girl she was at the age of fifteen and a half, when, in her telling, she first met her Chinese lover on a ferryboat crossing the Mekong River. It is the fifty-five-year gap between those two evoked faces that opens up the extended exercise in experimental, autobiographical fiction—neither quite autobiography nor quite fiction—that *The Lover*, in fact, is.[6]

Although there are no photographs of the kind that are put on display in the opening pages of *Roland Barthes*, Duras's fictionalized memoir goes on to become almost as much of a family album as Barthes's work. Both writers put images of self and family into the public sphere and both employ distancing techniques, but Duras has no sympathy for the discretion characteristically deployed by Barthes. Moreover, Duras chooses to interrogate her autobiographical material by using fictional techniques that include shifting constantly between the present of her writing and a handful of potent and recurring images from a delimited period of her past.

Further, Duras begins with what is the negative of a photograph in a new sense—a sense that is related to John Berger's identification of a historical opposition between photography and memory. The image of her fifteen-and-a-half-year-old self on the ferryboat crossing the Mekong River derives its power as image for the narrator from the fact that it is the equivalent of a photograph not taken: "It is to this quality of not having been taken that the image owes its virtue, that of representing an absolute, of being its creator."[7]

There is some ambiguity in the way the issue is formulated here. It is, however, clear from the context that the power of the remembered image is recalled in association with the pleasure taken in a mirror image, in an act of jubilant self-imaging, in fact, of the kind that for a long time now has been associated with Lacan's imaginary register. "I'm fifteen and a half," a passage begins and is repeated in a number of variations that accumulate additional details as the work of memory proceeds, focusing less on face or figure than on articles of clothing—the dress of natural silk, the leather belt, the high-heeled, gold-lamé shoes and the man's hat ("a man's flat-brimmed hat, a brownish-pink fedora with a broad black ribbon" [11–12]). It is above all the latter that, the narrator claims, confers not just an air of calculated ambiguity but of wholeness on an adolescent girl's body that had previously been associated with a defect or lack—"the awkward thinness of the figure, the characteristic defect of childhood, became something different." The hat, in fact, functions as a fetish: what it does to the body is precisely to overcome its lack, to complete it, and to put it into circulation as a fully gendered and desirable body: "Suddenly I see myself as another, as another would be seen, outside myself, available to all, available to all eyes, in circulation for cities, journeys, desire. I take the hat and am never parted from it. Having got this hat that all by itself makes me whole, I wear it all the time" (12–13).

Expressed here is an exhilarating sense of a fullness of self whose illusory nature is confirmed by the fact that it depends on masquerade but is nonetheless pleasurable in spite of that. These wonderfully suggestive passages evoke, in fact, what is for Duras a kind of evanescent yet persistent "ur-image," an image that stands behind all those other images of Duras that, over the past couple of decades or so, she has allowed to be put into circulation by the publishing and related industries, and that have turned "the writer" into a media star. The girl who sees herself for the first time with the man's hat in a shopkeeper's mirror as a fully achieved, gendered subject is, on more than one level, in a state of innocence. And it is the same girl who stands on the Mekong River ferryboat shortly before she meets the Chinese lover who will initiate her into the passion and morbidity of sexual desire and sexual difference.

Fifty-five years later, the narrator of *The Lover* is, of course, far from such a state of innocence. It is therefore impossible to avoid reading into the choice of certain words in the passage just quoted Duras's experiences of a lifetime as woman and as "writer." Concentrated in that key notion of visual "availability"—"available to all, available to all eyes, in circulation for cities, journeys, desire"—is not so much youthful prescience as mature knowledge of what it potentially means to be both a woman and "a writer" in the modern world, and of how, for Duras, these two categories are collapsed together. Although the passage concerns a youthful awakening, it also points forward to what we know from other sources, namely, the extent to which Duras is aware that her status as "woman writer" makes her doubly the object of desire, and the challenge she finds in that situation; the choice of words alone confirms the eroticized charge that may come from being in "the public eye," of seeing oneself as the object of another's look, both on the local level, as woman, and on the national or international scene, as "writer." Many of the characteristics subsequently concentrated in Duras's authorial persona are already present in the cultivated ambiguities of that represented French girl who knowingly adopts a form of masquerade for her sexual "coming out" in colonial Vietnam at the beginning of the 1930s. "The writer" savors in retrospect the emergence in the girl she once was of her mature taste for self-interrogating exhibitionism and provocation.

The power of that "ur-image" over the narrator, then, is associated with completeness or fullness and is related in retrospect to the tale of first love that it introduces. Its brilliance is tied to the mythic suggestiveness of the larger scene, which implies an end as well as a beginning. The symbolism of a rite of passage is literalized in the crossing of the Mekong; the virgin girl on the deck of the ferryboat is poised to meet her first lover, whose apparent potency and allure is associated with an exotic difference of race and a large black limousine.

The end implied in the crossing of the river is that of childhood: the mysterious force of desire (Why this man? Why now and under these circumstances?) separates as well as joins; it abruptly reorients a young life away from family in the direction of something both potent and forbidden. The beginning is that of initiation into the strange knowledge of our selves as em-bodied, as desired and desiring flesh, that comes with sexual experience.

The "strangeness" of such self-knowledge is reinforced in *The Lover* by racial and cultural as well as gender difference that, in the context of French colonial Vietnam of the early nineteen-thirties, carry a transgressive charge. Here, as elsewhere in Duras's writings, racial difference eroticizes a sexual object. The thematic continuity between the interracial love affair of *The Lover* and the libidinal investments across a bitter national divide in, for example, *Hiroshima mon amour* and *War* is a commonplace of Duras criticism. In all cases the attraction of sexual otherness is heightened by an important element of the culturally taboo, which, as I suggest below, sometimes takes the extreme form of sleeping, or desiring to sleep, with the enemy. In any case, the dimension of the forbidden is given specificity in Duras's memoir novel of 1984 and associated with her personal experience in a number of ways, starting with the representations of the love scenes and the evocations of the Chinese lover's body.

Probably the most remarkable feature of those love scenes is their unusual split character, as a result of which the traditional pleasures of voyeurism are undercut by the reflective analysis. The "I" that sometimes mutates into "she" is both the girl who makes love to her first man and the narrator who represents it, both framer and framed. Moreover, as feminist critics have not been slow to point out,[8] the love scenes are characterized by the kind of role reversals in which the traditional dualities of male/female, active/passive, white/colored, adolescent/adult are in one way or another undermined or reversed.

It is, therefore, not surprising if the adolescent, female look to which the mature Chinese lover's male body is subjected is surprisingly cool and passionless: there is no question of her being romantically "swept away." Moreover, that same body is made to seem doubly other; its sex organ confirms that it is a male body, yet in the light of Western norms it appears androgynous—it is "unmasculine" in its apparent weakness and thinness, in its unexpected smoothness and its lack of body hair.

The weakness of men relative to women is, in fact, an important motif of *The Lover* and of other of works by Duras, including, for example, *Mr. Andesmas's Afternoon* and *Pain*—a weakness of gender that is located in psychobiology rather than in character or in the body. It is, moreover, a view of men that can be said to have begun with Duras's father, who died when she was only four, and with her brothers, both of whom depended on women and never made anything of their lives. In any case, the beginning of *The Lover* represents her first love as an affair of her own choosing; and in the end what is displayed is the girl's own strength in comparison with her older lover's passivity in the face of circumstances and the futility of her family. He becomes less the object of her passion than her compassion, and finally her indifference.

If Duras clearly takes pride in identifying her heroine as herself, it is apparently in large part precisely because she is stoically heroic in the way suggested earlier. The author thus associates herself with a line of fictional heroines who include the nameless survivor from Nevers of *Hiroshima mon amour*. Such women are represented as stronger than men not simply on emotional grounds but because their ethics is altogether less worldly; they have no fear of social opprobrium and they are without *pudeur*. On the one hand, "the poor little white girl" of *The Lover* seems to enjoy the apparent abasement suffered because of her reputation as a wealthy Chinaman's whore; on the other, she describes her sexual experiences and her acceptance of money and favors with a dispassion that is designed to disconcert. The "Marguerite Duras" of the autobiographical fiction could well have said, "I have the honor of having been dishonored." Indeed, much of the attraction for her of autobiography is to be found in such an aspiration.

Given that *The Lover* is about a rite of passage and a sexual awakening, about an end as well as a beginning, it is not surprising that, in spite of its title, it concerns Duras's disturbingly dysfunctional French family at least as much as her Chinese lover himself. And here, too, the overt autobiographical references confirm the way in which the author is determined to force the traditional distinctions between the private and the public and to reject what, were it not for Rousseau himself, comes increasingly to look like typically masculine "discretion."

The book's character as, in part, a family album of the kind that is not usually put on display is confirmed immediately after those opening pages in which Duras evokes the long-cherished picture of her adolescent self. From the verbal reconstitution of that first missing image, which had survived only in her memory, she goes on to evoke a series of other images, some of which apparently exist as actual photographs and others merely in her mind's eye. Thus the narrator passes directly and without transition from extended reflections on the ferryboat photo that was not taken to comments on photos of her son and her mother that were. What the juxtaposition suggests is the peculiar bondedness and the fatal power of generational succession: her son's body clearly derives from hers; much of the weight the narrator finds herself bearing in life—"that deep despondency about living" (14)—can be read into the distracted stance and attitude of that image of her mother surrounded by her three children.

There are subsequent strategic evocations in the work of other photos of members of the family, represented alone or in groups of two or more. There are also even more telling vignettes of Donnadieu family life that have the character of "domestic scenes" in both senses of those words: they are group pictures that express the desperation and rage which are integral to their collective life—her mother's depression, her elder brother's sadistic violence, her younger brother's helplessness, her own troubling ambivalences, her hate and incestuous longings.

Moreover, such material is often handled by Duras like scenes from a film. The organization of *The Lover*—without chapters and in units that are never longer than extended paragraphs or short groups of paragraphs, isolated by blank white spaces—seems itself to derive from the technique of cinema. One has the sense of shots or short montages of shots separated by more or less disconcerting cuts; the narrative combines a focus on the expanded present of the writing with flashbacks and flash-forwards, and with the equivalent of a voice-over commentary provided by the writer as narrator. The effect is that from the opening page images are allowed to come and go with the fluidity of film, apparently illuminated by the activity of memory and the play of associations; they may or may not recur as other, related images crowd in or fade. In other words, Duras's writing technique here borrows back from the tradition of filmmaking that she had helped initiate when she wrote the screenplay of what was, after all, an early New Wave film, *Hiroshima mon amour*.

Perhaps one of the most telling passages in the book on the subject of image making, however, again concerns still photography. Duras compares a photograph of her mother, taken in a commercial photographer's studio toward the end of her life, with the formal photographic portraits of elderly Vietnamese, made in preparation for death. The photograph in this case becomes, indeed, a substitute for memory—not personal memory, however, but familial memory: the carefully retouched images were destined to assure a local immortality within the home at the family shrine.

Given the deeply unhappy, centrifugal character of her own family, her mother's gesture has an even greater poignancy than do the Vietnamese portraits. Yet her mother's special case is also an example of a widespread but naive trust in modern culture in the power of the image to affirm and preserve the self—a trust that Duras by no means distances herself from, even as she obliquely comments on it. The photographic image constitutes the proof of a selfhood otherwise subject to doubt. On the one hand, as a private individual one can say, "I am, and shall continue to be, because my 'likeness' has been objectively recorded and mechanically reproduced"; on the other hand, as a person in the public eye one is able to affirm, "I am a celebrity because I see my 'likeness' massively reproduced and circulated." The aura of which Walter Benjamin once spoke is associated now not with "an original," but with a potential to generate endless lookalikes.

As anyone who has met a "star" in the flesh knows, compared to the image "the original" is almost always devoid of aura, even insipid.

If the opening paragraphs of *The Lover* confirm the degree to which Duras is at home in our image-culture, they also show that central to her writing is a project of self-representation and self-revelation that involves narrating episodes from her life calculated to scandalize and shock. Like Gide, she, too, might well affirm, "I come to disturb." For most of her career, she carried out such a program through fictional surrogates, through a series of women characters all of whom have an uncanny resemblance to each other; at a certain point they cease to be women and become "woman." In the more recent works under discussion here, the "she's" and "I's" she employs have Marguerite Duras, author, as their referent.

In *The Lover* the reader is drawn in from the beginning with the promise that long-kept secrets concerning the author herself are to be revealed: "Previously I spoke of periods of clarity, those on which the light fell. Now I'm talking about the hidden stretches of that same youth, of certain facts, feelings, events that I buried" (8). Moreover, in this passage Duras explicitly associates writing itself with "a basic unseemliness," defines it as an activity undertaken against a familial and national literary culture that traditionally placed a high value on *pudeur,* or "discretion," and understatement.

The social role of "the writer" that Duras inherits, on the other hand, is associated not with hiding but with showing and telling: showing and telling, on the basis of highly personal experiences, what life in time does to a human body or what extraordinary or disturbing things we are driven to do to others and others to do to us, both individually and collectively, with or without the excuse of war. Implicit throughout Duras's work is the notion that writing is by definition indecent—*impudique*—less understatement than overstatement, at least as far as explicitness is concerned. It is thus no accident, first, that Duras opens *The Lover* by holding up to the world a self-portrait at age seventy and, second, that that image should be one of "devastation." The whole point of that portrait is "to make a public spectacle of herself," to be pitiless in her self-representation.

If her unknown admirer claims to find a superior beauty in the look of age, it is because he has learned from a long tradition in European painting as well as twentieth-century photography (from Rembrandt to Walker Evans, say) that nothing is more resonant with meaning and photogenic beauty than a worn and textured face. In any case, whereas at a certain point in her life the aging film star Marlene Dietrich wilfully withdrew her image from public circulation by banishing the camera,[9] Marguerite Duras assumes her task as "writer" by presenting her own face in close-up so that all the marks of age are visible; and she contrasts that with the brief but resplendent moment, some fifty-five years before, when she was understandably in love with the image of her own still immature body poised to enter its relatively short period of fullness and wholeness.

It is not just harsh representations of herself that Duras projects in *The Lover*, however; her immediate family is subjected to a similar treatment. Although she makes the obligatory modernist disclaimer that "the story of her life doesn't exist" (8)—in the rather superficial sense that it lacks purposefulness and linearity—the story of her family certainly does, to the point at which, in her telling, we encounter something less like Freudian family romance than Greek myth. In the age of psychoanalysis and the confessional talk show, everyone knows that to tell the story of oneself is to reveal the secrets of one's family. And in Duras's case it is a story of neglect, wasted lives, irrational love, hate, pain, violence, madness, and, above all, death: the death of her father when she was four, the death of her own stillborn child shortly after her first marriage, the death of her mother, of her hateful elder brother, and of her beloved younger brother, at whose death, she claims, she also wanted to die.

It is, moreover, this relationship to her younger brother even more than to the lover of the title that suggests the kind of mythic antecedents Duras seems to be implicitly invoking. *The Lover* is in more ways than one a work of mourning, and nowhere is this more evident than in what it says about her younger brother and her passionate attachment to him. If there is one transcendent mythic figure in the Western tradition who fits Duras's conception of specifically feminine heroism, it is Antigone, and it was Antigone's fate to assume the task of carrying out the prescribed funeral rites for a dead and disgraced brother. The classic interpretation of Antigone's heroism is that of someone brave enough to sacrifice herself in the cause of a higher law than the law of the city. In *The Ethics of Psychoanalysis*, however, Jacques Lacan offers a reading of Sophocles' play that discovers within its heroine not a martyr of sweetness and spiritual light but a wild and untamable creature driven by a different kind of sacred principle, that of "desire," in the strong psychoanalytic sense he gave the word.[10] In either case, it is above all Antigone, who at the moment of her death might well have said before Duras, "I have the honor of having been dishonored."

Just as Antigone discovered the separateness of her destiny, so the Durasian persona in *The Lover* is shown to be motivated throughout by a different piety from the piety of her family's social world. Thus the telling of her family's story has something of the character of a sacred obligation that is also a settling of accounts; against her mother and her elder brother, she pays fitting public homage to the brother they victimized and she loved. The price of heroism in Antigone's case was opprobrium in the eyes of the world and the sacrifice of self; on a different level, that is the same price Duras is willing to pay for a modern and "writerly" form of heroism. Self-display is, after all, the means to martyrdom as well as its point.

The reference to the mythic model of Antigone is also a reminder of the characteristic rhapsodic style of *The Lover*; its consciously trancelike quality makes it radically different from most of the other works discussed in this volume, with the exception of parts of Rousseau's *Confessions* and some of Baudelaire's poetry. In the article quoted from earlier, Julia Kristeva attributes Duras's idiosyncratic style to her experience of World War II and the virtual incommunicability of pain that requires her to subvert the traditional "festive rhetoric" of literature: "If there is an exploration of form, it is subordinated to the confrontation with the silence of horror within the self and in the world. Such a confrontation leads to an aesthetic of *awkwardness* on the one hand and to a *noncathartic literature* on the other" ("The Pain of Sorrow," 140).

On the discursive level, in any case, the style of *The Lover* reads as both very old and very new. It contrives to be doubly powerful because it harks back to the speech of certain female seers in Greek literature and because it suggests the monological insistence of the analysand's speech in psychoanalysis. Truth in both cases is assumed to arrive from elsewhere. Thus, apparently working from deeper levels of her psyche, the narrator of *The Lover* is posited as less speaker than spoken.

The persona Duras projects of herself, then, is that of lone survivor and brooding chronicler, who is finally freed by so much death to do what no self-respecting member of a traditional family would have dared do (but that is the stuff of mythic Greek families), namely, "wash its dirty linen in public." After Stendhal and Sartre, in particular, Duras's theme is once again the theme of "the horror of home" that Baudelaire had affirmed almost a hundred years earlier to be a malady of the modern age. There is even a sense in which *The Lover* updates an old and insalubrious subgenre, *memoires à clef,* by providing her readers with all the keys they need from the outset. In many ways the character of Duras's "writerly" project here might best be summed up in the single word "scandal." Yet such an effect is attenuated precisely because the work implicitly assumes, with our culture at large, that it is proper to place a much higher value on truth telling than on "discretion."

Along with a kind of unembarrassed self-scrutiny, the other characteristic feature of *The Lover* is the way it combines the rhapsodic style of narration just referred to with the effect of spontaneity and intimacy: since that age of sentimentality to which Rousseau belonged, spontaneity in Western culture has been metonymically linked to truthfulness, and the offer of intimacy to a form of virtue that is of the heart. Thus one finds in *The Lover* stylistic features derived from familiar speech (ellipsis, repetition, and the use of the historical present, for example) that are designed to suggest the unbidden play of associations involved in the work of memory, as well as the unedited character of what emerges: "Another thing I should tell you . . ." (*Que je vous dise encore . . .*) (11). Such deictic markers are made the signifiers of an authorial presence that implies closeness both to the source of truth within and to the reader who reads.

At the same time, the author, like Rousseau before her, knowingly makes a confidant of the reader. We are made privy to information that was apparently both so personal and so important that it has remained a secret up to now: "I often think of the image only I can see now, and of which I've never spoken. It's always there, in the same silence, amazing *[émerveillante]*. It's the only image of myself I like, the only one in which I recognize myself, in which I delight" (3). The body of the work goes out of its way to sustain the tone of intimacy introduced here and the privileged relationship to the reader implied by it.

In a work that specializes in a form of scandal, nothing is perhaps more scandalous in the context of its time than the revisionist assertion that the beliefs of collaborators during the German occupation of France were no different from Duras's own commitment to the French Communist Party after the Second World War: "The Fernandezes were collaborators. And I, two years after the war, I was a member of the French Communist Party. The parallel is complete and absolute. The two things are the same, the same pity, the same call for help, the same lack of judgment, the same superstition, if you like, that consists in believing in a political solution to a personal problem" (68).

The passage is striking for a number of reasons. First, Duras is indirectly attacking *résistantisme*—the myth, associated in particular with Gaullism, that France under the German occupation was a nation largely united in its resistance but misled by a clique of political leaders and betrayed by a minority of collaborators. Second, this sounds like the kind of recantation that even in the mid-eighties was relatively rare among former Communist intellectuals. Third, the dismissal of politics as a means of solving fundamental human problems implies an end to *engagement* in the Sartrean sense. But what is most surprising is less the views expressed about the uncoupling of "the personal" from "the political" than their categorical character; the surprise is in the adjectives: "The parallel is *complete and absolute.*"

As a result, the attitude expressed turns out paradoxically to be not very different from that which it denounces. The politics Duras is rejecting here is politics of a revolutionary and/or salvationary kind, the kind that promises to produce new men and women in a new world, the kind she apparently once believed in herself. However, it is clear both from the context and from her other writings that the reason she rejects it is not because she puts any faith in the mundane politics of liberal democratic societies—a politics of public debate, parties and elections, compromise and competing interest groups—but because she looks outside of politics altogether for the solutions to human problems—that is, if the idea of such solutions makes any sense at all.

The passage is particularly significant for my purposes because it introduces the themes and deeply ambiguous moral climate of the occupation years which constitute the material of the work that was published a year after *The Lover,* in 1985, *Pain.* The improbable claim is made in a prefatory note that it was actually written much earlier, at a place and time that the author no longer recalls. The usefulness of this fudging of the actual date of composition is that it lends verisimilitude to Duras's frequent assertion that she does not write her works consciously and critically, but that they come to her from elsewhere, pass through her. And given that *Pain* is in many ways one of the most troubling of her compositions, the mystery of its origin only enhances its power.

If *Pain* seems to have been much less of a popular success than *The Lover,* that is hardly surprising. To begin with, it widens the range of that which is touched by scandal from the sphere of self and family to that of self and French society at large. Baudelaire's "horror of home" becomes, under the conditions of the German occupation, "the horror of human society," and in both cases the complicity of individuals, including also that of the narrator, is the point of departure. Furthermore, the autobiographical narratives of *Pain* have none of the attractions of romantic love that is, in spite of everything, still part of the appeal of *The Lover,* nor can they be recuperated as feminist stories of "empowerment" and triumph over male-made circumstances. Nowhere more than in *Pain* does Duras's taste for provocation overwhelm the discourse of political correctness to the point where, in one of the most notorious narratives of the volume, she seems to be illustrating the misogynist assertion that "every woman loves a fascist." Moreover, the provocation is enhanced by the very fact that the author presents the material as confessions of her own scandalous acts and desires.

As noted above, some of the Second World War material had already been worked through in *Hiroshima mon amour,* particularly in connection with the experience of the *femme tondue* from Nevers. And something of the strange heroism evoked in the published appendixes to the scenario of that film reappears in *Pain.* By the end the author/narrator and protagonist of the later work can claim, like the young woman from Nevers, "Shame has disappeared from my life" (*Hiroshima,* 132).

The six texts published together under the title *Pain* all have to do with aspects of life during the German occupation of France in 1940–1944, but the last two, and least significant, are described by the author as "invented"—in effect, mere "literature." The first four, on the other hand, "Pain" *(Douleur),* "Mr. X, Known Here as Pierre Rabier," "Albert from Capitals," and "Ter the Militia Man," are claimed to derive from the author's own wartime experiences. They have what is for Duras the superior status of direct personal testimony. It is thus only logical that they take the form of a journal, of what in a prefatory section preceding "Albert from Capitals" and "Ter the Militia Man" is referred to as "The Journal of *Pain*" (in the original French, the word used is again *la Douleur*).

The personal, confessional nature of the two episodes the narrator then

goes on to evoke is emphatically affirmed in the extraordinary short paragraph that follows. Once again the hold of the text over a reader is made
to depend on the promise of long-kept secrets about to be disclosed, secrets that transcend fiction because they concern the author: "I am Thérèse.[11] I am the woman who tortures the informer. At the same time, I am
the woman who wants to make love to Ter, the militia man. I give you
the woman who tortures along with the other texts. Learn to read: these
are sacred texts" (134).

The peculiarly solemn and hortatory note sounded in the last sentence
finds its justification in what precedes. On the one hand, the affirmation
of identity of author and character—"Thérèse, c'est moi."—is a way of
signalling that the texts that follow are beyond fiction, are somehow of a
higher seriousness because they are directly connected to a life; on the
other hand, that affirmation is itself a rhetorical gesture whose purpose is
to disarm the reader. No one was more aware than Flaubert that the heroine of his fiction was not himself; Emma Bovary could never have said,
"Flaubert, c'est moi." In any case, it is once again the preliminary auto-
accusation of "Albert from Capitals," this time of an unusual gravity, that
is calculated to dispel the reader's skepticism.

The view of "literature" as merely fictional and worldly, and therefore
incapable of expressing certain truths of experience—the most profound or
"sacred" truths, in this case—is, as we have seen, typical of that "writerly"
tradition inaugurated by Rousseau and expressed most forcefully by him
in the *Letter to D'Alembert on Theater*. It is a view that Duras had already
expressed in this volume, in the brief introductory remarks to the first
text derived from her wartime experiences, the title story, "Pain." Having
explained there how she came across "the Journal" many years after it
was written in an old *armoire* in her country house, and how she was
incapable of explaining the time of its writing or the mystery of its loss,
the author concludes with another categorical statement about the limits
of "literature." She begins with an assertion of value and an account of
the emotion she felt on rereading her own mystery text: "*Pain* is one of
the most important things in my life. The word "piece of writing" [*écrit*]
doesn't describe it. . . . I found myself in the presence of a phenomenal
disarray of thought and feeling that I didn't dare touch, and relative to
which literature seemed to me shameful." In other words, there is a kind
of writing that is more than writing because, in its immediacy and connection to the pain and suffering of personal experience, it transcends "literature."

What Duras is seeking is suggested best in the surprise of that word
"sacred" in the passage quoted earlier: "these are sacred texts." Yet given
her generation, as well as her personal and intellectual commitments, it is
perhaps not so surprising after all. The pursuit of the "sacred" in the modern Western world had, of course, resurfaced intermittently in French literary and artistic circles from at least the time of surrealism. It is a notion

that is central to Antonin Artaud's influential, avant-garde theory of theater as expressed in such essays as "The Theater of Cruelty" and "The Theater and the Plague." [12] A passionate interest in the sacred was also at the center of the activities sponsored by the short-lived but influential Collège de Sociologie and promoted by such contemporary midcentury Parisian intellectuals as Georges Bataille, Roger Caillois, and Michel Leiris. They had preceded Duras in their contempt not only for "literature" and the whole sphere of aesthetic production in general but also for the novel in particular; the latter was taken to be the genre par excellence of modern, desacralized, liberal democratic society and of a despised bourgeois individualism. [13]

Moreover, in Duras's case, as in theirs, the most immediate path to self-transcendence appeared to pass through encounters with exotic forms of human life outside Europe, transgressive erotic acts, or the encounter with death. In other words, the idea of regeneration through violence that is central to the revolutionary tradition in France is also to be found in a different form among those who sought renewal through spiritual experiences outside politics. The approach to the sacred was typically assumed to be through limit situations in which the stability of the self was threatened by disruptive forces within or without, or when one's own body or another's was subjected to extremes of pleasure or pain. The task of "the writer" in pursuit of the self-transcendence associated with such "sacred" knowledge was thus to put him or herself to the test of agony or ecstacy, and to report back on that experience. Given such expectations, it is also not surprising that the journal, autobiography, and the first-person, fictionalized memoir were the preferred genres. [14]

Two examples from different texts in *War* serve to illustrate how crucial such material was for Duras. The first concerns the descriptions of her first husband's body and bodily functions, immediately after he was brought back to Paris from the concentration camp at Dachau at the end of the war; the second has to do with the torture of the suspected informer, Albert, that "Thérèse," the Resistance fighter, conducts during the days following the liberation of Paris. Both episodes concern male bodies observed or acted upon by a woman, broken bodies that have ceased to be the object of any possible desire but that have become instead objects of a horrible fascination. Thus it is the horror of two bodies, to both of which she has a special relationship, that Duras "the writer" deliberately puts on lurid display—the horror of a body she had once loved, made love to, and, at the time, had already made up her mind to give up, and the body of a stranger whose bloody beating she supervises. In both cases Duras goes out of her way to emphasize how far she is beyond shame by directly associating herself with both episodes.

There is also a typical equivalence established between both episodes, a material as well as a moral equivalence of the kind referred to earlier in connection with Duras and the Fernandezes. The two passages report on transgressive acts of an order that are normally only encountered in time of war or when all social restraints have broken down. Both concern men who are reduced to total impotence as a result of torture or the severest kind of abuse and deprivation, which amounts to the same thing. The first, Robert L., as Duras's husband is known in the narrative, was the victim of the Nazi terror machine; the second, Albert, is shown to be the victim of the author acting as an embodiment of the zeal of the French resistance in their campaign for revolutionary justice and the purification of the national body politic.

Duras is concerned here both with what, in her experience, women no less than men are capable of doing to fellow human beings, and with that point at which the body is so traumatized and fragmented that it crosses over into something that is no longer human. Thus the equivalence is focused in the representation from a position of power of two bodies in the throes of a kind of martyrdom that defines the outer limit of human existence, immediately beyond which they become merely material, die, or otherwise cease to be. The effect of the passages concerned is also to confirm that horror, unfortunately, is an ambivalent emotion: it can turn into disgust and even contempt as easily as into compassion. It is this provocative ambivalence that is communicated by Duras in the two passages, evoking Robert L.'s return and Albert's torture, respectively:

> For seventeen days the sight of that shit didn't change. It was inhuman. It separated him from us more than his fever, more than his thinness, more than his nailless fingers, or the marks of SS beatings. We gave him golden yellow pap, infant's pap, and it reemerged from his body dark green like mud from a marsh.

> They have hit him hard. His eye is a mess, blood is flowing down his face. He is crying. Bloody snot issues from his nose. He groans, "Aah, aah, aah," without interruption. He has stopped answering. His breast is split open at the level of his ribs. He keeps on rubbing himself with his hands and covers himself with blood.[15]

With reference to the first passage, which, for obvious reasons, I chose for my epigraph, one notes the narrator's distance in a clinical curiosity determined, for the sake of bearing true witness, to spare no one. The practice of the "writerly" ethic of beyond shame obliges her to disclose everything, down to the color and consistency of her husband's shit.[16]

As far as the second passage is concerned, the shock effect of the fantasmatic episode is, if anything, even greater. And that is not just because we are made to share the point of view of the torturer—postwar cinema has turned that experience into a banality. The shock effect is rather in the fact that we are given access to another of the esteemed author's guilty secrets. What "the writer" reports is that, for a moment at least, the parallel she saw with regard to collaborators and communists was indeed absolute: "Thérèse" the resistance fighter is interchangeable with an SS interrogator. At the same time it is difficult to avoid reading into the scene a fantasm of brutal revenge in which Duras, as woman, took pleasure in exercising her power over an insignificant but evil little man, precisely because he was both insignificant and evil; behind Albert stands the image of her elder brother, who was also vaguely suspected of having been an informer during the Occupation.

It is difficult to avoid seeing in this perverse, sado-masochistic scenario an ironic reversal of the one that in Freud goes under the heading "a child is being beaten." [17] The difference, obviously, is that in Duras's case the sentence is active, not passive, and that the subject, the beater, is female and the object of the beating male: it is not so much "a man is being beaten" as "I, Marguerite Duras, am beating a man." The boldness of the torture scene is thus bound up with the fact that this is not simply a case of the pornography of violence in which gender roles are for once reversed; as with the love scenes of *The Lover,* the scene is framed so that the spectator observes the torturer as well as the tortured. The true spectacle is the spectacle of the pleasure/shame of "Thérèse".

As far as Robert L. is concerned, however, we can see that what also interested Duras in this material was its quality of "passion," in the Christian sense of the word. Thus, alongside the horror and the compassion and the disgust, including self-disgust, there is also an aspect of wonder. This emerges most clearly in connection with a form of dignity that Robert L. retained, even at the cruellest moments of his agony, and with the gradual rebirth of a "man" from the subhuman body of the returned deportee. At the heart of the mid-twentieth-century European darkness, Duras for once bears witness to something like the brief effulgence of the nobility in the creature that was once a husband: "Everything, or almost everything, let go, even the fingers that were no longer able to hold on to nails that also let go. The heart, however, continued to hold on to its contents. The heart. And the head. Hagard yet sublime, alone, it rose up out of this cadaver, emerged, remembered, recounted, acknowledged, demanded. Talked and talked" (68).

If disgust is coolly registered, homage is also briefly paid on those rare occasions when, as here, it seems due. The paradox the passage contains—a paradox that goes to the heart of Duras's representations of human existence—is that something of the original sacredness of human life shows itself only under the most harrowing of conditions: the glimpse vouchsafed of "a sublime body" depends on the prior reductive spectacle of the body as a mess of flesh.

Most of the time, however, and not only in *Pain,* Duras finds there are few aspects of human life to celebrate, beginning with herself and her own conduct. In the morally ambiguous climate of the German occupation, the Nazis she encounters are less than demonic, and those who work for the

Resistance, including herself, are complex human subjects whose motivations do not bear too close a scrutiny. Such heroism as does emerge from the pages of *Pain* has nothing to do with the national struggle against fascism. It is instead a heroism of the "writerly" kind.

The character of Duras's late works is, in fact, that of "a before of literature"; that is to say, their focus is explicitly on the author and her living—on her relationships, her deeply ambivalent or self-destructive behavior, her disturbing fantasms, or the repressed material that returns—to the point where all the rest, all that is "invented" or formally elaborated, is indeed just "literature." In many ways Duras takes the confessional tradition inaugurated by Rousseau further than anyone else discussed here in the direction of the Orphic, although one can find in her work important echoes of, say, Antonin Artaud, Georges Bataille, and even Céline. But unlike them she starts from the specificity of her situation and her power as woman.

There is, then, in the end, something provocatively masochistic and consciously sacrificial in the way Duras offers herself up to public scrutiny, in the way in which she knowingly makes a public spectacle of deviance and private pain. Committed to the ethic of hiding nothing and sparing no one, she performs a kind of moral and emotional striptease. Why else represent herself in turn as a mercenary Lolita figure; as a guilty and unfaithful waiting wife; as a woman drawn to certain male fascists, if not to fascism, and therefore as a collaborator on the level of desire; as a torturer who enjoys the gradual raising of the ante on the body of her futile victim; and, in *M.D.*, as an alcoholic suffering the pangs of withdrawal while she dries out? [18]

Duras's work effectively reaffirms the view first made explicit by Rousseau that for "the writer," bearing witness, like charity, should begin at home. And in her case that means at the level of observations of the material body—her own as well as the bodies of those who are close to her— of the drives that traverse it and the cravings that inhabit it. If she so frequently puts bodies of both sexes and a variety of ages on display, therefore, frequently under extreme conditions, it is because bodies testify in the end, like Dorian Gray's, to the uses and abuses of life in time and to something beyond them that inhabits them.

On the other hand, the reason why Duras is able to discover power in her situation as woman is that she challenges from within the traditional feminine virtue of modesty and exploits for her own purposes the traditional feminine vice of vanity. Like Marlene Dietrich, she is immoderately immodest in the way she focuses the world's attention on her image; unlike Marlene Dietrich, she does not in old age seek to avert the eyes of others from the face she is obliged to wear; indeed, she flaunts it. She knowingly continues to make herself visually available—"available to all, available to all eyes"—since "the writer's" narcissism is located elsewhere than that of the film star. Duras derives her satisfaction from a claim to "writerly" moral superiority that is also a provocation; the demand for attention in a space beyond shame is justified on the grounds of the pitilessness that, in the opening paragraph of *The Lover*, holds up the image of the author's own "devastation" to the world.

In an important sense, to make oneself "available to all, to all eyes" is what a rock star also does. There is a way in which Madonna, in a film such as *Truth or Dare*, which is the documentary journal of a rock tour, is Duras's scandalous mass-market double. As the title indicates, the claim made in the film is that risks are to be taken and that total artistic freedom to tell the truth is to be exercized; as artist Madonna affirms her right to show and tell all about herself. Consequently, she waxes indignant when the "fascistic" Toronto police attempt to ban the scene in which she simulates masturbation to music.

The case of Madonna relative to Marguerite Duras, or of the latter relative to Rousseau, confirms Bourdieu's idea that in the literary and artistic field there is a progressive diminution of the cost to the individual producer of competing for a position as innovator: "The more the autonomizing process advances, the more possible it becomes to occupy the position of producer without having the properties—or not all of them, or not to the same degree—that had to be possessed to produce the position; the more, in other words, the newcomers who head for the most 'autonomous' positions can dispense with the more or less heroic sacrifices of the past." [19] As far as Madonna is concerned, the appearance of artistic heroism has led to huge economic reward at little personal cost.

In any case, to return to the serious issues raised by Duras, though she is no feminist in a programmatic and political sense, one of the central submerged motifs of her works is the superiority of women. It is not a question of intellectual superiority over men, and even less, perhaps, of moral superiority, of a traditional kind, at least. Duras's women do not think or behave better. It has to do instead, on the one hand, with a determination to go to the end of one's desire and, on the other, with a readiness to represent oneself doing it before an audience. The ethics implied by the stance of "the honor of dishonor" is Rousseau's heroic shamelessness.

That is why the image of "the writer" Duras embraces is suggested, appropriately enough, by an image from a film on which she collaborated and that is a specifically female image. Like the young Frenchwoman of *Hiroshima mon amour*, who did sleep with the enemy and, before the age of punk, had her head forcibly shorn, Duras proudly exhibits the marks of her shame along with those worn by people close to her. Moreover, Resnais's filmic image suggests an even more famous one that proves to be unexpectedly relevant here: the shorn head of "Elle" in the Duras/Resnais film is the sign of an unsexing and a public humiliation to which the most famous woman of French history, Joan of Arc, was also subjected before she was burned at the stake. That image, as incarnated by Maria Falconetti in Carl Dreyer's 1928 avant-garde masterpiece, *The Passion of Joan of Arc,* became in France an icon and ideal ego with a multilayered significance for our modern age.

Since the discovery of Dostoyevski, himself a disciple of Rousseau in more than one respect, French writers have often been preoccupied with saints and sinners, and with the short distance that often separates them. And Dreyer's film was very much a document of its time and place in this respect because it associated the traditional idea of the sacred with a new and experimental art. Thus his treatment of Joan of Arc's story, taken largely from the actual transcripts of the trial, constitutes in its own way "a before of literature" of the kind Duras favors: its referent is the life of an astonishing, heroic woman who went to the end of her desire and, in doing so, confronted male weakness and defied the authoritarian male world of Realpolitik, social order, and institutionalized religion.

Above all, Dreyer's *Passion of Joan of Arc* concerns precisely a "passion" in which images of remarkable physical beauty confront images of devastation: from a visual point of view, nothing is more celebratory, or more pitiless, than Dreyer's famous angled close-ups and extreme close-ups of Falconetti's unmade-up face. The paradox of the Danish director's cinematographic art has, in fact, a special affinity with Duras's late works. Among other things, it illustrates the proposition that the appearance of "the sublime body" is preceded by the death of the flesh, or, in other words, that the ultimate stardom—that is, sainthood—depends on the agonizing, sacrificial spectacle of a body publicly mutilated and shamed. No wonder Duras enjoyed evoking the image of her devastated face at the beginning of *The Lover.*

References to the sacred are, as we have seen, frequent throughout much of Duras's work, although it seems typically to have retreated from external life inward. Moreover, as so often in past eras, it is interpreted as being in the keeping of women, including, in particular, apparently mad or outcast women. In the interviews Duras did with Michelle Porte for French television, for example, entitled *Marguerite Duras's Places (Les Lieux de Marguerite Duras)*, she cites Jules Michelet approvingly on the subject of witches.[20] She goes on to praise women's capacity for silence and for listening, as well as for a preternatural intelligence that communicates with the nonhuman. More specifically, women are held to have an uncanny bond with place, including especially such charged locations as "the home," on the one hand, and those primordial places that originally surrounded the home, like the forest and the sea, on the other. Women also continue to be the guardians of household deities as well as the repositories of familial memory. Above all, because they give birth, they live with the impossible knowledge that is inherent in an organic connection to the primal pain of existence.[21]

In light of all this, it is not surprising that Duras once again implicitly defines herself as "a writer" by expressing contempt for "literature" as such. In the same way that she professes to have no interest in meaning, syntax, or grammar when she writes, she also apparently cares nothing for traditional fine writing or the formal qualities associated with the different genres. "Literature" is, in fact, once again defined negatively, this time as a form of "plagiarism" and as male gendered; it suffers from the sin of belonging to the worldly sphere of culture and artifice that Rousseau had denounced in his own time and, by implication, to the public sphere first associated with Enlightenment liberalism. In any case, to the concept of male "literature" Duras opposes that of female "translation." Nothing distinguishes her work more obviously from that of her poststructuralist male contemporaries, in fact, than the essentialist notion that a woman writing as a woman is engaged in an activity that is both a listening and a translating: "I think 'feminine literature' is an organic, translated writing . . . translated from blackness, from darkness."[22]

As Duras's interviews with Michelle Porte also make clear, such writing depends in turn on a definition of woman as "desire" ("Woman is desire") and the conviction that she writes from a different "place": "We don't write at all from the same place as men. And when women don't write from the place of desire, they are not writing; they, too, are plagiarizing" (*Marguerite Duras's Places*, 102).

Although in their insistence on the specificity of the feminine such affirmations seem to be rooted in the new feminist consciousness that began to emerge in the late sixties, on another level they constitute a return to Rousseau. Indeed, it is part of my argument in this book that with Marguerite Duras we have come full circle. At the core of her self-understanding and self-representations as "writer" is the notion of an essential "porousness" or "opennness" that shuns the idea of a necessary detour through artistic form and is the contemporary equivalent of Rousseau's pursuit of transparency and immediacy. The eighteenth-century philosopher also sought in his way to transcend literary culture and "literature" as practiced in his time. The *Confessions* is itself predicated on a retreat from worldliness: Rousseau, too, affirms his openness both to the sacred within and to the divine in nature without; Rousseau, too, claims to tell his readers of his innermost feelings without artifice. In the same way that he believed in an original, natural language—an onomatopoeic, gestural language that preceded symbolization and human culture—he also pursued the goal of what one might call "a natural literature," one he associated with direct communication and the "genreless" genres of letter writing (*The New Héloïse*) and autobiography (the *Confessions*).

In the late twentieth century Duras's metaphor for her relationship to writing is that of an echo chamber, a hollow space which receives and passively re-emits messages that arrive from elsewhere; like Joan of Arc, she may be said to believe in her voices in opposition to male politics and male culture, even if those voices are no longer associated with angelic presences. In short, though it is expressed in forms, or even media, specific to her age, her belief in "a before of literature" has a long prior history.

When he was already marked for death and in hiding, Salman Rushdie wrote a lecture, which was actually delivered by Harold Pinter, entitled "Is Nothing Sacred? "[23] Rushdie's use of the word is, of course, ambiguous. His response turns out to be a kind of profession of faith or defense of literature at a time of extreme personal duress; literature, he argues, is the best we can hope for in a postmodern world in which God is long dead. And, unlike Duras, what he means by the word is a mediate space of celebration and fantasy, irony, commentary and debate, between a lost sacred realm and brute material existence, a space of "festive rhetoric". Thus, in terms of the opposition established by Kundera—with which I began—between "the novelist" and "the writer," Rushdie is on Kundera's side, on the side of "the novelist." Moreover, he takes the novel to be the model of all that is most important in contemporary literary art.

Thus his answer, in effect, amounts to a refutation of Duras, for whom the sacred does exist and is separate from the sphere of the literary. Where she thinks in terms of writing as a listening or translating, he is attached to the idea of poesis or a making. In the late twentieth century, it seems that one final refuge of the "the writer" in her postpolitical incarnation is in the championship of sacred (female) writing over profane (male) literature.

CHAPTER 7

Epilogue:
From Althusser's Theory of a
Murder to Foucault's
Aesthetics of Existence

[B]y the time of the emergence of the modern intellectual community, France, thanks to the Revolution, had become a universal model, her experience part of the collective European memory. Being French gave Parisian writers a uniquely dual identity and thus authorized them to bear a special burden. Henceforth, their marginality, their opposition, their elective condition of revolt and protestation within France itself was what elevated and integrated them into a superior, trans-national community and defined their cultural significance (in France and abroad); from Dreyfus on, this special confidence of French intellectuals would distinguish them from their peers in other cultures.

TONY JUDT

Judt's description of the unique role French intellectuals seemed destined to play on the world stage in the twentieth century as a result of their historical legacy of revolution corresponds remarkably well to the lives and careers of both Louis Althusser and Michel Foucault. Both were intel-lectuals in the classic French sense that their remoter ancestors were the eighteenth-century philosophes and their role vis-à-vis the state was rede-fined for modern French public life by the events of the Dreyfus Affair. Yet by the end in both cases that was not enough.

It took a personal tragedy and some ten years of silence before Althus-ser reemerged at his death as something more than an intellectual and the guru of high Marxist theory in his time, that is, as "a writer." In Fou-cault's case, on the other hand, it seems that, first, the experience of the events of May 1968 and, second, the gay rights movement led him to challenge the role of the classic universal intellectual and, through a series of critiques and self-critiques, to distance himself increasingly from macro-politics in the direction of micropolitics, local initiatives, and, finally, an ethics that was also an aesthetics of existence.

If I set Althusser and Foucault in opposition to each other in this epi-logue, then, it is because one points to an end and the other to a beginning.

Louis Althusser
(Photo J. Pavlovsky. Sygma)

Michel Foucault

That is, whereas the former was still identifying himself with a philosophical and "writerly" tradition that is as old as Roussear, the other knowingly distanced himself from that tradition; whereas one still takes political emancipation and sexual liberation to be dual aspects of a single cause, the other uncouples them; and, finally, whereas one embraces Rousseau's example in pursuit of the truth of the self to the point of writing his own *Confessions,* the other conducts a counterhistorical critique of the Western practice of confession, and in the process both connects Rousseau to Freud and undermines their importance under the rubric of the post-classical age's "will to know."

As for Althusser, the revival of interest in him in the early 1990s was the result of the publication of a single autobiographical work *The Future Lasts a Long Time, (L'Avenir dure longtemps),* published posthumously in France in 1992. Its success was, of course, in large part that of a *succès de scandale* insofar as it explained the circumstances under which he murdered his companion and wife of over thirty years, the former Hélène Rytmann, in their apartment at the Ecole Normale Supérieure in Paris. Surprisingly, like a classic crime thriller, Althusser's own narrative begins with an evocation of the murder scene:

> Here as I remember it fully and precisely down to its minutest details, engraved within me throughout all my ordeals and for ever more—between two nights, the one I was emerging from without knowing it and the one I was about to enter, of which I will explain the when and how—here is the murder scene as I lived it.[1]

Such is the long and convoluted opening sentence of Althusser's autobiography. There follow two pages in which the author does indeed evoke with some precision, and in the narrative present, the time, place, and circumstances of the murder. This short first chapter then breaks off with the author's rush to get help from the resident physician at the Ecole and his own dispatch under sedation to Saint Anne's Hospital.

Such a beginning is likely to surprise anyone who has any familiarity with Althusser's name and reputation. The mystery and horror called up is of the kind one expects from the opening scene of a thriller but not from the nonfiction account of a life by the most famous Marxist theorist of his generation, even if that life had involved the commission of a murder. Yet such an introductory strategy was apparently adopted self-consciously for maximum effect, for it becomes clear that, as in a thriller, every detail of the scene is designed to signify in the fullness of understanding which comes with the denouement once all the material has been worked through.[2]

Chapter 2 immediately interrupts the flow of the narrative in order to focus on the writer and on the scene of writing itself. It answers the question why, roughly five years after the fact, the author decided to write his own account of what had occurred for future public consumption. Having been deprived of his day in court because, for a combination of reasons, the case was never brought to trial—he benefited from what under French law is called a non-lieu (non-event)—against the advice of many of his friends he sets out to tell his side of the story. That "the silence and the public death" (*Future,* 23) to which he was, in effect, condemned by the medical-judicial process in lieu of a trial was unbearable for him is confirmed by his metaphor of "the tombstone"—a metaphor that, with its implications of the possibility of resurrection, has a peculiar resonance in this context. In any case, Althusser makes it his purpose to explain "publicly"—the word is repeated a number of times in its adjectival and adverbial form—what he takes to be all the significant factors that led up to the murder. And in order to do that, he finds it necessary to go a long way back and narrate the salient emotional episodes in his life, not just from his birth but, for reasons that will be apparent later, from some time before his birth.

The Future Lasts a Long Time has, then, the character of a substitute text which has the stature of works which only reach the reader from beyond the grave, a late twentieth-century equivalent of François René de Chateaubriand's *Memoirs from Beyond the Grave.* In it Althusser undertakes his own defense, though not as on a witness stand but in the time-honored mode of a literary genre that in France, at least, came under suspicion almost from the moment it emerged as such in the eighteenth century.

He makes no attempt to deny his guilt; the task he sets himself is rather to explain the forces within himself and without that contributed to the commission in his early sixties of the monstrous act. Althusser has a theory of the murder he committed, a theory that is specific to intellectual life in post–World War II France; and it will be the overriding purpose of his book to lay out that theory at the same time that he illustrates it from his own life. The resulting work is what might be called an *autobiographie à thèse.*

But why should that be of interest to anyone outside the circle of friends to whom the work is ostensibly addressed or outside that often distressingly self-preoccupied Parisian intellectual world in which he lived the greater part of his life? The answer in this context is that because in interrogating his life in public from the perspective of his late sixties and after the murder, Althusser also gives the reader the opportunity to interrogate his text and along with it the tradition of political advocacy and confessional writing, stretching back to Rousseau, from which it derives. It is clear that with his posthumous work Althusser realizes the ambition of becoming "a writer" in the full sense I have given the word here, that is, someone who is committed to the regeneration of self and society and whose characteristic modes of expression are political theory and cultural critique, on the one hand, and autobiography, on the other. With Althusser, too, in the end the stance of *j'accuse* is united with that of *je me confesse* in a general conception of writing as advocacy and orientation to a future imagined as both more just and more egalitarian than the disappointing present—a future, moreover, in which the transparency of self to self is emphasized.

Althusser was institutionalized immediately after his wife's death in 1980, and he ceased to play any kind of public role, even after his release, down to his death in 1990. Foucault died in 1984. Yet in the context of that modern French intellectual and cultural history with which I am concerned here, their deaths do not bear a comparable symbolic value. Whereas in retrospect the retreat and death of Althusser does seem to signal the end of an era, Foucault at the time of his disappearance still seemed to be open to the future. The critical philosophical problematic of *The Future Lasts a Long Time* remains that of the French philosophical mainstream in the 1960s. It is as if for Althusser the experience of 1968 had meant nothing, whereas for Foucault it signified a great deal. Two deaths, then, but, for reasons that I shall suggest, only one of them was described at the time as "untimely."[3]

Nevertheless, as is clear from a memorable statement of purpose halfway through his work, the issues as Althusser formulates them could hardly seem more pertinent or more crucial to all those engaged in one way or another with the academy, politics, or the intellectual life in our time: "[W]hat I owe my reader, because it is what I owe myself, is the elucidation of the subjective roots of my specific attachment to my profession as a Professor of Philosophy at the Ecole Normale Supérieure, to philosophy, politics, the Party, my books and their influence or, in other words, how I came (and it wasn't a matter of lucid reflection but of something obscure and to a great extent unconscious) to invest and inscribe my subjective fantasms in my objective and public activities" (152). In other words, political, social, literary, intellectual, and individual psychic history are made to overlap and interpenetrate in the work in ways that should not surprise, coming from the Marxist theorist who gave a whole new meaning to the originally psychoanalytic concept of "overdetermination."

Whether we like it or not, Althusser is clearly very much our contemporary, although one whom recent political history is rapidly distancing us from. Thus his posthumous work of confession affords an opportunity to reflect on some central preoccupations of the last decade that transcend his milieu or even the France on which Althusser's story is centered.[4] It is no longer as difficult as it was a few years age to defamiliarize his material and to discover there culturally and historically specific modes of critique and interpretation, self-understanding and self-presentation. In an influential article on the relationship between art and ideology, Althusser once claimed that the function of art was to put ideology on display, and it is a curious fact that in his autobiography he does something similar for theory,[5] though in ways of which he himself does not seem to be aware.

What kind of book is *The Future Lasts a Long Time* and what does it tell us about the man and his generation of French intellectuals? To begin with, in spite of the author's denials it is an autobiography that is a radical departure from the kind of critical philosophical and political writing Althusser had engaged in up to the time of his criminal act. But, as he himself acknowledges in Chapter 2, it is by no means without precedent in the French tradition. He self-consciously refers there to two works that clearly served in very different ways as models, namely, the extraordinary master text of French autobiography, Rousseau's *Confessions,* and the life history of the obscure, early-nineteenth-century Norman peasant and murderer Pierre Rivière, which Michel Foucault discovered and published in the early 1970s, *I, Pierre Rivière, having slaughtered my mother, my sister, and my brother . . . : A Case of Parricide in the nineteenth Century.*

What connects these earlier works and what connects them to Althusser's own project is the dimension of scandal. All three are in one sense *oeuvres d'occasion* insofar as all three establish a link between criminal acts to be explained and the confessional genre. Under the circumstances Althusser's denial, "Alas, I am not Rousseau" (25), is no doubt accurate as far as literary significance is concerned, but it is more than a little disingenuous relative to content and meaning.

There is more than one important sense in which he *is* Rousseau, or at least takes Rousseau as his model, even beyond the general determination to tell the whole truth about himself, which he paraphrases as follows: "I will affirm loud and clear: this is what I did, what I thought, what I was" (25). To begin with, although Althusser cannot, like Rousseau, claim to have undertaken "a project that has never been attempted before," he does affirm the originality of his work: he hopes to be able to explain himself to himself and, in the process, lead others to reflect on "a concrete experience whose critical 'confession' is virtually without precedent (apart from the admirable confession by Pierre Rivière that Michel Foucault published). . . ."(24) Like Foucault's peasant, but unlike Rousseau, Althusser stands before his public as a confessed murderer; in that sense, at least, he can be said to have scooped them both.

Nevertheless—and this is the second respect in which he resembles his model—in both cases the decision to write an autobiography was triggered by the urge to respond in public to the accusation of wrongdoing. The reason the eighteenth-century "antiphilosophe" undertook to write his *Confessions* is that he felt the need to justify himself, his writings, and his conduct in the face of perceived persecution by a cabal of his enemies, including in particular Voltaire's charge in an anonymous pamphlet that Rousseau had abandoned the five children Thérèse Levasseur had borne him to a foundling hospital at their birth. Although he makes no attempt to deny the fact, the author of the eighteenth century's most memorable treatise on education from birth to adulthood, *Emile,* could hardly fail to try to explain what was, if not a crime, at the very least an unnatural act, likely to undermine his public's faith in his morals and integrity as well as in his ideas.

Third, although, since his case did not go to trial, nothing obliged Althusser to explain his behavior in a public forum, he decided to do so in a confessional mode that rivals Rousseau's in the intimate details of his life he chooses to narrate, including his psychic and sexual life down to his phobias, obsessions, frequent clinical depressions, hospitalizations, and the painful misadventures of his body and even his penis (he suffered from phimosis). "The unprecedented daring" (25) he admired in Rousseau is something he knowingly attempts to inject into his own work, starting with the foregrounding of the climactic act that ended Hélène's life and changed his own.[6] It should be noted that even if it had occurred to him, Rousseau himself was not in a position to break what is in many respects the ultimate taboo and describe his own act of uxoricide.

Fourth, Althusser is also following in Rousseau's footsteps to the extent that, like the author of the *Confessions,* he identified himself within philosophy as an *"antiphilosophe".*[7] In a discussion in the middle of his autobiography Althusser makes it clear that for him the task of philosophy was practical, political, and interventionist. Thus, in opposition to Marx's comment in his famous thesis on Feuerbach that philosophers had previously only interpreted the world and not sought to change it, Althusser argues that *"all the great philosophers* have wanted to intervene in the course of world history, either to transform it or to make it regress or to conserve and strengthen it in its existing form against the threats of a change judged to be dangerous" (164). Like Rousseau over two hundred years earlier, Marx in the last century, and Mao Tse-tung in this, Althusser is, in effect, affirming that politics should be put in command of philosophy as well as of everything else.[8]

He might also, again like the author of the *Confessions,* have called himself a "righter of wrongs" *(redresseur de torts)* if that eighteenth-century phrase could have been used without embarrassment in the late twentieth century. In Althusser's case the broader ambition manifests itself initially in the desire to protect and care for his mother in her martyrdom—what he calls his "sacrificial task" *(tâche oblative).* And later his love for Hélène, another victim of a "bad mother," is characterized by a similar missionary zeal to save her from the suffering she had known in the world.

Related to this is the idea that he is a man with a more general interventionist mission, something that is apparent, first, in his preoccupation as a young Catholic with what was known as "the social question" and, second, in his maturity, in his championing of the cause of the working class and his longstanding membership in the French Communist Party. Moreover, the connection he makes between "subjective fantasms" and "objective and public activities" is apparent in a general attitude, manifested in a variety of situations, that he describes as an "obsessional pattern of behavior" to be his "father's father" or his "mother's father" (100).

Finally, in both his autobiographical work and his critical writings, Althusser is visibly in the tradition of Rousseau in an attitude toward art and literature that could be characterized as one of suspicion. It is no accident that he should praise Rousseau for, among other things, his understanding of the role played by ideology in the sociopolitical sphere and, in particular, the fact that he was the first theorist of culture to focus on the question of hegemony (although the eighteenth-century philosopher does not, of course, use either term): "I take Rousseau to be the first theorist of hegemony—after Machiavelli" (212).[9] In both cases a "writerly" suspicion of high culture and its relationship to established power is integral to the project of "writer."

Rousseau was, then, a powerful model. But the very structure Althusser gives his work is an indication that he has something different and more specific in mind than Rousseau did, something that reveals in retrospect the hidden pattern of a life but that is in its way no less "daring." The fact is, Althusser might equally well have proclaimed, "Alas, I am not unlike Rousseau." Apart from everything else, Rousseau was the first in the modern world to connect the defiant pose of the accuser with that of the self-accuser or confessor. In the process, he was also the first to associate confession itself with a new form of heroism, the heroism of disclosing the most intimate, disturbing, and even shameful aspects of one's private life in the cause of truth. The originality and influence of Rousseau's autobiography appears nowhere more clearly than in his self-portrait of the taboo-breaker as hero—what, in connection with Marguerite Duras, I have called a heroic shamelessness.

That Althusser identified himself with such a tradition in autobiographical writing is confirmed right off by the narrative technique already referred to—the technique of opening with the murder scene and then, after a chapter of justification and critical commentary, going back in time to the story of his grandparents and parents and his own birth in 1918, only to return by a circuitous route some 250 pages later to the point where he began. However awkward and even melodramatic Althusser's technique may seem, it is clearly intended to focus his text on the event that set him apart from almost all other men, and not only those of his status and profession.

Althusser is understandably single-minded, even going so far as to deny that his work is an autobiography at all: "[W]hat follows is neither a journal nor memoirs nor autobiography. Sacrificing everything else, I simply wanted to recover the impact of the emotive affects [*sic*] that have marked my existence and given it its form" (25).

From the point of view of 1985, of the moment five years after the murder when Althusser wrote most of *The Future Lasts a Long Time,* there is in a sense only one question that interests him, one question that he sets out to answer, and it is the one posed by the spectacle of the dead woman's body—in a robe, half on and half off the bed, with a fixed look in her eyes and the tip of her tongue sticking out between lips and teeth—described in the opening chapter.

One question, then, but he will give it two very different kinds of answers. First, he has to find a way to explain how the man who, as he claims, took upon himself a protective and even sacrificial role from very early in his life could be transformed into someone as destructive and/or self-destructive as to murder his wife. What was the source, in his own psyche or in the social world, of the conflicting impulses that could explain such antithetical forms of behavior? How, in short, does a guardian angel become a murderer? The second answer is of a much more general kind, namely, to explain the significance of the murder for French political and intellectual culture. How was the murder to be read in terms of the man, his way of life, his morals, his thought and influence as a teacher of philosophy, for over thirty years at France's most prestigious institution of higher learning?

Given his lifetime of commitment to the intellectual enterprise and to critical philosophy of a highly theoretical kind, it is not surprising that Althusser should resort to "theory" in order to answer the question posed by Hélène's murder. Given his generational affiliation, it is also not surprising that the two bodies of theory that prove to be indispensable are psychoanalysis and Marxism, in that order.

The explanatory power of psychoanalysis invests the whole work. Before the age of psychoanalysis, it is not uncommon to find autobiographies in which many of the fundamental scenarios of psychoanalytic theory are shown to be acted out, especially in representations of the early lives of the subjects—along with Rousseau himself, the example of Stendhal springs to mind. But with Althusser we have the case of a twentieth-century intellectual who not only evokes such scenarios but who also knowingly interprets them in light of the fundamental concepts of psychoanalysis. Althusser was especially well positioned to interpret his past in such terms because he had himself been in analysis for many years and clearly drew on the experience and insights afforded by that analysis in telling the story of his life.[10] He also had significant familiarity with psychoanalytic theory as developed in Paris in the middle decades of the century in Lacanian circles.[11]

It is psychoanalytic theory that explains the narrative structure and enables Althusser to draw a straight line between the murder committed in November 1980 and the birth that occurred sixty-two years earlier. What that theory also illuminates for him is the simultaneous banality and extraordinariness of a life: patterns of behavior are laid down in infancy and repeated compulsively through adulthood, but the familial dynamics and the individual psychic response in each case have their own singularity, their own form and texture.

Both the banality and the extraordinariness are there from the beginning in his narrative of a flawed birth—flawed, that is, in a psychic and not a physiological sense. The flaw was in the fact that the place he was born to occupy was not his. And that is why the autobiography proper begins a year or two before the author's birth, with his mother and with the original Louis Althusser, his father's brother and his mother's only true love, who was killed at the front in 1917. The foundation for the murder in 1980 was, so to speak, prepared by the trauma suffered by his mother over sixty years before.

It is as a consequence of this death that the narrative Althusser tells is the story of two overlapping and ultimately conflicting desires, his mother's and his own. The murder is read in retrospect as a symptom that helps uncover the hidden secret of a life in the fact that the young Louis was never able to recognize in himself the object of his mother's desire. There is a sense in which everyone is born into the wrong place at the wrong time—born, that is, into another's fantasmatic scenario and therefore alienated from one's own desire—but Althusser reads his situation as pathological, inasmuch as he was never valorized by his mother's love and therefore never able to believe in his own independent existence.

That his was an extreme case is confirmed for him by the exercise in naming to which he was subject. Not only was he the bearer of the Nom du Père ([No]Name of the Father), Charles Althusser, his given name, Louis, was also spoken for, since it had been that of his dead uncle. Although Althusser does not put it in these terms, it is as if the Oedipal rivalry is displaced onto the dead uncle and for that reason can never be worked through. However, in light of this Althusser implicitly acknowledges the importance of Lacan's insights into the role of signifiers in an individual's psychic life and explains his own hatred of his given name and his preference for Jacques: Louis is a signifier of weakness and of nonpossession of his body since it always says "oui"; Jacques, on the other hand, signifies someone who is in possession of his body in its wholeness and sexual potency—Jacques (e)jaculates.

In formulating the issues in these terms, Althusser is affirming his theoretical debt not only to psychoanalysis but also to the tradition whose beginnings Foucault, in an interview, traces back to the seventeenth century, although with the *Confessions* Rousseau clearly gave new impetus to it, that of locating the secret of a life in sex: "I think that people still consider, and are invited to consider, that sexual desire is able to reveal what is their deepest identity." [12]

Thus it is that everything else in Louis Althusser's infancy, adolescence, and adulthood is shown to follow from the negatively charged circumstances of his birth. It is, the author claims, because when his mother looked at him she looked through him at her dead lover that he sought to make himself the lost object of her desire; he set out to charm and seduce her by making himself what he was not. Moreover, it was a mode of behavior that stayed with him throughout his lifetime. It was because of her horror of sex, fear of contamination, and cult of bodily purity that he became the good student, chaste in mind and body, at least until his confinement in a German prisoner-of-war camp. It was because of her that he never made love to a woman or even kissed one until he met Hélène when he was almost thirty. It was because of the castration complex she induced in him that he had a phobia of a woman laying her hands on him.

The crucial point about this psychoanalytic interpretation from the point of view of the murder is that the persona he claims to have fabricated in order to please his mother was a persona in contradiction with his own desire. If everything he did, including his academic achievements, his books, his friendships, and his loves, was a function of masquerade, of what he repeatedly refers to as "artifice" and "imposture," then the truth of his life is that of his own radical inexistence: "Having no real existence, I was in life a being of artifice, a being of nothing, a dead man who could only manage to love and be loved through artifice and imposture of a kind derived from those whom I wanted to love me and whom I sought to love by seducing them" (82). And it is in essence on these grounds that he explains his impulse to destroy all those things and people who were closest to him in order to destroy the inauthenticity of a self that did not exist as such.

Whether or not Althusser's interpretation of his past is accurate or is itself the consequence of the secondary revisionism fundamental to autobiographical narratives we can in a sense never know. What is significant from my point of view is his interpretation as such and the theory he uses to explain his behavior.

It is in light of the theory that the trick of representing the murder scene twice becomes significant, once right at the beginning and once close to the end, when the life has been narrated up to that point. What had seemed merely horrible and incomprehensible at the beginning looks very different the second time around. The ambiguous details are made in the end to yield up a clear meaning. If it was a very gentle murder in Althusser's telling, that is because it was a murder of a very special character, so special, in fact, that it is hardly distinguishable from a lover's caress. The only weapon was a pair of hands that a moment before had been performing a customary massage. There were no signs of resistance and the victim's neck showed no marks of strangulation. In short, it is represented as the kind of murder that under certain extreme conditions a mother or a lover might have committed. It was what might be called a "consensual murder," or the kind of tender death one might wish upon oneself at a time of depression. In any case, the scene as represented becomes a confirmation of Althusser's theory of "a suicide by means of an intermediary" (*un suicide par personne interposée*) (260).

Psychoanalysis, then, is made to carry the main burden of explanation for the crime. However, Althusser would not be Althusser if he did not also turn to Marxism in order to give a larger context to the lives of the half-dozen principal characters evoked in his work. Far from contradicting the psychoanalytic reading, Marxism, or at least his own sophisticated version of Marxist theory, is intended to give a social and political perspective to the personalities involved and to the fatal relation between himself and Hélène. Yet, as I shall suggest later, the effort to reconcile the two theoretical discourses that in modern times have done the most to undermine faith in human agency gives rise to other problems.

Marxism obviously allows Althusser to connect in another way the psychic and the private with the social and the public. It gives a historical context to existences that would otherwise seem to float in interpersonal space. That is why he begins the narrative of his own affective life with the history of the transplanted French peasants that were his maternal grandparents as they arrive in Algeria as part of France's wave of colonial expansion.

From a theoretical point of view, central to the account of his life are, first, the concept of "overdetermination" that he had developed earlier in order to rescue Marxist thought from the crude determinism of dialectical materialism[13] and, second, his own theory of ideology and "Ideological State Apparatuses."[14] As far as his own life and behavior are concerned, the concept of overdetermination allows him to think in a general way of the complexity of the superstructure and its various practices as advancing unevenly, and relatively autonomously, so that any given act, even including a murder, is always at the point of a number of intersecting determinations. The idea of Ideological State Apparatus, on the other hand, has a very specific relevance to his life because it illuminates in particular what was for him the sociocultural function of the family in bourgeois society and its deeply pathological character. If Althusser was destined to undergo a flawed birth and spend the rest of his life trying to adjust to its consequences, it was, he claims, on account of the social institution of the family as well as the unpredictable course of modern European history (the "War to end wars" that killed his mother's true love).

As noted previously, hatred of family has a central place in French avant-garde culture extending back to the early nineteenth century and coming down through Baudelaire, Gide, and Sartre. But in the wake of Gramsci, Althusser focuses on what is for him its hegemonic and peculiarly malevolent power: "What the experience of captivity also taught me was the pleasure of no longer living in the company of Mom and Dad and in the world (so closed to the outside) of the university, of the school, and of the family apartment; in short, of no longer living under *the terrible, and I mean terrible, can you hear me Robert Fossaert? can you hear me from your horrible tomb, Gramsci? the terrible, horrifying, and most frightening of all the Ideological State Apparatuses,* which in any nation where the state exists, is *the family"* (95–96).

The reference in this passage to school and university, those parallel institutions of social and ideological reproduction, is also significant, since the young Althusser excelled there as well, apparently by means of artifice and imposture; but even more significant was the experience of his captivity. It is, in fact, ironic that if history first condemned him to live a certain life as a *pied noir* in a dysfunctional French petit bourgeois family in Algeria and France, history also rescued him from that fate.

Although he does not formulate his situation in such terms, it is apparent that Althusser was in an important sense the child of two world wars. He was born less than a month before the end of the first and, like so many of his generation—including another *normalien,* Sartre—little more than twenty years later he was profoundly marked by the experience of the Second World War, of mobilization, occupation, imprisonment, and the idea of resistance and collaboration. It was through such extreme circumstances that he was exposed to a very different set of institutions, a prison camp directly and the Resistance indirectly, and finally the French Communist Party.

In their different ways those institutions seemed to have been for him what might be called Utopian Ideological Apparatuses (assuming, as he did, that we are always "in ideology"), that is to say, the Ideological Apparatuses of a state that did not yet exist but whose ideal future form might be extrapolated from the fraternal relations between men and between men and women that at their best they promoted. It was in particular Hélène who provided him with this connection to the idea of heroic resistance—"a world of solidarity and struggle, a world of action illuminated by great fraternal principles, a world of courage" (123). It is no accident if this utopian glimpse of transparent interpersonal relations in a context of achieved social harmony harks back in its way to Rousseau's archaizing dream of the classical polis reborn in eighteenth-century Europe.

What Althusser fails to note is that the kind of egalitarian and fraternal relations experienced by human beings under the simplifying circumstances for which Albert Camus employed the metaphor of the plague may not be reproducible under the normal conditions of communication and exchange in the modern world. Moreover, such observations in the autobiography help make clear that at the heart of Althusser's apparently tough-minded brand of Marxism lurks the kind of countermodernism that Jürgen Habermas has recently associated with a form of conservatism.[15]

In this connection it is characteristic that, eliding almost entirely the role played by De Gaulle, the Free French, and the Allies, Althusser in 1985, like so many other French intellectuals of his generation, still posits a France whose national honor was saved by a largely communist resistance movement and its working-class allies after being betrayed by its pro-fascist and defeatist bourgeoisie: "Plutôt Hitler que le front populaire."

What *The Future Lasts a Long Time* has to come to terms with in the end is, of course, the fact that all the promise and all the hopes were never realized, either on the personal or on the sociopolitical level. At the end of Althusser's life there remains instead the brutal fact of the murder and the need he felt to account for it in terms of the two complementary bodies of contemporary theory that he had championed as a critical philosopher—two bodies of theory apparently best adapted to exposing "false consciousness" and "absent causation" in the individual psyche or in a social formation.

And as far as he is concerned, they stand him in good stead. They furnish him with the two different kinds of answers needed to the question posed by the murder. On the one hand, they enable him to reconstruct the crime itself and trace its point of origin back to the trauma in his mother that preceded his own birth; on the other, they revalidate theory as such in opposition to those who sought to represent the crime as an indictment of critical thought in general and the structuralist Marxism with which he was associated in particular. As a result, he is able both to exculpate himself and to restore faith in his philosophy at the same time.

Althusser attributes the murder of his wife to a complex of causes and circumstances, but it is surprising to note that in a final chapter he gives the last, summarizing, word to "an old physician friend," who remains anonymous and who employs an authoritative medical-psychiatric discourse in order to confirm the author's own view of the matter and to explain how overdetermined the act was—overdetermined, in fact, to the point that it might never have happened had a physician's letter been received and his hospitalization begun immediately. Nevertheless, the murder turns out to be the symptom that confirms the dark forces and unconscious patterns in Althusser's behavior throughout his life; it was always potentially there.

On the one hand, therefore, there is the idea of a "suicide by means of an intermediary"; it is affirmed that he killed Hélène in order to put an end to imposture and to prove to himself and others his own nonexistence. On the other hand, there is also the suggestion that he was committing for her the suicide she did not have the courage to commit for herself. The idea of a "suicide by means of an intermediary" cuts both ways; Hélène's death was the point of intersection of not just one but two alienated desires.[16] In short, Althusser reaffirms the belief that sex is the secret of life or, as Foucault formulates it ironically in the interview quoted earlier, "Tell me your desires, I'll tell you who you are" ("The Minimalist Self," 11).

The answer Althusser gives to the question of the relationship of his crime to theory itself, or what two recent critics have called "la pensée 68,"[17] is for those outside the author's immediate circle of greater moment than the explanation of why he murdered his wife. The scandal of the murder clearly concerned Louis Althusser the man but it also concerned the Parisian intellectual milieu to which he belonged and the critical philosophy of a generation. It was as if the "theoretical antihumanism" Althusser had championed had come home to roost and revealed itself as dangerous and not simply theoretic. His personal scandal was also that of contemporary theory, since a continuity could be observed between that (dehumanizing) theory and the criminal act.

Much of the raison d'être of the autobiography springs from the fact that, from its author's point of view, Hélène's murder not only deprived him of all his civil liberties but, if left unexplained, also had the power to undermine a lifetime of philosophical and political work and the work of those he was in one way or another associated with—among others, his colleagues at the Ecole Normale and his students as well as most of the most famous names in post-fifties French theory, such as Lacan, Foucault, and Derrida, all of whom receive honorable mention in the body of the work, including especially the last two.[18]

Perhaps the most important task of the autobiography in this case is, therefore, to demonstrate the truth and power of contemporary theory. In opposition to the idea of the scandal of theory, the work is structured and designed to consecrate the triumph of theory. There is for him discontinuity, not continuity, between theory and the murder. The causes of that act are elsewhere: in the human psyche as it comes to be constituted from infancy through the passage into language and culture, and the emergence of the split subject alienated from its desire; in the potentially tragic entrapment within the fantasmatic family dynamics into which every child is born; in the institutions by means of which bourgeois society reproduces itself at great cost to the collectivity and to individual mental health.

For Althusser contemporary theory provides us with the means of understanding so much that would otherwise have remained inaccessible and incomprehensible, including the most monstrous acts of which we are capable. Perhaps what is most remarkable about *The Future Lasts a Long Time* is that at bottom it has the simplicity of an allegory designed to communicate the idea that theory saves.

With the autobiographer's assistance, it can also be said to save itself. And it is in this connection that Althusser may, in effect, be observed to be repeating once more with his autobiography the "obsessive pattern of behavior" to which he refers a number of times in his text, namely, that of playing the role of "father's father" or, as he reformulates it in connection with his career as political philosopher, "the master's master"—or even "the master's mother": "To be the 'master's master' always quietly haunted me, but to do so at a distance that was protected by the masters from whom I also situated myself at a distance, where I was happiest; I was always in a perverse relation where I was not the 'father's father' but the mother of my supposed master, thereby imposing on him the task of realizing my own alienated desire through the intermediary of his own person and desire" (159).

Given this taste for "the number-two spot" *(la position seconde)*—which on the basis of his own experience he implicitly seems to identify with "the mother's spot"—it is no wonder that Althusser's favorite classical thinker, even beyond Spinoza, Hobbes, and Rousseau, is Machiavelli, the pure political thinker, adviser and éminence grise to any proper prince. Like Gramsci before him, Althusser identified that prince in modern times with the Communist Party, in relation to which he may be said to have stood perversely in "the mother's spot," trying to force it to do the work of his own alienated desire. Such an attitude also makes it clear why two of his most important books of critical essays, *For Marx* and *Lenin and Philosophy,* carry in their titles dedications to master political thinkers, whose legacy he still wants to "mother" from beyond the grave.

That is probably why he also remains unrepentant, not with respect to the murder of Hélène, of course, but in his belief down into the age of Gorbachev in Soviet-style communism as the repository of social hope. As his dismissive comments on left-wing radical *groupuscules* and spontaneous action suggest, 1968 does indeed seemed to have meant nothing to him. Unlike Foucault, who went on to embrace many of the new social movements that escaped Marxist categories and to formulate bold new concepts and modes of analysis—relative to the disciplinary society, technologies of the subject and of subjectivication, the end of the universal intellectual, local forms of action and strategies of empowerment—Althusser in the mid-eighties seems scarcely to have changed his positions from those he had adopted in the late forties and fifties.

That he failed to update his theories of historical process and political action, or even his own role as party intellectual in light of contemporary events and major social change, also sheds some light on the significance of his "return to Marx." To look for an understanding of the modern world in virtually a single nineteenth-century text, as he does in his *Lire le Capital (Read Capital),* was not only to ignore the new directions taken by Foucault and even Sartre, it was also to occlude all the work done in Germany since the turn of the century relative to the processes of modernization and to that bifurcation of an eighteenth-century idea of reason into "repressive" and "emancipatory" reasons, which goes under the broad name of "dialectic of Enlightenment." There is a sense in which Althusser, if not a man of a single book like the Rousseau of *Emile (Robinson Crusoe),* was a man of some half a dozen: *The Prince, Leviathan,* the *Discourse on the Origin of Inequality, Capital* itself, some Spinoza, and, toward the end of his life, the *Confessions.* In any case, Althusser seems to have gone to his grave having paid very little heed to the fact that Soviet-style communism turned out to be the triumph of instrumental reason in the form of massive bureaucratization, as Weber had warned,[19] or to the reality of state terror—unlike another French literary intellectual of an earlier generation, André Gide, who on his return from a visit to the Soviet Union in 1936–37 was haunted by the cries of the political prisoners.[20]

Althusser's final work is nevertheless a complex and ambiguous piece of autobiographical testimony that is of great interest to anyone concerned with French social and cultural history in the twentieth century, the role of the intellectual in Western democracies, or the relationship between politics and theory. But as an *autocritique*, like his earlier *Eléments d'autocritique*,[21] it leaves a lot to be desired. Some of its limitations I have already touched upon, but among the problems it glosses over there are two that seem to me to be of particular significance: on the one hand, the work does not explore the problematic relation it implies between psychoanalytic theory and Marxism; on the other, it fails to deal with the fact that autobiography is always potentially a mystificatory literary genre that is typically at pains to deny its own literariness.

First, then, Althusser is still immersed in that 1960s problematic which attempted to forge a synthesis out of psychoanalysis and structuralist Marxism—a synthesis deriving from the faith that the political and the sexual revolutions were, in fact, one. As a result, he does not raise the possibility that the psychoanalytic interpretation he offers of his life history throws a strange light on his Marxist philosophy of history. The fact is, by demonstrating so convincingly the way in which his "subjective fantasms" are inscribed from the beginning in his "objective and public activities," Althusser implicitly acknowledges that all his adult commitments to people, philosophy, politics, and causes are fundamentally contingent in character from the point of view of the social whole; that is, they derive "in the last instance" from individual psychic accommodations to the accident of his birth to a peculiarly traumatized mother. Like all dysfunctional families, including Marguerite Duras's, his family was dysfunctional in its own way, but the power it exercised over him into maturity had the character of a Greek familial destiny to which the question of relations of class, for example, seem relatively marginal.

In effect, Althusser gives a psychoanalytic reading of his life history that implies he would have evolved very differently had he as an infant been a player in a different alien fantasm—he might even have emerged as a Gaullist or at the very least as the kind of university professor of pure philosophy he despised. His work, in effect, updates the existentialist ethics of Sartre to imply that we are the sum not only of our acts but also of our unconscious desire and of our obsessive fantasms as well as of those who marked us in our infancy. Even in his peculiarly privileged case, it seems that only protracted exposure to analysis and to massive ideological critique enabled him to see the light.

As for the second problem, as I noted at the beginning, *The Future Lasts a Long Time* has the character of a substitute text that, in lieu of his appearance in a court of law, undertakes its subject's defense by producing *après coup* the narrative of his life and the theory of that narrative, whether all the evidence is admissible or not. Thus in spite of the author's demurrals, it clearly belongs to the recognizable literary genre of autobiography, albeit one with something specific to prove. In no previous work is Althusser so conscious of functioning as a writer—in the generic as well as in my more specialized sense.

In this connection, it is symptomatic that at one point in the work he notes with pleasure that one of his admirers had told him specifically he was something more than the author of works of critical philosophy, "that I had a 'style,' that I was in my way a writer" (164). And nowhere is the ambition implied by his response more evident than in *The Future Lasts a Long Time,* starting with its epigrammatic title and the opening description of the murder scene. Like Rousseau's *Confessions,* the function of Althusser's work is to tell his side of "the story," to persuade his readers of the truth of his version of events, even if it is for theory's sake as much as his own. And this inevitably involves him in the practice of writing as an art of persuasion.

What is less immediately obvious is that he connects the success of the philosopher's task in general to the work of the writer. Those "great philosophers" he refers to whose ambition was "to intervene in the course of world history" had imposed themselves on their public through a thought characterized by clarity of presentation and a mastery of language that constitutes a "style."

That is why in the end *The Future Lasts a Long Time* embodies a significant paradox. The man who claims to have murdered his wife in order to put an end to artifice and imposture, as well as to escape from the tyranny of his mother's desire, finds himself repeating the same pattern of artifice, apparently unself-consciously, in a genre that from Stendhal to Valéry, Sartre, and Roland Barthes was understood to be notorious for its promotion of deception and self-deception. A more consistent response to the murder, as some of Althusser's friends seemed to realize, would have been silence. All writing seeks to persuade, but autobiographical writing is frequently pure seduction.

In that sense it is not unlike the classic French academic exercise that he learned to excel at in his lycée in Lyons in the late 1930s, the *dissertation,* rhetorical mastery of which was and remains crucial to a successful career in the French university in the humanities and whose secret he explains ironically as: "first, the most extreme clarity in the writing, and then the art (another artifice) of composing on any subject whatsoever, a priori and by deduction in a vacuum, a dissertation that is consistent with itself and that convinces" (86). He learned then to please his teachers by writing as they would have written, just as with the autobiography he makes himself lovable after all to his friends.

That there was something problematic about his autobiographical project did occasionally occur to Althusser in the course of the writing, but such an awareness appears in his text chiefly in the form of denials and in one epigrammatic aside, the force of which goes undeveloped and leads to no substantial critique. He simply notes, "Naturally, avoiding mere anecdote or the stuff of journals or bad literature that is nowadays de rigueur in autobiography (that is, the unprecedented decadence of literature), I will simply stick to the *essential*" (152).

One can agree with his suggestive phrase that autobiography is often enough "the unprecedented decadence of literature," but note that, from the point of view of psychoanalysis and the structuralist Marxism that were so important to him, "the essential" is that to which one simply cannot stick. This is something of which Althusser had once shown himself to be aware in a famous essay on art, where he argued, "The structure which controls the *concrete* existence of men . . . can never be depicted by its presence, positively, in relief, but only by traces and effects, negatively, by indices of absence, *in intaglio*."[22] And what is true of structural causality in the social realm also holds, of course, for the unconscious. Moreover, it is the naive romantic faith in the possibility of "sticking to the essential" that as much as anything else produces the "bad literature" of which he complains.

In this connection, finally, the theory of hegemony is important, because that theory validates submitting art to a political test. If in early modern Europe Rousseau was indeed the first theorist of hegemony, as Althusser claims, that is because he was suspicious of Enlightenment high culture in his time, as Althusser was of the high culture of his. In the name of a different though equally stern morality Althusser, like his great predecessor, had similar censorious, not to say terroristic, attitudes toward literary and artistic activity. The only value Althusser discovers in art is in its capacity to perform the function of ideological critique.

In this respect, his position is notably different from that of such major theorists of the Frankfurt school as Benjamin, Adorno, and Marcuse, who, in a modern world dominated by repressive instrumental reason, looked specifically to art as the realm where radical utopian impulses might still be formulated and the ends of emancipatory reason pursued. The idea, articulated by Habermas and derived from his understanding of the Enlightenment, that "aesthetic rationality" exists in the modern world as an autonomous sphere of critical human activity alongside the two other forms of rationality, the scientific-technical and the practical-moral, is alien to Althusser's ultimately reductionist, Marxian account of all forms of superstructural practice[23]—in spite of all he had to say on "the relative autonomy" of the different practices that make up a social formation.

In the essay on Cremonini, as well as in the "Letter on Art in Reply to André Daspre," Althusser had argued for the power of great art and literature to make ideology visible. But neither there nor in his autobiography does he suggest what characterizes such art in general; he has nothing to say on what must be present in order for it to produce the "interior distance" that he claims enlightens. If he had reflected further on the issues, he could hardly have avoided focusing on the importance of formal values in the whole sphere of the aesthetic. Even from the limited point of view he adopts to praise art and to distinguish it from ideology, he would have needed to take account of such issues as form, genre, convention, intertextuality, self-referentiality, tradition and innovation, play, experiment, transgression—in a word, "artifice." But this is, of course, what his theory of his poor, flawed self makes it impossible for him to do. Yet there is obviously no writing without artifice, as the occasional artfulness of the narrative of his own life demonstrates. If autobiography is typically "bad literature," that is because it takes itself to be "natural"; it does not believe in the necessary detour through art; it is not literary enough. The final unintended lesson of *The Future Lasts a Long Time* might be rendered with the deeply un-Rousseauist and "unwriterly" formulation *Vive l'imposture!*

If in this brief study of the trajectory of a normative idea of "the writer" across some two and a half centuries of French cultural history I choose to end with a few comments on Foucault, that is because he has turned out to be the most complex and influential of France's late-twentieth-century thinkers, and one who gave a decisive new inflection to the idea of "the writer" I have been describing here. Whereas Althusser, like Sartre before him, is in so many respects living off Rousseau's legacy, Foucault detached himself from it in the course of his career, without, of course, formulating his development in the terms laid out in this book; from this point of view, the single most important work is *The Will to Know,* the first volume of *The History of Sexuality.* On the one hand, as noted earlier, he was the first to undertake a systematic critique of "confessionalism" in Western culture, going back to the Middle Ages but especially since the Counter-Reformation, and, on the other, he attacked the concept of ideology that was traditionally at the heart of Marxist cultural studies until it was joined by hegemony. Moreover, it is in their very different understanding of the sphere of aesthetic activity that the distance between Althusser and Foucault is especially apparent.

Foucault, of course, was himself a critical philosopher and intellectual of the self-confident French type described by Tony Judt in the epigraph to this chapter. In a series of substantial, provocative, and highly original works, he ranged widely in the course of his career over the historical past and present, and was nowhere more an intellectual than when he was criticizing the practices and self-understanding of the traditional, universal intellectual. At the same time, in place of that suspicion of the aesthetic that characterizes Althusser, one finds from the beginning a profound respect for those works of art and literature that have a certain transfiguring or transcendent force. And by the end of his life, he was developing a notion of aesthetics as crucial to a critique of power and the sphere of the political. Furthermore, it is no accident that Foucault also died without ever writing an autobiography or any equivalent, even if in his later life he did respond increasingly in interviews to questions on his personal life and to the relations between his life and work.

With respect to those relations, I quoted in my introduction two sentences from a 1983 interview in which the ambiguity of his position is made clear: "As far as my personal life is uninteresting, it is not worthwhile making a secret of it. By the same token, it may not be worthwhile publicizing it."[24] Rousseau, like those "writers" who came under his influence, had, of course, assumed that his life was of a unique interest, and he was determined to publicize it to the world down to its most intimate details. This was not, of course, Foucault's way. Nevertheless, although he admired them, he by no means consistently identified with those retiring authors I referred to in my introduction as "counterexamples" to "the writer," such as Maurice Blanchot and Samuel Beckett.

On the contrary, the paradox of Foucault in this respect is that by the last decade or so of his life the man who had first acquired a reputation as a grey archivist on the margins of French intellectual life had assumed a highly visible public persona. He had developed by then a whole art of self-presentation that included a readiness to hold press conferences and grant frequent interviews—and, whenever possible, to edit those interviews himself for publication. The Foucault the world came to know cultivated a personal *image de marque* consisting of a startling baldness, steel-rimmed glasses, an intense look, white polo-neck sweaters, and a taste for black. In many respects, for reasons I shall touch on later, this public persona was a late-twentieth-century equivalent of Baudelaire's nineteenth-century dandy. Such, in any case, was the image that was endlessly reproduced and widely circulated, appearing not only on the covers and dust jackets of his books but also on posters and in a wide variety of journals and newspapers. Finally, that air of a singular, postmodernist guru was reinforced for a long time by a certain mystery and the rumor of scandal in his private life. The composite figure he projected seemed to be at one and the same time historian, activist, publicist, and aesthete of a new and programmatic kind.

The complex way Foucault is positioned relative to the idea of "the writer" derives to a great extent from beginnings that were outside the French intellectual mainstream as it was constituted in the 1950s and 1960s, as he himself has indicated.[25] From *Madness and Civilization* on, Foucault's published works tended to exhibit a highly original and frequently disconcerting combination of apparently heterogeneous bodies of thought or modes of writing that often had the effect of problematizing the discursive ground on which he stood.

Thus, to begin with, in the heyday of existentialism, phenomenology, and Marxism this former student of Althusser was drawn to the material and the critical approach of such important French historians of science as Gaston Bachelard, Georges Canguilhem, and Georges Dumézil, although the focus of his inquiries was the dubious sciences of man, as opposed to the noble sciences of the physical and natural universe. Second, Foucault came to combine the extensive archival work that historical research implies with a strong interest in the insights afforded by art and literature into human experience at its limits, notably in connection with death, madness, sexuality, and criminality. In this respect his taste in authors is relatively similar to Duras's; his personal pantheon of those who wrestled with a "beyond of reason that reason knows not of" includes such figures as the Marquis de Sade, Antonin Artaud, Raymond Roussel, Georges Bataille, and Maurice Blanchot. Third, the discovery of the philosopher of the will to power and of the theory of genealogy or counterhistory, Friedrich Nietzsche, opened up for him a whole new way of conducting historico-practical critiques of Western rationality and morality, historical change, and the constitution of subjectivity since the seventeenth century that was notably at odds with the prevailing existentialism, phenomenology, and Marxism. Finally, the preoccupation with language systems associated with French structuralism from the late fifties on, and with what Frederic Jameson once called "the prison house of language," led him, in the style of a Kantian critique, to identify from a historical point of view different discursive regimes and the limits of knowing and doing that those regimes implied, in order, wherever possible, to seek to transcend them. From *Madness and Civilization* on, Foucault was centrally preoccupied with the unthought and with modalities for thinking outside prevailing cognitive and cultural norms.

Whatever else such a restless intellectual eclecticism implied, therefore, it was an expression of the belief that the road to human emancipation in the modern world presupposed a form of patient historical critique with the systematic practice of transgression. The apparent contradiction that gave rise to is memorably evoked by Jürgen Habermas in a paper whose focus is Foucault's lecture "What Is Enlightenment?" What impressed Habermas when he met Foucault for the first and last time, in 1983, was a tension "that eludes familiar categories, between the almost serene scientific reserve of the scholar striving for objectivity on the one hand, and the political vitality of the vulnerable, subjectively excitable, morally sensitive intellectual on the other." [26]

Because he was always ready to begin again and to rethink philosophical practice from its limits and in light of his empirical research, Foucault from his student days was dissatisfied with the kind of totalizing system building associated with the previous generation of French intellectuals. No wonder, then, that if Foucault did suffer from an anxiety of influence, as James Miller argues persuasively in *The Passion of Michel Foucault*, it was in connection with Jean-Paul Sartre. An important part of Miller's reading of Foucault's life, in fact, involves explaining his determination to be an anti-Sartre, which, of course, also implies that from my point of view he also strove to be an "anti-writer."

That this is the case appears most clearly in his writings and his behavior in the last decade or so of his life, although it is already apparent in the famous affirmation that concludes the introduction of *The Archaeology of Knowledge:* "Do not ask who I am and do not ask me to remain the same: leave it to our bureaucrats and our police to see that our papers are in order. At least spare us their morality when we write."[27] This is a repudiation of our contemporary politics of identity even before it was fully formulated.

The passage is often quoted without its final sentence, but that sentence is of obvious significance in this context precisely because it connects a certain practice of writing for a public with what was for him a specific, unacceptable morality—a morality whose origins in the modern world I trace back to Rousseau and to all those who, directly or indirectly, were subject to his influence. It is what in this context I would call "a writerly morality," precisely because it demands a declaration of who the writer is, entails the affirmation of an identity that connects the outer man who writes to the inner truth of his being, and assumes continuity of that pre-given identity over a lifetime. As Rousseau was aware and as Derrida, in effect, once pointed out, from such a perspective writing is also seen as an imperfect form of dictation in which the externality of the written word is forever inadequate to render the full presence of a self.

In any case, the morality of writing Foucault substitutes for Rousseau's was for a long time one in which the author is no longer presumed to be the founding subject of a text, as he once argued in "What Is an Author?" In the substitution of the concept of "author function" for "author," one recognizes a particular instance of a more general project to undermine a traditional humanist confidence in human agency and to posit instead a historically bounded humanity caught up forever in the toils of discursivity. Foucault diagnoses a link between writing and "sacrifice," and takes pleasure both in the effacement of that "writing subject" who had achieved fame and heroic status from the romantic movement on and in a return, in the age of poststructuralism, to something like the anonymity that had typically characterized literary production in the Middle Ages. As far as the relation between author and text is concerned, it is difficult to imagine a greater difference than that between the self-affirming subject of autobiography and the writing subject that consciously "cancels out the signs of his particular individuality."[28]

Finally, at the end of "What Is an Author?" Foucault looks forward to "discourses" that would develop "in the anonymity of a murmur. We would no longer hear the questions that have been rehashed for so long: Who really spoke? Is it really he and not somebody else? With what authenticity or originality? . . . Instead, there would be other questions like these: What are the modes of existence of this discourse? Where has it

been used, how can it circulate? . . . And behind all these questions, we
would hear hardly anything but the stirring of an indifference: What difference does it make who is speaking?" (119–20). That final question not
only radically demarcates Foucault from an attitude toward writing that is
as old as Rousseau, it also underlines the distance that separates him from
Althusser's confessional writing practice in *The Future Lasts a Long Time.*

The theoretical attitude toward a relation between work and author
that we normally associate with structuralism/poststructuralism gives rise
in Foucault's own works to complex texts that draw on a great deal of
heterogeneous material and are written in shifting stylistic registers. What
disconcerted many of his early readers, including the director of his Doc-
torat d'Etat thesis, Georges Canguilhem, were the references to works of
radically different orders and the moves back and forth between the expos-
itory prose of traditional scientific discourse and dark purple passages,
flights of lyric ecstacy, and gnomic gloom. In the academy, as in the French
intellectual milieu in general, it did apparently matter who was speaking.

However, after the histories of madness, psychiatry, penology, and sexuality, and the theories of regimes of discursivity, of the disciplines and
the processes of normalization, the technologies of the self, and the constitution of subjects, there emerged toward the end of his life a Foucault who
became preoccupied above all with ethics. And it is here that one sees the
decisive turn he took against that historically bounded idea of "the writer"
that has concerned me in these pages.

The ground for this turn was, however, prepared in an important way
by the first volume of the *History of Sexuality, The Will to Know.* The
broad significance of that work in the present context is in the way in
which it radically redefines the relationship between sex and power. Far
from interpreting the latter as that which says no to sex, Foucault argues
that what he calls the "apparatus of sexuality" was, in fact, constitutive
of sex as we know it and that that apparatus depended on the emergence
of a *scientia sexualis* in the West in which the will to power takes the
form of "the will to know." The effect, in any case, has been the establishment of a whole network of overlapping institutions and practices that
constitute a system of subjectivication and control. Moreover, in mounting
his challenge to the "repressive hypothesis"—that modern orthodoxy
which argued that the rise of sexual repression since the seventeenth century paralled that of capitalism for the good reason that there was a symbi-
otic relation between them[29]—Foucault is led to formulate his historical
critique of confession in general.

By implication, his genealogy of modern sex also sheds new light on
that specifically literary practice of confession which interests me here. In
the persistence of that tradition from Rousseau down through Althusser
one finds, on the one hand, confirmation of Foucault's thesis that modern
man is "a confessing animal" *(une bête d'aveu)* (*Will to Know*, 80) and,
on the other, an expression of the faith, which he contests, that "confes-

sion makes you free" (78). From a Foucauldian point of view, it is only natural that Althusser should have recourse both to Rousseau and to psychoanalysis in order to illuminate the buried truths of his own psychic life. In *The Will to Know*, far from representing a rupture with a Western understanding of sex and the pathologies associated with it, psychoanalysis is represented as no more than the modern and most theoretically sophisticated form of a single "confession science" *(science-aveu)* that is, in fact, older than Rousseau and has no trouble accommodating itself to the work of Freud. From this point of view, both the eighteenth-century philosopher and the turn-of-the-century inventor of psychoanalysis are no more than major contributors to the longstanding and continuing institutionalization of the incitement to speak, or of "giving a discursive form to sex" (48). In a single incisive sentence Foucault dismisses the idea that to talk openly about one's intimate sexual life is in itself subversive; and in the process he also deflates the tacit faith I have been concerned with here in the heroism of confession: "Isn't it in order to incite us to talk about it, to talk about it over and over again, that it is made to shimmer at the outer limit of all actual discourse, as the secret that one absolutely must ferret out, as something that has been wrongly reduced to silence and that it is both difficult and necessary, dangerous and very important to say" (48).

As for the turn taken by Foucault in his later work, it is perhaps best understood as a return not simply to Nietzsche, but beyond Nietzsche to Baudelaire and, in a different way and even further back, to Kant, which is also to say *not* to Rousseau. What came to appear central to Foucault was the idea of self-transformation and self-transcendence through the exercise of one's freedom combined with a will to self-mastery. The significance of this turn is particularly apparent in the relatively late essay, referred to in chapter 3, that takes its title from Kant's famous "What Is Enlightenment?" of 1784. It is something of a surprise that the author of *Madness and Civilization* and *The Order of Things* should make the case for the importance of the way in which Kant poses the problem of Enlightenment and "modernity" in connection with his historical present, and for the continuing relevance of Kant's understanding of the philosopher's task for our own present.

Having summarized the German philosopher's conception of Enlightenment as humanity's coming of age and the courage to take responsibility for one's life as an autonomous and reasonable human being—the famous *Aude sapere*—Foucault goes on to take his cue from Kant in thinking about the task of philosophy and its relation to "modernity" in our own time. As a result, he envisages "modernity" less as a historical period than as an "ethos" in the Greek sense, and a style of philosophical interrogation conceived as "a permanent critique of our historical era" that Kant was the first to embody so fully. It is moreover an ethos that Foucault typically finds to be in opposition to what he calls "countermodernity."

He then goes on to develop the significance of Kant's formulation of the issues in some brilliant pages on the first major theorist of aesthetic modernism, Baudelaire. It is there that Foucault begins to adumbrate the possibility of a modernist ethics and to distance himself from the posing of the problems of our own historical present in purely political terms. From his point of view, the specificity of Baudelaire's understanding of his time is to be found in "the will to heroize the present." The role of poet and artist is understood by Baudelaire as the effort "to extract from fashion whatever element it may contain of poetry within history." Thus a work of art created in the ethos of "modernity" operates a transfiguration of contemporary life that Foucault describes as "a difficult interplay between the truth of what is real and the exercise of freedom; 'natural' things become 'more than natural,' 'beautiful' things become 'more than beautiful.' . . . For the attitude of modernity, the high value of the present is indissociable from the desperate eagerness to imagine it, to imagine it otherwise than it is." Baudelairean modernity "simultaneously respects this reality and violates it."[30]

In other words, Foucault discovers surprising continuity between the project of the Enlightenment as defined by Kant and Baudelaire's aesthetic theory and practice in mid-nineteenth-century France. In both cases, starting from his historical present an autonomous individual exercises his freedom in a project of rethinking that present with the expectation of transforming it and, in the process, himself. Furthermore, in Baudelaire's case a comparable modernist poetic/philosophical ethos prevailed both in the practice of poetry and in the celebration of a certain style of life. The nineteenth-century poet's ideal type for the time was, of course, the dandy, but the dandy conceived not as a mere narcissistic man of fashion. "The doctrine of elegance" as practiced by Baudelaire's dandy is also an ethics—an ethics, moreover, that is a form of asceticism. In the same way that a banal reality may be transfigured in art and poetry, a human being may transform himself into something finer through a discipline of the self that is not a subjectivication. In brief, with respect to self-fashioning or self-refashioning, an ethics may take the form of an aesthetics. In at least one important sense, therefore, Baudelaire's dandy prefigures Nietzsche's superman.

The interesting point in this context is that Foucault tends to leave open the question as to whether Baudelaire was right in separating his aesthetics from a politics: "This ironic heroization of the present, this transfiguring play of freedom with reality, this ascetic elaboration of the self—Baudelaire does not imagine that these have any place in society itself, or in the body politic. They can only be produced in another, a different place, which Baudelaire calls art" ("What Is Enlightenment," 42). The least that can be said about this is that, if Foucault is not agreeing with Baudelaire in pointing to the end of a certain salvationist idea of politics, he is definitely in the process of reevaluating the significance of politics as we know it and limiting its reach by virtue of the fact that he sets it in opposition to ethics and aesthetics. What is certain is that the ethical and the aesthetic are no longer posited as reducible to the political. Moreover, art is acknowledged by Foucault, as by Adorno and Marcuse before him, as a peculiarly privileged mode of transcendence of the given that should not be subordinated to some normalizing political law.

In the end, Foucault summarizes the continuing relevance of Enlightenment thought as mediated by Kant as "the principle of critique and a permanent creation of ourselves in our autonomy" (43), and he clearly sees there a connection with the Nietzschean project of self-surpassing. So much is clear from the ringing declaration with which Foucault concludes his homage to the greatest of the Enlightenment philosophers and affirms his relevance to our historical present: "The critical ontology of ourselves has to be considered not, certainly, as a theory, a doctrine, nor even as a permanent body of knowledge that is accumulating; it has to be conceived as an attitude, an ethos, a philosophical life in which the critique of what we are is at one and the same time the historical analysis of the limits that are imposed on us and an experiment with the possibility of going beyond them" (50).

As his choice of words shows, there is no doubt that Foucault gives a modernist aesthetic gloss to Kant here; he connects him, surprisingly, to those romantic and postromantic "experimental" artists and writers whom Foucault admired and who exercised their freedom by testing the established limits of human experience to the point of risking life and sanity. Yet what in large measure explains Habermas's tribute in the paper he wrote shortly after the French thinker's death, "Taking Aim at the Heart of the Present," was the balance struck in Foucault's Kant essay between morality and aesthetics, or, in other words, between Kant himself, on the one hand, and Baudelaire and Nietzsche, on the other. The originality of late Foucault, and the reason he seems to be striking out in a new direction, is perhaps no more evident than in such a synthesis. In any case, the Kant essay makes clear that Foucault was the first of the major postwar thinkers in France not to assume that twentieth-century German thought was entirely dominated by Nietzsche and Heidegger and, without giving up his admiration for Nietzsche, to connect his own project with a very different affiliation in German thought and with the origins of French aesthetic modernism.

As Habermas points out, Foucault identifies in Kant the origin of a critical tradition in philosophy that "leads through Hegel, Nietzsche, and Max Weber to Horkheimer and Adorno," and also "surprisingly" to Foucault himself ("Taking Aim," 174). And one can only assume that it is modesty which prevents Habermas from inserting his own name in the list, between Adorno and Foucault. In any case, the skeptical genealogist and aesthete of the self has joined hands with the Kantian believer in attempting to further the incomplete project of Enlightenment. It is as if, after all the critiques of reason as manifested in the human sciences, Foucault had finally discovered his own "dialectic of Enlightenment" from the positive side—discovered, that is, that there was an emancipatory rationality as well as a perverse, instrumental kind and that the autonomy of art was, after all, worth celebrating.

What is important from my point of view, however, are the omissions as much as the inclusions in Habermas's list. In acknowledging that he was also an heir of Kant's Enlightenment—or, more precisely, that he henceforth refuses "the blackmail" of being for it or against it in its wholeness—Foucault ceases to defer to either Marx or Freud. Whereas, as we saw, they remained for Althusser the master thinkers of our age until the end, they have disappeared from sight in Foucault's late profession of faith. A suspicion of the masters of suspicion—a doubt relative to theories become dogma and the validity of their truth claims—had already appeared obliquely in the designation of them as "founders of discursivity" in "What Is an Author?"

In any case, the abandonment of the closed horizon of understanding of an earlier generation implied by the disappearance of Marxism and psychoanalysis does point in the direction of something radically new. As far as Marx is concerned, the reasons for his disappearance are explicit in Foucault's own "What Is Enlightenment?" Although Marx is not mentioned by name, like Rousseau before him he is connected with those "programs for a new man that the worst political systems have repeated throughout the twentieth century." It is in opposition to this that Foucault affirms his commitment to "a historico-critical attitude" that "must also be an experimental one." And he goes on: "This means that the historical ontology of ourselves must turn away from all projects that claim to be global or radical" ("What Is Enlightenment," 46–47) The alternative, of course, is transformations that are local and cumulative.

The significance of Foucault's return to Kant and partial reconciliation with the heritage of the Enlightenment he embodied is at least twofold. On the one hand, it points in the direction of a paradigm change in modern French culture relative to "the writer," as is clear from the last two volumes of *The History of Sexuality*. In those volumes and in related writings and interviews Foucault went on explore, among other things, the ethics of the Stoics, the principal aim of which, in his reading, is an aesthetic one. The purpose was, as he put it in a late interview, "to live a beautiful life." This is what Foucault understands by "an aesthetics of existence." [31]

On the other hand, the return to Kant may signify something more mundane in French political culture itself. The emergence of a new consensus style of political thought and the belated resurgence of French liberalism suggest that that culture is perhaps in the process of being "normalized"—if one understands by "normal" a politics and a public life of an unheroic, quotidian Anglo-American kind, the kind that appears in an idealized form in Habermas's theory of "communicative rationality." What François Furet failed to find in the French political tradition in 1977 has perhaps begun to emerge since: "French thought essentially knows nothing of appeals to the final harmony of interests and the common value of particular conflicts; . . . it needs to incarnate the social sphere in a unified image, which is the rational authority of legal despotism. That is because it always comes back to a political vision of the social, and poses the problem of origins and of the legitimacy of the social contract."[32] Such was the kind of political culture that was put in place by the tradition of revolution, a tradition in which "the writer" flourished. Is it possible that a political culture of a more liberal kind will have little use for such a figure?

More recently Pierre Bourdieu has argued that what contemporary French cultural life needs is less philosophy and more sociology, less indulgence in the exercise of the supposedly pure and free speculative intelligence and more concrete social-scientific studies that focus on specific institutions and forms of collective behavior. And given what sometimes passes for philosophy in Paris—and not only in the media—he is probably right.[33] Moreover, Tony Judt in part confirms the qualitative change in French intellectual life that he associates with a new respect for "institutional attachment and disciplinary conventions" and a revival of the prestige of academic styles of learning and writing that manifests itself in "the decline of the great public intellectuals and the resurrection of the professors."[34] Given the focus of his book, it is not surprising that Judt has nothing to say about the function of literature in the emerging public culture. Bourdieu, on the other hand, has made his position clear in a recent important work that provocatively challenges the whole concept of literary value and aesthetic reason from the point of view of social scientific rationality.[35] But his line of argument and its tradition constitutes a different story that is worthy of a book of its own, although it is worth noting that at least in the distrust expressed for art and literature, Bourdieu often seems to echo Rousseau and beyond him Plato.

One final point. That in the years before his death Foucault was engaged in transforming his own self and his role is clear from his various writings and interviews, and is confirmed by James Miller's descriptions of his life and of the impact California and its gay culture had on him. That he thereby, like Barthes before him, was at the same time drawing attention to the obsolescence of a certain idea of "the writer" is, in my view, also apparent. And nowhere is this more obvious than in the implied contrast between a project of self-transformation focused on the concept of "the beautiful life" and confession. Such self-transformation is oriented toward the future in a sense that is no longer political; moreover, it is discontinuous, open-ended, ethical, and aesthetic. Confession, on the other hand, is oriented toward the past and believes in the possibility of a summum; it is continuous, self-identical, moral, and anti-aesthetic. Confession also implies a belief in the potential transparency of self to self, and finds the question "Who am I?" a legitimate one.

Ethico-aesthetic self-transformation is, then, a deeply un-Rousseauist and un-Althusserian idea; it is associated with play, masquerade, experiment, artifice, and even imposture, if imposture were not a concept derived precisely from moral essentialism. At one limit it is Dionysian and might well engage a subject in shattering Sadean fantasies or in the personal "theater of cruelty" of sado-masochism, as apparently was the case with Foucault toward the end of his life. At the opposite limit it is Apollonian and opens onto stoical self-mastery and what Baudelaire called "the science of pleasure." In any case, whatever the risks—and the manner of Foucault's death is a warning that they are not negligible—from the point of view of the aesthetics of existence, the truth is not so much a given to be revealed as a choice to be made or essayed.

Was Foucault toward the end of his life contributing to "the death of 'the writer' " in the same way that he had earlier theorized "the death of the author"? And was he in the process testing the possibility of a new normative type for a new historical era, although obviously not with the boldness and brilliance Rousseau may be said to have done so some two and a half centuries earlier? It is certainly too early to say. One long chapter in French sociopolitical and cultural history may have closed with his and Althusser's deaths—that is, if historical chapters ever fully closed. Whether a new one is opening is for a future present, not for the mere author of a critical essay, to judge. There is, however, no doubt that after Foucault the process of overcoming what I take to be a central flaw of Rousseauism—the failure to respect the autonomy of scientific and aesthetic reason, respectively, and to subsume ethics to politics—can begin in France, as it has elsewhere.

Notes

INTRODUCTION

1. See, for example, Tony Judt's cogent observations on "rights-talk" in the context of a discussion of the marginalization of liberal thought in French political life. "Liberalism, There is the Enemy," in *Past Imperfect: French Intellectuals, 1944–1956* (Berkeley: University of California Press, 1992). See also Marcel Gauchet, *La Révolution des droits de l'homme* (Paris: Gallimard, 1989).

2. See on this subject Judt's well-documented account of the years 1944–56 in *Past Imperfect*, as well as Jean-François Sirinelli's *Intellectuels et passions françaises* (Paris: Fayard, 1990), Herbert R. Lottman's *The Left Bank: Writers, Artists, and Politics from the Popular Front to the Cold War* (Boston: Houghton Mifflin, 1982), and Ariane Chebel d'Appollonia's *Histoire politique des intellectuels en France, 1944–1954* (Brussels: Editions Complexes, 1991).

3. That was also the context in which François Furet wrote, in a highly influential essay, "I am writing these lines at the end of the spring in 1977, at a time when the criticism of Soviet totalitarianism, and more generally of all forms of power claiming to be founded on Marxism, has ceased to the monopoly or the quasi-monopoly of right-wing thought, and has become a central theme of left-wing thinking." "La Révolution française est terminée," in *Penser la révolution française* (Paris: Gallimard, 1978), 27–28. Unless quoted from English-language editions, translations from French texts are my own.

4. A significant sign of such revisionist tendencies is to be found in the collective work *La République du centre: La Fin de l'exception française (The Centrist Republic or the end of French Difference)* (Paris: Calmann-Lévy, 1988), by François Furet, Jacques Julliard, and Pierre Rosanvallon, the very title of which substitutes for the idea of France's normative historical destiny or special guiding role among nations that of a return to normalcy.

5. Michel Foucault, "Truth and Power," in *The Foucault Reader,* ed. Paul Rabinow (New York: Pantheon Books, 1984), 67. See also, among so much else, the discussion between Michel Foucault and Gilles Deleuze, "Intellectuals and Power," in *Language, Counter-Memory, Practice: Selected Essays and Interviews by Michel Foucault,* ed. Donald F. Bouchard, trans. Bouchard and Sherry Simon (Ithaca: Cornell University Press, 1977).

269

A decade after 1968, Jean-François Lyotard's *La Condition Postmoderne* (Paris: Editions de Minuit, 1979) also devoted itself to surveying the so-called discourses of legitimation of modernity, only to find them all wanting, including particularly the master narratives of historicism which the French Left had lived off at least since the mid-thirties and in some respects much longer.

6. What it had signified for so long is briefly summarized by Furet as follows: "The French Revolution is not only the Republic. It is also an indefinite promise of equality and a privileged mode of change. It is enough to regard it not just as a national institution but as the matrix of universal history in order to give it its dynamism and fascinating power. The nineteenth century believed in the Republic, the twentieth in *the* Revolution. The same founding event is at the origin of both images." "La Révolution française est terminée," 18–19.

7. A decade earlier, Furet had spoken of a kind of a "boomerang effect" in a formulation that is characteristically trenchant: "Solzhenitsin's work raised everywhere the issue of the Gulag at the heart of the revolutionary project; it is, therefore, inevitable that the Russian example returns to strike its French 'origin' like a boomerang." In other words, it reopened the whole question of the relationship between the French Revolution and the Terror. "The French Revolution Is Over," 29.

As far as the notion of historical "breaks" is concerned, Michel Foucault has typically warned us of the kind of generational conceit involved in assuming that we live in a present "of rupture, or of high point, or of completion, or of a returning dawn. . . . I think we should have the modesty to say to ourselves that, on the one hand, the time we live in is not *the* unique or fundamental or irruptive point in history, where everything is completed and begun again." ("Critical Theory/Intellectual History," trans. Jeremy Harding, in *Politics, Philosophy, Culture: Interviews and Other Writings, 1977–1984,* ed. Lawrence D. Kritzman [New York: Routledge, 1988], 35–36.) Nevertheless, the weight of the historical evidence that a two-hundred-year tradition of investing social hope in global revolutionary change has come to an end in our time is overwhelming.

8. Mona Ozouf, "La Révolution française et l'idée de l'homme nouveau," in *The French Revolution and the Creation of Modern Political Culture,* vol. 2, ed. Colin Lucas (Oxford: Pergamon Press, 1988), 214–15.

9. For the oft-told tale of the emergence of the general intellectual in France at the time of the mobilisation of progressive opinion in connection with the Dreyfus Affair, see Pascal Ory and Jean-François Sirinelli, *Les Intellectuels en France, de l'affaire Dreyfus à nos jours* (Paris: Armand Colin, 1986).

10. In an essay that focuses on the philosophes' conception of universal knowledge, "Philosophers Trim the Tree of Knowledge," Robert Darnton summarizes first Voltaire's and then D'Alembert's heroic view of the philosophes and *gens de lettres* as the principal agents of the progress of civilization and of enlightenment before going on to point to the cluster of related categories associated with those concepts: "Throughout the 1750s, in pamphlets, plays, journals, and treatises, the *philosophes* came to be recognized or reviled as a kind of party, the secular apostles of civilization, in opposition to the champions of religion and orthodoxy. Many of them contributed to the *Encylopédie*—so many, in fact, that *Encyclopédiste* and *philosophe* became virtual synonyms, and both terms crowded out their competitors—*savants, érudits, gens d'esprit*—in the semantic field covered by the

general expression *gens de lettres.*" *The Great Cat Massacre and Other Episodes in French Cultural History* (New York: Vintage Books, 1985), 208.

11. "We do not construct 'a philosophical author' as we do a 'poet,' just as, in the eighteenth century, one did not construct a novelist as we do today" ("What Is an Author?" in *The Foucault Reader*, 110.) Moreover, in Foucault's reading, the nineteenth century's conception of the author/creator as originator and guarantor of a work of art is perceived not as the norm but as something of an aberration.

12. Roger Chartier, *The Cultural Origins of the French Revolution*, trans. Lydia G. Cochrane (Durham: Duke University Press, 1991), 12. See also Keith Michael Baker, *Inventing the French Revolution: Essays on French Political Culture in the Eighteenth Century* (Cambridge: Cambridge University Press, 1990).

13. Milan Kundera, "The Jerusalem Address: The Novel and Europe," in *The Art of the Novel*, trans. from the French by Linda Asher (New York: Harper & Row, 1986), 157.

14. Kundera, "Sixty-three Words," in *The Art of the Novel*, 143–44.

15. See Jacques Julliard, *La Faute à Rousseau: essai sur les conséquences historiques de l'idée de souveraineté populaire* (Paris: Le Seuil, 1985).

16. Pierre Bourdieu's major contributions to the human science of culture extend from *La Distinction: Critique sociale du jugement* (Paris: Editions de Minuit, 1979) through *Les Règles de l'art: Genèse et structure du champ littéraire* (Paris: Le Seuil, 1992). See also his "The Field of Cultural Production" and other theoretical essays that have a particular relevance for literature in *The Field of Cultural Production: Essays on Art and Literature* (New York: Columbia University Press, 1993), ed. Randal Johnson.

17. See in this connection James Miller's discussion of "self-effacement" in Blanchot and Foucault in *The Passion of Michel Foucault* (New York: Simon and Schuster, 1993), 153–55.

18. Apart from the works to be discussed here, including, for example, Simone de Beauvoir's *Les Mandarins* (Paris: Gallimard, 1954), Philippe Soller's *Femmes* (Paris: Gallimard, 1983) and Julia Kristeva's *Les Samouraïs* (Paris: Fayard, 1990) in France, and Philip Roth's *The Facts: A Novelist's Autobiography* (New York: Penguin, 1988), Susan Sontag's *Illness as Metaphor* (New York: Farrar, Straus, and Giroux, 1978), and William Styron's *Darkness Visible: A Memoir of Madness* (New York: Random House, 1990) in the United States.

19. See, for example, Robert Darnton, "The High Enlightenment and the Low-Life of Literature," in *The Literary Underground of the Old Regime* (Cambridge, Mass.: Harvard University Press, 1982), and "The Facts of Literary Life in Eighteenth-Century France," in *The French Revolution and the Creation of Modern Political Culture*, vol. I, ed. Keith Michael Baker (Oxford: Pergamon Press, 1987).

20. Simone de Beauvoir, *Mémoires d'une jeune fille rangée* (Paris: Gallimard, 1958), 196.

21. Stendhal, *Vie de Henry Brulard* (Paris: Garnier, 1961), 12.

22. In a discussion of the importance of "the image of great predecessors," Bourdieu quotes the following revealing passage from a novel by Flaubert's contemporaries the Goncourt brothers, *Manette Salomon*, in order to emphasize that "what attracts and fascinates in the occupation of artist is not so much the art itself as the artist's life: 'At heart, Anatole was called by art much less than he was

attracted by the artist's life. He dreamt of the studio. He aspired to it with a schoolboy's imaginings and the appetites of his nature. He saw in those horizons of Bohemia which enchant from a distance: the novel of Poverty, the shedding of bonds and rules, a life of freedon, indiscipline and disorder, every day filled with accident, adventure and the unexpected.'" ("Field of Cultural Production," 65–66).

23. "Critical Theory/Intellectual History," 44–45.

24. *A New History of French Literature,* ed. Denis Hollier (Cambridge, Mass.: Harvard University Press, 1989).

25. Roland Barthes, *Roland Barthes* (Paris: Le Seuil, 1975), 81.

26. In reflecting on the current situation, Judt takes the argument a stage further by pointing to "the decline of the great public intellectuals" and "the resurrection of the professors." *Past Imperfect,* 297.

27. Louis Althusser, *L'Avenir dure longtemps* (Paris: Stock/IMEC, 1992). The title of the American edition of Richard Veasey's English translation, *The Future Lasts Forever: A Memoir* (New Yoir: New York University Press, 1992), sounds like an overstatement; I prefer to use the more literal rendering here.

28. Foucault, "The Minimal Self," in *Politics, Philosophy, Culture,* 16. It is, of course, a remark calculated to give pause to any future biographer, as James Miller shows himself to be well aware.

CHAPTER 1

1. I should perhaps mention at once that the word "writing" here is not intended as a synonym for "textuality," with the very different problematic that that word implies in modern critical theory. That is in part why my focus is not the same as Thomas M. Kavanaugh's in his absorbing recent study *Writing the Truth: Authority and Desire in Rousseau* (Berkeley: University of California Press, 1987). His concern, as he notes in his preface, is the following: "Rousseau's 'life,' as it interests us here, *is* itself an act of writing. And Rousseau's 'writing' *is* the essential adventure of his life, an impossible attempt to state not only his own but a universal truth" (x).

2. Roger Chartier sums up the argument for the idea of a new political culture as follows: "Thanks to the constitution of a public whose judgments were not necessarily those of academic authority or the princely patron, thanks to the emergence of a market for cultural products that permitted at least a partial autonomy to those who created those products, and thanks to the widespread diffusion of skills that made possible a large circulation of the written word, people acquired habits of free judgment and contradictory criticism. The new political culture that arose after 1750 was the direct heir of those transformations in that it substituted for an all-powerful authority, which decided in secret and without appeal, the public manifestation of individual opinions and the will to examine freely all established institutions. Thus a public was formed that, more sovereign than the sovereign, obliged the king to confront contrary opinions." *The Cultural Origins of the French Revolution* (Durham: Duke University Press, 1991), 166–167.

3. Mona Ozouf, "La Révolution française et l'idée de l'homme nouveau," in *The French Revolution and the Creation of Modern Political Culture,* vol. 2, ed. Colin Lucas (Oxford: Pergamon Press, 1988), 213–14.

4. Jean-Jacques Rousseau, *Les Confessions,* ed. Jacques Voisine (Paris: Garnier, 1964), 3.

5. Among the abundant secondary literature on autobiographical writings, see the following relatively recent works on the French tradition: Philippe Lejeune, *L'Autobiographie en France* (Paris, 1971) and *Le Pacte autobiographique* (Paris, 1975); Huntington Williams, *Rousseau and Romantic Autobiography* (Oxford: Oxford University Press, 1983); Leah D. Hewitt, *Autobiographical Tightropes: Simone de Beauvoir, Natalie Sarraute, Marguerite Duras, Maryse Condé* (Lincoln: University of Nebraska Press, 1990); Michael Sherringham, *French Autobiography: Devices and Desires—Rousseau to Perec* (Oxford: Oxford University Press, 1993); John Sturrock, *The Language of Autobiography: Studies in the First Person Singular* (Cambridge: Cambridge University Press, 1993).

6. See Robert Darnton's discussion of the new intimacy Rousseau established in his relationship with his readers ("He transformed the relation between writer and reader, between reader and text"), "Readers Respond to Rousseau: The Fabrication of Romantic Sensitivity," in *The Great Cat Massascre and Other Episdoes in French Cultural History* (New York: Vintage Books, 1985).

7. Rousseau, *Discours sur l'origine de l'inégalité,* in *Oeuvres complètes,* ed. Bernard Gagnebin and Marcel Raymond (Paris: Pléiade, 1964), 3:460.

8. Foucault actually associates this idea with the nineteenth century: "I think that the idea of characterizing individuals through their sexual behavior or desire is not to be found, or very rarely, before the nineteenth century." Michel Foucault, "The Minimalist Self," in *Politics, Philosophy, Culture: Interviews and Other Writings, 1977–1984,* ed. Lawrence D. Kritzman (New York: Routledge, 1988), 11.

9. In this connection, it is interesting to note that in her discussion of revolutionaries' views of the emergence of "the new man," Mona Ozouf distinguishes between two oppositional attitudes, namely, "the miraculous conception and the workaday conception of the Revolution, grace and work, supernatural and patient" ("La Révolution française et l'idée de l'homme nouveau," 225). It need hardly be said that the connection between the first conception and the works of Rousseau is no coincidence.

10. Louis Althusser, "Ideology and Ideological State Apparatuses," in *Lenin and Philosophy and Other Essays,* trans. Ben Brewster (London: Monthly Review Press, 1971).

11. See, for example, Voisine's note in *Confessions,* 426–27.

12. "Rousseau even attempted to teach his readers how to read and, through reading, tried to touch their inner lives. This strategy required a break with conventional literature. Instead of hiding behind the narrative and pulling strings to manipulate characters in the manner of Voltaire, Rousseau threw himself into his works and expected the reader to do the same. He transformed the relation between writer and reader, between reader and text." Darnton, "Readers Respond to Rousseau," 228.

13. That is why I find it hard to agree with Priscilla Clark that Rousseau represents the category of "private" writer, in opposition to Voltaire, a "public" one. *Literary France: The Making of a Culture* (Berkeley: University of California Press, 1987).

14. The notable exception is, of course, his immensely successful epistolary

novel *Julie, or The New Héloïse*. Yet, given his own reservations about the morally corrupting power of the genre and the fact that the work is, in part, a fantasized refiguration of erotic relationships from his life, it is in many ways the kind of exception that proves the rule.

15. See, for example, Voisine's comments on the two meanings of confession in the Catholic tradition, the *confessio laudis,* or profession of faith, and the *confessio peccati,* or confession of sins, in *Confessions*, vi.

16. "I should like to be able in one way or another to make my soul transparent to my reader's eyes, and that is why I am attempting to show it to him from every point of view, to illuminate it on every day, to write so that not a single operation occurs there that he does not perceive, so that he may judge by himself the principle that produces them" (*Confessions*, 198). See Jean Starobinski, *Jean-Jacques Rousseau: Transparency and Obstruction*, trans. Arthur Goldhammer (Chicago: University of Chicago Press, 1988). See also Robert Darnton's essay on "the history" of Starobinski's work, "History and Literature" in *The Kiss of Lamourette: Reflections in Cultural History* (New York: Norton, 1990).

17. Rousseau, *Discours sur les sciences et les arts,* in *Oeuvres complètes,vol. 3* (Paris: Pléiade, 1964).

18. Althusser, *L'Avenir dure longtemps* (Paris: Stock/IMEC, 1992).

19. See chapter 7 for a discussion of Althusser's stance on these issues.

20. The phrase in Rousseau's French is "Peuples policés," which, before the age of modern "policing," conflates without ironic intention the idea of "polis," "polite," and "police" itself.

21. Althusser's highly influential text here is, of course, "Ideology and Ideological State Apparatuses." In effect, Rousseau also problematized the notion of autonomy in cultural production that is so important to Bourdieu by asserting the autonomy of the cultural producer from state power and its agents, while at the same time rejecting the idea of the autonomy of the work of art relative to the field of power as the postromantic generations would come to affirm it in France.

22. The First Discourse pays particular homage to the great classical orators and incorruptible guardians of public morality from Socrates and Demosthenes to Fabricius Luscinus and Cato the Censor.

23. Immanuel Kant, *Kant's Political Writings,* ed. Hans Reiss, trans. H. S. Nisbet (Cambridge: Cambridge University Press, 1970), 59.

24. Michel Foucault, "What is Enlightenment?" in *The Foucault Reader,* ed. Paul Rabinow (New York: Pantheon Books, 1984), 47–48.

25. See, for example, Richard Rorty's "Habermas and Lyotard on Postmodernity," in *Habermas and Modernity,* ed. Richard J. Bernstein (Cambridge, Mass.: M.I.T. Press, 1985), 161.

26. See Robert Darnton's use of this phrase in "The Kiss of Lamourette," in *The Kiss of Lamourette*, 10.

27. It is noteworthy in the light of recent debates that, in a sympathetic reading of Rousseau's *Letter* in the introduction to his own translation of the work (*Politics and the Arts: Letter to D'Alembert on the Theater* [Ithaca: Cornell University Press, 1960]), Allan Bloom points out that Rousseau belonged to the classic tradition of political philosophers who assumed that, in order to survive, republics required a more virtuous and more self-disciplined citizenry than other forms of government. Furthermore, Bloom describes Rousseau as "one of the last great voices in favor of censorship" and makes the rather extravagant claim that *The*

Letter is "as complete a treatment of the arts in relation to politics as has ever been produced" (xi-xvi).

28. "Notice how in order to elicit laughter this man disturbs the social order; how scandalously he overthrows all those sacred relations on which it is founded; how he makes fun of the respected rights fathers have over their children, husbands over their wives, masters over their servants." Rousseau, *Lettre à D'Alembert sur les spectacles* (Lille: Librairie Giard, 1948), ed. M. Fuchs, 46.

29. See, in particular, the chapter entitled "Che Vuoi?" in Slavoj Zizek, *The Sublime Object of Ideology* (London: Verso, 1989), esp. 185–87.

30. The idea of the libidinal and even transgressive character of cognitive inquiry is given a particularly lapidary formulation in the *Discourse on the Origin of Inequality:* "We seek to know only because we desire to take our pleasure [*jouir*]" (143).

31. "What! Plato banished Homer from his Republic and we should tolerate Molière in ours!" *Letter*, 157.

32. For a recent illuminating discussion of the concept relative to the French eighteenth-century context, see Keith Baker's "Defining the Public Sphere in Eighteenth-Century France: Variations on a Theme by Habermas," in *Habermas and the Public Sphere,* ed. Craig Calhoun (Cambridge, Mass.: M.I.T. Press, 1992).

33. See Stuart Schram, *The Thought of Mao Tse-tung* (Cambridge: Cambridge University Press, 1989), 132.

34. François Furet, "Révolution française et tradition jacobine," in *The French Revolution and the Creation of Modern Political Culture,* vol. 2, ed. Colin Lucas (Oxford: Pergamon Press, 1988), 336.

35. See also in this connection Keith Michael Baker, "On the Problem of the Ideological Origins of the French Revolution," in *Inventing the French Revolution: Essays on French Political Culture in the Eighteenth Century* (Cambridge: Cambridge University Press, 1990).

36. Furet makes the general point that "Rousseau is in no way 'responsible' for the French Revolution, but it is true that he constructed without his knowing it the cultural materials of the consciousness and practice of revolution." François Furet, "La Révolution française est terminée," in *Penser la Révolution Française* (Paris: Gallimard, 1978), 58.

37. Lynn Hunt, *Politics, Culture, and Class in the French Revolution* (Berkeley: University of California Press, 1984), 11. There is the suggestion of such an attitude in the *Letter* in the idea of constant mutual surveillance as a civic responsibility. With reference to the institution of women's circles or clubs in Geneva, Rousseau comments that those involved "have, as it were, the function of Censors in our town. In a similar way in Rome's great age Citizens observed each other closely and accused each other out of a zeal for justice." *Letter*, 143.

38. Part 1 of Lynn Hunt's *Politics, Culture, and Class in the French Revolution,* "The Poetics of Power," is particularly suggestive of the form "cultural revolution" took during the course of the French Revolution.

39. Mona Ozouf notes that fraternity "made its entry into offical language through the back door, in a supplementary article to the Constitution of 1791, which envisioned fraternity as a remote product of future national holidays. Those holidays were instituted in order to 'foster' fraternity, which was thought of as the goal of a long-term project to shape the civic spirit." "Fraternity," in *A Critical Dictionary of the French Revolution,* ed. François Furet and Mona Ozouf,

trans. Arthur Goldhammer (Cambridge, Mass.: Harvard University Press, 1989), 694.

For Rousseau the idea is already represented with the seductive power of a memory from childhood: "Oh! where are the games and the festivals of my youth? Where is the concord among citizens? Where is public fraternity? Where is pure joy and true merriment? Where are peace, liberty, equity, innocence?" *Letter,* 178–79.

40. Robert Darnton evokes the moral temper of the French revolutionaries in this respect in terms that are decidely Rousseauist: "At the height of the Revolution, however, from mid-1792 to mid-1794, virtue was not merely a fashion but the central ingredient of a new political culture. It has a puritanical side, but it should not be confused with the Sunday school variety preached in nineteenth-century America. To the revolutionaries, virtue was virile. It meant a willingness to fight for the fatherland and for the revolutionary trinity of liberty, equality, and fraternity." "The Kiss of Lamourette," 10.

41. The preface goes on: "No chaste girl has ever read a novel, and I gave this one a clear enough title so that when one opened it, one knew what to expect. She who in spite of the title dares to read a single page is a lost girl" (*Julie, ou La Nouvelle Héloïse* [Paris: Garnier, 1960], 3–4). See also Rousseau's much longer "Preface to *Julie,* or commentary on the Novel, which is usually published as an appendix to the novel. For a recent discussion of these and related issues, see Joan De Jean, "*Julie:* The Well-Ordered House" in *Literary Fortifications: Rouseau, Laclos, Sade* (Princeton: Princeton University Press, 1984).

42. Rousseau, *Emile,* in *Oeuvres complètes* (Paris: Pléiade, 1969), 4:362–63.

43. The important work is, of course, Foucault's *Discipline and Punish,* trans. Alan Sheridan (New York: Vintage Books, 1977).

44. Ozouf, "La Révolution française," 225. See chapter 7 for a discussion of these issues in connection with Foucault's own Kantian essay "What is Enlightenment?"

45. It is in his strangely literal reading of "The Crow and the Fox" that Rousseau reveals a kind of tone deafness to the play of what Roman Jakobson once called "the poetic function" of language.

46. Robert Darnton, *The Literary Underground of the Old Regime* (Cambridge, Mass.: Harvard University Press, 1982).

47. Some of the key words in Plutarch's biography of Cato are "gravity," "dignity," "simplicity," and "self-discipline." The power for Rousseau of Cato's example is evident from the way in which Plutarch praises his way of life even more than his oratory: "His powers of expression merely set a standard for young men, which many of them were already striving to attain. But a man who observed the ancestral custom of working his own land, who was content with a cold breakfast, a frugal dinner, the simplest clothing, and a humble cottage to live in, and who actually thought it more admirable to renounce luxuries than to acquire them—such a person was conspicuous by his rarity." Plutarch, *Makers of Rome,* trans. Ian Scott-Kilvert (London: Penguin Books, 1965), 123.

48. Saint Augustine offers a retrospective narrative of his life that, in effect, tells two stories in one. On one level, it is a human story of sinfulness, self-deception, philosophical inquiry, spiritual quest, and conversion that is written from the point of view of the mature convert. On another level, it is a narrative of God's hidden purposefulness and mercy, a rereading of the narrator's own past that uncovers the previously overlooked signs of providential intervention and ex-

plains it, in large part, in terms of the efficacy of a good mother's prayers: "You were guiding me as a helmsman steers a ship, but the course you steered was beyond my understanding." Saint Augustine, *Confessions,* trans. R. S. Pine-Coffin (Baltimore: Penguin Books, 1961), 84.

Saint Augustine's *Confessions* are, however, only intermittently a narrative, because they take the form of a prayer. Their addressee is, therefore, God himself, who, since he is omniscient, already knows what his creature has to tell him, but nevertheless requires a full accounting as a purifying spiritual exercise. Consequently, Augustine is at least as much concerned to offer up praise and solicit forgiveness in the present of the writing as he is to report in detail on his fallen past, although there are, of course, a number of wonderfully suggestive anecdotes that do just that.

Individual prayer is traditionally assumed to be for God's ears only, in the same way that confession is for the ears of a single priest. To write down one's confessions for circulation is, therefore, also to address a wider audience, which is something Augustine acknowledges: "I need not tell all this to you, my God, but in your presence I tell it to my own kind, to those other men, however few, who may perhaps pick up this book. And I tell it so that I and all who read my words may realize the depths from which we to cry to you" (45). If he writes, so to speak, for publication, then, it is as a form of Christian witness, so that his own life story may serve as an example of his moral and spiritual misadventures and God's mercy.

49. One symptom of the decadence in our time of the tradition of literary confession that Rousseau inaugurated is to be found in the Madonna film of the same title, *Truth or Dare.* See chapter 6.

50. See also the description of the great pleasure he found when still a boy in submitting himself to the chastisements of Mademoiselle Groton (*Confessions,* 28). In a recent book Peter Brooks briefly discusses the Mademoiselle Lambercier episode in the context of the early "erotic marking" of the body. *Body Works: Objects of Desire in Modern Narrative* (Cambridge, Mass.: Harvard University Press, 1993), 38–43.

51. Denis Diderot, "Eloge de Richardson," in *Oeuvres* (Paris: Pléiade, 1951).

52. "I could not imagine how a girl and a boy managed to make love to each other." *Confessions,* 160.

53. Milan Kundera, "Sixty-three Words," in *The Art of the Novel,* trans. from the French by Linda Asher (New York: Harper & Row, 1988), 150.

54. In light of such episodes it is little wonder that Edmund Burke regarded Rousseau as "a philosopher of vanity" and "a man who blended 'metaphysical speculation' and 'the coarsest sensuality.' " See Harvey Mitchell's "Burke, or Why a Revolution?" in *The French Revolution and the Creation of Modern Political Culture,* vol. 3, ed. François Furet and Mona Ozouf (Oxford: Pergamon Press, 1989), 9.

55. In the early 1920s, in a short autobiographical piece entitled "Old Bloomsbury," Virginia Woolf was, in a sense, paying a debt to Rousseau when she both recorded aspects of her and her friends' sexual affairs and celebrated the feeling of liberation they experienced in discussing them. The fact that Lytton Strachey could point to a stain on Vanessa Bell's dress and ask, "Semen?" constituted in Edwardian England an opening onto a post-Victorian world: "Can one really say it? I thought and we burst out laughing. With that one word all barriers of reticence

and reserve went down. A flood of the sacred fluid seemed to overwhelm us. Sex permeated our conversation. The word bugger was never far from our lips. We discussed copulation with the same excitement and openness that we had discussed the nature of the good." Virginia Woolf, *Moments of Being: Unpublished Autobiographical Writings,* ed. Jeanne Schulkind (New York: Harcourt Brace, 1976), 173–74.

56. Philip Roth, *The Facts: A Novelist's Autobiography* (London: Penguin Books, 1989), 167.

57. Furet comments that "Rousseau probably had the greatest genius for anticipation that has ever existed in intellectual history, given all those things he invented or guessed that were to obsess the nineteenth and twentieth centuries." "La Révolution française est terminée," 58.

58. In "Révolution française et tradition jacobine," François Furet explains succinctly the significance of the Jacobin legacy throughout the nineteenth and into the twentieth century in terms that both recall Rousseau's influence in this respect and transcend it: "From the Restoration up to the foundation of the Third Republic, it [Jacobinism] forms part of the baggage of the republican party in different forms and ways; it constitutes an undivided heritage in which one finds at the same time the idea of sovereignty of the people one and indivisible, the all-powerful Assembly elected by universal suffrage, the French nation as figurehead in the task of the emancipation of all peoples, hostility to the Catholic church, the religion of equality, and finally the secret or public society, depending on the circumstances, of professional activists of political revolution. But it also contributes the idea of the Terror as inseparable from the First Republic and from the bloody dictatorship exercised in the name of virtue" (335–36).

59. With reference to the generation of Parisian intellecuals that dominated French intellecutal life during the decade following the Second World War, Tony Judt identifies what he calls six tropes that were central to their discourse, namely, violence and struggle, sexualized imagery, treason, collaboration, resistance, and the enemy. (*Past Imperfect: French Intellectuals, 1944–1956* [Berkeley: University of California Press, 1992], 49–55.) Equivalents of these six tropes are, of course, to be found in the discourse that was formulated from the early 1790s on.

60. According to Plutarch (the source of a great deal of Rousseau's knowledge of Greco-Roman society and politics), Cato, too, combined his attack on luxurious living—"Valerius Flaccus was the only colleague . . . with whom he could make some progress in cutting away and cauterizing the hydra-like luxury and degeneracy of the age"—with a determination to banish the philosophers—"Cato made up his mind to find some plausible excuse for clearing the whole tribe of philosophers out of the city" (*Makers of Rome,* 137, 145). On Rousseau's role in the formation of the discourse of revolution, see Carol Blum, *Rousseau and the Republic of Virtue: The Language of Politics in the French Revolution* (Ithaca: Cornell University Press, 1986).

61. Rousseau, *Les Rêveries du Promeneur Solitaire* (Paris: Pléiade, 1959), 1014–15.

62. Rousseau, "Preface to *Julie,* or Commentary on the Novel," in *Julie* (Paris: Garnier, 1960), 514–15.

63. The by-now classic references are, of course, Jacques Derrida, "Differance," in *Speech and Phenomena,* trans. David B. Allison (Evanston: Northwestern University Press, 1973), and, with specific reference to Rousseau, "Nature,

Culture, Writing," in *Of Grammatology*, trans. Gayatri Chakravorty Spivak (Baltimore: Johns Hopkins University Press, 1976).

64. Roger Chartier notes that the Kantian idea of the "public" is a universalist one that depends precisely on "the circulation of written works" and on modes of representation of a kind that Rousseau rejected: "Nor was [Kant's] 'public' constituted in reference to the ideal of the city in classical antiquity, which presupposed being able to listen to the spoken word and deliberate in common, and which involved the physical proximity of all members of the body politic. For Kant only written communication, which permitted exchange in the absence of the author and created an autonomous area for debating ideas, was admissible as a figure for the universal." *Cultural Origins of the French Revolution*, 26.

65. *Le contrat social*, in *Oeuvres Complètes* 3:360.

66. *Inventing the French Revolution*, 4.

67. Voltaire, *Lettres Philosophiques, ou Lettres Anglaises* (Paris: Garnier, 1988), 54.

68. That the potentially generous and emancipatory significance of the word could be perverted in ways that echo Rousseau's own political discourse is indicated by Colin Lucas: "*Patrie* was the word of 1792–94, replacing the earlier reference to nation. In the hands of a Robbespierre or a Saint-Just, *Patrie* was specifically a moral imperative: only those who had *vertu* belonged. Thus, the once indivisible nation was divided into the good and the bad: and the former were the citizens ("citoyens actifs" in a new sense) and they constituted the *patrie* which was both object and product of their of their solicitude: the incorrigibly bad were excluded and in this way the indivisibility of the nation was reconstituted in the *patrie*. Exclusion became the handmaiden of unanimity. . ." *The French Revolution and the Creation of Modern Political Culture* 2:xiv.

69. See Simon Schama's account of these events in *Citizens: A Chronicle of the French Revolution* (New York: Vintage Books, 1990), 561–66.

70. Quoted by Furet. In the absence of any practical exercise of power, the price of such authority was high, as Furet notes: "The men of letters tended to substitute law for fact, principles for the balance of interests and the calculation of means, values and ends for power and action" ("La Révolution française est terminé," 65–67). In the mid-1940s Jean-Paul Sartre formulated the change of attitude that occurred among French writers of the classical age and those of the mid-eighteenth century as a discovery of "the present": "The passionate sense of the present preserves him from idealism; he is no longer simply content to contemplate the eternal ideas of Liberty or Equality. For the first time since the Reformation, writers intervene in public life, protest against an injust decree, demand the reopening of a trial or, in other words, decide that the sphere of the spiritual is in the street, at the fair, at the market, in a courtroom, and that one should not turn away from the temporal but, on the contrary, constantly return to it, and transcend it at every possible moment." *Qu'est-ce que la littérature?* in *Situations*, II (Paris: Gallimard, 1948), 154.

71. That is why Blake was wrong—although by no means alone among subsequent generations—when he coupled their names in a celebrated poem, "Mock on, mock on, Voltaire, Rousseau." It is understandable that the English romantic poet, possibly inspired by the famous Houdon bust of a grinning Voltaire, would want to demonize the great sceptic, but Rousseau is in another category altogether, as the romantic generation of poets and writers as a whole was well aware.

72. But see, for example, "The Imagery of Radicalism," in Lynn Hunt's *Politics, Culture, and Class in the French Revolution.*

73. Alexis de Tocqueville, *The Old Regime and the French Revolution*, trans. Stuart Gilbert (New York: Doubleday Anchor, 1955), 12–13. This passage occurs in Part 1, chapter 3, under a heading that itself says so much: "How, though its objectives were political, the French Revolution followed the lines of a religious revolution and why this was so."

74. The case for Proust as "novelist" resisting the powerful influence of the eigtheenth-century "writer" would involve a two-pronged argument: on the one hand, the dimension of sociopolitical *engagement* is obviously alien to his whole moral and aesthetic sensibility; on the other, although twentieth-century France's most celebrated work of fiction, *Remembrance of Things Past*, clearly draws on the experiences of its author's life, it is not an autobiographical novel. It is, if anything, a critique of autobiography in the Rousseauist vein. Indeed, the whole impact of Proust's fictional practice, as well as of his critical writings, was to refocus attention not on the artist but on the process of the making of a work of literary art, not on the contingencies of a life but on their magical transcendence. As he made particularly clear in a famous essay, "The Method of Sainte-Beuve" (an influential critic who was in his own way a "Rousseauist"), Proust denied a continuity between the self that lives in the world and the one that writes: "[A] book is the product of another *self* than the one which we display in our habits, in society, and in our vices" (*Contre Sainte-Beuve* [Paris: Gallimard, 1954], 137). And with reference to what I am calling "Rousseau's legacy," it is the last phrase, "in our vices," that has a special resonance.

It is understandable, therefore, if, in a late essay, Roland Barthes decides that the central theme explored in *Remembrance of Things Past* is not a life but "that of the desire to write" itself. And he goes on to identify Proust's great work as belonging neither to the genre of the novel nor to that of the essay but to "a third form" whose structure is "rhapsodic": "rhapsodic, that is to say, from an etymological point of view, 'sewn together.' . . . [T]he work is made like a dress; the rhapsodic text implies an original art like that of a seamstress: patches, pieces are arranged in a network, a pattern, a system of cross-references. A dress is not a patchwork any more than is *Remembrance of Things Past.*" "Longtemps je me suis couché de bonne heure," in *Le Bruissement de la langue* (Paris: Le Seuil, 1984), 317.

CHAPTER 2

1. See Milan Kundera, "Sixty-three Words," in *The Art of the Novel* trans. from the French by Linda Asher (New York: Harper & Row, 1988), 143–44.

2. Alexis de Tocqueville, *The Old Regime and the French Revolution*, trans. Stuart Gilbert (New York: Doubleday, 1955), 207–8.

3. Stendhal, *La Chartreuse de Parme*, (Paris: Pléiade, 1952), 25.

4. Dennis Porter, "Stendhal: Histoire et mythe personnel," *Stendhal Club* 82 (January 1979).

5. See, for example, Françoise Mélonio's discussion of this question in "Tocqueville: Aux Origines de la démocratie française," in *The French Revolution and the Creation of Modern Political Culture*, vol. 3, *The Transformation of Politi-*

cal Culture, 1789–1848, ed. François Furet and Mona Ozouf (Oxford: Pergamon Press, 1989), 599.

6. With regard to the beginnings of the emergence of modern political culture at the moment of the French Revolution, Robert Darnton describes the process as follows: "The French did not have much of a political vocabulary before 1789, because politics took place at Versailles, in the remote world of the king's court. Once ordinary people began to participate in politics—in the elections to the Estates General, which were based on something approximating universal male suffrage, and in the insurrections of the streets—they needed to find words for what they had seen and done. They developed fundamental new categories, such as 'left' and 'right,' which derive from the seating plan of the National Assembly, and 'revolution' itself. The experience came first, the concept afterward." "The Kiss of Lamourette," in *The Kiss of Lamourette: Reflections in Cultural History* (New York: Norton, 1990), 4–5.

7. The two works on Napoleon, the *Life of Napoleon* and *Memoirs on Napoleon,* were written some twenty years apart, in 1817–18 and 1836–38, respectively, and were unpublished during Stendhal's lifetime. It is in the relatively late *Memoirs* that he notes, "My love for Napoleon is the only passion that remains; but that does not prevent me from seeing the faults of his mind and the petty weaknesses of which he stands accused" (*Napoléon,* ed. V. Del Litto [Lausanne: Editions Rencontre, 1961], 256). It is also in the *Memoirs* that Stendhal emphasizes that 1797 marked a decisive break: "In 1797 one could still love him passionately and without reservation; he had not yet stolen his country's liberty; nothing as great had appeared in centuries" (257). For Stendhal, it was finally 1803 and Napoleon's coronation as emperor that marked the end of "heroic times" (309).

8. In a classic of an earlier age of American literary criticism first published in 1957, *Politics and the Novel,* Irving Howe follows his Introduction with a chapter entitled "Stendhal: The Politics of Survival."

9. His earliest Italian travel book is entitled *Rome, Naples, and Florence in 1817* and the significance of that immediate postimperial moment is what the book largely explores.

10. Stendhal, *Le Rouge et le noir,* in *Romans et nouvelles,* vol. 1, ed. Henri Martineau (Paris: Pléiade), 575–76.

11. See Françoise Mélonio's discussion of the concept of "the grey society" and the emergence of modern mass society in Tocqueville, owing to the progressive leveling of social conditions both under the ancien régime and since. "Tocqueville," 602.

12. It is interesting to note that by the 1850s Tocqueville was blaming "despotism" for the single-minded pursuit of wealth in modern society that he had once associated with American democracy: "Love of gain, a fondness for business careers, the desire to get rich at all costs, a craving for material comfort and easy living quickly become ruling passions under a despotic government." *The Old Regime and the French Revolution,* xiii.

13. In 1784, at a point approximately halfway between the American Revolution and the French one, Immanuel Kant issued his own warning about the fact that there is no shortcut to enlightenment and that revolutions merely tend to replace new prejudices for old: "[A] public can only achieve enlightenment slowly. A revolution may well put an end to autocratic despotism and to rapacious or power-seeking oppression, but it will never produce a true reform in ways of think-

ing. Instead, new prejudices, like the ones they replaced, will serve as a leash to control the great unthinking mass." Kant, "An Answer to the Question: What is Enlightenment?" *Political Writings*, ed. Hans Reiss, trans. H. S. Nisbet (Cambridge: Cambridge University Press, 1991), 55.

14. Stendhal, *Vie de Henry Brulard* (Paris: Garnier, 1961), 12.

15. Stenhal, *Rome, Naples, et Florence en 1817*, ed. V. Del Litto (Paris: Le Divan, 1956), 5.

16. As far as Rome is concerned, he notes, "There is nothing but decadence here, nothing but memory, nothing but death. Active life is in London and Paris" (27).

17. Like Stendhal before him, Tocqueville paints a negative picture of democratic societies in comparison with aristocratic ones as far as disinterested meditation, artistic creativity, and the cultivation of "noble pleasures" are concerned. His summary of the difference goes a long way to explain the distrust felt for the American experiment in democracy by the nineteenth-century French liberal elite as well as by literary and artistic circles: "It would be to waste the time of my readers and my own if I strove to demonstrate how the general mediocrity of fortunes, the absence of superfluous wealth, the universal desire for comfort, and the constant efforts by which everyone attempts to procure it make the taste for the useful predominate over the love of the beautiful in the heart of man. Democratic nations, among whom all these things exist, will therefore cultivate the arts that serve to render life easy in preference to those whose object is to adorn it. They will habitually prefer the useful to the beautiful, and they will require that the beautiful be useful." *Democracy in America*, trans. Henry Reeve, ed. Phillips Bradley (New York: Vintage Books, 1945), 2:50.

18. Dennis Porter, *Haunted Journeys: Desire and Transgression in European Travel Writing* (Princeton: Princeton University Press, 1991), 135.

19. Virginia Woolf, *The Years* (San Diego: Harcourt Brace, 1965), 399. In this work, first published in the monstrously overpoliticized decade of the 1930s, the character, North, goes on to muse on a very different kind of life in a manner that Stendhal would have understood: "For him a life modelled on the jet (he was watching the bubbles rise), on the spring, of the hard leaping fountain; another life; a different life. Not halls and reverberating megaphones; not marching in step after leaders, in herds, groups, societies caparisoned" (410).

20. Philip Roth, *The Facts: A Novelist's Autobiography* (New York: Penguin Books, 1988), 172.

21. Kundera, "Sixty-three Words," 144. Compare Joseph Brodsky's comment in an essay on Derek Walcott: "Poets' real biographies are like those of birds, almost identical—their real data are in the way they sound. A poet's biography is in his vowels and sibilants, in his meters, rhymes, and metaphors." "The Sound of the Tide," in *Less Than One: Selected Essays* (New York: Farrar Straus Giroux, 1986), 164.

22. Referring to his passionate feelings for Alberthe de Rubempré in 1828, Stendhal notes that they were no different from what he felt for his mother at the age of six: "My way of pursuing happiness had in no way changed" (*Henry Brulard*, 26).

23. Roland Barthes, *Roland Barthes* (Paris: Le Seuil, 1975), 62.

24. It is interesting to note that Virginia Woolf adopted a similar approach in her essay-length memoir: "I write the date, because I think that I have discovered

a possible form for these notes. That is, to make them include the present—at least enough of the present to serve as platform to stand upon." "A Sketch of the Past," in *Moments of Being: Unpublished Autobiographical Writings,* ed. Jeanne Schulkind (New York: Harcourt Brace Jovanovich, 1976), 75.

25. Stendhal, *Romans,* ed. V. Del Litto (Paris: Pléiade, 1952), 1:1515.

26. Jeanne Schulkind used the phrase as the title for her collection of Woolf's autobiographical writings. It is opposed to the "moments of non-being" in which we are plunged most of the time on any given day. See "A Sketch of the Past," 70.

27. Keith Michael Baker, *Inventing the French Revolution: Essays on French Political Culture in the Eighteenth Century* (Cambridge: Cambridge University Press, 1990), 4.

28. Joseph Brodsky, *Less than One: Selected Essays* (New York: Farrar, Straus, Giroux, 1986), 28–30.

CHAPTER 3

1. Milan Kundera, "Sixty-three Words," in *The Art of the Novel,* trans. from the French by Linda Asher (New York: Harper & Row, 1986), 143–44.

2. It is interesting to note that in two short early essays, "Comment on paie ses dettes quand on a du génie," ("How One Pays One's Debts When One Is a Genius") and "Conseils aux jeunes littérateurs," ("Advice to Young Writers"), Baudelaire is preoccupied with the difficulty of earning money and with the problem of creditors. *Oeuvres complètes,* ed. Claude Pichois, vol. 2 (Paris: Gallimard, Bibliothèque de la Pléiade, 1976).

3. Baudelaire's thoughtful introductory essays on such social poets of the 1840s as Pierre Dupont and Auguste Barbier speak to his consciousness of the difficult lives led by urban workers and the peasantry, and of his openness to the idea that literature in general, and poetry in particular, might deal with such issues. The journal of which he was the coeditor, with Champfleury, the theorist of literary realism, and Charles Toubin in February 1848 was *Le Salut public.* See Claude Pichois's notes in *Oeuvres complètes* 2:1553–63; chapter 14, "We Must Go and Shoot General Aupick," in the Pichois's biography, *Baudelaire,* trans. Graham Robb (London: Hamish Hamilton, 1989); and Marcel Ruff, "La Pensée politique et sociale de Baudelaire," in *Littérature et société; Recueil d'études en l'honneur de Bernard Guyon* (Paris: Desclée de Brouwer, 1973).

4. Walter Benjamin, *Charles Baudelaire: A Lyric Poet in the Era of High Capitalism,* trans. Harry Zohn (London: Verso, 1983). See also the illuminating study by Susan Buck-Morss, *The Dialectics of Seeing: Walter Benjamin and the Arcades Project* (Cambridge, Mass.: M.I.T. Press, 1991).

5. See Marc Eigeldinger, "Baudelaire juge de Jean-Jacques," and Melvin Zimmerman, "Trois études sur Baudelaire et Rousseau," in *Etudes Baudelairiennes,* vol. 9 (Neuchâtel: A la Baconnière, 1981), for discussions of Baudelaire's views on Rousseau.

6. Valéry's brief summary of the singular importance for Baudelaire of the discovery of Poe has never been surpassed: "The demon of lucidity, the genius of analysis, and the inventor of the most novel and most fascinating combinations of logic and imagination, of mysticism and calculation, the psychologist of exceptional states, the literary engineer who explored and utilized all the resources of

art, appeared to him in the person of Edgar Poe and enchanted him." Paul Valéry, "Situation de Baudelaire," in *Oeuvres* (Paris: Pléiade, 1957), 1:599.

7. Michel Foucault, "What Is Enlightenment?" in *The Foucault Reader,* ed. Paul Rabinow (New York: Pantheon Books, 1984), 32.

8. In a short and influential essay that has the character of a manifesto, "Modernity—an Incomplete Project," Jürgen Habermas gives the following specifically German philosophical definition of "modernity" as "project": "The project of modernity formulated in the eighteenth century by the philosophers of the Enlightenment consisted in their efforts to develop objective science, universal morality and law, and autonomous art according to their inner logic. . . . The Enlightenment philosophers wanted to utilize their accumulation of specialized culture for the enrichment of everyday life—that is to say for the rational organization of social life." *The Anti-Aesthetic: Essays on Postmodern Culture,* ed. Hal Foster (Seattle: Bay Press, 1983), 9.

9. Michael Fried, "Painting Memories: On the Containment of the Past in Baudelaire and Manet," *Critical Inquiry* 10 (March 1984): 510.

10. Baudelaire, "Salon de 1846," in *Oeuvres complètes* 2: 415, 432.

11. Following a long line of literary and philosophical commentators, Habermas puts it this way: "By the time of Baudelaire the *promesse de bonheur* via art, the utopia of reconciliation with society had gone sour." "Modernity," 10.

12. This is something, ironically, that Louis-Napoleon World Exhibition of 1855 was meant to highlight, with its exhibition spaces devoted to a half-century of French art alongside the displays of technological invention (see "Exposition Universelle, 1855, Beaux-Arts," in *Oeuvres complètes,* 2:575–97). The event provided a stimulus for Baudelaire's reflections on non-European ideas of beauty in the form of Chinese artifacts that violated the canons of a doctrinaire Western aesthetics, artifacts that for him nevertheless belonged to "universal beauty," and that he found pleasing precisely because they exhibited the element of "strangeness" he invariably associated with beauty: "Beauty is always strange" (578). Given that the exhibition as a whole was inspired by the belief in progress associated with a kind of scientific triumphalism as well as with the assumption of Western cultural superiority, Baudelaire also found there a pretext to pose the question of what in a subtitle he refers to as "The Idea of Progress applied to the Fine Arts."

13. That he did not take Balzac to be a realist is apparent from his celebration of that writer at the end of the last section of the Salon of 1846, with its famous title "The Heroism of Modern Life": "Oh! you, Honoré de Balzac, you, the most heroic, the most extraordinary, the most romantic, and the most poetic of all the characters that you drew from your bosom" ("Salon de 1846," 496).

14. Poe's "It is a happiness to wonder" becomes "C'est un bonheur d'être étonné."

15. Baudelaire, "Fusées," *Journaux intimes,* in *Oeuvres complètes,* ed. Claude Pichois (Paris: Gallimard, Bibliothèque de la Pléiade, 1975), 1:658.

16. "The study of a masterpiece from that period and of that type will not teach him [the painter] the attitude, the look, the grimace, or the vital aspect of one of these creatures that the dictionary of fashion has classed in succession with the crude or mocking names of 'the impure,' 'kept women,' 'lorettes,' and 'biches.' " ("Le Peintre de la vie moderne," in *Oeuvres complètes* 2:696.) The brilliance and provocation of Manet resides, of course, in the fact that he painted such figures from his age in poses borrowed from the great renaissance artists. Baude-

laire created poetic equivalents of the painter's modern nudes in poems such as "Les Bijoux" ("Jewels") from the *Pièces condamnées,* which opens with the memorable lines "La très chère était nue, et, connaissant mon coeur, / Elle n'avait gardé que ses bijoux sonores" ("My beloved was naked and, knowing my taste, / She had retained only her sonorous jewels") *Oeuvres complètes* 1:158.

17. In the chapter entitled "Cultivation of the Arts" in the second volume of *Democracy in America,* Tocqueville notes that one effect of "the democratic principle" is that it "not only tends to direct the human mind to the useful arts, but it induces the artisan to produce with great rapidity many imperfect commodities, and the consumer to be content with these commodities." As for the fine arts, he concludes that although it does not necessarily follow that "a democratic social condition and democratic institutions" diminish the number of those who cultivate them, democracy does influence the way they are cultivated. The result, in any case, is that "the number of consumers increases, but opulent and fastidious consumers become more scarce." Alexis de Tocqueville, *Democracy in America,* trans. Henry Reeve, ed. Phillips Bradley, (New York: Vintage Books, 1945), 2:52–53.

18. However, specifically in connection with Baudelaire, Habermas does recognize the emergence in the nineteenth century of a new and "radicalized consciousness of modernity which freed itself from all specific historical ties" ("Modernity," 4). And he identifies Baudelaire as the pioneering figure of an age that exalted its present and rebelled against the normalizing function of tradition.

19. "As for religion, I deem it useless to speak about it or seek out what remains, since wasting one's time denying God is the only scandal left in the whole business." *Oeuvres complètes* 1:666.

20. In his remarkable reading of *Madame Bovary,* Baudelaire praises Flaubert for "the wager" he engaged in, that of creating beauty out of the banal material of provincial middle-class adultery. "Madame Bovary" in *Oeuvres complètes,* vol. 2.

21. See T. J. Clark's discussion of the new Paris in *The Painting of Modern Life: Paris in the Art of Manet and His Followers* (New York: Knopf, 1984), especially the chapters "The View from Notre Dame" and "The Environs of Paris."

22. See Benjamin's discussion of these figures, along with the apache, the ragpicker, and the conspirator, in *Charles Baudelaire,* 97–101.

23. Benjamin, who, with reference to Poe, associates the new cultural type of "the detective" with the flaneur, also distinguishes between the precise observations of the former and the mere gaping of the *badaud.*

24. For a critical discussion of Baudelaire's praise of the dandy from the point of view of existentialist commitment, see Jean-Paul Sartre's discussion in *Baudelaire,* trans. Martin Turnell (Norfolk, Ct.: New Directions, 1950), 133–34. Sartre, in effect, expresses a puritanical disdain for such masquerade.

25. Jean-Jacques Rousseau, *Oeuvres complètes* (Paris: Gallimard, Bibliothèque de la Pléiade 1964), 3:138.

26. Baudelaire, *Le Spleen de Paris,* dedication, "A Arsène Houssaye," in *Oeuvres complètes* 1:275–76.

27. Baudelaire, *Correspondance* ed. Claude Pichois (Paris: Gallimard, Bibliothèque de la Pléiade, 1973), 2:141, 182. It is interesting that a writer whose work was important to Baudelaire, Thomas De Quincey, also distanced himself from Rousseau's example in the preface "To the Reader" with which he begins his *Con-*

fessions of an English Opium Eater (1821), which Baudelaire was to translate. Although Rousseau goes unnamed, De Quincey clearly has his *Confessions* in mind when he condemns those so lacking in propriety that they shamelessly publicize their most intimate thoughts and experiences. Having thus explained that his purpose is to be "useful and instructive," he goes on: "In *that* hope it is, that I have drawn it up: and *that* must be my apology for breaking through that delicate and honourable reserve, which, for the most part, restrains us from the public exposure of our own errors and infirmities. Nothing, indeed, is more revolting to English feelings, than the spectacle of a human being obtruding on our notice his moral ulcers and scars, and tearing away that 'decent drapery,' which time, or indulgence to human frailty, may have drawn over them: accordingly, the greater part of our confessions (that is spontaneous and extra-judicial confessions) proceed from demireps, adventurers, or swindlers: and for any such acts of gratuitous self-humiliation from those who can be supposed in sympathy with the decent and self-respecting part of society, we must look to French literature, or to that part of the German, which is tainted with the spurious and defective sensibility of the French" (*Confessions of an English Opium Eater* [London: Penguin Books, 1986], 29). For De Quincey, writing in the early 1820s, "gratuitous self-humiliation" in the literary sphere was identified as a French disease whose source was to be traced back to Rousseau. The English writer's revelations were largely restricted to his experiences as an addict in a society where opium was routinely prescribed for various medical conditions, and to his inner life and the drug-induced fantasies to which he was subject—what Baudelaire was to call "artificial paradises."

28. Baudelaire, "Fusées," *Journaux intimes*, 652.

29. Baudelaire, "Hygiène," *Journaux intimes*, 668.

30. The first quotation is from Benjamin himself, the two following from Buck-Morss's summary of his position. *The Dialectics of Seeing*, 105.

31. See Léon Cellier "Baudelaire et George Sand," *Revue d'histoire littéraire de la France* 67, no. 2 (April–June 1967): 343–56. Baudelaire associated Sand with Rousseau directly in connection with the claim both made to live their life in accordance with an injunction from Juvenal, *Vitam impendere vero* ("Make one's life depend on nothing but the truth"): "To my knowledge three people have adopted that austere motto: Jean-Jacques, Louis Blanc, and George Sand. Joseph de Maistre says somewhere (in his *Considerations on France*, I believe), 'If a writer adopts as his motto *Vitam impendere vero*, there is a good chance he is a liar.' " "Pensées d'album," *Journaux intimes*, 709.

32. See *The Dialectics of Seeing*, 36–39 and 336–38, for a summary of Benjamin's perception of his own critical task.

33. "Modernity," 9 (emphasis mine). Habermas's narrative of the way in which "the project of modernity" has been misunderstood through an almost exclusive focus on the aesthetic sphere and the supposed failure of even the twentieth-century avant-garde to revitalize "the life world" is, in many ways, more convincing. It is difficult to argue against the idea that aesthetic modernism is only one dimension of modernity and that one cannot expect an "emancipatory effect" in society at large from art alone, divorced from similar efforts in the instrumental-scientific and moral-practical spheres. However, perhaps because he seems to be relying too heavily on Peter Bürger's understanding of the European avant-garde (*Theory of the Avant-garde*, trans. Michael Shaw [Minneapolis: University of Minnesota Press, 1984]), he also tends to turn Baudelaire into a cultural villain.

As far as Bürger's book is concerned, there is a superficial plausibility to establishing a continuity between late-eighteenth-century German aesthetics and late-nineteenth-century French aesthetic modernism on the basis of a common belief in the autonomy of the work of art. He does so in order to establish the important break as that of Dada and surrealism, since those movements effected a critique of the institution of art with the supposed purpose of returning it to social life. Given his thesis, it is not surprising that Bürger hardly mentions the work of Baudelaire, the complexity of whose writings taken as a whole anticipate so many aspects of the twentieth-century avant-garde while at the same time looking back to European romanticism. It is, for example, difficult to imagine André Breton's *Nadja* or Louis Aragon's *Paysan de Paris* in the absence of Baudelaire's phantasmagoric urban poetry in verse and prose poems.

34. "Let Them Read Proust," *The Economist*, 13 October 1990.

35. One meaning of what Habermas calls "the inner logic" of art is suggested by Valéry, who, of course, belonged to the tradition in French poetry that was inaugurated by Baudelaire. In the essay referred to above, "Situation de Baudelaire," he defines the task of the poet in the following terms: "The duty, the work, the function of the poet are to render both evident and active those powers of movement and of enchantment, those stimulants of the affective life and of the intellectual sensibility that are mixed up with the signs and means of communication of ordinary, banal life in normal language. The poet devotes and consumes himself in the construction of a language in language . . ." (611).

36. See Gisèle Freund's discussion of this cultural milieu in her chapter on "The First Portrait Photographers," in *Photography and Society* (Boston: Godine, 1980).

37. In her absorbing study *French Daguerreotypes* (Chicago: University of Chicago Press, 1989) Janet E. Buerger notes that "[a]n astonishing twenty-one million daguerrotype plates were manufactured in 1851 in Paris alone" (3).

38. For a recent selection of paintings and images associated with Baudelaire, see Yann le Pichon and Claude Pichois, *Le Musée Retrouvé de Charles Baudelaire* (Paris: Stock, 1992)

CHAPTER 4

1. Tony Judt, *Past Imperfect: French Intellectuals, 1944–1956* (Berkeley: University of California Press, 1992), 249.

2. Jean-Paul Sartre, *Situations, X: Politique et Autobiographie* (Paris: Gallimard, 1976), 64.

3. *L'Existentialisme est un humanisme*. The title of the English translation, *Existentialism and Humanism*, trans. Philip Mairet (New York: Haskell House, 1948), loses the insistence of the "is."

4. The necrological portraits he drew of his distinguished friends and contemporaries, including Albert Camus, Maurice Merleau-Ponty, Paul Nizan, and Frantz Fanon, are also illuminating of Sartre's understanding of the responsibilities of the intellectual and writer. For detailed studies of Sartre's theory and practice in the genre of biography, see Douglas Collins, *Sartre as Biographer* (Cambridge, Mass.: Harvard University Press, 1980), and Sterling Haig, ed., *Sartre and Autobiography, The French Review* (special issue) no. 55, 7 (summer 1982).

5. "Simone de Beauvoir interroge Jean-Paul Sartre," in *Situations, X;* Simone de Beauvoir, *La Cérémonie des adieux, suivi de Entretiens avec Jean-Paul Sartre (août-septembre 1974)* (Paris: Gallimard, 1981).

6. Most memorably by Charles De Gaulle when he was head of the French state, at the height of protests against the Algerian war: "You do not imprison Voltaire." Quoted by Annie Cohen-Solal in *Sartre: A Life,* trans. Anna Cancogni (New York: Pantheon Books, 1987), 415.

7. "When I left the Ecole Normale . . . I was 'man alone,' that is to say, the individual in opposition to society by virtue of the independence of his thought but who also owes nothing to society and over whom society exercises no power because he is free." Jean-Paul Sartre, "Self-Portrait at Seventy," in *Situations X: Politique et autobiographie* (Paris: Gallimard, 1976), 176.

8. See *Sartre: A Life,* 159–78.

9. Since the romantic period at least there have, of course, been transcriptions of conversations with great men, such as Goethe's *Conversations with Eckermann.*

10. Later in the same interview, he also notes, "[W]e know well that the distinction between private and public life does not, in fact, exist, that it is a pure illusion, a mystification. That is why I cannot claim to have a private life, that is to say, a hidden, secret life; it is also why I answer your questions." "Self-Portrait at Seventy," 176.

11. *Sartre: un film* (Paris: Gallimard, 1977), 81.

12. See "Sixty-three Words," in *The Art of the Novel,* trans. from the French by Linda Asher (New York: Harper & Row, 1988), 143.

13. Pierre Bourdieu, "The Field of Cultural Production," in *The Field of Cultural Production,* ed. Randal Johnson, (New York: Columbia University Press, 1993), 45. In this connection also, Denis Hollier has noted that committed literature is a call to action in the present that "simultaneously condemns any modality of action that might resort to means smacking of what could be called symbolic effectiveness. The writer addresses the reader's freedom, and that suffices for the writer to rule out any will to trouble him, plunge him into excessively violent feelings, or overwhelm him. He must not call the magic of words into play." *The Politics of Prose: Essay on Sartre,* trans. Jeffrey Mehlman (Minneapolis: University of Minnesota Press, 1986), 4.

14. I am, of course, referring to *The Eighteenth Brumaire of Louis Bonaparte* and *The Civil War in France.*

15. Sartre does not mean "autonomous" in the same way that the aesthetic movement, for example, affirmed art to be autonomous, as will be clear from the discussion that follows.

16. *Qu'est-ce que la littérature?* in *Situations, II* (Paris: Gallimard, 1948), 176. It is as if Sartre's hostile view of the avant-garde derives from a temptation denied. After all, the fact is that during his years as a lycée teacher in Le Havre and Paris he did come close to living the marginal, experimental, parasitic life he associated with the nineteenth-century French aesthetes whose principal preoccupations outside art itself were, according to him, love, travel, and war. Their radically antisocial, nonutilitarian attitudes typically took a destructive and even self-destructive form: "He [the fin-de-siècle writer] frequently even regards his life as a tool to be destroyed. In any case, he puts it at risk and is willing to lose it: alcohol, drugs, everything is grist to his mill" (170).

17. See Julien Benda, *La Trahison des clercs* (Paris: 1927). Benda was, of

course, responding at the time to the increasing political polarization of French cultural life as a consequence of the Dreyfus Affair.

18. See *Sartre: A Life,* 68.

19. Jean-Paul Sartre, *Search for a Method* trans. Hazel E. Barnes, (New York: Vintage Books, 1968), xxxiv.

20. In another context, he sets up the opposition in these terms: "Existentialism and Marxism . . . aim at the same object; but Marxism has reabsorbed man into the idea, and existentialism seeks him everywhere *where he is,* at his work, in his home, in the street." *Sartre: un film,* 28.

21. That is also why he can assert without irony and over the objections of his young Maoist collaborators that his unfinished three-volume critical biography of Flaubert might eventually "serve the masses." *Sartre: un film,* 130.

22. For a helpful discussion of Sartre's conception of alienation, see "Praxis and Nature," in Mark Poster's *Existentialism and Marxism: From Sartre to Althusser* (Princeton: Princeton University Press, 1975). The book is also a good introduction to the theme announced in its title. See also "Sartre," in Fredric Jameson's *Marxism and Form: Twentieth-Century Dialectical Theories of Literature* (Princeton: Princeton University Press, 1971).

23. *Les Mots* (Paris: Gallimard, 1964), 3.

24. It actually gets worse: "In my whole life I have never given an order without laughing. That's because I am not devoured by the canker of power; I was never taught to obey" (13).

25. The idea of the freedom enjoyed by the bastard had been explored in his fictional works by Gide in the previous generation, but for the leading French existentialist the absence of a father seems to have simplified the task of discovering his freedom to be the master of his fate. That Sartre assumed that a son bears the heavy responsibility of exploring critically his paternal inheritance is clear throughout *Words*. It is also discussed in detail in *The Critique of Dialectical Reason,* where the situation of the bourgeois son as heir, both inside metropolitan France and in relation to the long colonial adventure, is analyzed; the heir is defined as even more guilty than the father if he passively assumes his inheritance and fails to analyze the exploitation to which he is a party and to make an attempt to end it. That is why the notion of paternity is also associated with that of property: a son inherits, and from that circumstance typically derives his sense of solidity. In both *Words* and The *Critique,* then, the function of the father is that of occupying a place his son will learn to occupy in his turn and, therefore, that of assigning his son a mission in life. The role of the son who is determined to take responsibility for his choices and his actions is to refuse the mission.

26. In this and a great many other respects, Sartre clearly enjoys directing his well-known talent for vituperation against his youthful self. He was, he comments, "[a] stupified vermin who was without faith or law, reason or purpose, and who therefore escaped into the theater of family life, running hither and thither from one form of impostorship to another" (75).

27. "What is no longer possible for me is something that a lot of young people now scorn, namely, style; that is to say, the literary way of rendering an idea or a reality. That necessarily demands corrections. . . ." "Self-Portrait at Seventy," 135–36.

28. Sartre's attempts to do work for French television toward the end of his life gave rise to a series of frustrations and finally came to nothing.

29. The final references to the progressive degeneration of Sartre's body, however, are Simone de Beauvoir's. It is she who records, in *The Ceremony of Farewell,* his periods of mental confusion, his loss of independence and of physical control, she who focuses on the spectacle of a Sartre who dribbles as he dozes off. See *La Cérémonie des adieux,* 51–52, 84.

30. See *Sartre: A Life,* 216–18.

31. "It is natural to be *immersed* in language because language is in itself the bearer of truth." *Sartre,* 61.

32. See Jacques Derrida, *Of Grammatology,* trans. Gayatri Chakravorty Spivak (Baltimore: Johns Hopkins University Press).

33. See also part 1 of *Situations, III* (Paris: Gallimard, 1949).

34. It is comments such as this that caused Judt to remark about France's midcentury intellectuals, "Their reputations may have dimmed with time but not to the point that we can read without discomfort of their insouciance in the face of violence, human suffering, and painful moral choices." *Past Imperfect,* 3. See especially his part III, "The Treason of the Intellectuals."

35. Quoted in "First Reactions," *Le Monde,* 17 April 1980. On the other hand, Pierre Nora, quoted in the same article, placed him in a somewhat different canonical succession: "Voltaire or Flaubert? The 'little man' is a giant who belongs to two ages of literature and of the intelligence. On one side, he is, with Malraux, the last representative of a race that has died out with them, the sacred monster, the man whose truth is founded on sensibility alone and is therefore profoundly moral and political. But Sartre is also the first who by a coup d'état has displaced the literary center of gravity from the writer to the intellectual, from the man of letters to the man of learning, from outside history to inside history." I am, of course, arguing that such a coup d'état had already been initiated in the very different historical context of the eighteenth century by Rousseau.

36. A phrase that Jacques-Laurent Bost characteristically denounces: "I hate that word [*sic*]." *Sartre,* 112.

37. Simone de Beauvoir notes that Sartre was on top form for the making of the film: "He was animated, gay, at his best." *La Cérémonie des adieux,* 39.

38. It is notable that in summarizing the arguments Sartre makes in the film, Beauvoir resorts to the discourse of permanent revolution to interpret his second conversion, to contestation and self-contestation. (*Cérémonie,* 15.) Sartre did not, in fact, change his way of life or abandon all links with his literary and intellectual past, as his obsessive determination to finish the monumental Flaubert biography attests.

39. For an overview of Sartre's shifting stands on ethical questions, see Juliette Simont, "Sartrean Ethics," in *The Cambridge Companion to Sartre,* ed. Christina Howells (Cambridge: Cambridge University Press, 1992).

40. *Existentialism and Humanism,* 32.

41. See James Miller, *The Passion of Michel Foucault* (New York: Simon & Schuster, 1993), 38, 52–54; see also Martin Jay, "In the Empire of the Gaze: Foucault and the Denigration of Vision in Twentieth-Century French Thought," in *Foucault: A Critical Reader,* ed. David Couzens Hoy (New York: Oxford University Press, 1986).

42. Foucault, quoted in *The Passion of Michel Foucault,* 41.

43. Louis Althusser, *L'Avenir dure longtemps* (Paris: Stock/IMEC, 1992), 168.

44. Jean-François Lyotard, *La Condition postmoderne: Rapport sur le savoir* (Paris: Editions de Minuit, 1979), 7–8.

45. Alexis de Tocqueville, *The Old Regime and the French Revolution*, trans. Stuart Gilbert (New York: Doubleday Anchor, 1955), 147.

46. Milan Kundera, "Sixty-three Words," in *The Art of the Novel*, trans. from the French by Linda Asher (New York: Harper & Row, 1988), 131.

CHAPTER 5

1. Roland Barthes, *Roland Barthes* (Paris: Le Seuil, 1975). Among the many critical works on Barthes, two that are particularly relevant to the issues discussed here are Steven Ungar, *Roland Barthes: The Professor of Desire* (Lincoln: University of Nebraska Press, 1983), and Louis-Jean Calvet, *Roland Barthes, 1915–1980* (Paris: Flammarion, 1983).

2. Milan Kundera, "Sixty-three Words," in *The Art of the Novel*, trans. from the French by Linda Asher (New York: Harper & Row, 1988), 143–44.

3. Barthes, "Longtemps je me suis couché de bonne heure," in *Le Bruissement de la Langue* (Paris: Le Seuil, 1984).

4. Susan Sontag, *On Photography* (New York: Dell, 1973), 22–24.

5. John Berger, "Uses of Photography," in *About Looking* (New York: Pantheon Books, 1980), 51–52.

6. Eve Kosofsky Sedgwick, *Epistemology of the Closet* (Berkeley: University of California Press, 1990).

7. The gap that separates Barthes from Foucault in these matters is apparent in two sets of observations. In *Incidents* Barthes expresses his great irritation at the suggestion that he must be denying part of his sexuality if he does not engage in sadomasochism: "[T]his fashion, this doxa, that would set up sadomasochism as a norm, or as normal, and then require one to explain deviance from it, is discouraging" (*Incidents* [Paris: Le Seuil, 1987], 96). Foucault, on the other hand, once expressed his total indifference to the kind of "middle range pleasures" that were so important to Barthes: "A pleasure must be something incredibly intense. . . . I'm not able to give myself and others those middle range pleasures that make up everyday life. Such pleasures are nothing for me and I am not able to organize my life in order to make place for them." Michel Foucault, "The Minimalist Self," in *Politics, Philosophy, Culture: Interviews and Other Writings, 1977–1984*, ed. Lawrence D. Kritzman (New York: Routledge, 1988), 12–13.

8. Charles Baudelaire, "Jouir est une science," in *Oeuvres complètes*, ed. Claude Pichois (Paris: Gallimard, Bibliothèque de la Pléiade, 1976), 2:415.

9. See "Sixty-three Words," 131.

10. Joseph Brodsky, "The Sound of the Tide" in *Less Than One: Selected Essays* (New York: Farrar, Straus, Giroux, 1986), 164.

11. He refers to her a number of times with the tender neologism "Mam," and on one occasion finds himself instinctively returning to the old apartment they had shared but in which he no longer lives.

12. In "Broken Heart," the final section of his short essay *Bringing Out Roland Barthes* (Berkeley: University of California Press, 1992), D. A. Miller points to the stereotype of "The Sad Old Queen" that Barthes both represents and distances himself from.

CHAPTER 6

1. Marguerite Duras, *Hiroshima mon amour: Scénario et dialogue* (Paris: Gallimard, 1960), 105. In an article entitled "The Pain of Sorrow in the Modern World: The Works of Marguerite Duras," which, at least on the historical level, overindulges in the contemporary rhetoric of crisis ("Never has a cataclysm been so apocalyptically exorbitant"), Julia Kristeva makes the claim that "all of Marguerite Duras's oeuvre may be found in the text of *Hiroshima, mon Amour,* whose action takes place in 1957, twelve years after the atomic explosion. *Hiroshima* has everything: suffering, death, love, and their explosive merging in the mad melancholy of a woman." *PMLA* 102 no. 2 (March 1987): 139, 143.

2. "Unfortunately" because it displaces the focus from the highly personal, anguished way the German occupation was lived through by the protagonist onto the objective phenomenon itself. *The War: A Memoir,* trans. Barbara Bray (New York: Pantheon, 1986).

3. A relatively complete Duras bibliography is to be found in a thoughtful study of her works through *Le Vice-consul* and *L'Amour,* Sharon Willis's *Marguerite Duras: Writing on the Body* (Urbana: University of Illinois Press, 1987).

4. As its title suggests, this is to some extent the theme of Leah Hewitt's book *Autobiographical Tightropes* (Lincoln: University of Nebraska Press, 1990). Its very helpful chapter on Duras is entitled "Rewriting Her Story, from Passive to Active: Substitutions in Marguerite Duras's *The Lover.*"

5. Susan Sontag, *On Photography* (New York: Dell, 1980), 24.

6. The case seems to confirm John Berger's assertion that what preceded the invention of photography in the 1820s and 1830s was not other modes of visual representation but human memory. However, Duras's reflections confirm, if confirmation were needed, that the image making of memory has persisted alongside the photographic kind. It should also be noted that there is frequently a complicity between them: as was apparent in *Roland Barthes,* memory feeds on the images it would otherwise be unable to retrieve. See John Berger, "Uses of Photography," in *About Looking* (New York: Pantheon Books, 1980), 50.

7. Marguerite Duras, *The Lover,* trans. Barbara Bray (New York: Harper & Row, 1986), 10. In the quoted extracts from this book I have modified Bray's translation when it was necessary to emphasize a different aspect of the original.

8. See, for example, Leah Hewitt's reading of these scenes in *Autobiographical Tightropes.*

9. This is, of course, true even of the filmed interview, *Marlene,* she allowed Maximilian Schell to do not long before she died. The camera pans and tracks throughout her apartment, one sees her interviewer and hears her voice, but not once are we allowed to catch a glimpse of that once celebrated face and figure.

10. See Jacques Lacan, "The Essence of Tragedy: A Commentary on Sophocles' *Antigone,*" in *The Seminar of Jacques Lacan,* Book VII: *The Ethics of Psychoanalysis, 1959–1960,* trans. Dennis Porter (New York: Norton, 1992).

11. Her actual sentence, echoing Flaubert, is "Thérèse, c'est moi."

12. See Antonin Artaud, *Le Théâtre et son double* (Paris: Gallimard, 1938).

13. See, for example, Denis Hollier, ed. *The College of Sociology, 1937–39* (Minneapolis: University of Minnesota Press, 1988).

14. Leiris, of course, advocated a literature that was a form of bullfighting. See

"De la littérature considérée comme une tauromachie," in *L'Age d'homme* (Paris: Gallimard, 1939).

It should also be pointed out, as Hollier notes (*The College of Sociology,* xxv), that the founding members of the *collège* saw nothing honorific in the designation "writer." The fact is, however, that they were using the term in its generic sense as more or less synonymous with *littérateur* or "man of letters."

15. Marguerite Duras, *La Douleur* (Paris: Editions de Minuit, 1985), 69, 152.

16. One of the climactic episodes of Philip Roth's account of the slow and painful death of his father as the result of a brain tumor concerns a comparable confrontation with shit. See *Patrimony: A True Story* (New York: Simon & Schuster, 1991), 171–75.

17. On this question, see in particular Catherine Clément, "De la méconnaissance: Fantasme, scène, texte," *Langages* 31 (1973), 36–52, and Madeleine Borgomano, "On bat un enfant, ou l'ambivalence de la mère," in her psychoanalytic and thematic study *Duras: Une Lecture des fantasmes* (Petit Roeulx, Belgium: Cistre-Essais, 1985).

18. That the figure of "the writer" is still very much with us is, in effect, confirmed by the fact that detailed narratives of writers' physical and mental illnesses, or of those to whom they are intimately related, have become a minor genre of our time; apart from writings by or on Duras herself, one thinks immediately of relatively recent works by Simone de Beauvoir (on her mother and on Sartre), Susan Sontag (on her experience with cancer), Phillip Roth (on his father), and William Styron (on his depression).

19. Pierre Bourdieu, "The Field of Cultural Production," in *The Field of Cultural Production: Essays on Art and Literature,* ed. Randal Johnson (New York: Columbia University Press, 1993), 45.

20. *Les Lieux de Marguerite Duras* (Paris: Les Editions de Minuit, 1977) is derived from two programs prepared for French television by Michelle Porte on the basis of extensive interviews with the author. It is composed of a relatively heterogenous body of photographic images—pictures of her country house and garden or of herself and members of her immediate family, and stills of characters or locales from her films—that are located at intervals or grouped within written transcripts of the interviews and short passages of dialogue from Duras's films.

21. "It's true, it [to give birth] is to commit murder. The child is completely happy. The first sign of life is a cry of pain. As you know, when air first enters the cavities of the child's lungs, it causes great suffering; the first manifestation of life is pain. . . . They are the cries of someone whose throat is being slit, the cries of someone who is being killed, murdered; the cries of someone who refuses." *Les Lieux de Marguerite Duras,* 23.

22. Quoted by Sharon Willis in *Marguerite Duras,* 15, from Susan Husserl-Kapit, "An Interview with Marguerite Duras."

23. "The Herbert Read Memorial Lecture: 6 February, 1990," (London: Granta, n.d.).

CHAPTER 7

1. Louis Althusser, *L'Avenir dure longtemps* (Paris: Stock/IMEC, 1992).

2. The technique of opening with a murder scene will remind a great many

readers of Hollywood crime thrillers of the forties and fifties. There, too, the opening scene was that of a murder committed and, after a wavy dissolve, it was followed by a protracted flashback in which the events leading up to the crime were
reconstructed with the greatest possible precision down to the present of the opening scene.

3. In a paper on a lecture of Foucault's that I discuss later, Jürgen Habermas
notes, "Even from a distance, one experiences Foucault's death at fifty-seven as an
event whose untimeliness affirms the violence and mercilessness of time—the
power of facticity. . . ." "Taking Aim at the Heart of the Present: On Foucault's
Lecture on Kant's *What Is Enlightenment?*" in *The New Conservatism: Cultural
Criticism and the Historians' Debate,* trans. Shierry Weber Nicholsen (Cambridge,
Mass.: M.I.T. Press, 1989), 173.

4. James Miller, *The Passion of Michel Foucault* (New York: Simon & Schuster, 1993), focuses on some of these issues.

5. Althusser writes, "What art makes us *see,* and therefore gives to us in the
form of *'seeing,' 'perceiving,'* and *'feeling'* (which is not the form of *knowing*) is
the *ideology* from which it is born, in which it bathes, from which it detaches itself
as art, and to which it *alludes.*" "A Letter on Art in Reply to André Daspre," in
Lenin and Philosophy and Other Essays, trans. Ben Brewster (London: Monthly
Review Press, 1971), 222.

6. "Finally, I found in the *Confessions* the unique example of a kind of 'autoanalysis,' entirely devoid of self-satisfaction, in which Rousseau manifestly made
discoveries about himself in the process of writing and of reflecting on the most
significant experiences of his childhood and his life, and, for the first time in the
history of literature, *on sex* and on the admirable theory of the 'sexual supplement'
that Derrida has given a remarkable analysis of as a figure of castration." *The
Future Lasts a Long Time,* 212–13.

7. "What I admired in him [Rousseau] was his radical opposition to the es-
chatological and rationalist ideology of the Enlightenment, that of the philosophes
who hated him so . . . ." *Future,* 213.

8. "I tried to reconcile this radical critique of philosophy as an ideological
imposture . . . with my experience of philosophical practice, and at first I ended
up with formulas such as the following: 'philosophy represents science in the
sphere of politics and politics in that of science,' and later 'philosophy is in the last
instance the class struggle in theory.'" *Future,* 161.

9. Althusser discovers the theory of hegemony in the *Discourse on the Origin
of Inequality.* Rousseau is, however, even more explicit on the subject in his first,
prize-winning discourse, the *Discourse on the Sciences and the Arts,* where he
writes, "Whereas the Government and Laws provide for the security and the well-
being of the collectivity of men, the Sciences, Letters and the Arts, though perhaps
less despotic and less powerful, hang their garlands of flowers over the iron chains
that weigh them down, stifle in them the feeling for the original liberty they seemed
born for, make them love their slavery, and turn them into what are known as
civilized Peoples". Jean-Jacques Rousseau, *Discours sur les sciences et les arts,* in
Oeuvres complètes, ed. Bernard Gagnebin and Marcel Raymond (Paris: Pléiade,
1964), 3:6–7.

10. This does not prevent him from denying that he is engaged in a form of
"autoanalysis," of course, and from warning off those who would interpret his
behavior in light of psychoanalytic theory: "Believe it or not, but neither here nor

elsewhere do I engage in autoanalysis. I leave that to all the smart alecks with their 'analytical theory' to carry out in light of their own obsessions and fantasms. I simply report the different 'affects' that have marked me for life in their initial form and in their succesion after the fact." *Future,* 42.

11. It should be noted, however, that in the body of his text he pleads ignorance of psychoanalytic theory: ". . . in spite of all my psychoanalytic borings and all my experience as an analysand, I have never been able to enter into any of Freud's texts! Nor those of any of his commentators." *Future,* 159–160.

12. Michel Foucault, "The Minimalist Self," in *Politics, Philosophy, Culture: Interviews and Other Writings, 1977–1984,* ed. Lawrence D. Kritzman (London: Routledge, 1988), 11. See also the final pages of "L'Hypothèse répressive," in *Histoire de la sexualité,* 1, *La volouté de savoir* (Paris: Gallimard, 1976).

13. See Althusser, "Contradiction and Overdetermination" in *For Marx,* trans. Ben Brewster (London: Verso Editions, 1979).

14. "Ideology and Ideological State Apparatuses," in *Lenin and Philosophy.*

15. See Jürgen Habermas, "Modernity—an Incomplete Project," in *The Anti-Aesthetic: Essays On Postmodern Culture,* ed. Hal Foster (Seattle: Bay Press, 1983), and *The New Conservatism: Cultural Criticism and the Historians' Debate.*

16. It is interesting to note in this connection that Rousseau claims it was also chiefly for their sake that he abandoned his children to the foundling hospital at birth—so that they would not be exposed to the corrupting influence of his in-laws.

17. See Luc Ferry and Alain Renaut, *French Philosophy of the Sixties: An Essay on Antihumanism,* trans. Mary Schnackenberg Cattani (Amherst: University of Massachusetts Press, 1990).

18. As the response to James Miller's biography of Foucault reminds us, we still have a predatory, Victorian taste for presumed scandal, and in many circles a writer's or a thinker's life is still invoked in order to invalidate his art or ideas. Paul Johnson's *Intellectuals* (New York: Harper & Row, 1988), containing short debunking biographies of Western intellectuals from Rousseau and Shelley to Victor Gollancz and Lillian Hellman, is representative in this respect.

19. See Albrecht Wellmer's illuminating discussion of these issues in "Reason, Utopia, and the *Dialectic of Enlightenment,*" in *Habermas and Modernity,* ed. Richard J. Bernstein (Cambridge, Mass.: M.I.T. Press, 1985).

20. See André Gide, *Retour de l'U.R.S.S., suivi de Retouches à mon retour de l'U.R.S.S.* (Paris: Gallimard, 1978).

21. Althusser, *Eléments d'autocritique* (Paris: Hachette, 1974).

22. Althusser, "Cremonini, Painter of the Abstract," in *Lenin and Philosophy,* 237.

23. See Martin Jay, "Habermas and Modernism," in *Habermas and Modernity,* as well as Richard J. Bernstein's helpful introduction.

24. "The Minimalist Self," 16. It is noteworthy that the editor of the collection containing this essay, Lawrence Kritzman, entitles the first section of the book "Self-Portraits."

25. The academic and cultural milieu in which Foucault was immersed as a student and young researcher in Paris is very well described by James Miller in the early chapters of *The Passion of Michel Foucault.*

26. "Taking Aim at the Heart of the Present," 173–74.

27. Foucault, *The Archaeology of Knowledge,* trans. A. M. Sheridan Smith (New York: Harper & Row, 1972), 17.

28. Foucault, "What Is an Author?" in *The Foucault Reader,* ed. Paul Rabinow (New York: Pantheon Books, 1984), 102.

29. In this respect, as one of most celebrated lines of *The Will to Know* reminds us, far from emancipatory, talking openly about one's sexual life is interpreted as a mystification: "One must not assume that in saying yes to sex, one is saying no to power." The *History* of Sexuality, 1:207–8).

30. Foucault, "What Is Enlightenment," in *The Foucault Reader,* 41–42.

31. Foucault, "On the Genealogy of Ethics: An Overview of Work in Progress," in *The Foucault Reader,* 341–43. See also the interview entitled "The Aesthetics of Existence," in *Politics, Philosophy, Culture.*

32. François Furet, "La Révolution française est terminée," in *Penser la révolution française* (Paris: Gallimard, 1978), 56.

33. See, for example, Pierre Bourdieu, "A propos de Sartre . . . ," *French Cultural Studies* 4 (October 1993). Reflecting on Sartre's generation of *normaliens,* he observes, "Pure products of a triumphant scholastic institution that accorded its 'elite' unconditional approval, making out of a competitive examination for the recruitment of school teachers (the *agrégation* in philosophy) a body for the consecration of the intellect. . . . these apparent child prodigies discovered that at twenty years old the privileges and obligations of genius had been conferred upon them. . . . Armed with their intelligence alone, they were unencumbered by positive bodies of knowledge . . ." (211).

34. Tony Judt, *Past Imperfect: French Intellectuals, 1944–1956* (Berkeley: University of California Press, 1992), 297.

35. Pierre Bourdieu, *Les Règles de l'art: Genèse et structure du champ littéraire* (Paris: Le Seuil, 1992).

Index